A SENSE OF POWER

A SENSE OF POWER

The Roots of America's Global Role

John A. Thompson

CORNELL UNIVERSITY PRESS   ITHACA AND LONDON

First published 2015 by Cornell University Press
Printed in the United States of America

Library of Congress Cataloging-in-Publication Data

Thompson, John A. (John Alexander), 1938– author.
  A sense of power : the roots of America's global role / John A. Thompson.
    pages cm
  Includes bibliographical references and index.
  ISBN 978-0-8014-4789-1 (cloth : alk. paper)
  1. United States—Foreign relations—20th century.   2. Power (Social sciences)—United States—History—20th century.   3. Politics and war—United States—History—20th century.   4. Intervention (International law)—History—20th century.   5. Great powers.   6. World politics—20th century.   I. Title.
  E744.T485 2015
  327.73009'04—dc23   2015010884

Cornell University Press strives to use environmentally responsible suppliers and materials to the fullest extent possible in the publishing of its books. Such materials include vegetable-based, low-VOC inks and acid-free papers that are recycled, totally chlorine-free, or partly composed of nonwood fibers. For further information, visit our website at www.cornellpress.cornell.edu.

Cloth printing   10 9 8 7 6 5 4 3 2 1

For Peter Clarke and Stefan Collini, longtime friends and advisers

Contents

Preface

This book has been long in the making. Indeed, its origins go back to my puzzle-ment during the Vietnam War as to why the United States was fighting it. The costs of doing so were clearly very great—not only the direct costs in terms of casualties, money, and the disruption of young lives but also the damage to the country's internal harmony and its international moral standing. These costs were being incurred to prevent a communist takeover in South Vietnam, but it was hard to see how such a takeover would significantly diminish either America's safety from the danger of external attack or its economic prosperity. Yet, as a graduate student participating in the heated discussions of the time, I was struck by how much the arguments on both sides focused on security or economic interests. From the president down, proponents of the war argued that it was nec-essary for the sake of America's own security.[1] Opponents of the war, especially the radical young, were convinced that it was being fought to make the world safe for American capitalism.

Although my own research at that time was on the early twentieth-century progressive movement, my interest in the issue led me to turn my atten-tion as a historian from domestic reform to U.S. foreign policy. When I did so, I found that the arguments over Vietnam in contemporary debate were reflected in the two most widely held historical explanations for the global policy that had led the United States to fight such a controversial war in Southeast Asia. Most mainstream historians saw this policy as a response to threats to the nation's security—a policy adopted with a reluctance that had been overcome only by the painful experience of forced involvement in two world wars. Revisionists, on the other hand, saw the policy as the product of an internally generated drive to create and maintain an "Open Door world" in which American exports would find the profitable markets necessary to sustain the domestic prosperity that legitimated the capitalist system. I found neither of these explanations persuasive, for reasons I set out in general terms in the introduction and more fully with respect to crucial historical moments of decision in later chapters.

This left me with the task of providing an alternative explanation for the great expansion of America's overseas involvement and commitments, and this book is my attempt to do that. In substance, it is a study of the evolution of U.S. foreign policy, and the internal debate about it, between the late nineteenth century and the mid-twentieth century. It starts when the United States, through the remarkable growth of its economy, first acquired the capacity to exert a significant influence on great-power politics—a capacity that it had certainly lacked before the Civil War. The narrative ends at the point when the United States had assumed commitments and responsibilities across the globe and had also developed the institutions and capabilities that have enabled it to play a uniquely extensive and influential world role ever since.

During the intervening period, the extent to which the United States involved itself in the politics of other continents oscillated. It became a major player in great power politics under Woodrow Wilson's leadership during and after World War I but then withdrew from active commitment during the 1920s and 1930s. Involvement gradually increased again in the years before World War II, and entry into that conflict led not only to what remains by far America's largest and most demanding overseas intervention but also to a consensus that the United States should adopt an "internationalist" policy thereafter. It was only in the postwar years, however, that this developed into a readiness to assume potentially costly long-term commitments and a continuing and growing involvement across the globe.

Because my object is to try to explain how and why the nation came to make such costly efforts to achieve foreign policy objectives, my analysis focuses most intensively on these turning points and the reasons for the crucial decisions made then. I have not aimed to provide a comprehensive narrative of America's foreign relations in these years. The history of U.S. foreign policy in this period has been very thoroughly studied by scholars and, as will be apparent from the notes, my account is much indebted to the extremely impressive body of existing work. Nor have I attempted to uncover new documentary sources, which seemed unnecessary since so much significant documentation has been published. But, although this is a "big picture" book, I have sought to ground it in empirical particulars.

In developing my interpretation, I have drawn on the work of political scientists, who are perhaps more inclined than historians to address large explanatory questions and more inclined to seek systematic answers. The approach of the Realist school in particular has helped to structure my analysis, particularly its focus on the fundamental part played in international politics by the relative power capabilities of states, as well as on the primary concern of all states with their own security and survival. Somewhat paradoxically, however, this attempt to place U.S. foreign policy in a broader theoretical and empirical context left me all the more impressed by the unique character of America's position in the world since the late nineteenth century. Completely outranking all other states in the basic sinews of power while at the same time enjoying a quite exceptional degree of security from the danger of serious external attack, the United States has been largely free from the systemic pressures emphasized in some versions of Realist theory. Potentially able to wield an unparalleled influence in world politics but essentially self-sufficient strategically and economically, the United States has had an unusually wide range of choice between viable options in the field of foreign policy.

The way the case for American involvement has often been made has tended to obscure this reality. In contemporary debate, a distinction is commonly made between "wars of choice" and "wars of necessity." It is part of the thesis of this book that since the late nineteenth century, there have been no "wars of necessity" for the United States. Arguing this has sometimes been mistaken for a justification of noninvolvement or "isolationism," but it is certainly not intended to be so. The most crucial of the decisions examined here was the one to become involved in World War II. Coming from Britain, I can only be profoundly thankful that Americans made this choice, as were millions of non-Americans across the world. The insistence that it was nonetheless a *choice* is rather to counter the tendency of Americans to disguise from each other and themselves the real reasons for their actions—the "deceit and self-deceit" to which Henry Luce referred in one of the less remembered parts of his famous essay on "the American Century" (written at the time of the Lend-Lease debate).[2]

As we shall see, the concerns and sentiments that have led Americans to favor strenuous actions to affect events abroad have been complex and varied—though interpretations of experienced history have often been crucial. These concerns and sentiments are best examined on a case-by-case basis. But in looking for a more general cause of the global role the United States has assumed, I return to the sheer scale of the nation's potential power. Not only has this provided the indispensable means for effective action, but consciousness of it has also shaped the state of mind with which Americans have approached the choices they have had to make. My belief in the often-overlooked importance of this dimension is reflected in the title of this book.

Acknowledgments

Over the twenty years this project has taken to complete, I have incurred numerous and heavy debts. I began work on it when I was a Fellow at the National Humanities Center in North Carolina in 1993–94, and I am grateful to Bob Connor, Kent Mullikin, and the staff there for providing such an ideal environment for academic work and also to some of the other Fellows at the time, particularly Mark Mazower and Fritz Ringer, for enlightening and stimulating conversation. As I was venturing into the political science literature, an invitation from John W. Chambers and Warren F. Kimball gave me an opportunity to try out my ideas in a forum that included political scientists at the Rutgers Center for Historical Analysis. It was in that year, too, that I came to know Melvyn P. Leffler, whose thorough and critical reading of early sketches of the argument presaged his steady and friendly encouragement over the years. He was also one of the several friends, themselves scholars working in a variety of fields, who made helpful comments on successive book proposals as the project took different forms. These others include Marvin R. Cox, Campbell Craig, William W. Dusinberre, W. Bruce Leslie, David Lieberman, Fredrik Logevall, H. B. Ryan, and Jay Sexton. Once I started writing, a number of people took the time to give my drafts a critical reading. The introductory chapter benefited from the thoughtful observations of Timothy W. Guinnane and Adam Humphreys, as well as those of Christopher Clark and Ira Katznelson, who also read and commented on some of the other chapters. Gillian Sutherland cast an experienced and discerning eye over the first three chapters. Patricia Williams did the same for the preface and conclusion. Brooke Blower's thoughtful questions and suggestions on chapters 3 and 4 reflected a deep knowledge of the period they cover, as did those of James T. Patterson for chapter 6. Luke Fletcher helped me navigate the complex historiography regarding NSC-68. Finally, an anonymous reviewer of the manuscript for the Cornell University Press made suggestions that helped me to improve the final version significantly. To all of these people, I am most grateful.

My greatest debt is to the four friends whose advice I have sought at every stage of the project and whose insightful and detailed comments on chapter drafts greatly improved the final product, as well as encouraging me along the way. The book's dedication is an acknowledgment of how much the friendship of Peter Clarke and Stefan Collini has meant to me over the years. The book has benefited greatly from the experienced judgment of Robert W. Tucker, who profoundly influenced my thinking on this subject before we developed a friendship that I greatly value, while Andrew Preston's shrewd advice and steady support rather reversed the customary relationship of teacher and student.

It was great good fortune that I was led to the Cornell University Press and, once there, to Roger Haydon, not only an expert and committed editor but also an encouraging, understanding, and patient one.

My wife Dorothy gave the whole text a very careful reading at a late stage, but this was the least of her contributions to this project, which would not have been brought to completion without her loving support, practical help, and sometimes impatient encouragement.

A SENSE OF POWER

THE PROBLEM

In the early twenty-first century, the power of the United States in world affairs has generally been recognized to be without historical precedent in its scale and scope. Most obviously, its armed forces possess an unparalleled striking power and range. With significant numbers of American troops stationed in sixty-five countries, the United States guarantees the security of countries across the globe, including such wealthy ones as Japan and Germany as well as threatened ones like Taiwan and Israel.[1] Its influence in such organizations as the United Nations (UN), the International Monetary Fund (IMF), the World Bank, and the World Trade Organization (WTO) has been far greater than that of any other country, and the regimes such institutions seek to maintain and promote embody American values, for the most part. The position taken by Washington is an important factor in international issues everywhere in the world and, for many countries, in domestic ones too.

This power is no novel phenomenon. Indeed, it did much to shape the history of the twentieth century. In all three of the twentieth century's major geopolitical conflicts, the role of the United States was decisive. In World War I, the allies had become dependent on American supplies and finance even before the United States became a belligerent, but in the end the American military contribution also became vital. When, following the collapse of Russia, the Germans made their final thrust on the western front in 1918, the French and British would have been hard-pressed to turn the tide without the rapidly increasing flow of fresh troops from across the Atlantic.[2] In World War II, the brunt of the land fighting against Germany was borne by the Russians, but it was the productivity of the American economy that gave the allied powers the tremendous superiority in *matériel* that carried them to victory on all fronts. By 1943, about 60 percent of their combat munitions was being manufactured in the United States, while Lend-Lease aid made a significant contribution to the production of the rest.[3] The victory over Japan was almost entirely due to American power. In the Cold War, the United States not only largely organized the effort to contain Soviet and communist power, it also provided the major part of the resources.

In more peaceful enterprises, too, the United States played a leading role. No doubt, broader forces lay behind the development of the League of Nations and the United Nations (and their associated agencies), the IMF, the World Bank, and the WTO, but as a matter of historical fact these international organizations were all the products of American initiative and leadership. Whatever the economic importance of Marshall aid per se, it is hard to imagine the postwar recovery and integration of western Europe without American assistance and encouragement, to say nothing of the confidence generated by the security guarantee institutionalized in NATO. The development of modern Japan was likewise much affected by U.S. policy both during the occupation and after. The American role has been crucial in the creation and survival of the state of Israel. And across Latin America and other parts of the "Third World" as well as in those countries formally allied to the United States, the activities of the U.S. government and its agents—indeed, mere signals and rumors of what Washington wants, in some instances—have had a significant influence on the course of events.

The global role of the United States has, of course, aroused diverse reactions and responses. The record of U.S. foreign policy has certainly not been one of unbroken success in achieving its objectives, and the benignity of those objectives has been variously assessed, both at home and abroad. Such an assessment is not the purpose of this book, which is addressed to the question of *why* the United States has played such an active part in world politics. This is an important issue, not only because of the huge influence of U.S. actions on world history over the last century but also because the necessity or wisdom of its continuing to play such a role is a matter of current domestic debate.[4] It is also a question that is not susceptible to an easy or simple answer.

In practice, answers to this question, too, tend to be related to value judgments on the merits or virtues of the American role. Critics of U.S. policy have often sought to expose it as the product of an internally generated agenda; defenders have often claimed that it was a necessary response to external threats. But the question of how far it has been a matter of choice between practicably viable options has an intellectual interest independent of any value judgments. This is all the greater because there are serious problems with both the main types of explanation usually offered—those that focus on contingent external events and those that emphasize more general and continuous factors.

The first sort of explanation focuses on the external threats that arose in the 1940s. At first view, this is a natural approach because by the end of the turbulent and momentous decade framed by the fall of France in June 1940 and the outbreak of the Korean War in June 1950 the United States had assumed the global role that it has played ever since. The threats posed successively by the conquests of the Axis powers and by Soviet/communist expansionism have often been seen as sufficient in themselves to explain the abandonment of "isolationism" and the adoption of policies that involved a much wider projection of American power.

In a longer perspective, however, these threats are not an adequate explanation for the great expansion in the scope and scale of the nation's perceived foreign policy interests between the late nineteenth and the late twentieth centuries. This expansion began long before the 1940s; the view that the United States was "isolationist" before Pearl Harbor is a popular misconception. Clearly some other explanation is needed to account for the sending of an army of two million men to France in 1917–18 and for the acquisition of an overseas empire in 1898. And just as the focus on the 1940s tends to ignore or misrepresent much of the earlier history, so it has some difficulty explaining the character of United States policy since the end of the Cold War. For in the period between the end of the Cold War and the terrorist attacks of September 2001 it became apparent that America's commitment to the exercise of world power did not depend on a sense of existential crisis or challenge. In these years, the United States continued to maintain armed forces of an order of magnitude and striking power far beyond that of any possible rival or combination of rivals. Those forces were deployed across the globe and were actively involved during this period in the Middle East, Africa, and the Balkans. In addition, the United States extended its security guarantee through NATO to formerly communist countries in eastern Europe.

If specific external events do not seem adequate to explain the long-term nature of America's world role, this suggests the need for a more general explanation. Several such explanations have been offered. One is that the extent of America's involvement in world politics arises inevitably from the preeminent scale of its power in terms of material resources. A rather different form of Realism attributes the expansion of American interests to the increased demands of national security, consequent upon developments in military technology and external changes in the configuration of world power. Alternatively, economic interests and the need to make the world safe for American capitalism are seen as the driving forces of U.S. policy by many, particularly by those critical of it. To others, the ideological character of American nationalism and the belief that the country has a mission to promote freedom and democracy in the world provides the key. Yet each of these general explanations is open to serious objections.

Power as an Explanation

A very common view is that America's global role has inevitably arisen from the sheer scale of the nation's power—that is, its abundant possession of the capabilities or resources that can be used to influence other states.[5] America's preeminence in this respect has ultimately rested on the disparity between the size and productivity of its economy and that of any other country. America overtook Britain as the world's leading producer of manufactured goods in the 1880s, a position it retained throughout the twentieth century. Indeed, for most of that century, its manufacturing production was more than twice as great as that of its nearest rival; for some years after World War II, it was almost equal to that of the rest of the world combined. At the beginning of the twenty-first century, its GNP still amounted to more than a fifth of world output, more than twice that of Japan or China, the next-largest economies.[6]

There is no question that the scale of this productive capacity, in combination with advanced technology and a large and comparatively well-educated population, has provided the United States with the means to play the role that it has. It has enabled the country not only to build its formidable military strength but also to exercise effective diplomatic leverage and influence through the provision (or withholding) of military and other aid and the threat of economic sanctions. It is the size of the American economy that has made the United States by far the biggest contributor to the United Nations and given it its dominant role in the IMF and the World Bank and its leading one in the WTO. The United States would certainly not have been able to adopt such an extensive role without its great economic and financial strength.

For some, America's preeminent possession of power resources not only furnished the means for the United States to play such a large and active role in world politics but also provides a sufficient explanation for its doing so. Expressing a common view, Michael Mandelbaum sees the course of U.S. foreign policy since 1945 as "the Natural History of a Great Power": "American expansion followed a pattern common to other countries similarly situated in the international system. . . . There is a family resemblance between the United States, the Soviet Union, and Great Britain, on the one hand, and ancient Rome, on the other. The Romans in their day were also stronger than others. They too dispatched soldiers and governors far from the imperial city."[7] "As the power of a state increases, it seeks to extend its territorial control, its political influence, and/or its domination of the international economy," the political scientist Robert Gilpin has written. "The phenomenon . . . is universal."[8]

To the question of why great powers are bound to expand, various answers have been given. Some see it as simply a consequence of human nature. "Of the gods we believe and of men we know that it is a necessary law of their nature that they rule wherever they can," Thucydides has the Athenians telling the Melians. This aphorism is cited by Hans J. Morgenthau in support of his assertion that the drive to dominate is one of "those elemental biopsychological drives by which in turn society is created."[9] Such an assumption apparently underlies the common image of power as a sort of liquid substance, flowing automatically into hollows and "vacuums." Realist writers quote Lord Acton's dictum that "power tends to expand indefinitely, and will transcend all barriers, abroad and at home, until met by superior forces."[10]

To other scholars, however, the imperatives of power derive less from some internally generated drive to dominate than from the demands of the international system. Kenneth Waltz, for example, observes that "in a world of nation-states, some regulation of military, political, and economic affairs is at times badly needed." In Waltz's view, such regulation and the provision of other "collective goods" inevitably falls on the shoulders of the larger states, since "great power gives its possessors a big stake in the system and the ability to act for its sake."[11] The idea that the international system imposes special tasks on its most powerful members has been most developed in the version known as "the theory of hegemonic stability." According to this theory, a multilateral trading system can only function successfully when there is a "hegemon" to manage it, ensure an acceptable distribution of benefits, and, when necessary, enforce adherence to the rules. In the century or so leading up to 1914, it is said, this role was played by Britain; since World War II it has been assumed by the United States. Such a dominant power, Gilpin insists, is "a necessary . . . condition for the full development of a world market economy."[12]

Whether they focus on internal or external dynamics, theories that assume that the possession of power will automatically lead to its exercise are open to the objection that they neglect the costs of wielding power. For, of course, almost every means by which a state can exert leverage in international affairs involves some sacrifice on its part.[13] This is obvious in the case of wars, where the price comes in the form of casualties as well as money. But it also applies to the deployment (or even maintenance) of armed forces and to military or other foreign aid. Even economic sanctions or preferential terms for trade or investment always involve some sort of opportunity cost.[14] As Gilpin concedes, "This is a point that political realists tend to forget in arguing that states seek to maximize their power."[15] Recognizing that the exercise of power requires effortful activity involving the sacrifice of other desirable goods makes it much less plausible to view it as a universal human instinct. The psychological restraints on the drive to domination do not consist only of altruistic feelings and ethical considerations; they may also include the desire for an easy and comfortable life. Since this desire is likely to be higher among the priorities of ordinary citizens than of heads of state, it might be assumed to be particularly salient in democracies like the United States.[16]

Similarly, the mere fact that a state possesses the capability to provide collective goods for the international system will not necessarily provide it with the motivation to do so. The Realist assumption that states act in accordance with a rational assessment of their self-interest should surely lead one to expect that potential power will be exercised only if it is believed that doing so will yield the country taking the action benefits greater than the costs involved. The assessment of benefit will depend on the importance attached to the interests at stake. Waltz asserts that a state's stake in the international system increases with its relative power, but this is surely an empirical matter that cannot be assumed *a priori*. Indeed, international trade is generally more important for small countries than for great powers because the proportion of their economic activity that involves foreign transactions is almost always higher. The same is likely to be true for the comparative importance to them of such other public goods as international law and a reliable system of collective security.

Given the inadequacy of these general explanations, it is not surprising that the historical record shows that, as Gideon Rose puts it, "there is no immediate or perfect transmission belt linking material capabilities to foreign policy behavior." Yet Rose also insists that "over the long term the relative amount of material power resources countries possess will shape the magnitude and ambition—the envelope, as it were—of their foreign policies: as their relative power rises states will seek more influence abroad, and as it falls their actions and ambitions will be scaled back accordingly."[17] As a historical generalization, this is hard to dispute, but the pattern still calls for explanation.

Part of the explanation may well lie with a point that Gilpin makes—that the relative cost of exercising leverage internationally declines as a state's power increases.[18] In this respect, the United States provides a good illustration of a general proposition. The global political influence that the United States has enjoyed has been acquired at a comparatively low cost. One measure of this is the price in human life and military casualties. Victory in the Second World War established the United States and the USSR as the dominant powers in the world: it cost the latter roughly seventeen million dead, the former 323,000.[19] Part of this disparity may be accounted for by a greater sensitivity to this particular kind of cost; certainly American leaders have consistently sought to minimize casualties by using air and naval rather than land power wherever possible and by being prepared to spend money on extensive rescue and medical facilities as well as sophisticated weaponry.

However, the sacrifices demanded by the deployment of American power have been moderate in other respects also. Even during the nation's greatest military effort in the twentieth century, the domestic standard of living continued to rise between 1940 and 1944.[20] Whereas in Britain total personal consumption had fallen by 1943 to only 70 percent of that of 1938–39, in the United States the wartime nadir (in 1942) was some 5 percent *higher* than it had been in 1940. The difference was equally marked in terms of the disruption of normal social patterns. It has been estimated that in Britain and the Soviet Union during World War II only about 30 percent of women aged fourteen and over remained "at home" whereas in the United States the proportion was about 70 percent.[21] In the later 1940s and 1950s the burden of the substantial overseas expenditures on economic aid, security assistance, and the maintenance of U.S. forces abroad was greatly eased by America's accumulated gold reserves and regular surplus on the nongovernmental balance of payments. With the disappearance of these assets, foreign aid of all kinds fell from 2.4 percent of GNP in 1949–52 to 0.5 percent in the early 1980s.[22] Even so, because of the size of its economy, the United States in 1983 provided twice as much overseas development assistance as any other country, even though the proportion of its GNP devoted to such expenditure was the lowest of any industrial country except Austria.[23]

Growth in a nation's wealth, then, can make foreign policy objectives that would have been judged not worth the price of the effort to achieve them come to seem affordable. "According to the law of demand, as the power of a state increases, so does the probability of its willingness to seek a change in the system," Gilpin writes. "Regardless of its goal (security or welfare), a more powerful state can afford to pay a higher cost than a weaker state."[24] It is still the case, of course, that such a state may choose not to spend its additional resources on exercising power abroad at all but instead use them to improve the quality of its domestic life—as the United States very largely did before the 1940s. The comparatively reduced cost of achieving foreign policy objectives is a facilitating factor; it may encourage their pursuit, but by no means does it create an imperative on its own.

Moreover, the explanatory power of this factor in the American case is reduced by the substantial character of the costs the United States *has* paid for exercising its global role. In human terms, America's foreign wars have taken the lives of well over a half-million servicemen and wounded over a million more.[25] Many of these servicemen were enlisted through a draft, a form of which was in force for thirty-five years in the twentieth century (1917–18, 1940–47, 1948–73). In financial terms too, America's attempts to influence the course of events beyond its borders have been expensive. While a belligerent in World War I (1917–18), United

States devoted over 10 percent of GNP to war expenditure. During World War II (1941–45) an average of 31.9 percent of GNP was committed to the military, and during the forty-two years of the Cold War (1947–89), the average figure was 7.4 percent.[26] (By comparison, calculations of the percentage of net national product allocated to defense expenditure by the countries in Europe's armed alliances before World War I range from 2.8 percent in Austro-Hungary to 4.6 percent in Russia.)[27] In the early twenty-first century, the Pentagon's budget accounted for 40 to 45 percent of global military spending—more than double the proportion of America's share of world output.[28] Substantial further resources have been devoted to a large and sophisticated apparatus for the conduct of foreign policy, including the gathering of intelligence.

The commitment of the country's resources on this scale over many decades to means for exerting influence abroad cannot, therefore, be seen as an automatic concomitant of its economic and financial preeminence. It suggests that important national interests must have been perceived to be at stake in the achievement of foreign policy objectives. For all states in the international system, the most important interests are generally recognized to be physical security and economic prosperity. Each of these has provided the basis for a widely accepted explanation for America's global role.

Security as an Explanation

The provision of security is the prime *raison d'être* of all states. That physical security is for a state an interest as paramount as self-preservation is for an individual is particularly stressed by scholars in the Realist tradition, but it is also generally recognized outside the academy and across cultures.[29] In the UN Charter, "the inherent right of individual or collective self-defense if an armed attack occurs" (Article 51) is the only qualification on the undertaking by member states to "settle their international disputes by peaceful means" (Article 2(3)). Just as in domestic law it is the most acceptable justification for killing another individual, so, for many people, self-defense possesses a unique moral status as a justification for the use of military force.

It is often claimed that it was for the sake of this simple and supreme value that the United States was compelled to adopt a more active and extensive role in world politics. According to this view, the traditional policy of non-involvement was only made possible by the "free security" that the United States had enjoyed before the twentieth century. The historian C. Vann Woodward, who coined the phrase, saw that security as resting on two pillars—the protection provided by the difficulty of crossing any of the three great oceans surrounding North

America, and British sea power.[30] The European balance of power that prevailed between 1815 and 1914 has often been seen as constituting a third factor protecting North America from the danger of an attack. According to the influential Realist scholar N. J. Spykman, for example, the former colonies of Britain, Spain, and France "obtained and preserved independence both in North and South America, because there was never a united Europe to gainsay them and because no single European state ever obtained sufficient freedom of action to throw its whole military weight into a struggle in this hemisphere."[31]

All these conditions of "free security," it is argued, were progressively removed during the late nineteenth and early twentieth centuries. The barrier constituted by the oceans was first reduced, and then virtually eliminated, by advancing technology in the form of steamships, aircraft, and intercontinental missiles. Thus, it has been claimed that "the great technological-military revolution, which began about 1855, for the first time created the physical and logistical conditions for forceful and large-scale interventions from Europe—even against determined opposition on American shores."[32] British control of the Atlantic became dependent on American assistance, as was shown in 1917, more dramatically in 1940–41, and unmistakably with the sharp decline in British capabilities in the post–World War II period. The maintenance of a balance of power in Europe (or Eurasia) similarly came to require the throwing of America's weight onto the scales. To many, this provides the basic explanation for America's entry into two world wars and also for the policy of containment during the Cold War.[33]

In this view, the expansion of America's role in the world was not due to a greater ambition in its assessment of its interests. The object of American policy remained the same as it had always been—protection of the homeland from the danger of attack. That this required a balance of power in Europe has been recognized, it is claimed, ever since the time of the Founding Fathers. Jefferson's remark in 1814 that he did not wish to see "the whole force of Europe wielded by a single hand," Arthur Schlesinger observes, "defined the national interest that explains American intervention in the twentieth century's two world wars as well as in the subsequent Cold War."[34] In this interpretation, the difference between America's actions in the Napoleonic era and in the twentieth century was due to changes in the configuration of power in the rest of the world and in the technology of warfare.

In assessing the plausibility of this explanation of America's adoption of a world role, it is important to distinguish two variables—the degree of security enjoyed by the United States and the price paid to obtain it. It has been common to see the two as moving in tandem, but a strong case can be made that, while the twentieth century has undoubtedly seen a rise in the costs America has needed to pay to be safe from external attack, the degree of security it has thereby obtained has been higher than it was earlier.[35] Geography alone had never been an adequate shield, as was amply demonstrated by both the Revolutionary War and the War of 1812. The friendly disposition of Great Britain and the preservation of a balance of power in Europe were matters largely beyond the control of the U.S. government during the first century or so of the nation's existence. In this period, in fact, British sea power was more commonly viewed by Americans as a potential threat than as a bulwark.[36] If America's security then was "free," it was also somewhat precarious.

With the great growth in its population and economic strength, the nation has come to depend on its own power, together with the continuing advantages presented by its geographical location. The basis of its security has thus been brought more under its control, insofar as previously it was dependent on British policy. It has also become firmer. In part, this is because many of the technological advances in warfare have tended to make a transoceanic attack not less difficult, but more so. The transition from sail to steam, for example, circumscribed the range of battleships rather than enlarging it. The "wooden walls" of Nelson's day, as the military historian John Keegan delights in pointing out, had a range far greater than that of later "fossil-fuel fleets" constrained "by the capacity of their coal bunkers or oil tankers."[37] The logistical problems of a transoceanic military expedition also grew as armies became more dependent on sophisticated and customized munitions. As Spykman observed in 1941:

> In the good old days, armies carried little equipment and could live off the land. This meant that they could be landed in small boats on beaches and open coasts and, once ashore, could establish bridgeheads and move inland. All of this has changed. A modern army carries a large amount of heavy machinery which takes up a great deal of cargo space and can be landed with ease only in ports with adequate docking facilities, and, because it does not live off the land, it must be able to maintain an uninterrupted line of oceanic communication with its home base.[38]

Moreover, as Spykman recognized too, the development of aviation also aided the defense more than the offense, despite frequent claims to the contrary. Given the advantage of operating from nearby bases, the United States could be confident of its ability to maintain command of the air over its coasts, making it virtually impossible for an amphibious expedition to effect a successful landing.[39] The later development of intercontinental bombers and missiles did, of course, render the American homeland vulnerable to devastating attack in a way that it had never been before. But this did not increase the strategic need for foreign policy commitments. The only source of security against a transcontinental missile attack has been the deterrent effect of a capacity to retaliate, and the retaliatory capacity of the United States has not only been unsurpassed in scale but also entirely self-generated; it has not depended on the actions of allies or the balance of power in the rest of the world.

This analysis suggests that changes in the conditions of American security had implications for the nation's defense posture but not for its foreign policy. Guarding against the danger of external attack came to require devoting more resources to its military establishment than the remarkably low proportion assigned to that purpose through most of the nineteenth century.[40] But the United States did not need the assistance of allies in order to protect itself. The scale of its own power in combination with the continuing advantages of its geographical location rendered America self-sufficient in terms of security—more so, indeed, than it had been earlier in its history. So on the face of it there would appear to have been no security requirement impelling the nation to abandon its traditional policy of noninvolvement in political matters beyond the Western Hemisphere.

It is often maintained that to concentrate in this way on the capacity for national self-defense is to adopt too minimalist a view of America's security requirements. The simplest argument is that there are degrees of security and that a higher level of safety can be achieved by adopting a forward strategy. Why prepare only to fight in the last ditch when there is the possibility of establishing a buffer zone? As a military planner observed in 1945, it is preferable to fight one's wars "in some one else's territory."[41] "It is the capacity of the strong to act in order to preempt events far away that distinguishes their international conduct from that of other states," Michael Mandelbaum writes. "It is simply an effort to establish a margin of safety. It is not unlike the precautions people take in their daily lives. They insure themselves against imaginable but unlikely disasters. They wrap packages with more padding than normal handling would require. They build houses to withstand greater shocks than are expected. They vaccinate their children against diseases that have all but died out. The world operates according to the principle that it is better to be safe than sorry. How much safety a person enjoys often depends on how much he or she can afford."[42]

What Mandelbaum portrays as a natural preference is seen by proponents of the theory of "offensive realism" as a necessity imposed on states by the character of the international system. "States seek to survive under anarchy by maximizing their power relative to other states, in order to maintain the means for self-defense," John Mearsheimer argues. "The international system forces great powers to maximize their relative power because that is the optimal way to maximize their security. . . . Only a misguided state would pass up an opportunity to be the hegemon in the system because it thought it already had sufficient power to survive."[43]

These general arguments that the search for security impels great powers to expand are vulnerable both in terms of their logic and in the light of history.

There are ways in which attempts to maximize a state's military strength or territorial control can actually diminish its security, either by alarming other states into counter-actions or by leading to "imperial overstretch."[44] Contrariwise, some states have failed to expand their power as far as they could have done and suffered no harm thereby. Notable examples are Victorian Britain with regard to continental Europe and the United States in the late nineteenth and early twentieth centuries. Mearsheimer admits that these cases apparently run counter to his thesis but responds that the behavior of Britain and the United States in these years was the result of their insular position and "the stopping power of water." However, these factors did not inhibit imperial Japan from projecting its power in the interwar period or, indeed, the United States itself in both world wars and since 1945.[45] It would seem more persuasive to attribute the restraint to a well-founded belief that no security advantage was to be gained by expansion. As for Mandelbaum's homely analogies, they may be questioned in their own terms. The amount of padding people use in parcels, for example, surely correlates with other variables at least as much as their income, such as their temperament or the quality of the local postal system.

It cannot, then, be assumed that expansion will always enhance security. Whether or not it does will depend on the circumstances facing particular states at particular times. In the case of the United States in the twentieth century, reliance on the nation's preeminent strength in economic and potential military terms, in combination with its advantageous geographical position, would seem sufficient to produce an extremely high level of security. Mearsheimer himself observes that "the United States is probably the most secure great power in history, mainly because it has always been separated from the world's other great powers by two giant moats—the Atlantic and Pacific Oceans."[46] Why, then, did it have to enter into overseas commitments and project its power to other continents?

Mearsheimer's own answer to this question is that the United States, as a regional hegemon in the Western Hemisphere, has been determined to prevent the emergence of "a potential peer competitor" in Europe or East Asia.[47] The connection between this concern and American security is generally made by the argument that, if a hostile power were to gain control of the resources of the whole of the Old World, the United States would find itself outmatched and vulnerable to attack. The genealogy of this scenario can be traced from Halford Mackinder's geopolitical speculations early in the twentieth century through the arguments of interventionists and President Franklin D. Roosevelt himself in the years before Pearl Harbor to the wartime books of writers such as Spykman and Walter Lippmann.[48] By the end of World War II, it had become an axiom of official U.S. strategic thinking that "the potential military strength of the Old World in terms of manpower and in terms of warmaking capacity is enormously greater" than that of the Western Hemisphere, and that it was therefore a vital security interest to prevent any single power gaining control of all these resources.[49] This continued to be the basic strategic rationale for America's overseas commitments through the Cold War and beyond.[50]

This rationale can only be accepted as an adequate *explanation* for the assumption of these commitments, however, to the extent that its premises were rational in the light of the available evidence. Only when beliefs meet this test can adherence to them be seen as self-explanatory. When they do not meet it, the question arises of why they are held. The belief that American security required ensuring that the Old World not fall under the control of a hostile power or coalition is surely not self-explanatory in this sense. The reality of the posited danger was too questionable.

In the first place, there was the improbability of a single power gaining control of all Eurasia, let alone of the entire world beyond the Western Hemisphere. If, as some analysts argue, states naturally tend to balance against power, or at least against threats, that would be one obstacle.[51] Another would be the likelihood of nationalist resistance to any such exercise of imperialism. Second, even if this improbable eventuality were to come to pass, it is not clear that the consequences for American security would be so grievous. It would remain true that an amphibious transoceanic invasion is not a practical possibility in modern conditions, as Spykman acknowledged as early as 1941. Even if a hostile power were to gain control of a preponderance of the globe's resources, it is difficult to see why it would choose to embark on such a difficult, hazardous, and costly enterprise as attacking the United States. The only motive suggested is a general desire to conquer or dominate the whole world. Although some Realist political scientists assume that this is as natural a goal for a great power as monopoly is for a commercial company, it is doubtful if any regime (with the possible exception of Hitler's) has ever entertained such a grandiose ambition.[52] In any case, it is difficult to dispute Mearsheimer's conclusion that "except for the unlikely event wherein one state achieves clear-cut nuclear superiority, it is virtually impossible for any state to achieve global hegemony. . . . Even if Moscow had been able to dominate Europe, Northeast Asia and the Persian Gulf, which it never came close to doing, it would still have been unable to conquer the Western Hemisphere and become a true global hegemon."[53]

Those who have insisted on the importance for American security of the European balance of power have sometimes conceded that the United States would always be capable of deterring or defeating a direct attack. But they maintain that the price of doing so in the face of a hostile world would be exorbitant. In such circumstances, it is argued, the United States would have to become "a garrison state." "Security . . . involves more than national survival," the historian Melvyn P. Leffler insists. It includes the protection of "domestic core values from external threats." Republican liberty and the free enterprise system are among these core values, and they would not survive the degree of military preparedness that would become necessary if the United States were isolated: "The United States, as Dean Acheson liked to say, might survive but it would not be the country he loved."[54]

But this belief, too, is not self-explanatory. It might well be thought that a military posture that limited itself to making North America an uninviting target for attack would be less costly in terms of both resources and domestic liberty than the achievement of preponderant global power. As we have seen, the costs of the extensive role that the United States has assumed have not been slight. The need to preserve the credibility of America's commitments was the most compelling reason for the nation's involvement in the conflicts in Korea, Vietnam, and other parts of the Third World.[55] It also underlay the nuclear arms race, since the concern to maintain a secure counterforce capability derived from the perceived needs of "extended deterrence."[56] It was generally acknowledged that resolve to protect American territory required less elaborate demonstration; in 1978, Robert Jervis estimated that "less than one per cent of the G.N.P. is devoted to deterring a direct attack on the United States."[57] It is perhaps not surprising that many of those—at both ends of the political spectrum—who have most feared the effects on American liberties of a "garrison state" have tended to oppose the extension of overseas military commitments.

Moreover, the "garrison state" argument implicitly assumed that an isolated United States would need to prepare for a protracted conventional war along the lines of World War II. It thus became even less self-evident in the nuclear age. "Discussions of security continue to reflect conditions that have not obtained for more than a generation," the political scientist Robert W. Tucker observed in 1981. "These discussions continue to reflect the calculations relevant to a conventional—that is, a prenuclear—balance of power system. . . . Since the great nuclear power can now destroy any other state or combination of states, nuclear-missile weapons have conferred what had hitherto proven unachievable: a surfeit of deterrent power."[58] In the case of the United States, this deterrent capacity has been generated entirely by the nation itself and has not been dependent on the maintenance of a balance of power in the Old World.[59] In these circumstances, it seems hard to take issue with Charles Krauthammer's brisk conclusion in 1986 that "if the security of the United States is the only goal of American foreign policy, all that is needed is a minimal deterrent arsenal, a small navy, a border patrol, and hardly any foreign policy at all."[60] Indeed, Tucker has gone further in observing that, once the Soviet Union had developed the capability to deliver a nuclear attack on the United States, America's overseas commitments and alliances had a negative effect on its safety: "Although the loss of allies, even the most important allies, would not significantly alter the prospects of an adversary surviving an attack upon the United States, the risks that might have to be run on behalf of allies could lead to a nuclear confrontation that would escape the control of the great protagonists." "Why," he asked, "should we persist in commitments whose sacrifice would not risk our physical survival but whose retention does?"[61]

Tucker's own answer to this question was that "nations, particularly great nations, have seldom been willing to equate their security with their physical dimensions alone."[62] Certainly, the term *national security* has often been used in American writings and speeches to cover much more than the protection of the United States itself from external attack. It has also often been taken to require the achievement of what Arnold Wolfers called "milieu goals" in distinction to "possession goals"—that is, those that relate to "the shape of the environment in which the nation operates."[63] The argument here is that the United States could not be truly secure in a hostile and unruly world. Therefore, it needs to concern itself with the nature of the regimes in other countries and with upholding norms of international conduct. Among the arguments for including these concerns in the category of security requirements is the assertion that the nation's "core values" of democracy and the free enterprise system would be hard to sustain if they were confined to North America.

The problem with encompassing these broader objectives under the rubric of national security, however, is that the concept loses the quality that makes it potentially a powerful explanation for American actions.[64] This quality is the general belief that the value is one that *has* to be protected at all costs. The milieu goals are both too ambitious and too disputable to have this quality. George W. Bush's assertion that "the survival of liberty in our land increasingly depends on the success of liberty in other lands" won diminishing assent as the difficulty of bringing democracy to the Middle East became apparent.[65] The same was true in the Vietnam years of Dean Rusk's declaration that "we can be safe only to the extent that our total environment is safe."[66] The disputable character of milieu goals is aggravated by the way in which the principles they give rise to often conflict with each other. Policy in particular situations will vary greatly according to the relative priority accorded to the support of democracy, the right of self-determination, the peaceful settlement of disputes, and the maintenance of the balance of power. In any case, policies aiming at these broader goals will lack the imperative sense of urgency and the unproblematic legitimation of the use of force that are uniquely attached to what FDR referred to as "the cause of self-evident home defense."[67]

Economic Interests as an Explanation

Whereas national security is an explanation for America's world role commonly advanced by its defenders and advocates, it has been critics of U.S. policy who have most often attributed it to economic interests. There are several ways in which this can be done. One is to argue that the nation's prosperity and growth have been dependent on its overseas economic interests and that these have required government support, directly in specific contexts or more generally through the maintenance of a liberal international economic order. A second approach sees the overseas economic interests that have shaped policy as those not of the nation as a whole but of influential elements within it. This interpretation of American diplomacy was developed by the historian Charles A. Beard in his writings in the 1930s.[68] Finally, there is the suggestion that the ideology arising from America's capitalist political economy produces a drive to establish an "Open Door world" regardless of the actual material importance of the interests involved. All these versions of the argument may be found in the influential writings of William Appleman Williams, though it is the last that his admirers have tended to emphasize in recent years.[69]

Attempts to attribute U.S. global strategy to the objective needs of the national economy face two major problems. The first is the limited scale in proportional terms of America's overseas economic interests, particularly in the period in which the traditional stance of non-involvement was abandoned and major foreign commitments assumed. The second is the difficulty of establishing a connection between these interests and American foreign policy.

Despite the emphasis in early formulations of the Open Door thesis on a desire to establish external markets for the nation's "surplus" production, this is probably the aspect of America's overseas economic interests that can least plausibly be seen as providing a motive for its political and military commitments. To a much greater extent than in most other developed countries, American production has been consumed at home. In the 1950s and 1960s, when America's commitment to influencing world politics was at its peacetime apogee, exports constituted only 4 to 5 percent of GNP. This figure, low as it is in comparative terms, would be even lower if the North American economy were to be regarded as a unit, since roughly a quarter of America's exports went to Canada and Mexico. Moreover, the importance of exports to the American economy was diminishing rather than growing as the nation's role in world politics expanded. In the decades after independence, merchandise exports are estimated to have amounted to between 10 and 20 percent of GNP, and the figure remained between 6 and 7 percent in the later nineteenth century; by the 1920s, this had fallen to around 5 percent.[70] (This trend was the result of industrialization, since a higher proportion of farm products than of manufactured goods was exported.) Since the 1920s, like the 1960s, was a period of prosperity, this suggested that the American economy did not need extensive export markets in order to flourish.

Some political actions can be seen as reflecting this situation, but they are hardly those that would lead the way to an "Open Door world." "Throughout the long era from 1861 to 1933," the economist Peter H. Lindert writes, "the United States competed with Russia as the most protectionist of the major powers."[71] Although U.S. exports in the 1930s slumped even more drastically than domestic demand, the recovery program of the early New Deal was for the most part strikingly inward-looking.[72] The Reciprocal Trade Agreements Act of 1934 was an exception and, although the agreements made under it before World War II were limited in number and scope, the congressional delegation of authority to the executive that it embodied was the mechanism through which tariff levels were to be much reduced in subsequent decades (despite the persistence of strong protectionist sentiment in Congress). In the 1940s, with the establishment of the Bretton Woods system and the General Agreement on Tariffs and Trade (GATT), the United States took the lead in institutionalizing a multilateral trading system, but it is an open question how far this executive-led policy was driven by a concern with America's own future prosperity or by wider foreign policy goals.[73] The latter clearly took priority in the post–World War II years; not only did the stationing of American forces abroad cause balance of payments difficulties but the United States also actively promoted steps toward economic union in western Europe that had the effect of disadvantaging U.S. exports.[74] In 1992, Alfred E. Eckes, former chairman of the United States International Trade Commission, argued that during the Cold War "the U.S. government sacrificed thousands of domestic jobs to create employment and prosperity elsewhere in the noncommunist world."[75]

Nor is it easy to see a connection between specific overseas actions and commitments of the United States and the nation's trade interests. The logic of such a connection seems clearest in the case of countries in the Third World, where a determination to protect the rights of property and enforce contractual obligations was most likely to lead to outside intervention. But in the period when the country assumed its global role, such places never absorbed more than a small proportion of U.S. exports, the great bulk of which went to other developed countries.[76] To have constructed the elaborate politico-military apparatus that the United States did in the post–World War II era for the sake of safeguarding markets for such a tiny fraction of American production would hardly satisfy the least exigent of cost-benefit calculations. In preventing discrimination against U.S. exports, particularly in the developed world, the greatest leverage has been provided by the size of the American market, which has meant that the trade in question has always been proportionally more important to the other countries involved than to the United States.[77] By contrast, when U.S. officials have sought to gain economic concessions from allies in return for the security commitments to them, as with Germany in the 1960s or Japan in the 1980s and 1990s, the results have been meager at best.[78] Moreover, there has been no reason to assume that other nations' interest in trade relations with the United States would cease if ideologically hostile regimes came to power; that was certainly not the case with the communist governments in Russia and eastern Europe.

American investment has been much more sensitive than trade to the political conditions obtaining in foreign countries. Unlike trade, too, it grew rather than diminished in scale as America's power in world affairs expanded. Yet, here again, the connections between the two processes have not been close. The first great growth in America's overseas investments occurred during World War I and the 1920s—by 1929, they were equivalent to over a fifth of GNP, a level not reached again until 1981.[79] Although private sector loans to the allies during the period of neutrality in World War I have been seen (rather misleadingly) as paving the way for America's intervention, the loans made during the 1920s (mostly to Germany) led to no political or military commitments. Indeed, by 1934 over 40 percent of American loans to Europe were in default, but the U.S. government took no responsibility for this situation.[80]

The great majority of direct investments abroad have not needed any governmental support; the desire of other countries for foreign capital has given U.S. corporations a bargaining position strong enough to protect their interests.[81] Although Washington has acted at times to promote or protect American business interests abroad, particularly in Latin America, this goal is rarely publicly avowed, as it tends to arouse domestic opposition. "It is singular," the British ambassador observed in 1913, "how the majority of Americans are more pleased than otherwise at the losses of rich Americans in Mexico."[82] The contrast with the United Kingdom implied here may have partly reflected the different importance of foreign investment to the economies of the two countries.[83] Whereas overseas investments provided as much as 8 percent of Britain's national income in 1910, the comparable figure for the United States in 1973 was 1.6 percent.[84] The proportion of American annual gross capital formation exported has never amounted to more than 2 percent of the total.[85] At times, officials have encouraged such investment for the sake of foreign policy objectives.[86] But at other times they have deplored the export of capital as damaging to domestic employment and growth and hence to the welfare of most Americans—a position also commonly expressed by labor leaders.[87]

The aspect of America's international economic relations that has most often been regarded as a truly national interest has been the importation of raw materials either not available at all in the United States or not in sufficient quantities to meet the country's needs. Historically, the government has been most concerned about materials needed by the armed forces. Fears about the adequacy of U.S. strategic supplies led Washington in the 1920s to prompt, as well as to back diplomatically, the development by U.S. corporations of oil resources in the Middle East and the Netherlands East Indies, and of rubber in Liberia.[88] Since World War II, the United States has built up great stockpiles of "strategic" and "critical" materials to guard against the danger of being cut off from overseas supplies.

Yet the American situation has never been remotely comparable to that of Japan, or Germany, or even Britain, where it is plausible to argue that the perceived need to gain overseas supplies of raw materials led to an expansionist policy. By contrast, the United States has been remarkably self-sufficient in this respect also. In the period 1900–29, domestic production accounted for 96 percent of all the minerals consumed, and as much was exported as imported.[89] Despite the enormous rate of consumption, the United States even in the mid-1970s was dependent on foreign sources for only 15 percent of its supply of critical nonfuel minerals, while western Europe and Japan had to import, respectively, 75 and 90 percent of their supplies.[90] Moreover, once again, the degree of self-sufficiency is even greater if the North American economy is considered as a unit. Canada has been a particularly important source of supply—notably, of nickel, one of the few minerals the United States has lacked. There have been periodic scares, but these have resulted from greatly underestimating the potentialities of substitution and the stimulating effects of wartime conditions on domestic output.[91] In 1942, for example, Spykman published tables showing how dependent the United States was on transoceanic sources of "strategic" and "critical" raw materials, concluding that "the Asiatic Mediterranean [the South China Sea and Indonesia] is perhaps the most important single source of strategic raw materials for the United States, and its control by a single power would endanger the basis of our military strength."[92] Few of his readers can have anticipated that between 1941 and 1943, with the "Asiatic Mediterranean" entirely under the control of Japan, there would be a *more than eightfold* increase in American armaments production.[93]

Oil has, of course, come to be an obvious exception to this lack of dependence on raw material imports—although in this respect, too, the United States has remained much closer to a position of self-sufficiency than most other industrial countries. Nevertheless, its need in recent decades for an uninterrupted flow of plentiful supplies of imported oil at a reasonable price can be seen as the unique example of an overseas economic interest of clear national importance. One indication of its special status is that it is the only economic interest that has been invoked by those seeking to develop public support for military intervention abroad—particularly, at the time of the Persian Gulf War of 1990–91.

Generally, the argument that the nation was fighting for economic interests has been advanced by those who opposed the intervention rather than by those who supported it. Yet the degree to which U.S. policy, even in the Middle East, has been driven by a concern to maintain oil supplies at a reasonable price remains open to debate. And, in any case, this particular economic interest was at most a minor concern in the period when the United States assumed its world role.

If exports and other overseas interests have been proportionally quite limited in a national context, they have certainly been crucial for some sectors of the American economy. The resulting differences of sectional interest have clearly been reflected in divisions over trade policy, and some scholars see them as also crucially important in shaping attitudes to foreign policy commitments.[94] However, even if, for the sake of argument, we accept this interpretation of sectional divisions over foreign policy, it is not sufficient to explain America's assumption of a global role and the degree of political consensus that has made this possible. Neither the structure of the American economy nor the balance of power within it changed between 1914 and 1950 to anything like the extent that the scope and ambition of U.S. foreign policy did.

There remains the argument that U.S. policy has been shaped not by a direct concern with specific economic interests but by a worldview that reflects the structure and objective requirements of the capitalist system. It is, however, only the acceptance of a quasi-Marxist assumption that ideological "superstructure" reflects "the forces" and "relations" of production that brings such an interpretation under the rubric of economic interest. It seems more appropriate to consider ideology as an explanatory factor in its own right.

Missionary Ideology as an Explanation

There can be little doubt that the way in which Americans have viewed world affairs and the role their nation should play in them has been inflected by ideology. If there are countries whose foreign policy is entirely shaped by hard-nosed calculations of strategic and material interest, the United States is not one of them. This reflects the character of American nationalism, based as it is not on ethnicity, language, or religion but on allegiance to the land itself, the political system and the values these are seen as embodying. From colonial times, Americans have seen their experience as of universal rather than local significance. Here in this "New World" they could construct a society in which the deep human aspirations for freedom and fulfillment could at last be realized, unconstrained by the oppressive structures that had become established on other continents. The founding of the United States represented a new era in human history. "The

Declaration of Independence," Lincoln declared on the eve of the Civil War, "gave liberty, not alone to the people of this country, but, I hope, to the world, for all future time. It was that which gave promise that in due time the weight would be lifted from the shoulders of all men." That was why the Union represented "the last best hope of earth."[95]

Pervasive and deep in the culture though these ideological beliefs have been, they do not in themselves provide a sufficient explanation for America's assumption of such an active and extensive role in world politics. For, ever since the days of the Founding Fathers, the national mission has been invoked as a justification for avoiding involvement in overseas conflicts. From the classical republican and English Country Whig traditions of political thought, Americans inherited a belief that standing armies were a threat to domestic liberty as well as a burden on taxpayers; free societies should rely on a citizen militia for defense. The whole business of power politics, including professional diplomacy and espionage as well as war, came to be associated with the European social order—the means by which an essentially feudal ruling class justified both its privileges and the oppressive apparatus of states and empires. When such oppression was challenged by peoples who seemed to be following the example of 1776, there was usually some feeling that the United States ought to render them assistance, but the policy of non-involvement was upheld by the argument that this would endanger republican liberty at home.

This fear of the domestic effects of involvement in foreign conflicts shows that the predominance in the nineteenth century of the view that the nation's mission was only to provide an *example* of the blessings of liberty was not, as some have argued, simply a consequence of its lack of capacity to do more.[96] By the same token, the rise in the twentieth century of a more activist, interventionist interpretation of America's historic role and responsibilities should not be seen as an inevitable, predestined consequence of the growth of its power.

In any case, there are good grounds for doubting that the commitment of most Americans to the spreading of freedom and democracy abroad is deep enough to sustain strenuous and costly foreign policy enterprises. Although presidents and other policymakers commonly invoke these principles when seeking support for their policies, they almost invariably link them with other, more concretely self-interested objectives. Failure to do this persuasively tends to result in political defeat, as the experience of Woodrow Wilson and Jimmy Carter demonstrates. Studies of public opinion indicate that democracy promotion, although widely approved of as a general goal of U.S. foreign policy, is regarded by the majority as less important than America's own security or economic interests and as not, in itself, justification for enterprises involving significant human or financial costs.[97]

Seeking an Answer

The preceding argument has sought to show the difficulty of explaining America's assumption of a strenuous and wide-ranging global role in general or theoretical terms. The nation's preeminent economic strength and financial resources have endowed it with the means to play the role, but possession of the capacity is not sufficient in itself to explain its exercise, especially given the costs involved. Nor is the undertaking of this global role easily explicable in terms of a need to safeguard the nation's core interests of safety from external attack and economic prosperity.

When abstract analysis or theoretical propositions are unable to explain an historical phenomenon satisfactorily, examining *how* it came about is usually the best way to find out *why*. In this case, it is not difficult to determine the period on which such an historical inquiry should focus. Before the Civil War, the United States lacked the capacity to play a large role in international affairs even if it had wished to do so. During those decades, it developed a tradition of non-involvement in the great power politics of Europe and also a habit of devoting few resources to the conduct of foreign policy or, in normal times, to its armed forces. As late as 1890, military expenditures amounted to less than 0.5 percent of GNP, and only seventy-six people were employed by the State Department in Washington.[98] By then, however, America's rapidly growing economy had already become larger than that of any other nation, thereby bringing more ambitious foreign policy objectives within the sphere of realistic aspiration. When the Truman administration left office in 1952, tens of thousands of Americans were engaged in conducting the nation's diplomatic, intelligence, and foreign aid operations in a plethora of agencies under the aegis of the National Security Act of 1947. The country's leading role in international organizations such as the United Nations and the IMF was underpinned by their financial dependence on it. Bound by long-term treaties to protect the security of twelve west European countries, Canada, Japan, Taiwan, the Philippines, Australia and New Zealand, the United States had military bases across the globe while its massive navy dominated the oceans of the world. In the second half of the twentieth century, the nation's defense budget absorbed more than 5 percent of GNP on a regular basis (and in many years significantly more). Between 1890 and 1952, clearly, America's stance in world politics had been transformed.

This transformation was not the product of a sudden, abrupt change, either in the external environment or in the thinking of most Americans, but the result of a comparatively long process. The process was also an unsteady one, with more than one oscillation between advance and retreat. These changes of stance reflected shifts in the balance of opinion within the country on the central issue of how far the United States needed to—or should—accept the costs and risks of full-scale participation in world politics. The subject of this book, therefore, is what might be called "the long debate" over this question between the late nineteenth and mid-twentieth centuries. There had been fierce disagreements over foreign policy earlier, and there certainly have been since, but it was the successive debates of these years that were the most intense and consequential, leading ultimately to an enormous expansion of the nation's foreign policy commitments.

In the American system, public debate matters because it shapes the context within which the elected politicians who have the power to determine the nation's course make their decisions. Of course, politicians themselves participate in the public debate and seek to shape opinion, presidents being in a powerful position to do this through their deeds as well as through words that carry a special authority. But they know that it is impossible to sustain policies that make substantial demands on the nation's resources without public support. Because the behavior of the United States in the international arena is the product of this interactive process, any attempt to explain it must examine the factors that shaped public and congressional opinion as well as the thinking of "policymakers" (a category that grew greatly in size over the course of this period and thereafter). Public opinion and the thinking within government are distinguishable entities, and at times the gap between them has been significant. But the distinction can be drawn too sharply; the arguments deployed within government often mirrored those in the public arena.

In examining the successive stages of this long debate, I focus especially on arguments invoking threats to the nation's own safety and the part played by economic interests. There are two, perhaps related, reasons for this focus. One is that, as indicated earlier, each of these factors has been seen by many historians and commentators as the basic explanation of twentieth-century U.S. foreign policy. As argued above, the sufficiency of such explanations is reduced if it is questionable whether either the nation's security or the continued flourishing of its capitalist economy *really* depended on its foreign policy commitments. Yet the belief or perception that such a dependence did exist may still have been crucial in shaping people's foreign policy views or motivating the actions of the U.S. government. Historians adhering to one or other of these interpretations do, indeed, show that such beliefs or perceptions were often articulated. Hence there is reason to pay particular attention not only to the influence of such beliefs and perceptions but also to their origins and evolution. (This incidentally highlights how the historical interpretations themselves were developed in the context of earlier internal debates about foreign policy.)

Even without this historiographical background, it would seem natural to approach the subject by focusing on the role played by security concerns and economic interest. For these cross-cultural values are commonly assumed to shape the foreign policy of all states, not only by Realist theorists but also in everyday discussion. Assessing the extent to which this has been true in the case of the United States makes clearer what has to be explained in other ways— through exploring the various, more particular values and concerns that led Americans to favor the exercise of their nation's power to affect developments on other continents or the nature of the international system as a whole.

Ultimately, it is the sources of the will to exercise power that we are seeking— the reasons why the nation was prepared to make costly commitments to achieve foreign policy objectives. That there was a natural reluctance to make the sacrifices such commitments inevitably entailed is a central theme in what follows. But I argue that the extraordinary scale of the nation's relative power operated in a contrary direction. Partly, this was because it made the cost of foreign policy enterprises more bearable, in the manner outlined above. But, in addition to this objective effect, there were subjective ones. Americans at all levels were very conscious of their nation's great potential power—indeed, were more inclined to exaggerate it than to underestimate it—and this affected their views and attitudes in several ways. Most obviously, it engendered confidence in the ability of the United States to achieve ambitious foreign policy objectives—provided it made the necessary effort. This in turn fostered a sense of responsibility. If the United States possessed a unique—or at least exceptional—capacity to affect the course of events overseas, its failure to act would be as consequential as action—and, in some circumstances, morally culpable. Along with confidence, and a sense of responsibility, consciousness of the scale of America's relative power nurtured a very large conception of the nation's proper status and influence in world affairs—of its prerogatives, as it were. Varied as they were, all these assumptions and attitudes can be seen as reflecting a sense of power.

1

A NEW SENSE OF POWER

In the decades following the Civil War, the American republic grew so greatly in every respect that its status among the nations of the world was transformed. In physical terms, the United States had already acquired title to all of its present-day contiguous territory before the Civil War, but it was only after the war that the trans-Mississippi west was pacified, developed, populated by settlers, and linked to the rest of the country by railroads; by 1912 the whole of the region had achieved statehood, twelve new states having been admitted to the union since 1865. More U.S. land was settled between 1870 and 1900 (430 million acres) than in the previous three hundred years (407 million acres). The nation's population rose from thirty-six million in 1865 to a hundred million in 1915. This obviously contributed to the growth in the size of its economy, but a larger contribution was made by advances in efficiency; per capita productivity increased by almost 2.5 percent per annum between 1870 and 1910. By the latter year, the GNP was five times greater (in real terms) than it had been forty years earlier. There were twice as many cattle, hogs, and sheep on American farms, and the physical output of wheat and corn had increased by 250 percent. Impressive as this growth in agricultural production was, it was outstripped by the increase in mining and manufacturing. The tonnage of coal (including anthracite) mined in 1910 was twelve times that in 1870, while the output of steel rails was six and a half times greater. In industries that started from near zero, such as crude petroleum and steel ingots and castings, the growth was even more spectacular, rising respectively from 5.2 million to 209.5 million barrels and from 77,000 to 28 million short tons.[1]

These rates of growth were unmatched elsewhere, and they propelled the United States well ahead of all other countries. In 1850, Britain and France had each produced one and a half times as much as the United States. With its GDP doubling in only seventeen years, the United States had overtaken both by 1870, and by 1890 it was producing almost as much as the two combined. By 1913, the value of America's output exceeded that of Britain, France, and Germany combined and amounted to roughly two-thirds of that of all western Europe. By that date, it was producing 32 percent of the world's manufactured goods and 20 percent of its total output. At a time when steel production was regarded in Winston Churchill's words as "a rather decisive index of military power," America's output on the eve of the First World War was almost twice that of Germany, which in turn was producing more than Britain, France, and Russia combined.[2]

Realist theory as well as everyday assumptions would lead one to expect that this great growth of the nation's relative power would produce an expansion of its foreign policy objectives and the devotion of some of the nation's new wealth to efforts to exercise increased international influence. Such an expectation is to some extent borne out by the conduct of the United States in the half-century between the Civil War and World War I. Indeed, histories of U.S. foreign policy generally see expansion as the central theme in this period, highlighting the Spanish-American War of 1898 and the subsequent acquisition of an overseas empire. Many have attributed this expansion to the nation's economic interests, particularly the perceived need to secure overseas markets for "surplus" production. But, although such a need was often asserted, its actual impact on the nation's foreign or trade policy is hard to discern. Other analysts attach more weight to anxiety about the security of the Western Hemisphere in an era of European imperialism, but again, the influence of this anxiety, while real, was quite narrowly circumscribed. Rather, the record suggests that the main impetus for a wider and more assertive involvement in external affairs came from consciousness of America's new power and the belief that its enhanced international status entitled it to greater prerogatives and brought wider responsibilities. The political force of such beliefs, however, was both limited and episodic, and this was true also of the nation's foreign policy actions in these years. The United States remained largely detached from great power politics, exerting much less influence on them than its economic might would have enabled it to. However, there was an increasing consciousness of this discrepancy among educated Americans, and many of them anticipated that their nation would—and should—play a greater world role in the future.

The Expansion of U.S. Foreign Policy

It was with respect to the Western Hemisphere, and especially central America and the Caribbean, that the assertion of the nation's new power was most clearly manifest. From the 1870s on, there was increasing pressure for the repudiation of the 1850 Clayton-Bulwer Treaty with Great Britain, which had stipulated that any canal across the isthmus of central America should be jointly constructed and controlled. The United States also conducted its relations with the South American republics more high-handedly. When Chile was slow to apologize and offer reparation after two American sailors were killed and several injured by a mob in Valparaiso in 1891, President Benjamin Harrison threatened war; "the American Republic will stand no more nonsense from any power, big or little," one senator declared. In 1894, the United States sent a fleet to break a rebel blockade in Brazil, and a year later it intruded on a dispute between Britain and Venezuela over the boundary of British Guiana, insisting that it be arbitrated. In a Note justifying American intervention to the British government, Secretary of State Richard Olney declared that "today the United States is practically sovereign on this continent, and its fiat is law upon the subjects to which it confines its interposition ... because, in addition to all other grounds, its infinite resources combined with its isolated position render it master of the situation and practically invulnerable as against any or all other powers."[3]

This belligerent diplomacy may have gained added confidence from the development of American naval power in these years. In the aftermath of the Civil War, the navy had declined until it possessed only fifty ships capable of firing a gun, and these mostly un-armored, wooden sailing vessels; its impotence was demonstrated in 1873 by its inability to mount an effective challenge when Spain captured an American ship carrying contraband to Cuban insurrectionists and executed over fifty men, many of whom were Americans. The revival of the navy began in the 1880s with the building of steel cruisers, increasingly steam-powered, armored, and with rifled guns. That decade also saw the foundation of the Naval War College at Newport, Rhode Island, and the creation of embryonic intelligence organizations within the Navy and War Departments. A major transition was the decision in 1889–90 to build battleships capable of blue-water engagements with the capital ships of the major European powers; three such battleships were authorized by Congress in 1890, and six more in 1892–96.[4]

The building of a battleship navy was promoted by the theories of A. T. Mahan, whose *The Influence of Sea Power upon History, 1660–1783*, based on his lectures at the Naval War College, propelled him to international fame after its publication in 1890. In this book and a successor volume, Mahan attributed Great Britain's victories in war and its preeminence in peace to its command of the sea. Key to this was a concentrated fleet of capital ships capable of defeating any other navy in battle and of operating far from home, which in the age of steam required overseas coaling stations. Under this protection, a large merchant marine could carry the overseas trade that brought prosperity to a nation and furnished skilled seamen to man the battleship navy. In a series of articles during the 1890s, Mahan spelled out what he saw as the implications of this analysis for the United States. The primary requirement was to assert naval dominance over the Caribbean and Central America so that an isthmian canal would be a strategic asset rather than a liability. When in 1893 American residents in Hawaii overthrew the native queen and requested annexation of the islands by the United States, Mahan promptly argued that this was necessary to protect the West Coast and the Pacific approaches to an isthmian canal as well as the trade routes to China and Japan.[5]

Mahan's doctrines accorded with some existing currents of opinion in the metropolitan Northeast. In particular, they were taken up by two young Republican politicians, close friends, who were already firm believers in a strong navy and a vigorous foreign policy. Theodore Roosevelt of New York, author of *The Naval War of 1812* (begun while an undergraduate at Harvard), gave Mahan's historical works glowing reviews. Henry Cabot Lodge of Massachusetts drew on them in Senate addresses advocating the annexation of Hawaii. "The great nations are rapidly absorbing for their future expansion and their present defense all the waste places of the earth," he observed in a magazine article. "As one of the great nations of the world, the United States must not fall out of the line of march."[6] Apart from Hawaii, Lodge had no specific territorial acquisitions in mind. His driving concern, as he made clear on many occasions, was that the United States should take "rank where we belong, as one of the greatest of the great world powers." Roosevelt, too, repeatedly urged the United States to behave as a great nation should and, more than Lodge, stressed that this entailed a preparedness to fight.

> We ask for a great navy . . . partly because we feel that no national life is worth having if the nation is not willing, when the need shall arise, to stake everything on the supreme arbitrament of war and to pour out its blood, its treasure, and tears like water rather than submit to the loss of honor or renown.[7]

These developments were the background to the Spanish-American War and the subsequent acquisition by the United States of substantial overseas territories, including the Philippine archipelago as well as Hawaii and Guam in the Pacific and Puerto Rico in the Caribbean; a naval base was also established on Cuba, which became a protectorate. None of this would have happened, however, without the Cuban rebellion against Spanish rule that, following earlier uprisings, broke out in 1895. Although the administrations of Cleveland and McKinley strongly pressed Spain to resolve the conflict, which was impinging on American interests in various ways, they resisted demands that the United States recognize the rebels as the legitimate government of an independent Cuba. Unsurprisingly, Lodge and Roosevelt were early advocates of expelling the Spanish, but in this they were not representative of their fellow northeastern Republicans; it was Democrats and Populists from the interior who provided most of the congressional support for "Cuba Libre." By early 1898, however, the pressure in Congress for intervention had become general and overwhelming, fueled by public outrage at the deaths and suffering resulting from the brutal policies of the Spanish General Valeriano Weyler. Humanitarian sentiment was fused with traditional anticolonialism and a particular demonization of the effete Catholic monarchy of Spain. There was nothing new about these impulses and attitudes in themselves; the novel element was consciousness of the nation's power and the belief that this brought with it a moral obligation. "We cannot refuse to accept this responsibility which the God of the universe has placed upon us as the one great power in the New World," declared John M. Thurston (R–Neb.), weeping as he reported to the Senate on a fact-finding mission to the island. But it was a less high-minded sense of the respect that the United States could expect to receive from other powers that finally precipitated the conflict. The sinking of the battleship *Maine* in Havana harbor with the loss of 260 lives through an explosion that was widely attributed to Spanish agents, following the publication of a letter in which the Spanish minister in Washington made disparaging remarks about McKinley, provoked a storm of anger in the press at these insults to the nation's honor: "Remember the *Maine*, to hell with Spain!" became a popular rallying cry. At a more informed level, anticipations of an easy victory were strengthened as it was realized that Spain's hopes of effective support from other European powers would be disappointed.[8]

The war with Spain was clearly a response to external events rather than being motivated by an internally generated desire for overseas territorial expansion. Indeed, it began under the aegis of anti-imperialism; supporters of the Cuban cause often invoked the principles of the Declaration of Independence. It is true that others doubted the capacity of the insurgents to establish an effective government and that McKinley succeeded in blocking moves to make recognition of the Cuban republic part of the congressional resolution authorizing the use of military force. He did, however, accept the Teller Amendment committing the United States "to leave the government and control of the island to the people thereof" after it had been pacified. This was consistent with the president's earlier and repeated declaration that "forcible annexation" was "not to be thought of" because "by our code of morality, [it] would be criminal aggression."[9]

That the war, nevertheless, led to many annexations was the result of the inter-action of preexisting interests and concerns with unanticipated events that arose from the course of the conflict itself. The most consequential of these events was Admiral Dewey's destruction of the Spanish fleet in the Philippines at the very beginning of the war. This triumph in the western Pacific, together with the exu-berant atmosphere of war, strengthened support for the annexation of Hawaii, long favored by most Republicans including McKinley, and this was achieved by joint congressional resolution in July 1898. If, as Mahan had argued, Hawaii was needed to guard the approaches to an isthmian canal, the same was even more true of a base in the Caribbean, and this led to the seizure of Puerto Rico. Fol-lowing Dewey's victory, over ten thousand American troops were dispatched to Manila. The resulting need for intermediate coaling and cable stations provided not only an additional strategic rationale for annexing Hawaii but also one for taking the islands of Guam and Wake (an uninhabited atoll).

If acquiring such overseas supply bases represented the fulfillment (and extension) of a Mahanite program, assuming the government of the Philippine islands (with a population of eight million) constituted a form of European-style colonialism that had not been advocated before the war even by expansionists like Lodge and Roosevelt. Such men naturally sought to exploit the opportunity provided by the war to enhance both the scope of the country's international involvement and the place of foreign policy in American life by promoting what Lodge called "a large policy." Yet, although Roosevelt immediately and consis-tently wanted to annex the Philippines, Lodge himself wavered over this and at times, like Mahan, wanted to take only Manila and the island of Luzon. This was all McKinley asked for in his initial instructions to the American peace commis-sioners in September, but by late October the president had come to favor taking the whole archipelago, a position he insisted on during the negotiations with Spain. McKinley argued that this was the only practicable option. Leaving the islands under Spain's oppressive and incompetent rule would be a betrayal of the Filipinos, especially given the insurgency led by Emilio Aguinaldo with which U.S. forces had initially cooperated. But granting the Philippines independence would, observers reported, lead to anarchy and a scramble for influence among the European powers currently competing for concessions in China.

These external considerations may help to explain the change in the president's position but at least as important seems to have been his reading of American public opinion, which he had sought to gauge during a speaking tour through the Middle West in October. That there was indeed increasing domestic support for annexation was indicated by polls of press opinion: In August 1898, only 43 percent of a sample of sixty-five newspapers were for permanent retention of the Philippines, but by December a poll of 498 papers reported 61 percent in favor.

The latter poll showed the division to be largely along party lines and, relatedly, sectional, with Republican papers overwhelmingly for expansion, Democratic ones almost as strongly against, and the least enthusiasm for it in the South. There was a similar pattern to the voting in the Senate, where the treaty gained the requisite two-thirds majority by a margin of one vote in February 1899.[10]

These territorial acquisitions, following the quick and comprehensive defeat of Spain, were seen by many as a turning point that would lead to the United States' playing a much larger role in world politics. "We cannot return to the point whence we set out," wrote Woodrow Wilson, then a professor at Princeton. "We have left the continent which has hitherto been our only field of action and have gone out upon the seas, where the nations are rivals and we cannot live or act apart." Days after Dewey's victory, the London *Times* observed, "In the future America will play a part in the general affairs of the world such as she has never played before. . . . When the American people realize this, and they realize novel situations with remarkable promptitude, they will not do things by halves." In the next few years, more than one book was published on the United States "as a world power."[11]

In the regions where the war had been fought, these expectations were borne out to a greater or lesser extent. This was preeminently true of Central America and the Caribbean, where the United States moved steadily to establish its hegemony.[12] Indeed, the intervention in Cuba that led to the war can be seen as a part of this process, and the postwar treatment of that island made it clear that a controlling position there was the priority of American policymakers. Although the Teller Amendment's abnegation of annexation was adhered to, the military occupation did not end until the Cubans had written into their constitution the terms of the Platt Amendment of 1901. This not only forbade Cuba from forming ties with a foreign power but also granted the United States a naval base and the right to intervene to maintain "a government adequate for the protection of life, property and individual liberty." This right was to be exercised three times over the next twenty years, while a reciprocity treaty in 1903 added an economic dimension to this quasi-colonial relationship.

Policymakers' concern that Cuba should remain stable and free from foreign influence derived in good part from the projected isthmian canal, the strategic case for which had been reinforced by the acquisition of Hawaii and the Philippines and the consequent need to deploy naval power on both oceans. In the aftermath of the war, the British at last accepted the supersession of the Clayton-Bulwer Treaty and, at the Senate's insistence, granted the United States the right to fortify as well as to build and control an isthmian canal on the condition that it should be open to the vessels of all nations equally. The project now became a political priority, although choosing the route and obtaining the requisite territory proved a complicated business, resolved only after Panama, with implicit American support, broke away from Colombia and granted the United States sovereign rights over a ten-mile-wide zone. This opened the way to construction of the canal, which began in 1904.

In the same year, the United States explicitly claimed the exclusive right to exercise "an international police power" in its sphere. This was precipitated by the adverse public reaction to Anglo-German naval action against Venezuela in 1902–03 to enforce the claims of foreign creditors. The legitimacy of such enforcement was accepted by the administration, but in 1904 the president declared, in the so-called Roosevelt Corollary to the Monroe Doctrine, that when "intervention by some civilized nation" was required in the Western Hemisphere, the United States would assume the responsibility. In the following years, a variety of means were developed to exercise what Secretary of State Philander Knox was to call "benevolent supervision" of small countries in the Caribbean and Central America, including taking control of custom house receipts, empowering American experts to manage government finances, and persuading U.S. bankers to make loans. But behind all this was the threat, and in several cases the reality, of military intervention.[13]

In East Asia, the most immediate and substantial impetus to increased involvement came from the Philippines, where the United States had not only to bear the responsibilities of government but also to wage a protracted and unsavory war against Aguinaldo and his followers as they continued their fight for independence, now against their new colonial masters. By 1902, when it effectively ended, this conflict had cost the United States more than 4,000 dead and 2,800 wounded as well as $400 million; twenty thousand Filipinos are estimated to have been killed in action and as many as two hundred thousand from war-related causes. With the Philippines came greater concern with East Asian affairs generally. The difficulty of defending such far-flung possessions was to add an edge of anxiety to relations with Japan. More immediately, there was the perceived need to protect American interests in China, which for some had been a prime reason for keeping at least a base in the Philippines. The concessions recently granted to European powers in various parts of China had raised a fear that American exporters would be disadvantaged in what was seen as a growing market. In circular Notes to the powers in 1899 and 1900, Secretary of State John Hay affirmed America's commitment to the preservation of "Chinese territorial and administrative entity" and "the principle of equal and impartial trade with all parts of the Chinese empire." The second "Open Door Note" followed the participation of American troops (sent from the Philippines) in the eight-power military expedition to defeat the anti-western Boxer Rebellion and liberate the foreign legations besieged in Beijing.[14]

Not the least consequential aspect of the War of 1898 was the boost it gave to Theodore Roosevelt's political career. After resigning as assistant secretary of the navy to become lieutenant colonel in a volunteer cavalry regiment, Roosevelt became a national celebrity when he led a well-publicized charge up one of the heights overlooking Santiago Bay; he capitalized on this to win the governorship of New York in November. Two years later the Republicans sought to exploit his heroic status by putting him on their ticket as vice president, with the result that McKinley's assassination in September 1901 installed him in the White House at the age of forty-two. Taking energetic personal charge of foreign policy, Roosevelt broke new ground by involving himself in international disputes outside the Western Hemisphere in which the United States had no direct interest. During the Russo-Japanese War that broke out in 1904, he requested the belligerents to respect the neutrality and territorial integrity of China before offering his good offices in bringing the war to an end and then playing an active part in mediating the treaty that was signed in Portsmouth, New Hampshire, in September 1905. By this time, Roosevelt had become involved in private diplomatic exchanges regarding a Franco-German dispute over Morocco. This led to the United States' becoming a participant in the Algeçiras Conference of 1906 and a signatory of the resulting treaty.[15]

Roosevelt also sought to strengthen the nation's instrumentalities for exercising influence in the world, though here he was pushing forward a process that predated his administration and was to outlive it. Predictably, he paid particular attention to the navy, which doubled both its manpower and its budget during his tenure. As in Britain and Germany at this time, the chief focus was on building ever larger and more formidable battleships. When Roosevelt sent "the Great White Fleet" of sixteen battleships on a cruise around the world in 1907–09, it dramatized, both at home and abroad, the new power of the U.S. Navy. Although the army did not grow in the same way, the creation of an Army War College in 1900 and of a General Staff in 1903 helped to make both its ethos and its organization more professional and up-to-date. Elihu Root drove these changes as secretary of war, and he also accelerated a process of reform in the State Department after becoming secretary of state in 1905. Consuls began to be paid salaries and to be subject to inspection. The tradition of patronage was attenuated as consuls, and then diplomats, were selected by examination and promoted on merit, while the establishment of geographical divisions within the State Department fostered expertise. This last occurred under Roosevelt's chosen successor, William Howard Taft, but Roosevelt himself was responsible for enhancing an administration's ability to conduct the nation's diplomacy swiftly and effectively by developing the use of executive agreements with foreign governments to circumvent the Senate's power to block treaties, notably in effecting the takeover of the Dominican customs house in 1905. Although such agreements went back to the 1817 Rush-Bagot Pact over the Canadian boundary, their use was to be vastly expanded in the twentieth century; by 1972, the United States was signatory to 947 treaties but 4,359 executive agreements.[16]

The Limits of Expansion

Real and impressive as was the expansion of America's foreign policy in this period, its continued limitations were also striking. These limitations were of three kinds. The first was geographical. The United States made hardly any attempt to exert influence across most of Asia, including the Middle East, and Africa—parts of the world that were, of course, at this time largely subject to European empires. Most importantly, it remained essentially detached from the great power politics of Europe. Theodore Roosevelt's role in the Moroccan crisis of 1905–06 might seem to provide an exception, but it illustrates the other two limitations on America's overseas actions—the reluctance to assume obligations or incur costs and a lack of continuity. After Roosevelt's private diplomacy led to the open participation of the United States in the Algeçiras Conference, the head of its delegation made it clear that his government signed the resulting treaty "without assuming obligation or responsibility for the enforcement thereof," a point Roosevelt reiterated in his annual message. Even so, the Senate ratified the treaty only after adding the explicit reservation that it involved no purpose "to depart from the traditional American foreign policy which forbids participation by the United States in the settlement of political questions which are entirely European in their scope." That this was the case was confirmed by the position adopted in later controversies and conflicts. The precedent Roosevelt had set was ignored when a second Moroccan crisis, more serious than the first, erupted in 1911. Reporting to Congress on the Italo-Turkish War of 1911–12 and the Balkan wars of 1912–13, President Taft observed that "the United States has happily been involved neither directly nor indirectly with the causes or questions incident to any of these hostilities and has maintained in regard to them an attitude of absolute neutrality and of complete political disinterestedness."[17]

In contrast to this principled detachment from the politics of Europe, the annexation of the Philippines and Hay's Notes on China clearly made the United States a player in the diplomacy of East Asia. But it exerted less influence in that region subsequently than the actions of 1898–1901 might have led one to expect. The talk of a major naval base in the western Pacific came to nothing. The idea of one in China was abandoned in the face of Japanese protests and doubts about its compatibility with the Open Door policy, and then the navy and the army were unable to agree on a site in the Philippines. Instead, Pearl Harbor in Hawaii was made into the fortified base of the Pacific fleet, and even such an ardent annexationist as Roosevelt came to recognize that strategically, the Philippines were not an asset but a liability—"our heel of Achilles"—and privately expressed a wish that they could be "made independent, with perhaps some kind of international guarantee." The further projection of military power to East Asia was limited to sending gunboats up the rivers of China to protect Americans and Europeans engaged in business or missionary activities and signaling the threat of some action in response to the Chinese boycott of American goods in 1905–06. When the boycott ended, the administration sought to improve relations with China by the use of soft power; it remitted its share of the indemnity imposed after the Boxer Rebellion, stipulating that the funds be used to establish an American school in China and to bring Chinese to study in the United States.[18]

The boycott had been a protest against the exclusion laws and mistreatment suffered by Chinese in the United States, and similar discriminatory measures directed against Japanese immigrants led to tension with that assertive new power and even a "war scare" in 1907–08. Unable under the federal system to do much to ameliorate the treatment of Japanese in California and under strong domestic pressure to further restrict Japanese immigration, Roosevelt sought to conciliate Tokyo by making concessions in East Asia. In secret agreements in 1905 and 1908, the administration implicitly gave Japan a free hand in Korea and recognized its preeminent interests in southern Manchuria. When the Taft administration went back on this policy by attempting to secure the internationalization of all railroads in Manchuria, Roosevelt warned his successor that the United States had neither the means nor the will to check Japanese ambitions there. The Open Door policy, he wrote, was "an excellent thing . . . so far as it can be maintained by general diplomatic agreement," but "as a matter of fact, [it] completely disappears as soon as a powerful nation determines to disregard it, and is willing to run the risk of war rather than forego its intention." Roosevelt's judgment was borne out when in January 1915 Japan took advantage of the European war to demand that China grant it further extensive concessions. President Wilson's advisor, Colonel Edward M. House, urged "great caution" because the United States was "not at present in a position to war with Japan over the 'open door' in China," and Washington eventually contented itself with stating that it could not "recognize any agreement or undertaking" that impaired the new Chinese republic's "territorial integrity" or "the open door policy."[19]

Even in the Western Hemisphere, the dominance of the United States was not as complete as Olney had claimed in his 1895 Note. Traditionally, South America had far closer cultural and economic ties with Europe than with the United States, ties that in some countries were strengthened by the influx of new immigrants, especially from Italy and Germany, in the late nineteenth and early twentieth centuries. It is true that as the balance of financial and economic power shifted across the Atlantic, American exporters and investors began to challenge Europe's economic predominance in the southern continent, but in 1912 their share of the import market in Argentina, Brazil, and Chile was still less than 15 percent. On the political front, too, the United States sought to reorient South America toward itself. The strengthening of hemispheric solidarity became a policy objective when Secretary of State James G. Blaine organized a pan-American conference in 1889–90 and attempted to promote tariff reciprocity and a mechanism for settling inter-American disputes peacefully. Further conferences were held in 1901 and 1906 from which arose a permanent organization, called the Pan-American Union from 1910 and provided with a headquarters in Washington. This was largely paid for by Andrew Carnegie, whose Endowment for International Peace also funded the American Institute of International Law that was created in 1912. But the movement faced serious obstacles, as was demonstrated when Woodrow Wilson attempted in 1914 to secure a pan-American pact in which all the "republics of the two Continents" would guarantee each other's territorial integrity and establish mechanisms for settling disputes between themselves peacefully. After meeting resistance from Chile, the project finally collapsed when Wilson sent a military expedition into Mexico in 1916. This illustrated the fundamental problem, which was the tension between the ideal of a free association of equally sovereign states and the implicit presumption that the United States occupied a superior position morally as well as in terms of power. As American politicians often stressed, the Monroe Doctrine was a unilateral policy, not a collective one, and the Roosevelt Corollary in particular aroused resentment and resistance to its hegemonial implications. In reality, the Corollary only effectively applied to the small countries of the Caribbean and Central America where the United States had the means easily to take control and where, too, law and order tended to be particularly fragile. The U.S. Navy's General Board warned in 1901 that it was "impracticable successfully to maintain naval control by armed forces beyond the Amazon." In the south of the continent, Washington's leverage was limited, and large countries like Argentina, Brazil, and Chile (the so-called ABC powers) were essentially able to set their own course. Privately, Roosevelt suggested that they should be treated as "guarantors of the [Monroe] doctrine as far as America south of the Equator is concerned."[20]

Relying similarly on states in the Caribbean and Central America, Roosevelt asserted, "would be about like asking the Apaches and Utes to guarantee it." Matters were certainly different in this region, although there was no further attempt to expand direct American rule after the acquisition of Puerto Rico and the Canal Zone and the rejection by the Danish legislature in 1902 of a bid to buy that country's Virgin Islands. The public support for the annexation of overseas lands inhabited by alien peoples had always been fragile, and it waned rapidly as the ugly war in the Philippines dragged on for years. Even Theodore Roosevelt, while privately contrasting the benefits Cuba had received from America's military government with the state of the Dominican Republic after "a hundred years of freedom," avoided assuming direct responsibility for the latter's government, picturesquely declaring that "I have about the same desire to annex it as a gorged boa constrictor might have to swallow a porcupine wrong-end-to." Nonetheless, by taking over the Republic's customs house and subjecting its finances to the control of an American economist, Roosevelt pioneered what has been called a "neo-colonial substitute" that was later to be applied elsewhere. Just as the United States came to be seen as a player in the internal politics of the small countries of the region, so its hegemonial position there was uncontested by the great powers of Europe and thus free of significant cost. Although much has sometimes been made of the nebulous and impracticable planning by some German naval officers for an expedition to the Western Hemisphere, this was completely abandoned in 1906. Britain too implicitly accepted the U.S. Navy's dominance in the Caribbean when it withdrew its capital ships from the West Indies to concentrate them in home waters against the German threat, and the Roosevelt Corollary was warmly received by the British press.[21]

If the scope of America's influence on world politics remained limited, so did the scale of the resources that the nation devoted to exercising such influence. Although its navy ranked third in the world in 1913, its army, with just over ninety thousand men, was less than a fifth the size of Bulgaria's. Nonmilitary means of achieving foreign policy objectives were even less well developed. Unlike some other executive departments, the State Department lacked a powerful self-interested domestic constituency to press its case in Congress, and it remained remarkably small. In 1913, only 213 people, including clerks, messengers, and manual laborers, worked for the State Department in Washington, while the entire force of the American diplomatic and consular services abroad numbered fewer than 450.[22]

Explaining the Limitations

Given the enormous growth in America's comparative economic strength in these years, it is not surprising that those who expect that the possession of power will lead to its exercise view U.S. foreign policy between the 1880s and 1917 as "underexpansionist." Fareed Zakaria, whose term this is, attempts to explain this apparent exception to the Realist hypothesis that states "expand when they can" because "a nation's interests are determined by its power" by modifying the theory. The crucial variable, he suggests, is not "national power" but "state power." This he sees as a function not only of the scale of a nation's resources but also of the state's capacity to extract those resources from the society and direct them toward the achievement of decisively chosen objectives. In these respects, Zakaria rightly points out, the American state remained very weak in the late nineteenth century compared to those of Europe. The strength of the state as an autonomous entity is greatest when there is a powerful bureaucracy and a centralized executive authority. In the nineteenth-century United States, the bureaucracy was tiny and subordinate, while the independent power of Congress limited the ability of presidents to pursue a consistent policy or achieve foreign policy goals. Treaties commonly failed to gain the necessary Senate approval, as with those involving the purchase of two islands in the Danish West Indies in 1868 and of Santo Domingo (or, alternatively, of a base there) in 1870. The federal government's limited sources of revenue as well as Congress's control of the purse strings made it difficult for the executive to raise the money required for the achievement of foreign policy objectives. However, Zakaria observes, the power of the state grew in the early twentieth century as a result of the progressive reforms adopted in response to pressures generated by economic growth and industrialization. The executive branch increased in size as the government assumed new responsibilities, new agencies were created, a federal income tax was enacted, and the president gained new authority. An expanding foreign policy, Zakaria argues, was the consequence.[23]

This argument is unconvincing. In the first place, the nature of the purported link between domestic reforms and overseas expansion is never really explained. How did the creation of such agencies as the Interstate Commerce Commission or the Pure Food and Drug Administration enhance the state's power to achieve larger foreign policy goals? More fundamentally, a wider view of history shows that when the political will has existed to achieve objectives judged to be really important by a broad and deep public consensus, the American state has been able to acquire the necessary resources and legal powers. As the United States mobilized for victory in the world wars of the twentieth century, the capacities, revenues, and legal authority of the federal government expanded enormously, and the overseas commitments assumed after 1945 served to sustain this expansion.

But earlier experience, too, had shown that the strength of the state in the United States should be viewed as a dependent variable rather than an independent one. During the Civil War, the federal government's spending rose by a factor of fourteen. Most of this was financed through the issuing of bonds facilitated by the establishment of a system of national banks. But the government also paid for its war effort by making paper money legal tender (and printing lots of it) and by imposing a variety of direct and indirect taxes that were collected by the newly created Bureau of Internal Revenue. As well as effectively extracting resources from the society, the Union government exercised extensive coercive powers over the citizenry. By issuing proclamations as commander-in-chief, President Lincoln suspended *habeas corpus* eventually over the whole Union, and in 1863 Congress enacted conscription. Little sign of a weak state here.[24]

However, these were emergency measures, and after the war most of the apparatus of state power was dismantled as rapidly as it had been erected. Although the authority of the national government had been permanently enhanced in many ways, Zakaria is right to emphasize that the American state in the 1870s and 1880s was hardly a "leviathan" and that its capabilities in the area of foreign policy were particularly undeveloped. At this time, the United States had no ambassadors. Its overseas representatives consisted of 31 ministers (some doubling as consul generals), 96 consuls paid so little (if at all) that they were allowed to engage in trade, and 418 lesser agents, usually native merchants. All the senior positions and those carrying a salary were filled on the basis of political patronage rather than aptitude for their assignments and, when the presidency changed parties (as it frequently did in this period), there were wholesale replacements. Those holding diplomatic posts rarely knew much about the country to which they were assigned or, indeed, of foreign affairs generally. Their communications with the small number of mostly transient officials in the State Department generally concerned routine and mundane matters, particularly cases involving American citizens (not least missionaries) who had gotten themselves into difficulties abroad. "Foreign relations," Robert Wiebe observes, "were composed of incidents, not policies—a number of distinct events, not sequences that moved from a source toward a conclusion." Nor did the nation have the capability of projecting power to other continents even if it had wished to. By the mid-1870s, the huge Union Army of the Civil War had been reduced to a force of less than thirty thousand, with most of its units scattered across the country to fight Indians or engage in engineering works. Before the 1890s, the state of the navy was no better.[25]

This very low base may be one reason why the role of the United States in world politics in 1914 remained so much smaller than it might have been given its preeminent economic strength. Another, related reason was the influence of tradition and ideology, particularly in shaping attitudes to affairs in Europe. George Washington's prudential advice to his countrymen in 1796 to avoid involvement through "artificial ties" in the "frequent controversies" of that continent had by the late nineteenth century acquired both an extraordinary aura of authority and a profound ideological accretion. It had become associated with the broad distinction between the New World and the Old World that was fundamental to the ideology of American nationalism as it developed after the Revolution and that had been drawn upon to justify the Monroe Doctrine of 1823. "The genius of our institutions, the needs of our people in their home life . . . dictate the scrupulous avoidance of any departure from that foreign policy commended by the history, the traditions, and the prosperity of the Republic," President Grover Cleveland insisted in 1885. Less sonorously, his secretary of state, Thomas F. Bayard, declared that "so long as I am head of this department, I shall not give myself the slightest trouble to thwart the small politics or staircase intrigues in Europe, in which we have not the slightest share or interest, and upon which I look with impatience and contempt."[26]

This tradition, together with the ideological justification for it, was to continue to play an influential part in American foreign policy debates well into the twentieth century. Yet that century would show that the tradition could be completely overridden when circumstances produced a strong and widely held desire to affect the course of events on other continents. It was because of the absence of such a consensual desire that U.S. foreign policy remained so limited before 1914.

One reason for this lack was internal disagreement about specific actions and lines of policy. The acquisition of the Philippines occasioned a major public debate, with many arguing passionately that it was a betrayal of the republican principles on which the nation had been founded. Charles Francis Adams condemned the adoption of "Old World methods and ideals"—which William Graham Sumner sardonically characterized as "the conquest of the United States by Spain." Although such New England Republicans constituted most of the leadership of the very active Anti-Imperialist League, in Congress the opposition was largely concentrated in the Democratic Party, whose predominantly Southern members had special reasons for resisting the incorporation of territories inhabited by nonwhite populations and whose products would compete with those of their own states. It was only after the party's presidential candidate William Jennings Bryan had urged ratification of the peace treaty with Spain so that the question could be put to the electorate that the necessary two-thirds majority in the Senate was mustered by a margin of one vote; it had been "the closest, hardest fight I have ever known," Lodge told Roosevelt. Although his denunciations of imperialism failed to help Bryan much in the 1900 election, the party stuck to its position as enthusiasm for retaining the Philippines subsequently waned among Republicans as well as the wider public; in 1912 the Democratic platform unequivocally condemned "the experiment in imperialism as an inexcusable blunder, which has involved us in enormous expense, brought us weakness instead of strength, and laid our nation open to the charge of abandonment of the fundamental doctrine of self-government."[27]

The scale and intensity of the debate over the Philippines was unique in this period but the broad difference of approach that underlay it was also manifested in other contexts, as were the related party and sectional divisions. Bryan Democrats and many Midwestern Republicans adhered to an anti-imperialist ideology that melded traditional Jeffersonianism with the antagonism to Wall Street and its corporate progeny expressed in the contemporary progressive movement. They tended to attribute U.S. interventions in the Caribbean and Central America (even Panama) to the influence of such banking and business interests and to characterize them as imperialistic. This perspective also stimulated opposition to naval expansion and indeed to practically all exercise of American power overseas.

Both traditionally and as a matter of contemporary observation, imperialism was associated with European powers, particularly Britain, and the division over America's own expansion was mirrored in divergent attitudes to Britain, which began in these years to play the central role in American foreign policy debates that they were to occupy for several decades. Although Olney, Roosevelt, and Lodge had been belligerent during the Venezuela boundary crisis of 1895–96, they and other members of the East Coast upper class took the lead in subsequently fostering an Anglo-American rapprochement. This process was facilitated by the accommodating nature of British policy at a time when the Empire felt overstretched in guarding against threats to its position in Asia and Africa and responding to Germany's naval challenge. In the Hay-Pauncefote isthmian canal treaties and the settlement of a disputed boundary between Alaska and Canada, as well as in withdrawing the Royal Navy from the Western Hemisphere, it was Britain that retreated and made concessions. But on the American side, too, there were influential people who wanted a closer relationship and wider partnership. None more so than John Hay, who became secretary of state in 1899 believing that "the one indispensable feature of our foreign policy should be a friendly understanding with England." Roosevelt himself wrote to Lodge that "the fact remains, in the first place, that we are closer in feeling to her than to any other nation; and in the second place, that probably her interest and ours will run on parallel lines in the future." The personal connections of such men with British politicians and opinion leaders facilitated informal cooperation, particularly over Far East policy. But this was not a policy with broad public support, and Roosevelt warned that "the less said about an understanding the better." The Democratic platform of 1900 had denounced the "ill-concealed Republican alliance with England," and a bilateral arbitration treaty negotiated in 1897 and promoted by both Cleveland and McKinley failed to gain Senate approval. Lodge observed sourly that "an administration which undertakes to respect and fulfill treaty obligations to England is an inviting object of attack."[28]

Antagonism to Great Britain had deep historical roots, of course, stretching back to the American Revolution. Politicians had long seen "twisting the Lion's tail" as a way of gaining popularity, particularly in some parts of the country. By the late nineteenth century, however, it was generally recognized that the most implacable hostility derived from specific ethnic groups, above all Irish-Americans, whose strength of feeling on this issue, together with their electorally strategic location in major cities, gave them an influence out of proportion to their numbers; in 1888, this influence was widely regarded as the cause of President Cleveland's defeat after the publication of a letter in which the British minister in Washington had favored his reelection. The great wave of Irish immigration had been in the 1840s and 1850s, and by the turn of the century Irish-Americans had become well established in American life and politics. The same was true of the much larger number of German-Americans, who also tended to view closer Anglo-American relations with suspicion—though the chief foreign policy interest of the prosperous German-Jewish community was action to alleviate the plight of Jews being subjected to pogroms in tsarist Russia. More recently arrived ethnic groups had little direct influence on U.S. foreign policy at this time.

However, the recent immigrants seem to have had a significant influence on the attitudes of others. Between 1880 and 1914 almost twenty-three million people entered the United States, with the result that between 1890 and 1920 around 15 percent of the American population were foreign-born and a further 25 percent were children of at least one foreign-born parent. The incoming flood peaked in the decade 1905–14, during which over ten million arrived, 70 percent of them from eastern and southern Europe.[29] The scale and provenance of this immigration disturbed many old-stock Americans, particularly among the northeastern upper class. In 1894, an Immigration Restriction League was formed in Boston with an executive committee composed almost entirely of wealthy Harvard graduates. It lobbied for the exclusion of immigrants unable to read and write in their own language, a measure Lodge shepherded through Congress in 1895–97. After it had been vetoed by Cleveland, Lodge regularly reintroduced the bill over the next decade. He argued for it principally on the grounds that the "new" immigrants were of inferior racial stock. In 1891, he had published an article in which he classified by "race" about fourteen thousand successful Americans and concluded that over 70 percent of them were of English descent and that nearly all of them traced their ancestry to some part of the British Isles or to other "Teutonic" countries. His most insightful biographer has written that "Lodge had a profound sense of dispossession, and felt that his country was being lost to those of his class and outlook who had played such a prominent role in its creation." Certainly, like others of his social background, he believed that the very identity of the United States depended on its retaining its "Anglo-Saxon" character.[30]

Yet Lodge's Anglophilia, like Roosevelt's, was moderated by his nationalism, in contrast to what Roosevelt called "the Anglomania of our social leaders and indeed of most of our educated men." The two men adopted a very militant stance against Britain in the Western Hemisphere, particularly during the Venezuela crisis of 1895–96 and over the negotiation of the Hay-Pauncefote treaties. Elsewhere in the world, however, they saw British imperialism as advancing the cause of civilization. In an era of racial thinking, the belief in a common Anglo-Saxon descent led to the assumption that the two nations not only shared basic characteristics and values but also were ultimately kin. Olney believed that "the American people . . . feel themselves to be not merely in name but in fact, part of one great English-speaking family" and insisted that "there is a patriotism of race as well as of country." Hay assured an English audience that "We are bound by a tie which we did not forge and which we cannot break."[31]

The diversity of perspectives, deeply rooted in ethno-cultural as well as ideological differences, made it difficult to undertake actions or commitments that went beyond the traditional lines of American policy, particularly if they involved taking sides in foreign conflicts. There was, however, one general goal that met with no significant opposition, and this was the promotion of international peace. In the two decades before World War I, organizations devoted to this cause proliferated. Although they did not have much impact on the general public's indifference to international affairs, they did benefit from the financial backing of Andrew Carnegie, which culminated in the $10 million with which he established the Carnegie Endowment for International Peace in 1910. There was in reality a fundamental difference of approach within the movement between conservatives seeking to create institutions to enhance the scope and authority of law in inter-state relations and those whose emphasis was on pacifism and disarmament, positions embodied respectively by Elihu Root and William Jennings Bryan. But all favored the development of nonmilitary means for settling international differences, and both Root and Bryan were among the succession of secretaries of state who negotiated treaties with other countries establishing some form of mechanism for the peaceful resolution of disputes with them. However, all these treaties suffered from serious limitations, either in their scope or in the firmness of the obligations incurred; these were largely due to the Senate's unwillingness to see any reduction either in its prerogatives or in the nation's future freedom of action. Similarly, although the United States participated in the Hague Peace Conferences of 1899 and 1907—and, indeed, Roosevelt prompted the calling of the second one—on both occasions it insisted that its adherence to the conventions on arbitration in no way affected its traditional "attitude toward purely American questions" and policy of non-entanglement elsewhere—the strongest reservation made by any of the signatories.[32]

The extremely cautious approach to arbitration illustrates the most basic constraint on the wider involvement of the United States in world politics—the unwillingness to take actions or make commitments that involved any sort of cost. This constraint arose from American public opinion, as this was interpreted by elected politicians, and was enforced by Congress. That it was a political reality was recognized even by those policymakers who most lamented it. "We have continually to accommodate ourselves to conditions as they actually are and not as we would wish them to be," Roosevelt reminded Taft. "I wish our people were prepared permanently, in a duty-loving spirit, and looking forward to a couple of generations of continuous manifestation of this spirit, to assume the control of the Philippine Islands for the good of the Filipinos. But as a matter of fact I gravely question whether this is the case." "Of course," he explained on another occasion, "I do not desire to act unless I can get the bulk of our people to understand the situation and to back up the action."[33]

The Role of Economic Interest

Clear evidence that a national interest generally agreed to be truly important demanded the achievement of a particular foreign policy goal might have overridden both the internal differences and the resistance to meeting the costs of a wider and more forceful exercise of America's potential power in world politics. That the clearest examples of such interests were the nation's economic prosperity and its safety from external attack is confirmed by the degree of attention paid to them both in contemporary debate and in subsequent historiography.

"American factories are making more than the American people can use; American soil is producing more than they can consume. Fate has written our policy for us; the trade of the world must and shall be ours." So declared the rising Republican politician Albert J. Beveridge as he foresaw in 1898 the planting of "the Stars and Stripes over an Isthmian canal . . . over Hawaii . . . over Cuba and the southern seas."[34] Beveridge was invoking the "glut theory," that the growth of the country's productive capacity had outstripped the capacity of the home market to absorb its output so that full employment and future prosperity now depended on a growth of exports. Historians who see a desire for overseas markets as the driver of an expansive foreign policy have shown that the theory was widely articulated, particularly during the severe depression that began in 1893. The National Association of Manufacturers (NAM), formed in the depth of this depression, devoted half its first manifesto to measures to increase foreign trade. Giving the keynote address at its founding convention, William McKinley, then governor of Ohio, declared that "we want a foreign market for our surplus products." In April 1898, the State Department's Bureau of Foreign Commerce declared, "It seems to be conceded that every year we shall be confronted with an increasing surplus of manufactured goods for sale in foreign markets if American operatives and artisans are to be kept employed the year round," and that this had "become a serious problem of statesmanship as well as of commerce."[35]

The State Department was using the need for exports to justify its claim for more resources, particularly for the consular service and the increasingly extensive information on overseas trade conditions that it was making available. Similarly, Beveridge and others invoked the glut theory when attempting to gain support for an expansionist foreign policy. However, the record shows that the argument had limited political traction. Advocates of foreign trade failed to achieve many of the government measures they called for, such as subsidies for overseas cables and, above all, support for the ailing American merchant marine. Whereas before the Civil War American ships had carried about 70 percent of the nation's foreign trade, by 1900 the figure had fallen to less than 10 percent. But the mail subsidies the federal government had provided to U.S. shipping companies were discontinued after a scandal during the Grant administration and, despite the pleas of the NAM and others, no further action was taken to counter the advantage foreign firms derived from having subsidized tramp steamers and contract lines at their disposal.[36]

The prime policy area bearing on foreign trade, however, was the tariff, a major issue in the national politics of this period. Indeed, the glut theory was developed by advocates of lower tariffs (notably the economist David A. Wells), and it was in this context that it was most commonly advanced. Here, too, however, it failed to win sufficient support to shape policy. Import duties rose sharply during the Civil War and remained at a high level afterwards. As the issues that had given rise to the Republican party gradually faded from political debate, the virtues of a protective tariff became increasingly central to the ideology of the dominant party in this era. It is true that some Republican leaders such as James G. Blaine and McKinley recognized the desirability of aiding exports to the extent of promoting treaties with other countries for the reciprocal lowering of tariffs, something stressed by those historians who attribute great influence to this concern. But the kind of reciprocity advocated is better seen as a variant of protectionism than as a move toward free trade.[37] In any case, few of these treaties were actually negotiated, and most of those that were failed to gain ratification in the Senate. Opponents argued that reciprocal rate reduction would lose more than it would gain, opening up the rich American market in exchange for poorer markets abroad.[38]

One reason why a concern with overseas markets did not do more to expand the scope of U.S foreign policy is that many saw no connection between the two. Thus, many of the leaders of the anti-imperialist movement in 1898, such as

Edward Atkinson, Carl Schurz, and W. G. Sumner, were strong proponents of foreign trade and lower tariffs. It is not surprising that such men saw no contradiction in the two positions, especially given the pattern of U.S. trade at this time. It is true that the value of goods sold to China and especially Japan grew greatly in the 1890s, but even by 1900 the whole of Asia absorbed only 5 percent of U.S. exports. By contrast, 75 percent went to Europe, which remained, as it had always been, by far America's biggest overseas market. With some exceptions, most notably the efforts successive administrations made to persuade Germany and France to ease barriers imposed (ostensibly on health grounds) against American meat imports, this transatlantic trade neither needed nor received support from the U.S. government. Although agricultural and other primary products continued to provide the greater part of U.S. exports to Europe, the most rapid growth here and elsewhere was in manufactured goods. Between 1890 and 1913, the U.S. share of the world trade in manufactures grew from 3.9 percent to 11 percent. In the lead of this expansion were giant firms like International Harvester, Westinghouse, and Singer. Enjoying competitive advantages through their large-scale production and advanced technology, such firms also built up extensive marketing organizations abroad. They sought to ease their entry into overseas markets by employing foreign nationals, and if disputes arose they commonly sought to resolve these without resort to the State Department. Indeed, the direct investment some corporations were making in distribution, assembling, and manufacturing facilities abroad was generally more welcome to the host government than to Washington.[39]

Nevertheless, farm lobbies and smaller manufacturers lacking the cost and capital advantages enjoyed by large corporations did seek greater assistance from the U.S. government in developing overseas markets, especially in Latin America and Asia. Although executive officials in the departments of State and of Commerce and Labor increasingly provided commercial information and occasional diplomatic support, Congress was generally unresponsive to such pressure. "As for the opening out of all possible new elements of trade by diplomatic activity and by positive legislation," Theodore Roosevelt explained to a correspondent, "it is astonishing how little public feeling there is for any such effort. I have tried once or twice to make such openings by diplomatic activity and I have had to fight tooth and nail to get either Democratic or Republican Senators to so much as even consider the treaties I have sent in, and generally they have rejected them, while the popular interest has been nil."[40]

This political reality surely reflected the fact that the great majority of businessmen and farmers derived their income largely or entirely from the home market. In absolute terms, U.S. exports grew fivefold between 1870 and 1914, and the U.S. share of world trade rose from 6 percent in 1868 to 11 percent in 1913. As a proportion of GNP, however, exports fell from around 7 percent in the 1870s to 5–6 percent in 1913–14. Nevertheless, from the 1870s the United States enjoyed a surplus on current account in most years as the unfavorable trade balances that went back to colonial days were reduced and then reversed. This was because the proportional fall of imports was greater than that of exports, as home-based industry increasingly met the demands of American consumers. Whereas in 1869 imports had supplied 14 percent of manufactured goods purchased in the United States, by 1909 the figure was only 5.9 percent. It is true that in bad times doubts about the capacity of the domestic market to absorb America's burgeoning production gained greater currency. But even in the depth of the depression in January 1895, McKinley stressed to the NAM that "we want our own markets for our manufactures and agricultural products; we want a tariff for our surplus products which will not surrender our markets and will not degrade our labor to hold our markets." And when prosperity returned and production boomed again, as it always did in this era, the glut theory lost much of whatever credence it had gained.[41]

The Issue of Security

If the promotion of exports was not widely regarded as a truly important national interest, preserving the American homeland from the danger of external attack, which had been seen as the prime responsibility of the federal government ever since its establishment, certainly was. So it is not surprising that those favoring the devotion of more resources to the armed forces or a more active foreign policy commonly made their case in terms of the requirements of national security.

Advocates of a stronger navy in the 1880s presented the argument in a stark and simple way—the need to protect the American coastline from direct attack. It was pointed out that the U.S. Navy was now outmatched not only by the navies of Britain and other European powers but also by those of several South American republics, particularly Chile. In newspaper articles and congressional speeches, the specter was raised of New York, San Francisco, and other port cities being shelled. In calling for the construction of a large force of "seagoing coastline battleships" in 1889, Secretary of the Navy Benjamin F. Tracy argued that "we must have the force to raise blockades . . . a fleet of battleships that will beat off the enemy's fleet on its approach." As the U.S. Navy began to rise from its nadir, it was necessary to envisage a more formidable opponent to justify its continued expansion. "Great Britain knows that the great ports of the United States, the great seaboard cities with their millions of wealth and inhabitants, lie absolutely at the mercy of her cruisers" and might "be put to a shameful ransom," Lodge warned the House of Representatives in 1891.[42]

Four years later, Lodge dramatized this danger by bringing a map onto the Senate floor with the British bases in Canada, Bermuda, and the Caribbean marked by heavy black Maltese crosses, and the much superior strength of the British navy to the American clearly indicated. He did this in the course of urging the acquisition of Hawaii on the grounds that otherwise Britain might take it to establish another naval station in the Pacific. While the United States should not "enter on a widely extended system of colonization," it "should take all outlying territory necessary to our own defense, to the protection of the Isthmian Canal, to the upbuilding of our trade and commerce, and to the maintenance of our military safety everywhere."[43]

Later that year, Lodge portrayed the British position in the Venezuela boundary dispute as a threat to America's vital security interests. The aim, he charged, was to gain control of the mouths of the Orinoco, which, together with its existing bases in the West Indies, "will give Great Britain control of the Spanish Main and make the Caribbean Sea little better than a British lake." This "acquisition of new territory in this hemisphere by a European power" was "an absolute violation of the Monroe Doctrine." If the United States acquiesced in it, "every other European power can do the same, and they will not be slow to follow England's example. We have seen them parcel out Africa, and if we do not interpose now in this case the fate of large portions of South America will be the same." The consequence would be that "we shall have formidable rivals all about us; we shall be in constant danger of war; and we shall be forced to become a military power with great armies and navies."[44]

Lodge was here alluding to the argument Olney had developed in his famous Note, the reasoning of which is usually disregarded. Olney did not present the unchallenged supremacy of the United States in the Western Hemisphere (which he portrayed in such extravagant terms) as in itself a justification for the administration's intrusion into the Anglo-Venezuelan boundary dispute but as evidence of his country's stake in the matter. If the United States allowed Britain to expand its colony's territory at the expense of Venezuela, he argued, "what one power was permitted to do could not be denied to another, and . . . the ultimate result might be the partition of all South America between the various European powers." The consequences of this for the United States would be "disastrous" because "thus far in our history we have been spared the burdens and evils of immense standing armies and all the other accessories of large warlike establishments, and the exemption has largely contributed to our national greatness and wealth as well as the happiness of every citizen." But were "the powers of Europe permanently encamped on American soil, . . . we too must be armed to the teeth; we too must convert the flower of our male population into soldiers and sailors, and by withdrawing them from the various pursuits of peaceful industry, we must practically annihilate a large share of the productive energy of the nation."[45]

In its firm and belated reply to Olney's Note, the British government pointed out that the Monroe Doctrine had no standing in international law and that "the dangers which were apprehended by President Monroe have no relation to the state of things in which we live at the present day," but in a belligerent message to Congress, Cleveland countered that the Doctrine was "strong and sound" and could "not become obsolete while our Republic endures." Like all American politicians, he knew that it had become established in the public mind as a basic principle of U.S. foreign policy, one that rested not only on strategic considerations but also on the New World's ideological distinctiveness. ("Europe as a whole is monarchical," Olney had observed.) Those wishing to develop political support for more assertive policies and a wider role in world politics sought to exploit rather than to challenge the Monroe Doctrine's axiomatic status. Thus Lodge opposed Mahan's proposal for making it coordinate with U.S. security interests by restricting its operation to the Caribbean area.[46]

With respect to the actions it covered, too, the public's understanding of the Doctrine's scope was broader than that of policymakers in the 1890s. Olney explicitly stated that "it did not relieve any American state from its obligations as fixed by international law nor prevent any European power directly interested from enforcing such obligations or from inflicting merited punishment for the breach of them." This was also the view of Lodge and Roosevelt; as the latter put it to the German diplomat Hermann Speck von Sternburg, "If any South American state misbehaves towards any European country, let the European country spank it." After becoming president, Roosevelt spelled out this position more formally in his first two annual messages. Accordingly, the administration raised no objection when informed by Britain and Germany in late 1902 that they were about to take coercive action against Venezuela for defaulting on debts owed to their nationals. However, when the action came to involve the sinking of Venezuelan vessels and naval bombardments as well as the imposition of a blockade, the outrage expressed in the American press at what many saw as not only high-handed bullying of a weak republic but also a violation of the Monroe Doctrine led directly to the issuing of the Roosevelt Corollary the following year.[47]

The opprobrium the punitive operation engendered in the United States was overwhelmingly directed at Germany, even though Britain had played the major role in it. Suspicious hostility of Germany had grown as relations with Britain improved in the aftermath of the 1895 Venezuela crisis, a process accelerated by what was seen as the two countries' antithetical reactions to the War of 1898 and particularly the actions of Dewey's fleet in the Philippines. As Germany embarked on its great naval-building program at the turn of the century, Roosevelt suggested to Lodge that "in a few years they will be in a position to take some step in the West Indies or South America which will make us either put up or shut up on the Monroe Doctrine; they are counting upon their ability to trounce us if we try the former horn of the dilemma." Whereas the early exercises of the Naval War College had been directed against England, by the turn of the century Germany was seen as the major threat by the newly established General Board. Its most detailed war plan envisaged a German attack in the Caribbean and expressed doubt that the navy would be able to defeat it. Taking no account of the limited range of Germany's new battleships, let alone of British command of the Atlantic, the plan had an unreal quality. In any case, anxiety about a German challenge to the Monroe Doctrine declined as it became clear that, like Britain, Germany had no intention of challenging American hegemony in the Western Hemisphere. As president, Roosevelt dropped his dire predictions and expressed his desire to cooperate with Berlin. "In considering possible wars with the great nations of the world," Mahan wrote in December 1903, "it seems to me inconceivable that any one of them should expect seriously to modify or weaken our position in this hemisphere. . . . Great Britain has abandoned the idea; who better than she could maintain it? . . . In brief, the American question, the Monroe principle, though not formally accepted, is as nearly established as is given to international questions to be."[48]

At this time, then, both public opinion and military doctrine saw security as involving no more than the defense of North America, or at most the Western Hemisphere, from external attack.[49] Perceived threats to the nation's security in this sense played a significant part in developing support for the expansion of America's international power that did take place in the late nineteenth and early twentieth centuries, particularly the build-up of the navy and the assertion of hegemony over Central America and the Caribbean. But, given that no other great power had either the intention or the capability of launching a full-scale transoceanic assault, safeguarding the nation's security interests legitimated the deployment of only a small proportion of its potential international power. No other goal was generally agreed to be important enough to justify the sacrifices—of lives, money, and even diplomatic independence—that more extensive and strenuous efforts to influence developments abroad were likely to entail. In a word, the scale of America's potential power greatly exceeded that needed to protect what were generally seen as its core interests.

The Sense of Power

Nevertheless, many Americans were highly conscious of their nation's new standing in the world, and this profoundly affected their attitudes to foreign policy issues in a variety of ways. Patriotic orators had, of course, long spoken of the republic's glorious future as well as of the global significance of its commitment to liberty and popular self-government. But by the end of the nineteenth century it was commonly being observed that the United States had entered a new phase of its history, one in which it should play a larger and more active part in international affairs. A common image was that of a youth grown to manhood. "A policy of isolation did well enough when we were an embryo nation, but today things are different," Senator Orville H. Platt (R–Conn.) declared in 1893. "We are sixty-five million of people, the most advanced and powerful on earth, and regard to our future welfare demands an abandonment of the doctrines of isolation." "We cannot avoid our destiny," Lodge explained to a correspondent. "We are too great to be any longer an isolated power." This line of thinking contributed to the War of 1898 and the acquisition of an overseas empire, and was in turn strengthened by them. "A nation hitherto devoted to domestic development now finds its first task roughly finished and turns about to look curiously into the tasks of the great world at large, seeking its special part and place of power," Professor Woodrow Wilson observed in 1901.[50] Twelve years later, President Taft developed this theme in his annual message:

> The Nation is now too mature to continue in its foreign relations those temporary expedients natural to a people whose domestic affairs are the sole concern. In the past our diplomacy has often consisted, in normal times, in a mere assertion of the right to international existence. We are now in a larger relation with broader rights of our own and obligations to others than ourselves.

It was not only the United States that had developed. It had done so in the context of a wider transformation brought about by dramatic advances in all forms of communication, so that not only goods but also information and ideas now moved rapidly between continents. "Isolation is no longer possible," McKinley declared in his last speech as he expatiated on these developments. "No narrow, sordid policy" would serve, only a "broad and enlightened" one. In particular, McKinley called for the settlement of international disputes through "the noblest forum" of arbitration. Endorsing this approach a decade later, Taft, like McKinley, cited the "wonderful" recent growth in the nation's foreign commerce as evidence of the nation's interest in the cause.[51]

Taft, as governor of the Philippines and then briefly of Cuba, had earlier been intimately involved with the foray into imperialism, which to his mind was another way in which the United States was actively promoting the cause of progress and civilization. As we have seen, no one believed this more strongly than Theodore Roosevelt, whose conviction that the advance of civilization was not an automatic process but one requiring effort and a readiness to use force survived his recognition that the direct administration of other countries for an extended period of time was not a politically viable policy for the United States. "More and more," he told Congress in 1902, "the increasing interdependence and complexity of international political and economic relations render it incumbent on all civilized and orderly powers to insist on the proper policing of the world."[52]

If Americans failed to play their part in this process, Roosevelt warned, "we shall become isolated from the struggles of the rest of the world, and so immersed in our material prosperity, so that we shall become genuinely effete." The view that its international behavior would be a test of the country's character was shared by many of those most conscious of the greater range of possible action opened up by its new economic strength. "The United States of America has not the option as to whether or not it will play a great part in the world," Roosevelt repeatedly argued. "All that it can decide is whether it will play that part well or badly." The nature of the performance would shape the way America was regarded by other countries—and by history. "Whereas the nation that has done nothing leaves nothing behind it, the nation that has done a great work really continues, though in changed form, to live for ever more," Roosevelt observed, citing the Romans in evidence. More than the prospect of lasting glory, however, Roosevelt stressed the claims of morality: "Our country, as it strides forward with ever-increasing rapidity to a foremost place among the world powers, must necessarily find, more and more, that it has world duties also."[53]

The belief that power brought with it responsibilities that went beyond narrow self-interest was deeply embedded in the Protestant culture in which most Americans were steeped. Of none was this more true than of the well-educated East Coast class from which most of those who paid regular and informed attention to world affairs were drawn. Overwhelmingly Anglo-Saxon in background, such men were participants in a literary and intellectual culture of which the capital was London and, as Ernest R. May has shown, their thinking about foreign policy was very much influenced by the trends of thought there. So it is not surprising that interpretations of America's international responsibilities tended to see these as involving some association with the role that Britain was viewed as playing in world affairs. "When we begin really to look abroad, and to busy ourselves with our duties to the world at large," Mahan wrote in 1897, "we shall stretch out our hands to Great Britain, realizing that in unity of heart among the English-speaking races lies the best hope of humanity in the doubtful days ahead." Despite Roosevelt's wariness about seeming to compromise America's diplomatic independence, he forthrightly declared in 1907 that "every true friend of humanity should realize that the part England has played in India has been to the immeasurable advantage of India, and for the honor and profit of civilization." And Brooks Adams foreshadowed what later became known as hegemonic stability theory by arguing that since 1815 Britain had upheld an "equilibrium" in the world's financial system. As its economic supremacy declined, Adams argued, Britain was becoming unable any longer to play this role, and so "we are forced to compete for the seat of international exchanges, or, in other words, for the seat of empire." But "there is no reason why the United States should not become a greater seat of wealth and power than ever was England, Rome, or Constantinople."[54]

Adams was also one of those who maintained that England had been, and was, "essential" for America's own security against "the enemies who fear and hate us, and who, but for her, would already have fleets upon our shores." Lewis Einstein, a former diplomat, argued that it had not only been Britain's command of the Atlantic but also its upholding of a balance of power in Europe that had allowed "on the Western Hemisphere the continuance of an economic development unhandicapped by the burden of extensive armaments." In making war on Britain in 1812 when it was engaged in fighting Napoleon, Americans had failed to realize "that England's fight was in reality their own, and that the undisputed master of Europe would not have been long in finding pretexts to reacquire the Louisiana territory which, except for England, he would never have relinquished." It followed that "it would hardly be wise statesmanship to remain passive if England should by any series of disasters be crushed. . . . A disastrous defeat inflicted by an opponent unwilling to use moderation in his victory should invite on the part of America a friendly mediation which in the last extremity might have to be converted into more effective measures."[55]

Einstein published these views anonymously in a British journal and, as we have seen, Americans seeking to develop political support for a wider international role were wary of publicly suggesting that this should involve alignment with any other country. Patriotic sentiment was better served by portraying a more active involvement as the way in which the United States could best fulfill its historic destiny to "show the way to the nations of the world how they shall walk in the paths of liberty" (as Woodrow Wilson put it). As we have seen, the hitherto dominant view was that this exemplary mission would be corrupted by entanglement in power politics and the accompanying evils of militarism and authoritarianism. Those advocating the exercise of American power abroad now argued that to interpret the nation's mission as simply demonstrative was inadequate and selfish. "Posing before less favored peoples as an exemplar of the superiority of American institutions may be justified and may have its uses," Richard Olney observed in 1898. "But posing alone is like answering the appeal of a mendicant by bidding him to admire your own sleekness, your own fine clothes and handsome house and your generally comfortable and prosperous condition. . . . The mission of this country . . . is not merely to pose but to act."[56]

It was commonly suggested that the United States was particularly qualified to play this altruistic role and to provide public goods to international society just because it was a satisfied power with no further territorial ambitions or impelling selfish interests of its own. "It is not true that the United States has any land hunger," Roosevelt publicly observed to Root in the year they promulgated the Corollary, and in Rio de Janeiro two years later Root more sonorously declared that "we wish for no victories but those of peace; for no territory except our own; for no sovereignty except the sovereignty over ourselves." In reassuring Latin Americans seven years later that "the United States will never again seek one additional foot of territory by conquest," Wilson as president declared that "we must show ourselves friends by comprehending their interest, whether it squares with our own interest or not. It is a very perilous thing to determine the foreign policy of a nation in the terms of material interest." "What are we going to do with the influence and power of this great nation?" he asked a year later. "Are we going to play the old role of using that power to our aggrandizement and material benefit only?"[57]

In a penetrating and prophetic analysis published in 1909, Herbert Croly explored at greater length the implications for America's historic democratic mission of its enormous economic advance, arguing that in foreign as in domestic policy this necessitated the abandonment of old shibboleths. The Monroe Doctrine retained a certain strategic logic in that geography should enable the United States to avoid entanglement in "the complicated web of European international affairs" and to establish "a peaceable American system" in the Western Hemisphere. But the ideological basis of the Doctrine was outdated, because the Holy Alliance of hereditary monarchs was long gone and "the emancipated and nationalized European states of today, so far from being essentially antagonistic to the American democratic nation, are constantly tending towards a condition which invites closer and more fruitful association with the United States." And with modern communications and the growth of international commerce, "Europe, the United States, Japan and China must all eventually take their respective places in a world system." If the United States was to be true to the democratic values from which it derived its national identity, it must contribute its influence "to the establishment of a peaceful system in Europe, America, and Asia," just because "a decent guarantee of international peace would be precisely the political condition which would enable the European nations to release the springs of democracy." This could bring with it "the obligation of interfering under certain possible circumstances in what may at first appear to be a purely European complication."[58]

By 1914, then, consciousness that the United States had developed the capability of playing a new and much larger role in world politics had led many

Americans to feel and think that it should do so. A variety of reasons and arguments had been articulated in support of this view, including almost of all of those that were later employed to justify and build political support for the global role that the United States assumed following World War II. In practice, however, the projection of American power overseas remained very limited in this period. It was continually asserted only in Central America and the Caribbean, where U.S. hegemony was uncontested by any major power and could be exercised without any significant commitment of American resources. Beyond this, successive administrations attempted to promote the peaceful settlement of international disputes, but Congress ensured that such attempts resulted in no significant diminution of America's own prerogatives. In no case did there exist the solid national consensus that would have been necessary if the United States were to make a meaningful effort to affect the course of events on other continents. This was partly because there were internal differences in the way these events were viewed and over what the most desirable outcome would be. The chief reason, however, was that few saw what happened across the oceans as posing any sort of threat to either the nation's security or its continued prosperity.

2

ADVANCE AND RETREAT, 1914–1920

The European war that broke out in August 1914 was to give rise to a major expansion of America's role in world politics. This expansion had two dimensions. One was an abandonment of the traditional abstention from involvement in the political affairs of Europe. President Woodrow Wilson had departed from this tradition, explicitly as well as implicitly, before the United States itself entered the war in April 1917, but belligerency greatly enhanced America's concern with and influence over the postwar European settlement, both of which were dramatically manifested by Wilson's personal participation in the Paris Peace Conference of 1919. Entry into the war led to the second dimension of the expansion—the massive and effective projection overseas of the nation's power. By the time of the Armistice, there were more American troops on the western front than either French or British troops. Even more important to the victory over Germany was the financial contribution of the United States—loans totaling seven and a half billion dollars to the governments of other countries in the coalition. Partly as a result of this, federal government expenditures increased by a factor of twenty-five over the prewar budget.[1]

Yet these developments proved short-lived. Not only was the huge army demobilized and the swollen budget slimmed (substantially, if not to prewar size), but the active participation in European affairs was also not sustained. The Treaty of Versailles failed to win Senate approval, leaving the United States outside the League of Nations that Wilson had done so much to establish. The immediate cause of this outcome was a highly partisan political conflict aggravated by personal feuds, but it also reflected a strong swing in public opinion against the undertaking of any overseas commitments that might prove costly. The presidential election of 1920 confirmed the breadth and depth of this sentiment.

Within this broad pattern of advance and retreat, U.S. policy toward the European war went through several phases. The initial attempt to maintain the traditional detachment from European quarrels gave way to an increasing engagement as Wilson proclaimed America's willingness to participate in a future league of nations and set out principles that should govern the postwar order. Yet within weeks of calling for "a peace without victory," Wilson led the country into war with Germany. These shifts were responses to the behavior of the belligerent powers, particularly Germany, and they can be understood only by tracing the course of events. The stand taken by the United States over the use of submarines against noncombatant vessels, which ultimately led to intervention, was influenced less by economic or security interests than by emotions arising in part from the strong feelings of connection that many Americans felt with Europe, and Britain in particular, but mostly from a concern with the nation's own honor and rightful prerogatives.

At a more structural level, the scale of America's productive capacity made whatever actions it took consequential for the outcome of the European conflict. Like many other informed Americans, Wilson came to believe that in these circumstances traditional non-involvement was no longer a viable policy. The president presented his program for a reformed world order as the way to prevent future wars that would inevitably draw in the United States—an argument that was to have great influence down the years despite Wilson's ultimate failure to achieve his vision. This vision was premised on America's capacity to provide world leadership, and Wilson's diplomacy consistently manifested great confidence in the nation's material and moral power and its consequent ability to achieve its goals and promote its values.

The European War and American Opinion

The war in Europe revealed both the importance and the complexity of the relationship between the United States and the continent from which the great bulk of its population had been drawn. Even more significant than the economic links (60 percent of the nation's exports went to Europe) were the emotional and intellectual connections. Americans' response to the awesome and appalling conflict was not uniform but reflected their own country's social and geographical diversity. Indeed, the divisions that developed at this time did much to set the context for the evolution of U.S. policy, not only during the war but also in the crucial decades that followed.[2]

The differences were both in the degree of involvement in the awesome conflict and in attitudes toward it. The depth of distress many articulate Americans expressed when the war broke out testified to the extent to which they felt themselves connected to Europe. As vivid reports brought home the horrors of all-out modern warfare, several confessed to having difficulty sleeping. "If civilized Europe were holding back India, for example, it would be comprehensible," *Harper's Weekly* observed. But "for Germans and French, with a whole complex and delicate civilization in common, to be using huge death engines to mow down men and cities is so unthinkable that we go about in a daze, hoping to awake from the most horrid of nightmares." The journalist Ray Stannard Baker noted in his diary, "These are our brothers who suffer." As one of the "muckrakers," Baker had become a prominent figure in the prewar progressive movement and, like it, had hitherto paid little attention to foreign affairs. With the European tragedy dominating the news agenda, however, leaders of the social settlement movement and other reform publicists turned their attention to the cause of international peace. New organizations were formed, notably the Woman's Peace Party, which, under the leadership of Jane Addams, took part in an international women's congress at the Hague in April 1915 that endorsed a program for immediate and lasting peace.[3]

Such an intense response to the war in Europe was not typical. The majority of Americans, especially west of the Appalachians and in small towns and rural areas, were much more detached from events across the Atlantic. The war was commonly seen as arising from the monarchical, caste-bound, and militaristic character of the Old World, and thus as further proof of the superiority of republican America—where, it was often observed, people from all the warring countries were living together in peace. "We never appreciated so keenly as now the foresight exercised by our forefathers in migrating from Europe," one Midwestern newspaper remarked.[4] The strongest impulse, therefore, was to retain this state of beatitude by keeping well clear of the horrific conflict unfolding on the mother continent. Quite quickly, attention reverted to more parochial and mundane concerns, although in the case of those for whom Europe provided an important market, particularly the cotton producers of the South, these included the effects of the war on their own economic interests.

Generally speaking, the strongest force making for a sense of involvement in the European war was identification with one or the other set of belligerents. The large and well-organized German-American community rallied to the Fatherland's cause not only through energetic public presentation of its cause but also by buying its war bonds and contributing to German war relief. (Almost 10 percent of the American population, according to the 1910 census, was either born in Germany or had at least one German-born parent.) Some other ethnic groups also tended to favor the Central Powers, notably Irish-Americans, Swedish-Americans, and Jewish-Americans. The bulk of articulate American opinion, on the other hand, sided with the Allies, particularly at the beginning when the attack on Belgium and the invasion of France seemed to show that Germany was the aggressor; many saw the conflict as one between militaristic autocracy and democracy. There were, however, great differences in the depth and durability of this pro-Allied partisanship. For the majority, it was secondary to the commitment to American neutrality and also tended to weaken over time as more complex views of the war's origins gained currency and the Allies lost some of their moral aura.

Others, however, identified with the Allied cause more wholeheartedly and consistently. These extreme pro-Allied partisans had influence beyond their numbers as their viewpoint was disproportionately represented in the Eastern metropolitan press and the nation's leading journals and magazines. It was much weaker in the Midwest than it was among the upper middle class on the eastern seaboard. Critics at the time and since have attributed this to sectional economic interest. But it is clear that more was involved than the profits that came to be made by certain bankers and munitions makers in supplying the Allies. Certainly J.P. Morgan and Co. actively aided the Allies' cause from the beginning, becoming their purchasing agent in North America and later raising loans on their behalf.[5] But Morgan's underwriting of the risky (and unsuccessful) Anglo-French loan of 1915 demonstrated that the partners were moved by considerations other than profit, and Wall Street firms whose leadership had less strong personal connections with Britain and lacked such Anglophile sentiment acted differently.[6] In any case, as Henry F. May points out, "the earliest and most consistent supporters of the Allies" were not "the business interests" but "the leading men of letters, the college presidents, the old-line publishers, the editors of standard magazines, and their friends."[7] The white Anglo-Saxon Protestant elite that created this subclimate of opinion in certain circles was defined by class and culture rather than particular economic interests.[8]

Most commonly, moral arguments were advanced for supporting the Allied cause; it represented civilization against barbarism, peace-loving democracies against militaristic autocracies, right against wrong. But pro-Allied partisanship was also often justified on the grounds of American self-interest. Most directly, it was suggested that if Germany won the war, it would then seek to attack the United States itself, raising the prospect of invasion. A more sophisticated way of suggesting that a German victory would diminish American security was articulated by Elihu Root. The international law that Germany violated in invading Belgium, Root argued, "was the protection of our peace and security. It was our safeguard against the necessity of maintaining great armaments and wasting our substance in continual readiness for war."[9] Root's argument was similar in structure to that Olney had made in his famous Note to Britain in the Venezuela boundary dispute: America's exemption from the burdens of power politics and the concomitant threat to republican values was dependent on the nature of its external environment. But to extend this argument from the need to uphold the Monroe Doctrine to the maintenance of a law-governed world order was to stretch it quite a long way.

Each of these arguments was carried into the political arena by northeastern Republican leaders who shared the pro-Allied perspective. The danger of invasion was stressed in the agitation for greater military "preparedness" that arose in the fall of 1914. "If Germany conquers France, England, or Russia, she will dominate Europe and will subsequently seek to extend that domination if she can to the rest of the world," Senator Henry Cabot Lodge declared in September 1914.[10] The United States would be particularly vulnerable because of its military weakness. "Unarmed, unready, undefended, we offer a standing invitation to aggression and attack," Lodge warned the Senate in January 1915. "The ocean barrier which defended us in 1776 and 1812 no longer exists. Steam and electricity have destroyed it."[11] As this campaign developed over succeeding months, alarmist scenarios of the invasion of North America were set out in magazine articles and books and even depicted on the movie screen.[12]

The argument that American security depended not only on the nation's own military strength but also on a law-governed world order fed into the calls for the United States to do more to establish and maintain international peace. In the autumn of 1914, Theodore Roosevelt spelled out the case for a "World League of the Peace of Righteousness" in which the major countries would unite to enforce with "collective armed power" the decisions of a judicial tribunal. Some activists in the prewar peace movement who had earlier advanced the idea of an international organization (sometimes described as a "world federation") seized the opportunity to promote their project. In the winter of 1914–15, ideas such as these were developed under the aegis of the New York Peace Society at a series of dinners and meetings attended by a number of prominent citizens including former president Taft and A. Lawrence Lowell, the president of Harvard University. The program they eventually agreed on was influenced both by the proposals of a group in Britain headed by Lord Bryce and by a prudent concern not to commit the United States to more than was politically realistic. The upshot was the launching of a new organization called the League to Enforce Peace in June 1915, with a short and definite program: The United States should "form a league of all the great nations," the members of which would enforce by joint economic and military action a commitment not to go to war before submitting any dispute (depending on its nature) either to "a judicial tribunal" or to "a Council of Conciliation."[13]

Wilson's Initial Policy

These various strands of opinion were very much in Woodrow Wilson's mind as he shaped the administration's policy toward the war. His chief objective seems to have been to minimize the effects of the war on America's own life. The threat that passionate partisanship presented to domestic harmony was a particular concern—Wilson later said that this had been "his main preoccupation during the first year of the war."[14] The official Proclamation of Neutrality on August 4, 1914, was automatic; no one suggested that the United States should do otherwise. But two weeks later the president followed it up by calling on his countrymen to be "impartial in thought as well as in action" regarding the conflict, stressing that "it is entirely within our own choice what its effects upon us will be." As he explained, Wilson issued the appeal because he feared that the country might become "divided in camps of hostile opinion, hot against each other," just because "the people of the United States are drawn . . . chiefly from the nations now at war" and so were naturally inclined to side strongly with one side or the other. The need to restore Europe to peace was, Wilson argued, a further reason for strict neutrality. America "should show herself in this time of peculiar trial . . . a nation that neither sits in judgment upon others nor is disturbed in her own counsels and which keeps herself fit and free to do what is necessary and disinterested and truly serviceable for the peace of the world."[15]

Wilson sought to override the divisive sentiments aroused by the European war by appealing to a higher loyalty to America. This, as he explained to his fiercely pro-Allied Ambassador in London, Walter H. Page, necessitated making it "demonstrably clear that we are doing everything that it is possible to do to define and defend neutral rights."[16] But this course carried its own danger of involvement. A century earlier, the young republic's defense of its rights as a neutral during a major European war had led to a war with Britain. By 1914, the great growth of America's economic power had exacerbated the problem by making the actions of the U.S. government much more consequential for the outcome of the European conflict itself. Both sets of belligerents were well aware that access to America's productive resources could decisively tip the balance of power between them. British policy reflected this awareness in two ways. On the one hand, the U.K. government quickly began placing substantial orders for munitions with American firms, and these were to amount to more than $20 billion over the next two years. On the other hand, Britain effectively cut Germany off from North American supplies through a naval blockade that was increasingly tightened over time.[17]

These British actions confronted the U.S. government with a series of issues. When in August 1914 Morgan's proposed raising a $100 million loan to the Allies in the American market, the administration went beyond the legal obligations of a neutral state by declaring that loans by American bankers to belligerent governments would be "inconsistent with the true spirit of neutrality." This was at the urging of Secretary of State William Jennings Bryan, who took the view that money was "the worst of all contrabands because it commands everything else." Yet a few months later Bryan was as firm as anyone in resisting a campaign, initiated by German- and Irish-Americans but enjoying quite wide public support, for an embargo on the export of munitions, arguing that such a departure from established law would in fact be an unneutral act.[18]

By far the most important and troublesome question was how the administration should respond to Britain's restrictions on trade. These not only went well beyond previous definitions of a blockade in both their scope and their means of enforcement but also impinged on American economic interests, particularly exporters of copper and foodstuffs, especially meat, to the German market. Yet Wilson avoided pushing the dispute with Britain to the point of confrontation. When in November 1914 the Royal Navy mined a large part of the North Sea and announced that neutral ships could traverse the area safely only if they submitted to guidance by Admiralty pilots, the U.S. government expressed no objection. Official Notes to London in December 1914 and March 1915 did refuse to accept the legality of the rules set out in successive Orders in Council, but they were couched in a friendly manner and contained no threat of any retaliatory sanctions.

Some have seen this effective acquiescence in the Allied blockade as a departure from true neutrality that inevitably led to America's eventual involvement in the conflict. By not asserting neutral rights firmly against the Allies, it is suggested, the United States provoked Germany into those violations of American rights that led to war in 1917.[19] This argument rests on the questionable assumption that, if the United States had succeeded in forcing the British to keep their restrictions on trade within the bounds of recognized legality, those in command of German policy in 1917 would have refrained from embarking on the unrestricted submarine campaign that they saw as the best chance of victory.

Rather than being a step on the road to war, Wilson's course was a reflection of his desire to minimize both the extent of America's involvement in the war and its effects on the nation's life. He evidently judged that it would not be possible for the United States to effect significant change in British behavior without accepting costs and possible risks quite disproportionate to the interests involved. The blockade was the principal means by which the British hoped to bring Germany to its knees, and they were deeply committed to it. At the least, credible threats to embargo exports to the Allies would have been necessary. This would have involved the sacrifice of economic interests that were always very much larger than those suffering from the British blockade and that were growing rapidly as a result of the Allies' purchases. This balance would have been significantly altered if cotton had been placed on the contraband list, but the British, aware of the commodity's political as well as economic importance to the American South, refrained from doing this until August 1915 and then undertook to make sufficient purchases to maintain the price.

Some historians have argued that Wilson's failure to resist the illegalities of the British blockade more firmly reflected a recognition of the nation's strategic interest in the continuance of British maritime supremacy and the prevention of a German victory.[20] That the president was averse to quarreling seriously with the British while they were desperately engaged in the European conflict is evident. This is not surprising given that most Americans (and Wilson himself) were at this time sympathetic to the Allied cause. But there is little reason to believe that this sympathy owed much to anxiety about America's own security. It is true that in the first month of the war, Wilson had agreed with House that "if Germany won it would change the course of our civilization and make the United States a military nation," but by early November he was arguing that "no matter how the great war ended, there would be complete exhaustion, and, even if Germany won, she would not be in a condition to seriously menace our country for many years to come."[21]

Wilson made this remark in the context of the agitation for military "preparedness." In his Annual Message in December 1914, Wilson declared bluntly that "no one who speaks counsel based on fact or drawn from a just and candid interpretation of realities can say that there is reason to fear that from any quarter our independence or the integrity of our territory is threatened." The nation should remain faithful to its traditional policy of eschewing "a standing army," or even "a reserve army," and continue to rely on "a powerful navy" and "a citizenry trained and accustomed to arms." To do more than this "would mean merely that we had lost our self-possession, that we had been thrown off our balance by a war with which we have nothing to do, whose causes cannot touch us." This passage of the president's speech was greeted with applause and cheers, indicating that it expressed the sentiments not only of his fellow Democrats but also of many Republicans.[22]

As he had with his appeal for an impartial neutrality, Wilson invoked as further justification the need to preserve America's unique position as a potential peacemaker. "We are, indeed, a true friend to all the nations of the world," he claimed, "because we threaten none, covet the possessions of none, desire the overthrow of none. . . . It is our dearest present hope that this character and reputation may presently . . . bring us an opportunity . . . to counsel and obtain peace in the world and reconciliation and a healing settlement."[23]

In this cause, House journeyed to Europe in early 1915, but in the instructions that he was to show the statesmen he talked to in London and Berlin, Wilson emphasized that "we have no thought of suggesting, either now or at another time, the terms and conditions of peace." And when the British foreign secretary, Sir Edward Grey, said that if American power were to be "actively and strenuously exerted for the making of a program of forcible security for the future—in that event England might consent to end the war as a drawn contest and trust to the subsequent discussion and world-wide agreement to secure safety for the future," House emphatically dismissed the suggestion. Such a commitment would be contrary to "not only the unwritten law of our country but also our fixed policy not to become involved in European affairs."[24]

House's statement clearly shows that six months of war in Europe had altered the basic shape of U.S. foreign policy as little as it had the nation's military posture. Neither the unprecedented scale and character of the conflict nor the great increase in America's relative power had disturbed the traditional pattern of its diplomacy in relation to the Old World. Indeed, the most salient recent development appeared to be the increased awareness of the implications of America's ethnic heterogeneity, and this had furnished an influential further reason for the commitment to neutrality. It is true that beneath the surface of policy the war had revealed how powerful and multifarious were the connections of the United States to Europe—and that various kinds of strong emotion as well as an increasing volume of goods were flowing across the Atlantic. These certainly had the potential to stimulate a more active intervention in the politics of Europe, and possibly costly commitments. But clearly there was also a strong desire on the part of most Americans—and the president—to avoid such involvement and commitments.

The Impact of the U-Boat

By January 1917, there had been both a great change in the nation's foreign policy and a significant strengthening of its military preparedness. President Wilson had committed the United States to participate in a postwar league of nations and then had made this readiness to underwrite European security conditional on a peace settlement that accorded with principles that he had unilaterally declared. Legislation passed in 1916 had authorized an enormous naval building program, doubled the size of the regular army, enlarged and more effectively federalized the National Guard, and created a Council of National Defense to advise the president on industrial mobilization.

The Response to Submarine Warfare

It was a decision made in Berlin that began the process that produced this "revolution" in American policy, as one historian has termed it.[25] As a reprisal for the British "food blockade," the German government announced in February 1915 that their submarines would seek to attack enemy merchant ships within a "war zone" around Great Britain; neutral vessels would not be directly targeted but would be at risk within this area. The United States immediately responded by informing Berlin that it would hold the German government to "a strict accountability" for any destruction of "an American vessel or the lives of American citizens."[26] In the summer of 1915 and again in the spring of 1916, the sinking by German submarines of Allied passenger vessels on which Americans were traveling led the United States to threaten Germany explicitly with the breaking of diplomatic relations and implicitly with war.

Neither the nation's economic interests nor its security requirements provide a plausible explanation of this confrontational approach, and there is no evidence that either figured among the considerations that led to it. There is no question that the maintenance of America's trade was an important national interest; exports to the Allies increased almost fourfold during the period of neutrality and clearly helped stimulate the economic boom that developed.[27] But this trade did not need the protection of the U.S. government. Because it was so important to their war effort, the Allies would have been bound in any case to continue to purchase American munitions and other supplies and to attempt to transport them safely across the Atlantic (as the British were to do in the face of much more formidable U-boats in 1939–41). It is true that American shipowners might have decided that the business was not worth the risk but, as proportion of the trade carried in U.S. vessels was very small, this would have made little practical difference.[28] In any case, the campaign was not seen as a major threat to transatlantic commerce in 1915 when the German navy had only a handful of modern, ocean-going submarines; indeed, its launching was welcomed by the British as providing justification for extending their blockade to prevent commodities of any kind from either reaching or leaving Germany.[29] So it seems highly unlikely that Wilson's stand was motivated, as one historian has suggested, by a desire "to lessen the effectiveness of the submarines against British trade" because he saw an Allied victory as serving America's security interests; there is certainly no evidence to suggest this was the case.[30]

The torpedoing of merchant ships by submarines, especially without warning, was clearly contrary to international law. Under this, a warship imposing a blockade had to observe the rules of "visit and search" when stopping either belligerent or neutral vessels; enemy merchantmen could be captured but could only be fought and sunk if they put up resistance. By early 1915 Roosevelt and other pro-Allied Republicans were criticizing the administration for not having protested Germany's violation of Belgian neutrality, and, as we have seen, Root and others argued that upholding international law everywhere was in America's own interest. Although Wilson himself did not wish to go beyond affirming America's own legal rights and obligations as a neutral state, he was strongly committed to upholding these. It was on this basis that he and Bryan had resisted the pressure for an arms embargo and why he had compelled his reluctant ambassador in London to deliver protests against the illegalities of the British blockade. But in those negotiations, the U.S. government, while reserving its position and seeking redress in particular cases, had not threatened to break relations when the Allies failed to bring their practices into line with its demands. Why did it resist German violations of the rights of Americans under international law so much more strongly?

The answer to this question has often been seen to lie in the different issues involved. "Debating the legality to destroy life and the legality to destroy property are very different things," Robert Lansing, then the State Department counselor, observed in April 1915.[31] However, as critics of the administration's policy at the time and later have pointed out, the only reason that the Allied blockade did not endanger life was that neutrals adjusted their behavior to it. British mines were potentially as lethal as a U-boat's torpedoes. From this point of view, the significant difference was not in the methods employed by the belligerents but in the American response to them. If Americans did not risk their lives sailing in the North Sea outside the authorized lanes, why should they do so in the waters where the U-boats were operating? The policy equivalent of the administration's effective acquiescence in the illegalities of the Allied blockade might seem to be an official warning to American citizens against traveling in the war zone on a ship of a belligerent country. However, Wilson never adopted this course of action even though it was advocated by Bryan at the time of the *Lusitania* crisis and later attracted much support in Congress.

The stand Wilson came to take over the submarine issue is better understood through a narrative than through abstract analysis. The wording of the "strict accountability" Note was ambiguous on the question of whether it applied only to American ships or also to Americans aboard ships belonging to a belligerent country.[32] In March, the administration was compelled to clarify its position on this issue when a small British liner, the *Falaba*, was sunk and an American engineer, Leon Thrasher, was among those who lost their lives. The case set off a fierce debate within the administration with Bryan arguing against the hard line being advocated by Lansing. Wilson was at first inclined to send a Note condemning the use of submarines against merchant vessels as inherently inhumane but was apparently impressed by Bryan's insistence that the American people would "be slow to admit the right of a citizen to involve his country in war when by exercising ordinary care he could have avoided danger." A month after the sinking, Wilson observed that "perhaps it is not necessary to make formal representations in the matter at all."[33] In his authoritative account of policymaking in both governments, Arthur Link concludes that "at this juncture the possibilities of an American adjustment to the submarine war were by no means remote."[34]

Less than two weeks later, on May 7, 1915, the premier British liner, the *Lusitania*, was sunk by a U-boat with the loss of 1,200 lives, including 128 Americans. After the horrors of the twentieth century, it requires an effort of historical imagination to understand how appalling this event seemed. It was, after all, little more than three years since the sinking of the *Titanic*, but this time the disaster was the result of a deliberate human act—"murder on the high seas" was a common description.[35] The denunciations of German barbarism by editorialists and commentators, particularly in the East, were no doubt heightened by the preexisting pro-Allied sentiments of many of them. The underlying feeling of such people that the United States ought really to be in the war strengthened demands for a strong American response to the *Lusitania* sinking.[36] Condemnation of the atrocity was mixed with a sense of outrage at what was seen as an unprovoked assault on the nation's own citizens. "It is inconceivable that we can refrain from taking action in this matter," Theodore Roosevelt declared, "for we owe it not only to humanity but to our own self-respect."[37] The political salience of such sentiments was brought home to Wilson by the criticism evoked by his incautious remark in an unrelated speech that "there is such a thing as a man being too proud to fight. There is such a thing as a nation being so right that it does not need to convince others by force that it is right."[38]

It was following this that Wilson himself composed a Note to Germany that was dispatched within a week of the *Lusitania* sinking. The Note stated that events had shown that it was a "practical impossibility" to employ submarines against commerce "without an inevitable violation of many sacred principles of justice and humanity" and demanded the abandonment of this method of warfare.[39] This was an extreme position in that it implicitly threw the mantle of American protection not only over American and other neutral shipping but also over the merchant vessels of the countries fighting Germany, even if these were transporting munitions or troops (as the *Lusitania* had done). Bryan resigned as secretary of state soon afterwards because he could not endorse a stand that he saw as a departure from neutrality that carried a serious risk of war with Germany. (Wilson appointed Lansing in his stead.)

Nothing suggests that Wilson gave any consideration to the effect of submarine warfare on the outcome of the European conflict as he deliberated over the issue. There is some indication that American credibility abroad did weigh with him. House, who was in London at the time, had cabled that failure to take a strong stand, backed if necessary by entry into the war, would diminish America's future influence over the peace, and the president observed to Bryan that "everything that affects the opinion of the world regarding us affects our influence for good."[40]

There seems little doubt, however, that the chief factor shaping the president's stance was his reading of American public opinion. "When I am almost overcome by perplexities," Wilson told the press at the time he was wrestling with the *Falaba* case, "what I try to remember, is what the people at home are thinking about. I try to put myself in the place of the man who does not know all the things that I know and ask myself what he would like the policy of this country to be."[41] Although this might seem no more than a piece of democratic piety, it reflected Wilson's longstanding view about the essentially representative and interpretative character of leadership in a democracy.[42] It also accorded with his personal political interest. Elected in 1912 because the Republican vote had been divided between Taft and Roosevelt, Wilson needed to broaden the base of his support if he was to be reelected in 1916. He knew that his political standing would be much affected by public perceptions of his conduct of foreign policy at this critical time. It was certainly helped by his *Lusitania* Note, which was greeted by the American press with almost unanimous praise.[43]

Shortly before Bryan's resignation, Wilson had written to him that "I wish with all my heart that I saw a way to carry out the double wish of our people, to maintain a firm front in respect of what we demand of Germany and yet do nothing that might by any possibility involve us in the war."[44] Whereas Bryan was unequivocal that the latter objective should have clear priority, Wilson had in effect subordinated it to the first. As Bryan warned, the position the president had adopted was a precarious one because it depended on Germany's acceding to his demands.[45] If Germany were defiant and the dispute escalated, it would be much more difficult for Wilson to avoid going to war now that he had put the nation's prestige (and his own) on the line.

In the last analysis, Wilson's course over the *Lusitania* rested on a confidence that he could force Germany to back down. Several elements may have contributed to this confidence—a genuine belief that the Germans, too, must have been shocked by the *Lusitania* sinking, an assumption that the U-boat campaign was more in the nature of a gesture than a serious weapon of war, and an underlying sense of America's power and of the shadow this must cast in Berlin. Writing to a supportive friend in late July, the president echoed the terms of his earlier letter to Bryan but with a significant addition: "The opinion of the country seems to demand two inconsistent things, firmness and the avoidance of war, but I am hoping that perhaps they are not in necessary contradiction and that firmness may bring peace."[46]

Wider Effects on U.S. Policy

It was in this context that Wilson reversed his position over "preparedness." That the president indicated an abrupt change of mind on the question within two weeks of the *Lusitania* sinking makes it clear that it was a direct consequence of the submarine dispute. But the crisis had also given a great boost to the public campaign for preparedness, with East Coast businessmen as well as college students eagerly enrolling for reserve officer training in summer camps at Plattsburgh, New York, and elsewhere. When Wilson first laid out the case for new measures in November 1915 he evidently anticipated broad public support for "reasonable" preparedness. Minimizing his change of stance, he reiterated both that he sought preparation only for defense, not for any more ambitious or aggressive policy, and that there was no immediate threat. When the scale and character of his program nonetheless aroused a nationwide movement of opposition and ran into trouble in Congress, particularly from Bryanite Democrats, Wilson took his case to the country in a series of speeches in early 1916.[47]

In this effort to rally public support, Wilson connected his change of position much more explicitly with the submarine dispute and also foreshadowed some of the ways in which he would later justify greater departures from traditional policies. Attempting to answer his critics' question, "preparedness for what?" he again emphatically repudiated any ambition to pursue a course of national aggrandizement. He also reiterated his commitment to neutrality, arguing that this was not based on a selfish desire to keep out of trouble but on the conviction that it was how the United States could best serve the world. But whereas "a year ago, it did seem as if America might rest secure without very great anxiety and take it for granted that she would not be drawn into this terrible maelstrom, . . . now no man can confidently say whether the United States will be drawn into the struggle or not." This, Wilson repeatedly stressed, was because of "the double obligation you have laid upon me"—of which he was "constantly reminded . . . by means of every voice that comes to me out of the body of the nation"—"to keep us out of this war" and "to keep the honor of the nation unstained." The actions of other countries might make it necessary to defend the Monroe Doctrine or "to use the force of the United States to vindicate the right of American citizens everywhere to enjoy the protection of international law." Specifically, these were the rights to travel and to trade across the world.

Implicitly recognizing that the interests these rights represented might well be judged insufficient to justify the costs of upholding them, Wilson linked such mundane privileges to more elevated and universal principles and to America's historic mission—"that flag stands for the rights of mankind, no matter where they be." Above all, he stressed the importance of America's "self-respect" and "honor": If his proposals were not accepted, "it may turn out . . . that I should have to suffer the mortification and you the disappointment of having the combination of peace with honor prove to be impossible."[48] Wilson invoked the claims of national honor in even more sweeping terms the following month in order to defeat moves in Congress to warn, or even prohibit, Americans from traveling on armed merchant ships.[49] His refusal to compromise over this issue may have reflected, as he implied, concern with the nation's international prestige, but at least as important, surely, was a desire to protect his political position in an election year at a time when leading Republicans were accusing him of weakness in standing up for American rights both in the submarine dispute and in Mexico.[50]

Although the president still needed to compromise with congressional critics on his return to Washington, both houses passed a bill doubling the size of the Regular Army (to over two hundred thousand men) and providing for a greatly enlarged National Guard under more effective federal control. The Navy Act of 1916 was even more impressive in authorizing the building of sixteen capital ships over three years—a larger program than any previously undertaken by any country. The preceding congressional debate revealed that these measures were the product of a feeling that the United States needed to strengthen its capacity to defend its existing interests (including the Monroe Doctrine and the rights of its citizens as well as its territory) rather than any sense that the nation had a stake in the outcome of the European conflict. Similarly, the forces created were not structured to project military power to other continents; the federalized National Guard, like the build-up of coastal defenses, was envisaged as a means to protect the nation's borders, while the emphasis on the construction of capital ships was ill designed to combat the challenge of the submarine. Likewise, the war plans of the army and the navy envisaged defending the United States from external attack; there was no planning for an expeditionary force to Europe until late March 1917.[51]

These increases in America's armed forces did not ensure that Wilson would be able to fulfill "the double obligation." As he warned an audience in St. Louis, "one reckless commander of a submarine, choosing to put his private interpretation upon what his government wishes him to do, might set the world on fire."[52] Germany had not yielded to Wilson's demand in the *Lusitania* Note, stubbornly adhering to the intrinsic legitimacy of its use of U-boats against enemy merchant vessels. Both sides made concessions at times when the dispute came close to the brink of conflict—Wilson in accepting the possibility that submarines could operate in a legal and acceptable manner against merchant ships, the Germans in pledging not to sink passenger liners in October 1915 and in suspending the campaign entirely in May 1916.[53] But these German undertakings were in the first case partial and in the second case conditional on the United States' securing future adherence to international maritime law on the part of the Allies also. The successive crises made it clear that Wilson had become dependent on the continued restraint of the German government to save him from having to make a painful choice between going to war and backing down from the stand he had taken, when backing down would be damaging to both his political standing at home and his diplomatic credibility abroad.

The president's desire to avoid such a choice intensified as he became more conscious of how averse the majority of Americans were to the prospect of involvement in the war. He had adopted his uncompromising position on submarine warfare at the height of public outrage over the *Lusitania*, when the loudest voices were those of East Coast newspapers and politicians. Two months later, Wilson sent to House, "as a sample of, I might almost say, all the letters I am receiving nowadays," one from a Democratic congressman stressing that "the mass of the people want peace" and questioning whether "the metropolitan press" spoke for the country.[54] When the torpedoing of another British liner, the *Arabic*, created another crisis in August, Wilson wrote emphatically to both his fiancée Edith Galt and House that it was "clear to me . . . that the people of this country rely upon me to keep them out of war."[55]

This appraisal of the balance of American opinion, together with the Germans' refusal to renounce the submarine campaign in principle, added urgency and force to Wilson's efforts to bring the war to an early end. This was, after all, the only secure way in which he could avoid being forced to choose between "peace" and "honor," and it became the dominating goal of his foreign policy from the fall of 1915 until America's own entry into the war in April 1917.

The manner in which Wilson first set about achieving this objective reflected how far the administration's position at this time was from that impartial neutrality for which he had called. In reality, Washington was much closer to London than it was to Berlin, not least because House had established a mutually admiring relationship with Grey, and this alignment was reinforced when the *Lusitania* sinking raised the possibility that the United States might enter the war on the Allied side. In August, the administration abandoned its opposition to loans to belligerent governments, which had already been somewhat relaxed. In advocating this change of policy, both Lansing and Secretary of the Treasury William G. McAdoo stressed the extent to which the nation's prosperity had become dependent on the Allies' purchases. These economic considerations were surely significant in this instance, but Wilson himself seems to have become persuaded—in the context of what Arthur Link calls "the overshadowing and ever-present threat of rupture with Germany"—that the ban on loans was an unwarranted infringement of the Allies' legal rights.[56]

In a letter to Grey in September 1915, House suggested that the president might now call for a peace "upon the broad basis of the elimination of militarism and navalism and a return, as nearly as possible to the status quo." After some delay, Grey responded by asking if Wilson would propose "that there should be a League of Nations binding themselves to side against any Power which . . . refused, in case of dispute, to adopt some other method of settlement than that of war?"[57] As we have seen, this was something that Grey had been urging for months, but now the response was very different than it had been the previous winter. This was clearly because the submarine dispute had in the meantime raised the possibility of American involvement in the war.

That prospect was not unwelcome to House himself, but he wanted the United States to fight for a better world order rather than simply in defense of technical neutral rights. He therefore concocted an elaborate plan whereby Wilson would call for peace when the Allies thought the moment was opportune and then force Germany, if necessary by war, to accept reasonable terms. When Grey made it clear that he would be interested in such a procedure only if the United States were prepared to join in upholding the subsequent settlement, Wilson permitted House to respond positively. There seems no doubt that this was because House had persuaded him that his scheme stood a good chance of bringing the war to an early end.[58]

Even as Wilson agreed to break with the tradition of non-entanglement, however, he sought to circumscribe the extent to which he did so. As House was about to sail to Europe to pursue his somewhat conspiratorial scheme, Wilson instructed him that "we have nothing to do with local settlements—territorial questions, indemnities, and the like—but are concerned only in the future peace of the world and the guarantees to be given for that. The only possible guarantees, that is, the only guarantees that any rational man could accept, are (a) military and naval disarmament and (b) a league of nations to secure each nation against aggression and maintain the absolute freedom of the seas." Thus, Wilson was limiting the nation's commitment both by disclaiming concern with the specific terms of a European settlement and by focusing on the future rather than immediate issues.

At the same time, the president made it clear that there was one immediate issue with which he *was* very much concerned. For him the purpose of House's mission was to employ American pressure in order to bring the European conflict to an end as soon as possible: "If either party to the present war will let us say to the other that they are willing to discuss peace on such terms, it will clearly be our duty to use our utmost moral force to oblige the other to parley, and I do not see how they could stand in the opinion of the world if they refused."[59]

Increasing Involvement and Commitments

Over the next thirteen months, Wilson's urgent desire to end the war led him publicly to proclaim America's willingness to take part in a postwar league of nations and also to extend the scope of his policy objectives to include the terms of the postwar settlement in Europe. This latter development was partly in response to pressure from abroad but mostly arose from the president's sense of American opinion.

The pressure from abroad came during House's negotiations in London. Grey would only consider the possibility of an early peace conference once House had agreed in a written memorandum that the subsequent settlement should include "the restoration of Belgium, the transfer of Alsace and Lorraine to France, and the acquisition by Russia of an outlet to the sea." When Wilson confirmed to Grey his agreement with the Memorandum, he in no way distanced himself from this statement, though he qualified the commitment to enter the war if Germany was "unreasonable" at the peace conference by inserting the word "probably." The Memorandum did constitute a tentative step toward involvement in the ordering of European affairs, but this secret document, which Wilson had no hand in drawing up, hardly constituted an official statement of America's foreign policy objectives and should not be read as an indication of what drove his policy.[60]

The real driver remained his desire to bring about an early end to the war, which was given additional impetus by the crisis following the sinking of the passenger ferry *Sussex* in March 1916, which brought the United States to the brink of war again.[61] Seeking to encourage the Allies to signal their readiness for him to call publicly for a peace conference in the manner set out in the House-Grey Memorandum, Wilson decided to make public the promise of American participation in an international organization to keep the peace and provide security to all countries. He did this in an address to the League to Enforce Peace on May 27, 1916.

In this speech the president sought not only to appeal to the Allied governments but also to justify to the American people this proposed departure from the time-honored policy of independent unilateralism. The main thrust of his case was that the war had demonstrated the impossibility of non-involvement in modern conditions: "Our own rights as a nation, the liberties, the privileges, and the property of our people has been profoundly affected. We are not mere disconnected lookers-on. . . . We are participants, whether we would or not, in the life of the world." Given the effects of the war on the United States, "we shall be as much concerned as the nations at war to see peace assume an aspect of permanence." Consequently, the president called for American participation in "an universal association of the nations . . . to prevent any war begun either contrary to treaty covenants or without warning and full submission of the causes to the opinion of the world—a virtual guarantee of territorial integrity and political independence."

Wilson relied primarily upon this essentially pragmatic line of argument on this occasion. He sought to minimize the break with tradition by reiterating that "we are in no sense or degree parties to the present quarrel," which should be concluded by "such a settlement with regard to their immediate interests as the belligerents may agree upon." But he also sought to forestall the objection that was to figure largely in the debate of 1919–20 and was revived with respect to the United Nations—that participation in such an organization to maintain the peace would commit the United States to upholding an unjust status quo. Thus, he proclaimed certain principles that should guide the settlement in addition to the fundamental one that nations should be secure against aggression:

> First, that every people has a right to choose the sovereignty under which they shall live. . . . Second, that the small states of the world have a right to enjoy the same respect for their sovereignty and for their territorial integrity that great and powerful nations expect and insist upon.

The latter principle, with its implicit reference to Belgium, may have been designed to mollify the Allied governments for the president's implicit backtracking from the territorial terms of the House-Grey Memorandum. But the former, which echoed the Declaration of Independence, linked Wilson's unprecedented commitment to America's historic values and objectives, as did his somewhat remarkable statement that the first object of the "association of nations" would be "to maintain the inviolate security of the seas for the common and unhindered use of all the nations of the world." This was also, as House had been quick to appreciate, an objective that would appeal to Germany.[62]

The speech failed in its immediate diplomatic purpose in that Grey made it increasingly clear that the Allies were not going to ask Wilson to call for a peace conference in the near future. Further causes of dissatisfaction with the Allies emerged in the summer of 1916, including the searching of American mail intercepted at sea and the plans for a postwar economic bloc agreed at a conference in Paris. British publication of a "blacklist" of U.S. and Latin American firms suspected of trading with the enemy with whom British subjects were forbidden to have any dealings was to Wilson "the last straw." By July he decided to terminate the covert cooperation with the Allies that House had promoted and conducted and to adopt a more independent approach that brought the American stance closer to "impartial" neutrality. When a note of protest to the British government remained unanswered, the administration secured congressional resolutions empowering the president to restrict trade with countries discriminating against American firms or illegally interfering with the movement of American goods or ships.[63]

The failure of the Allies to move for an early peace despite Wilson's public promise to participate in a postwar league of nations in no way diminished the president's commitment to the project. He evidently saw a league of nations as not only in the country's long-term foreign policy interest but also a way of achieving broad domestic support for more active involvement in world affairs. Hitherto, support for such involvement had come largely from northeastern Republicans; the leadership of the League to Enforce Peace was composed of such men. By presenting a future league of nations as a way of realistically achieving the maintenance of peace without participation in the existing system of power politics, Wilson had some success in persuading anti-militarist liberals and anti-imperialist Democrats to support his preparedness program as well as this international commitment. The president ensured that participation in a postwar league was included in the Democratic platform on which he would run for reelection.

Wilson built arguments for this commitment into his campaign speeches in the fall. Democratic spokesmen hailed him for achieving "peace with honor," and the president took advantage of the belligerent and implicitly pro-Allied speeches of Theodore Roosevelt to claim that "the certain prospect of the success of the Republican Party is that we shall be drawn in one form or another into the embroilments of the European war."[64] But he emphatically repudiated the imputation "that the people of the United States do not want to fight about anything." They did not wish to fight "for the ambitions of this group of nations as compared with the ambitions of that group of nations," but "America is always ready to fight for things that are American": "We are saving ourselves in order that we may unite in that final league of nations in which it shall be understood that there is no neutrality where any nation is doing wrong." "Some day we may have to use the physical force of this nation," he warned, because after the war "we have a distinct part to play in the world which we never played before." Placing this development in the context of America's growth and expansion, he explained that "we never had the opportunity to play it before. We never had the financial standing and position in the world that we have now. . . . We never had the industrial equipment and vigor and vision that we have now." In particular, the war's transformation of the United States from a debtor to a creditor nation had brought "a new responsibility."[65]

Notwithstanding this clear repudiation of the non-involvement tradition, it was as "the man who kept us out of war" that Wilson won his narrow victory in November. Both during the campaign and after the election, however, the president received messages from the German government warning him that it might soon feel compelled to revoke the conditional *Sussex* pledge and urging him to act quickly if he wanted to offer his services as a peacemaker.[66] With the election having demonstrated how widely and strongly the American people desired to keep out of the war, this prospect led Wilson to make his most open and determined move for an early peace. Both House and Lansing sought to dissuade him from this course because they feared that an American initiative would be welcomed by Germany and resisted by the Allies.[67] But the president's initial sympathy with the Allies had now evaporated, as he explained to Ambassador Page during the latter's home visit in September. "He described the war as a result of many causes—some of long origin," Page noted. "He spoke of England's having the earth, of Germany's wanting it."[68] In his election speeches, Wilson attributed the conflict to the European system as a whole rather than to Germany in particular.[69]

Indeed, such was Wilson's distance from the Allies at this point that he was prepared to weaken their war effort in the cause of an early peace. By this stage, the extent of their dependence on American finance as well as supplies had provided him with great potential leverage—as some at least in the British government recognized.[70] In late November, the president asked the Federal Reserve Board to strengthen a warning to American banks against investing in the short-term Treasury bonds on which the British and French governments were beginning to rely to finance their purchases in North America. "The object of course," the British Ambassador reported, "is to force us to accept [the] President's mediation by cutting off supplies."[71]

In December 1916, Wilson dispatched a Note to the belligerent powers pointing out the similarity of their war objectives as stated in general terms and calling on them to be more explicit about their specific goals in view of the appalling human costs of continuing the war, its effects on neutral nations, "and lest, more than all, an injury be done civilization itself which can never be atoned for or repaired."[72] Neither side replied helpfully to Wilson's Note. But the president had no intention of abandoning his peace offensive at this point. He continued through private diplomacy to seek more detail on Germany's expectations, and he also sought to increase the pressure on the belligerents through a major address to the Senate on January 22, 1917.[73]

In this speech, Wilson expressed more concern about the nature of the agreement the belligerents might reach between themselves than he had previously, saying that "it makes a great deal of difference in what way and upon what terms" the war was ended. Recognizing that, as a neutral state, "we shall have no voice in determining what these terms shall be," he nevertheless sought to influence them by making the commitment to participate in a future league of nations conditional. Arguing that "no covenant of cooperative peace that does not include the peoples of the New World can suffice to keep the future safe against war," Wilson warned the belligerents that "there is only one sort of peace that the peoples of America could join in guaranteeing." In specifying what that sort of peace was, the president reiterated some of the reforms in the character of inter-state relations to which he had referred earlier, such as "moderation of armaments," freedom of the seas, and "an equality of rights" between large, strong states and small, weak ones. But he went further by proclaiming some general principles that should govern also the territorial settlement. First, "that governments derive all their just powers from the consent of the governed, and that no right anywhere exists to hand peoples about from sovereignty to sovereignty as if they were property." Second, that "so far as practicable, . . . every great people now struggling towards a full development of its resources and of its powers should be assured a direct outlet to the great highways of the sea."

But the most important condition that Wilson attached to American readiness to guarantee the settlement was "that it must be a peace without victory" because "only a peace between equals can last." In arguing this case, Wilson stressed psychological factors:

> Victory would mean peace forced upon the loser, a victor's terms imposed upon the vanquished. It would be accepted in humiliation, under duress, at an intolerable sacrifice, and would leave a sting, a resentment, a bitter memory upon which terms of peace would rest, not permanently, but only as upon quicksand.[74]

The speech represented an intervention in European affairs unprecedented in American diplomacy. The peace terms Wilson outlined can be seen as an attempt to identify common ground between the antagonists and to balance objectives sought by the one side with those desired by the other. He evidently hoped that the promise of "an organized common peace" underwritten by American power would have general appeal, while he again sought to present his vision of the peace as fulfilling both Allied demands for the destruction of German militarism and the German objective of an end to British "navalism" and the freedom of the seas. And what distinguished the one territorial issue to which Wilson specifically referred, the restoration of an independent Poland, was that the general idea (if not the boundaries) could be accepted by both sides.[75]

In a newspaper interview two years earlier, Wilson had expressed the view that the best outcome of the conflict would be "a deadlock" that "will show to them the futility of employing force in the attempt to resolve their differences."[76] But there seems little doubt that he now made this formal call for a compromise settlement because of his urgent desire for an *early* peace and his recognition that the appetite for victory was the principal obstacle to its achievement. He sought to overcome this obstacle by openly appealing to war-weariness among the populations of the belligerent nations: "I would fain believe that I am speaking for the silent mass of mankind everywhere who have as yet had no place or opportunity to speak their real hearts out concerning the death and ruin they see to have come already upon the persons and the homes they hold most dear."[77]

Wilson's attempt to achieve greater diplomatic leverage from American participation in a postwar league of nations by making it conditional on the nature of the peace showed that the commitment remained for him, as it had been when he first made it privately through House, a means to the end of an early peace rather than the supreme objective of his policy. It also implied that it would be, as he put it, "a service" that the American people were offering to the troubled nations of Europe, rather than something that the United States needed to do for the sake of its own welfare and security.

Although Wilson's speech was greeted with indignation and distress in the Allied capitals, it was generally well received at home. However, speeches on the floor of the Senate by leading figures who represented significant bodies of opinion indicated that the president's interpretation of the national interest by no means commanded universal assent. Senator William Borah (R–Id.) challenged Wilson's bold claims that establishing a new foundation for world peace was an opportunity for which the American people had "sought to prepare themselves . . . ever since the days when they set up a new nation in the high and honorable hope that it might in all that it was and did show mankind the way to liberty" and that his program represented not the abandonment but the enlargement of such traditional policies as the Monroe Doctrine and the avoidance of entangling alliances. Borah introduced a Senate resolution reaffirming faith in the Monroe Doctrine in its original form and in Washington's and Jefferson's policy of non-involvement in European politics. From a different angle, Lodge launched an attack on Wilson's whole program, maintaining that its objectives were undesirable, unattainable, or both. As a pro-Allied partisan, he challenged the claim that only a peace without victory would be lasting. He also argued that if a league to enforce peace was to be truly effective, it would require an international police force of five million men: "In the present state of human nature and public opinion is it probable that any nation will bind itself to go to war at the command of other nations and furnish its army and navy to be disposed of as the majority of other nations may see fit?" The president privately confessed to a friend that he found these reactions rather disturbing, as "after all, it is upon the Senate that I have to depend for the kind of support that will make acts possible."[78]

Going to War

There is an oft-told story about the entry of the United States into World War I. According to this, Americans had come to have a considerable stake in the Allied cause by the spring of 1917. In different versions of the story, this stake is attributed to an increasing emotional and ideological sympathy, to an economic and financial interest constituted by the scale of American exports and loans to Britain and France, or to fear of the consequences for America's own security of a German victory. The unrestricted submarine campaign launched by Germany in February 1917 raised the likelihood of an Allied defeat, especially in the context of the impending collapse of the eastern front, the poor morale of the French army, and the near-exhaustion of Britain's financial resources. To prevent this outcome, the United States entered the war.[79]

This account makes perfect sense but suffers from the drawback of not being true. At the beginning of 1917, majority American opinion was markedly less favorable to the Allies than it had been earlier in the war. Initially, the Entente powers had been widely seen as simply responding to aggression, but this moral advantage had eroded over time. The ruthless nature of Britain's war effort, as manifested in the treatment of the 1916 Easter rising in Ireland as well as the conduct of the blockade, together with indications of the Allies' own postwar ambitions, had led many Americans to see the war more as a simple power struggle than as a contest between right and wrong. As we have seen, Wilson's own thought had followed this trajectory, and he saw himself as representative. In September 1916, Page recorded his saying that "at first everybody he met favored the Allies. Now he came across nobody who was not vexed with England."[80]

Passionate pro-Allied sentiment persisted in certain circles, particularly among the upper middle classes of the eastern seaboard. But the influence of such people was probably at a nadir in the winter of 1916–17. This was certainly true of their most prominent public representative, Theodore Roosevelt, whose speeches in the election campaign were generally judged to have been a liability for the Republican candidate, Charles Evans Hughes.[81] After his election victory, as we have seen, Wilson had invested his political capital in a determined effort to achieve "a peace without victory" in Europe.

But just ten weeks after coining this phrase in his address to the Senate, the president was on Capitol Hill again, calling on the whole Congress to declare war against Germany. The dramatic change in his policy was clearly the consequence of Germany's unleashing of its submarines to attack the ships of neutral as well as enemy nations in a wide zone around Britain, France, and Italy. But this was *not* because it was believed that the submarine campaign was likely to bring Britain to its knees and leave Germany in a position to threaten the United States itself. Although the suggestion that a victorious Germany would pose a threat to the United States had been made by pro-Allied partisans from the beginning and had helped inspire the preparedness campaign, the congressional debates over that issue in 1916 had shown that most Americans remained confident that the United States could defend its homeland unaided.[82]

It is possible that this confidence would not have withstood the imminent prospect of a triumphant Germany dominating Europe, but in the spring of 1917 Americans saw no such prospect. Once the Germans had failed in the first weeks of the war to crush France before Russia was fully mobilized, the great majority of American commentators on the European conflict seem to have envisaged only two possible results—an Allied victory or a stalemate. In February 1917, Frank H. Simonds, the most authoritative of such commentators, reported after a visit to the battlefields in France that the British army was superior to its foe in *matériel* and morale and was finally advancing after two years of holding the line. The March Revolution was widely seen as likely to strengthen Russia's commitment to the war by eliminating the influence of pro-German elements in the tsarist court. Nor was the new submarine campaign viewed as a winning weapon. Figures published at the beginning of March showed only slight increases in Allied tonnage losses. Indeed, some of the strongest supporters of intervention, including Lodge, feared that the British navy would defeat the campaign before it had produced the desired effect of bringing the United States into the war.[83]

Lacking any sort of foreign intelligence service, Wilson and the administration were no better informed than other Americans about the seriousness of the threat the U-boats constituted—or, indeed, about the French "crisis of reserves." In the intra-governmental discussions during the period of decision, those pressing for entry into the war never did so on the grounds that it was necessary in order to prevent a German victory. House saw the submarine campaign as a sign of desperation and predicted that Germany "will go to pieces before long." Lansing argued that for the sake of "peace and civilization," Germany had to be liberated from "Prussian militarism." From London, Ambassador Page warned that the feeling that the United States was "holding back . . . until the British Navy shall overcome the German submarines" would "interfere with any influence that we might otherwise have when peace comes."[84]

Page also suggested that America's own immediate interests were at stake by warning that the submarine threat would deter Britain from shipping gold to New York, resulting in "almost a cessation of transatlantic trade" and "a panic in the United States."[85] This emphasis on America's economic interest has been echoed by those historians who have seen the dependence of American prosperity on a threatened trade as the basic cause of the nation's entry into the war.[86] However, there are several problems with this argument, too. In the first place, it remained the case that only a small proportion of the nation's seaborne commerce (17 percent at the end of 1916) was carried in American ships.[87] Even had these stayed out of the war zone, therefore, the British would still have had the means, as they clearly had the will, to transport large quantities of goods across the Atlantic. Furthermore, some diminution in the volume of exports could well be seen as economically desirable for long-term reasons. As the Federal Reserve Board had recognized, there were dangers in a prosperity too dependent on the essentially temporary war trade. And Wilson himself had not only implicitly endorsed this view by approving the restriction of credit in November 1916 but had also explicitly argued that the boom America was enjoying could not be attributed to Allied orders.[88]

Even so, Page was right that a drastic and sudden reduction in Allied purchases would have had serious consequences for the American economy; in 1916, exports to Britain and France had absorbed close to 6 percent of the gross national product, contributing to a boom that saw growth of 7.8 percent in real terms during the course of the year.[89] Page was also right that the chief danger of such a reduction came more from the Allies' financial difficulties than from the U-boat threat. Addressing this issue, however, need not have entailed becoming a belligerent. Measures could have been taken to make it easier for the Allies to obtain the necessary dollars, just as in 1915 the initial ban on loans had been lifted after cabinet members had stressed its damaging effect on the American economy. Indeed, the Federal Reserve Board reversed its position not only on short-term treasury notes but also on unsecured long-term loans to the Allies in early March 1917, before the United States entered the war.[90]

However, for many at the time and since, it was not the prosperity of the nation as a whole so much as that of special interests within it that furnished the impetus for American intervention. American steelmakers and munitions makers, as well as the Morgan bank itself, had been making great profits from the war trade, as the Nye Committee of the 1930s was to show. When Senator George Norris (R–Neb.) declared that "we are going into war upon the command of gold," he was arguing that such moneyed interests had been able to manufacture sentiment through their control of the press.[91] But the previous two years had clearly shown that bellicose editorials in East Coast newspapers could not shape the opinion of the country—or of Congress. Nor was the administration likely to be sympathetic to the interests of the Morgan partners, who had openly backed the Republicans in the recent election.[92] Indeed, in the Progressive era, it would be a liability for any politician to appear to be doing the bidding of Wall Street—as Norris's comment implicitly showed.

When neither anxiety about a security threat nor a concern with economic interests impels a state to war, it is natural to ask what other foreign policy objectives its government was pursuing. In this case, no one at the time or since has doubted that "the government" meant Woodrow Wilson, and many historians attribute the president's decision to enter the war to his desire to achieve the objectives he had previously proclaimed. In Ernest May's words, "the same dream of peace that had entered into all his diplomacy finally led him paradoxically to a decision for war."[93]

There are several versions of this explanation. The least persuasive is that Wilson was driven, as he had been in advocating a peace without victory, by the desire to bring the war to an end as soon as possible.[94] But since Wilson's peace offensive had been designed to fend off the danger of American belligerency, this argument posits a dramatic reversal of his priorities. And there is no reason at all to believe that the failure to achieve peace at this time would have led him to declare war if Germany had not embarked on unrestricted submarine warfare.

A stronger argument is that Wilson's desire to shape the peace dictated a firm response to the German move because it created a greater concern with maintaining international credibility. The president clearly regarded an American promise to underwrite European security as both a key diplomatic asset and the bedrock of the lasting peace he envisaged. If the stern words and ultimatums he had addressed to Germany over the previous two years were now shown to be hollow, such a promise would lose credibility. In Patrick Devlin's words, "What weight could anyone attach to guarantees given by a nation that quaked at the thunder of the guns?"[95]

By contrast, belligerency would actually enhance Wilson's ability to shape the postwar order by making him a full participant in the peace conference. House and others had urged this consideration on him earlier, but it had not then weakened the president's desire to keep out of the war. Now, however, in the new context created by Germany's actions, it seems to have helped reconcile Wilson to intervention. Certainly, it was something he stressed to anti-militarist liberals who had been enthused by his "peace without victory" speech. In an interview with Jane Addams and other delegates from peace societies at the end of February, the president made the point that as head of a nation participating in the war he would have a seat at the peace table, but that otherwise he could at best "call through a crack in the door."[96]

These foreign policy considerations may well have weighed with Wilson, but his initial response to the German announcement of the submarine campaign did not suggest that maximizing his international influence was his chief concern.

He told House that "he would not allow it to lead to war if it could possibly be avoided," and he startled the cabinet by saying that if "in order to keep the white race or part of it strong to meet the yellow race—Japan, for instance, in alliance with Russia, dominating China—it was wise to do nothing, he would do nothing, and would submit to anything and any imputation of weakness or cowardice."[97] This was only one of the reasons Wilson gave at different times for his reluctance to take America into the war—the need for an uninvolved power to lead the belligerents to peace and the effects on the nation's domestic life were others—but the basic reason was surely his knowledge of the strength of non-interventionist sentiment in the heartland. He did not want to lead a divided nation into war.[98]

Notwithstanding this, Wilson never seems to have considered accepting the situation and warning American ships to keep out of the war zone—the course that diehard opponents of intervention were advocating, explicitly or implicitly. This was not among the options he presented to a group of Democratic senators before he broke diplomatic relations with Germany. The conference with the senators made it clear that, although most Americans did not wish for war, neither did they want to see their country behave in a craven manner.[99] And, whatever may have been the case for Wilson, it is certain that for the senators it was not the credibility of a future league of nations that was at stake but national honor, seen as a value in its own right rather than for any particular instrumental purpose. Although Wilson reproached some cabinet members in February for "appealing to the spirit of the *Code Duello*," he himself had invoked the nation's honor in defense of his positions on preparedness and the submarine dispute, and he clearly understood that he was leading what Lodge called a "proud and high-spirited nation."[100] Announcing the break in diplomatic relations to Congress, Wilson declared that there was "no alternative consistent with the dignity and honor of the United States." After an interview in mid-February, Herbert Hoover "came away convinced that the President earnestly, and even emotionally, intended to avail himself of any device to keep out, short of sacrifice of national honor." In his War Address Wilson emphasized that "there is one choice we cannot make, we are incapable of making: we will not choose the path of submission and suffer the most sacred rights of our nation and our people to be ignored or violated."[101]

Sensitivity about the nation's honor and the rights of its citizens had, of course, been a feature of U.S. policy since the early days of the republic.[102] Nevertheless, the growth of American power did widen the saliency of this value. Questions of honor are intrinsically related to perceptions of power. For nations as for individuals, not resisting injury or insult because of impotence is less dishonorable than failing to do so when one has the capacity. It has been generally recognized that for this reason the position of the United States in 1917 was different from that of the European neutrals. "Such small seafaring states as Denmark and the Netherlands suffered extensive losses from submarine warfare, and yet these governments did not feel themselves honor bound to declare war," the historian Ross Gregory has pointed out. "Interpretation of national honor varies with national economic and military strength. The more powerful the nation, the more the world expects of it and the more the nation expects of itself."[103]

Having ruled out the surrender of American rights, Wilson expressed no broader aim than their protection throughout February and March 1917. He still sought to achieve this goal without war. In breaking diplomatic relations with Germany, he stated that he would take no further action unless the Germans followed their announcement with "actual overt acts," and during February he continued to pursue the possibility of a negotiated end to the war in communications with the British and Austrian governments.[104] But when it became clear that American shipowners were unwilling to send their ships unprotected into the war zone, Wilson authorized the placing of naval guns and gunners on merchant ships, bypassing a Senate filibuster on the measure.[105] This "armed neutrality," it might be noted, would have done little to affect the outcome of the European conflict or to enhance Wilson's influence over the nature of the peace. But it broadened the domestic support for a firm stand by suggesting that it might be possible to uphold American rights without entering the European war. When Wilson adopted this stance no American ships had been attacked in an unacceptable manner, as he stated to Congress, and he could still have entertained a degree of hope that the Germans would continue to show such restraint or that somehow the war might be brought to an early end.

But Germany did not show restraint. When its leaders had decided on an unrestricted submarine campaign, they had anticipated that it would probably lead to war with the United States. On this assumption, Foreign Minister Arthur Zimmermann had offered Mexico an alliance in such an event, promising support for its re-conquest of lost territory in Texas, New Mexico, and Arizona. Handed over to Washington by the British after they had intercepted and decoded it, this "Zimmermann Telegram" was released to the press as Congress was considering the armed ship bill. Its publication discomforted even the most committed pro-German apologists and led to demands for war in newspapers across the country, notably in the previously indifferent Southwest.[106] In March, German submarines were authorized to deliberately target American ships, on March 18 news reached Washington that three ships had been sunk and fifteen lives lost.

Two days later, the president held a meeting of the full cabinet in which every member, including Secretary of the Navy Josephus Daniels, who was well known for his pacifist tendencies, said that war was now the only course. Although there were differences of tone and in views about the specific measures that should be taken, the common ground was that Germany was evidently determined to continue attacking American ships and killing American citizens and that war was the only appropriate response. In this, the cabinet was reflecting the great weight of press opinion; at the end of the month the *Literary Digest* reported that the only question being debated was "Shall we wage war with Germany independently of her other foes, or shall we wage it as an ally of the Allies?"[107] The suggestion by some historians that the country was so divided that the president could as easily have chosen peace over war is ill founded.[108] Wilson told more than one person at this time that he had been driven to the conclusion that there was "no alternative"; politically speaking, that was surely the reality.[109]

Yet Wilson was very conscious that there were still many Americans deeply reluctant to enter the war. At the cabinet meeting, Lansing reported, the president "spoke of the situation in this country, of the indignation and bitterness in the East and the apparent apathy of the Middle West."[110] This sectional division had been manifested in a vote in the House of Representatives at the beginning of March on an amendment to the armed ship bill prohibiting armed merchant ships from transporting munitions to a belligerent country. The divisions that vote reflected were not only regional but also ideological and ethnic, with support for the amendment coming particularly from progressive legislators and those representing constituencies with large numbers of German-Americans or Scandinavians.[111] As Wilson had long recognized, opposition to war derived at least as much from a desire not to become aligned with the Allies as from pacifist feeling. This was emphasized by the president's aide, Joseph Tumulty, in a note of guidance based on a study of newspaper opinion across the country: "If we are driven into war by the course of Germany, *we must remain masters of our own destiny*. If we take up arms against Germany, it should be on an issue exclusively between that Empire and this Republic; and . . . the United States must retain control of that issue from beginning to end."[112]

Tumulty's advice was reflected in Wilson's address to Congress on April 2, in which the president naturally sought to maximize support for the war he was calling for. He began by emphasizing the completely unrestrained character of the U-boat campaign and asked Congress to "declare the recent course of the Imperial German Government to be in fact nothing less than war against the government and people of the United States," and to "formally accept the status of belligerent which has thus been thrust upon it." But to those for whom the defense of the nation's rights and honor was an insufficiently broad and elevated justification for the suffering that war entailed, the president insisted that he was still committed to the establishment of the kind of peace that he had outlined in his address to the Senate in January.[113] However, he subtly re-described that objective in a way that met the drastically changed thrust of his policy by introducing a commitment to the spread of democracy: "A steadfast concert for peace can never be maintained except by a partnership of democratic nations. No autocratic government could be trusted to keep faith within it or observe its covenants." This followed from his insistence that the barbarism of Germany's conduct was attributable to the nature of its regime.

Making the government of Germany, rather than the country, the enemy served several purposes for Wilson. Stressing that "we have no quarrel with the German people" and that "we have no feeling towards them but one of sympathy and friendship" might make it easier for German-Americans to justify the president's declared confidence that most of them were "as true and loyal Americans as if they had never known any other fealty or allegiance." The distinction was also helpful in reducing the tension between the domestic and the external demands on policy. Domestically, as Tumulty had emphasized, it was important that this should be seen as America's war, entered into for the nation's own reasons and for its own purposes. Yet the practical reality was that war against Germany meant joining the Allies; indeed, at this stage, the only direct engagement the president proposed, apart from naval action against the U-boats, was the provision of material and financial assistance to those he referred to as "the nations already at war with Germany." Focusing on the iniquity of the German government gave the conflict an ideological dimension without entailing an unequivocal endorsement of the character and motives of the Allies.

The commitment to the spread of democracy contributed significantly to the sweeping, almost millennial, nature of the aims for which Wilson declared that America would be fighting. In his earlier speeches, his vision of the postwar order had been simply of a lasting peace, secured by some international organization. Now, he linked his program much more closely to the nation's historic sense of mission by adding the goal of universal freedom. America would fight not only "for the ultimate peace of the world" but also "for the liberation of its peoples, the German peoples included." The goal was "a universal dominion of right by such a concert of free peoples as shall bring peace and safety to all nations and make the world itself at last free."[114]

Wilson's address did not still debate but, in the context of Germany's conduct, it succeeded in securing overwhelming majorities in both houses of Congress for a declaration of war.[115] Even Borah and Hiram Johnson, western progressive Republican senators who would be prominent champions of isolationism in the 1930s, cast their votes in favor despite their considerable reservations about the Allied cause.[116] However, the complexity of Wilson's case for war did cause some confusion. When the president remarked a few weeks later that the United States had entered the war as "the friends and servants of mankind" rather than with a "special grievance of our own," he was challenged by a Democratic congressman.

In reply, Wilson drew a distinction between "the reasons" and "the objects" of America's war. "The objects" were to achieve the sort of peace he had outlined, but "the reasons" were "the very serious and long continued wrongs which the Imperial German Government had perpetrated against the rights, the commerce, and the citizens of the United States."[117] It is a useful distinction, but the manner in which Wilson made the decision for war shows that the explanation for American intervention lay with the "reasons" rather than the "objects." The debate in Congress confirmed that most of those who voted for war did so to uphold the nation's rights and honor rather than to achieve wider foreign policy goals.[118]

Fighting the War and Preparing for Peace

"I have exactly the same things in mind now that I had in mind when I addressed the Senate on the twenty-second of January last," Wilson declared in his War Message. Yet his call for a democratic international order, together with his unmeasured denunciation of Germany's rulers, dictated something other than "a peace without victory." Domestically, too, Wilson knew that the American people would tolerate the costs and sacrifices of war only if these were vindicated by military success. Achieving victory against the might of the Central Powers would require close cooperation with the Allies, but this would make it hard to maintain the cherished independence of America's war and the distinctiveness of its aims. These somewhat conflicting objectives and pressures shaped both the manner in which the war was conducted and the further development and elaboration of Wilson's peace program.

The first issue was the scale and nature of America's war effort. Adopting conscription from the outset, the United States was to raise an army of almost four million and transport two million soldiers to France by November 1918. Of these, 53,402 were to die in combat and 63,114 from other causes while 204,000 were wounded. (These casualty figures are higher in absolute terms than those for either the Korean or Vietnam wars, when the nation's population was almost twice as large.) Taking into account intergovernmental loans to co-belligerents amounting to more than ten billion dollars, the total cost of the war to the United States equaled (in current dollars) the total of all federal expenditures in the hundred years after the establishment of the Constitution. During the years 1917–18, spending on the war averaged 10.5 percent of GNP.[119]

Few Americans had expected such a major effort at the time that Congress voted for war. While members of the cabinet had been united in the meeting on March 20 in urging a declaration of war, they had disagreed over whether the United States should send an army to Europe. One newspaper survey found a two-to-one sentiment in Congress against sending any troops to Europe. In the Senate debate, Lodge observed that "we can not send a great army across the ocean, for we have no army to send." Since the U.S. Army, with a total strength of less than 130,000, ranked seventeenth in the world, he had a point. Lodge urged that the United States concentrate on furnishing the Allies with supplies and "large credits."[120]

The sending of such a large army to Europe has been attributed by some historians to an intention on Wilson's part to "dominate" the peace conference so that he could impose his own vision of the postwar order—"a conscious choice to accept what could amount to virtually unlimited sacrifices to achieve his transcendent ends."[121] But there is no evidence to support this interpretation, which seems to be another example of the tendency to see all Wilson's actions during the war as governed by a single long-term goal. After the United States became a belligerent, the president made it clear, both implicitly and explicitly, that the nature of the peace was not now his first priority. Some contemporaries pointed out, as have historians, that Wilson's potential leverage over the Allies was greater at this time than it would ever be again.[122] Although Wilson did deliberately avoid pledging not to make a separate peace, he apparently never contemplated exploiting the Entente powers' critical need for American support by making the extent of such support conditional upon their bringing their objectives into line with the principles he had set forth. This was certainly not because he did not recognize the discrepancy. On the contrary, he emphasized to House that "England and France *have not the same views with regard to peace that we have* by any means." But, while expressing confidence that "when the war is over we can force them to our way of thinking," he stated flatly that "we cannot force them now."[123] Quarrelling with the Allies would hardly be the way either to build domestic support for the war or to bring it to a swift and successful conclusion.

It was his determination to win the war that led Wilson to send a large army to Europe, which was the result not of a policy decision at the beginning but of an incremental process driven by unanticipated developments overseas. In his War Message, the president had called for an increase in the armed forces of "at least five hundred thousand men," to be "chosen on the basis of universal liability to service."[124] Conscription was the method of recruitment favored by the General Staff, and its advocates could point to the experience of Britain, which had been forced to resort to conscription the previous year.[125] Wilson also seems to have hoped that this demonstration of wholehearted commitment would have an "immediate moral effect" in Berlin, writing to one correspondent that "the more businesslike determination we use now the less likelihood there is that our men will have to be sacrificed in any great numbers."[126]

At this stage, Wilson remained uncommitted to any particular military strategy. The decision to send an American Expeditionary Force (AEF) to France resulted from the visit to Washington in April–May 1917 of Allied missions who revealed the seriousness of the position on the western front after the failure of the Nivelle Offensive and pleaded that some American troops be sent as soon as possible. A division under General J. J. Pershing was promptly dispatched.[127] The build-up in the following months was slow. However, the twin blows to the Allied cause in November 1917 of the Italian defeat at Caporetto and the Bolshevik revolution in Russia led the recently established Allied Supreme War Council to ask that twenty-four American divisions be sent to France by the end of June. The great German offensive following the collapse of the eastern front in the spring of 1918 produced a further impetus. As the British reeled back, Prime Minister David Lloyd George, in a hectic series of telegrams to Washington, pleaded for American reinforcements to be sent quickly: "It rests with America to win or lose the decisive battle of the war." The Americans became actively engaged in the fighting in early June, and by early July Pershing had more than a million men under his command. At the end of that month, Wilson approved a War Department plan to build the AEF up to eighty divisions (about three and a half million men) for the 1919 campaign (the Supreme War Council had requested a hundred divisions).[128]

Given the weakness of the Allies' military position in 1917 and the evident need to mobilize American power, it is not surprising that Wilson no longer looked with favor on proposals to bring the war to an early end. In May, the Petrograd Soviet called for "peace without annexations or indemnities on the basis of the self-determination of peoples," and in August the Pope appealed for the belligerent states to accept "a just and lasting peace" that would provide for disarmament, "the institution of arbitration," freedom of the seas, no indemnities, and the reciprocal restitution of occupied territory.[129] Although these proposals seemed to echo Wilson's plea in January for "a peace without victory," he rejected them firmly, principally on the grounds that "we cannot take the word of the present rulers of Germany as a guarantee of anything that is to endure." In private letters to friendly journalists in the autumn, the president deprecated "all discussion of peace at this time," and in a speech he stressed that "the war should end only when Germany was beaten."[130]

Such hard-line statements distressed some of Wilson's liberal supporters, both at home and abroad. Fears that American power was furthering imperialistic war aims were deepened and widened by the Bolsheviks publication of the secret treaties between the Allies in November 1917. Countering this suspicion was the immediate purpose of Wilson's Fourteen Points speech in January 1918, as it had been of one by Lloyd George to the British Trade Union Congress a few days earlier. Indeed, the desire to rally support for the war in several different quarters was reflected in the content of Wilson's speech. Speaking soon after the Bolsheviks had broken off negotiations with the Germans, he may even have hoped to induce them to continue the fight by stressing the need not only for "the evacuation of all Russian territory" but also for Russia to be granted the freedom to determine her own political development and such assistance as she might desire. At the same time, he sought to appeal to moderate opinion in Germany—and reassure liberals everywhere—by disclaiming any "jealousy of German greatness" or "wish to fight her either with arms or with hostile arrangements of trade," provided she were willing "to accept a place of equality among the peoples of the world, . . . instead of a place of mastery."

For Americans, the president reiterated his basic argument that the world had to "be made safe for every peace-loving nation which, like our own, wishes to live its own life, determine its own institutions, be assured of justice and fair dealing by the other peoples of the world as against force and selfish aggression." This was to be achieved not only through the establishment of "a general association of nations" to provide "mutual guarantees of political independence and territorial integrity to great and small nations alike" but also through the general acceptance of such liberal principles as open diplomacy, freedom of the seas, and the reduction and equalization of trade barriers.

But Wilson now went beyond his previous declarations of general principles by going into much more detail about the terms of the postwar settlement—an unprecedented American involvement in the political affairs of Europe. Despite his concern to remove any taint of the secret treaties from America's war effort, Wilson by no means repudiated all the territorial goals of his co-belligerents—whom he referred to as our "intimate partners," from whom "we cannot be separated in interest or divided in principle." Thus he called not only for the evacuation and restoration of all the territories occupied by the armies of the Central Powers but also for the rectification of "the wrong done to France by Prussia in 1871 in the matter of Alsace-Lorraine," the granting of autonomy to the nationalities of the Austro-Hungarian and Ottoman empires, and "free and secure access to the sea" for Serbia and an independent Poland. But the Points also represented an implicit repudiation of some other Allied ambitions, including those in the secret treaties. This was true of the calls for the frontiers of Italy to be readjusted "along clearly recognizable lines of nationality" (significantly less than had been promised by the Allies) and for the Dardanelles to be internationalized (rather than granted to Russia). The Point on Alsace-Lorraine was also deliberately worded so as to exclude the Saar Valley (lost to France in 1814). The balance between anti-imperialist principle and the sensitivities of the Allied powers was epitomized by the call for "a free, open-minded, and absolutely impartial adjustment of all colonial claims" in which "the interests of the populations concerned must have equal weight with the equitable claims of the government whose title is to be determined."[131]

"The self-determination of peoples" was what the Bolshevik peace agitation was calling for, and the principle of national self-determination underlay several of Wilson's Points. Despite his later reputation as its chief advocate, however, the president did not endorse it in every case—as his repeated use of the phrase "opportunity of autonomous development" indicated. In not more fully supporting the claims to sovereign independence of the nationalities within the Austro-Hungarian Empire, Wilson was continuing to take a different position than the European allies—and disregarding calls by Roosevelt for the United States to "insist on liberty for the subject races." The president's opposition to the dismemberment of the Habsburg Empire was of long standing and was strengthened by his hopes that Vienna might be induced to make a separate peace.[132] After it became clear in April 1918 that this was not going to happen, the American government became increasingly supportive of the claims of the Czechoslovaks and Balkan Slavs. By this time Wilson had also endorsed the general principle of national self-determination, although in a carefully qualified way: "all well defined national aspirations shall be accorded the utmost satisfaction that can be afforded them without introducing new or perpetuating old elements of discord and antagonism that would be likely in time to break the peace of Europe and consequently of the world."[133]

As set out in the Fourteen Points and embellished in later speeches, Wilson's peace program was ambitious, and all the more so because it was essentially a unilateral one. The president did not consult the Allied governments over any of his diplomatic communications (such as the reply to the Pope) or before making his speeches. The war effort did require considerable collaboration over issues of supply as well as naval and military action, but Wilson insisted that the resulting joint councils should confine themselves to technical and military matters rather than political ones. He resisted strong pressure from the Allies for American forces to be integrated with their armies at the unit level, supporting General Pershing's determination to maintain the independence of his command. Not only did the United States sign no treaty with the other states fighting Germany but Wilson was also very concerned to avoid even informal use of the term "our allies," complaining to Herbert Hoover when it appeared on Food Administration posters.[134] As Tumulty had advised, he was seeking to keep America's war distinct from the preexisting European conflict. In taking this position, the president was maintaining a more unequivocally nationalist line than such Republicans as Roosevelt and Lodge, who saw their country as joining Britain and France—shamefully late—in a common cause.

Indeed, as during the period of neutrality, Wilson held on to important aspects of the isolationist tradition even as he was leading the United States into commitments and actions that broke with it. In particular, the ideological contrast between the purity of the New World and the corruption of the Old remained basic to his thinking. Seeing the divergence over war aims as a specific manifestation of this contrast, he anticipated that it would lead to a fight at the peace conference. In September 1917, Wilson quietly began preparations for the postwar battle by asking House to assemble a group to "ascertain as fully and precisely as possible just what the several parties to this war on our side of it will be inclined to insist upon as part of the final peace arrangements, in order that we may formulate our own position either for or against them." This project, which became known as "the Inquiry" and was paid for out of the president's discretionary funds, consisted of a team of academics, mostly historians and geographers, working discreetly in New York.[135] As the war drew to a close, the president remarked that he wanted "to go into the Peace Conference armed with as many weapons as my pockets will hold so as to compel justice."[136]

Wilson expressed confidence about the anticipated confrontation. This reflected his high sense of American power, which he saw as multidimensional. Its basis was the economic strength that enabled the United States to finance the efforts of its co-belligerents so substantially. He had assured House that after the war the American government would be able to impose its will on the allies "because by that time they will, among other things, be financially in our hands."[137] By the time of the Armistice, Wilson saw America's newly demonstrated military power as a further source of leverage. On his voyage to Europe, he told the members of the Inquiry who were accompanying him that "it is not too much to say that at Château Thierry we saved the world, and I do not intend to let those Europeans forget it. They were beaten when we came in and they know it."[138] Of course, with Germany conclusively defeated, the immediate need for America's military assistance no longer existed, but the president evidently believed that, as Grey had indicated in 1914–16, the European powers set great store by an ongoing American commitment to their security. Accordingly, he felt that the threat not to make such a commitment would be a winning card in the negotiations. On the Atlantic crossing, Wilson said that he would tell the European leaders right at the beginning that "it must not be a peace of loot or spoliation" and that "if that is the kind of peace they demand, I will withdraw personally and with my commissioners return home and in due course take up the details of a separate peace."[139]

In addition to the hard power of financial and military strength, Wilson believed that he possessed the soft power of ideological appeal. He expressed confidence that "the peoples of all the Allies are with me in the sentiments that I have expressed" and that "if necessary I can reach the peoples of Europe over the heads of their rulers."[140] This belief had both deep roots and more immediate sources. Fundamentally, it reflected the longstanding national assumption that the values for which America stood were universal ones that would be shared by people everywhere if they were liberated from oppressive social and political structures—the assumption that had found expression in Wilson's conflation of "American principles" and "the principles of mankind" in his address to the Senate. In that same speech, Wilson also sought to make himself the spokesman for the deep loathing of modern warfare that he assumed had been engendered in "the silent mass of mankind everywhere" by their recent experience.[141] From the beginning, many Americans, particularly progressives, had seen the European war as the product of imperialistic and power rivalries that were of interest only to elites. The expectation that the common people of the devastated continent would rally to the vision of lasting peace on anti-imperialist principles that Wilson had articulated gained strength from the support for it in European socialist and labor circles; House received extensive accounts of this from Ray Stannard Baker, whom he had sent to report on it. In September 1918, Wilson claimed that "the common will of mankind has been substituted for the particular purposes of individual states" and that "statesmen must follow the clarified common thought or be broken." Recording the hostility of the Entente governments to the Fourteen Points, House noted that "the plain people generally both in America and in Europe are, I think, with the President."[142] This impression, however, was not simply an American illusion. Wilson's reception in Europe when he arrived in December 1918 to take part in the peace conference was extraordinary. British writers such as H. G. Wells and John Maynard Keynes recalled that Wilson had then been regarded by millions as "a Messiah" or "a prophet." Keynes wrote: "When President Wilson left Washington, he enjoyed a prestige and a moral influence throughout the world unequalled in history."[143]

The Limits of Power: The Paris Peace Conference

Keynes penned these words in a spirit of disillusionment. Like other liberals who had pinned their hopes on Wilson—and the Germans who had requested an armistice on the basis of the Fourteen Points and the president's other speeches—Keynes saw the terms of the Treaty of Versailles as a great betrayal. The chief objects of criticism were the severity of the settlement imposed on Germany, especially the large reparation payments demanded, and the disregard of the self-determination principle, particularly in the concessions to Italy in South Tyrol and Istria and to Japan in the Chinese province of Shantung. In the polemical tract that made him famous, Keynes attributed this outcome to Wilson's personal weaknesses—his lack of negotiating skill and determination. For the president, according to Keynes, had been in a strong position to shape the peace. In addition to his moral influence, "the realities of power were in his hands.... The American armies were at the height of their numbers, discipline, and equipment. Europe was in complete dependence on the food supplies of the United States; and financially she was even more absolutely at their mercy."[144]

To Keynes and many others, it followed that Wilson held a strong hand in the negotiations and so should have achieved more. Yet on closer examination, the "weapons" at the president's disposal look much less formidable than such critics assume or than he had anticipated. In the first place, the debts the Allies had incurred did not in themselves generate any particular diplomatic leverage. They could only have done so if the United States had been prepared to offer the possibility of their being reduced (or even written off entirely) if the debtor nations acceded to American wishes, for example on the size and terms of German reparations. But scaling down the Allies' debts was not something that Wilson could do, even if he had been so inclined. Soon after his arrival in Paris he was emphatically informed by the secretary of the Treasury that "Congress believes these loans are good and should be collected."[145] Such attitudes also severely constrained the extent to which further financial aid could be offered to European nations.[146] Nor, given the imperative political need to demobilize the conscript army, could Wilson contemplate any major or long-term military commitments in Europe. Keynes was not wrong about the unparalleled financial, economic, and potential military strength of the United States, but political willingness to meet the costs of translating those resources into effective international influence was lacking. Such willingness required a much stronger sense than yet existed of America's own stake in the future stability of Europe.

Unlike military commitments or financial assistance, soft power is cheap. In this regard, the weapon that Wilson was presumed to have had was the ability to appeal over the heads of his negotiating partners to their own populations.[147] But the belief that ordinary people everywhere would support Wilson against their own governments and national ambitions proved to be an illusion. Wilson's one attempt to use this tactic, his appeal to the Italian people over the issue of Fiume and other parts of the Dalmatian coast provoked such a hostile reaction in Italy that Americans were officially advised to keep their distance from the demonstrating crowds.[148] In all the Allied countries, the liberal left, the chief locus of support for a Wilsonian peace, lost ground to a surgent right after the war. In the United States, too, Wilson's position was weakened when the Republicans won majorities in both houses of Congress in the November 1918 elections after a campaign in which their leading spokesmen had denounced the Fourteen Points and demanded a dictated peace.[149]

A further bargaining counter that Wilson and others had believed he possessed was the threat to make a separate peace.[150] Wilson and House had raised this possibility during the negotiations to secure Allied agreement to an armistice based on the Fourteen Points.[151] But after the Armistice, the military terms of which made it virtually impossible for Germany to resume hostilities, it mattered less to the Allies if the United States were to make a separate peace. In these circumstances, threatening to do so was a high-risk tactic that could easily backfire. Indeed, in a paradoxical way, articulating the threat could diminish its potency. For its effectiveness now depended solely on the value that the other states placed on an American guarantee of the settlement, and this would in turn depend in part on the credibility such a guarantee possessed. Given the evident reluctance of the American military as well as public and congressional opinion to assume long-run commitments outside the Western Hemisphere, European statesmen were already inclined to put their trust in other, more traditional forms of security.[152] A move that emphasized the conditional nature of American involvement would thus be at least as likely to weaken as to strengthen their willingness to adopt Wilson's ideas. Moreover if the president, having threatened to withdraw, then felt compelled to do so, he would have utterly failed to achieve his goals. The political costs to Wilson of such an outcome were emphatically conveyed to him by Tumulty when, during the fraught negotiations over the Saar and the Rhineland, the president implicitly threatened to leave the conference by summoning his ship back to France.[153]

This incident also showed the illusory nature of the advantage that Wilson had hoped he would have in the negotiations as a result of America's lack of a direct interest in the terms of the settlement.[154] Although it was true that the United States did not have the kind of territorial or colonial ambitions that the other powers did, Wilson in fact had as large a political stake in the outcome of the conference as the other leaders. From the beginning and increasingly, America's war had been justified in terms of the new international order that it would produce. For many Americans, particularly Wilson's most fervent followers, failure to achieve this new order would render the costs and sacrifices of the war futile and the decision to intervene a mistake. On the other hand, if Wilson could cap the emphatic military victory with a peace based on his principles, he would enjoy the political triumph that his domestic opponents were fearing.

Given that the president could not afford to walk away and did not have the means to impose his will on every issue, he needed, like all negotiators, to prioritize his objectives. Neither at the time nor since has there been much doubt that his overriding goal was the establishment of the League of Nations as an integral part of the peace treaty.[155] This priority led him to give ground on some other issues. Thus, it has been persuasively argued that his early concession to Italy of a northern frontier incorporating a substantial German-speaking population was motivated by his desire for Prime Minister Vittorio Orlando's cooperation in the Commission drafting the League of Nations Covenant.[156] The most dramatic instance was Wilson's reluctant assent to the takeover by the Japanese of the rights previously enjoyed by Germany in Shantung. The president did not conceal from his associates that it was Japan's threat not to enter the League of Nations that had led him to yield on this (much to the disgust of Lansing).[157]

Reluctant though some of these concessions were, it is not difficult to understand why Wilson attached supreme importance to the establishment of a League of Nations. It was the embodiment of his promise that Americans had been fighting for a new world order that would put an end to such terrible wars. In his war address he had held out the prospect of a world both free and peaceful, but the latter feature was the more imperative objective. A free world might represent the fulfillment of the American mission, but it was a peaceful one that was required by the nation's own interests as these had been perceived by Wilson ever since the *Lusitania* crisis. To him, the submarine dispute and other dilemmas of neutrality had demonstrated that the traditional policy of remaining uninvolved in conflicts on other continents was no longer practicable. As Wilson saw it, this was principally because of the new scale of America's power: "By the sheer genius of this people and the growth of our power we have become a determining factor in the history of mankind, and when you have become a determining factor you cannot remain isolated, whether you want to or not."[158]

Over the years since 1914, Wilson's views about the origins and desirable outcome of the European contest had changed a great deal, but his commitment to the goal of ensuring that no such conflict would occur again had been steady from 1915 on. He had also consistently held that a settlement would be more stable if territories were assigned to states according to the wishes of their inhabitants, but even in his endorsement of the principle of national self-determination in 1918 he had made it clear that the claims of peaceful order should take priority over those of "liberty." Hence the overriding need for an effective international organization to resolve disputes and enforce norms of conduct.

Establishing such an international organization was no easy task, however, and it was made no easier by the motive that the United States had in promoting it. Fundamentally, this was a desire to be able to continue its longstanding pattern of national life undisturbed by events on other continents. A definite and potentially far-reaching commitment to use American power to maintain international order would appear to threaten this objective. On the other hand, without such a commitment a league of nations would lack the credibility it would need if states were to be induced to rely on it for their security, rather than on their own armaments and alliances. The difficulty here was brought home to Wilson in Paris when spokesmen for France and Belgium pressed for the authority of the League to be broadened and strengthened with provisions for an international force, or at least military staff, lest the organization be merely "a screen of false security" for states threatened with attack. Wilson firmly resisted such proposals, explaining candidly that "the argument which has been most employed against the League of Nations in America is that the army of the United States would be at the disposal of an international council, that American troops would thus be liable to be ordered to fight at any moment for the most remote of causes, and this prospect alarms our people."[159]

Wilson had long been conscious of the need to limit the specificity of American commitments if the Senate was to consent to joining a league of nations; he would have known of the difficulty that arbitration treaties had run into on this score. When discussing possible constitutions for a league with House, he had stated emphatically that "the United States Senate would never ratify any treaty which put the force of the United States at the disposal of any such group or body."[160] The Republican victory in the 1918 congressional elections had made it more certain that whatever Wilson brought back from Paris would face hostile scrutiny in the Senate; any doubt on this score would have been removed by the "Round Robin" resolution of March 1919 in which more than a blocking third of senators declared that the League "in the form now proposed" should not be accepted. Wilson's insistence on making the League an integral part of the peace treaty was surely motivated in part by the desire to make it more difficult for senators to vote against it. It also had the effect, however, of making attitudes toward the League even more closely linked to views about the justice of the treaty than they were bound to be. Thus, the adverse reaction of most articulate liberals to the terms of the Versailles treaty caused some, most notably the editors of the *New Republic*, to oppose American membership of the League. The greater part of liberal opinion, however, remained loyal to Wilson, with many taking comfort in the argument that the League was the instrument by which the injustices of the treaty could be rectified, after wartime passions had died down.[161]

In any case, liberal opinion was not what mattered most at this point. As Wilson's Wall Street ally Thomas Lamont observed in July 1919, "the critics who called the Treaty unjust were not dangerous to ratification" in the way that the Republicans were.[162] Republican leaders, having attacked the Fourteen Points and demanded an unconditional German surrender, were unlikely to criticize the harshness of the peace. Wilson's awareness of this apparently explains his unwillingness to revise the draft treaty, despite the protests of his liberal supporters and the second thoughts of Lloyd George. Tumulty, having reported that the treaty had been very well received by the American press, expressed his confidence that the president would not be "led astray" by "the pleadings of Germany for a 'softer peace.'" Ray Stannard Baker, after an unsuccessful attempt to persuade Wilson to listen to liberal objections, concluded "the President is evidently now keenly aware of his problem in getting the treaty—with the League—adopted by the American Congress" and that "it is plain that at every point the President is thinking of American public opinion."[163] Leading the United States into the new League of Nations that he had played such a crucial role in creating had become Wilson's sole real objective.

The Failure to Join the League of Nations

Both the causes and the significance of the American decision not to join the League of Nations have been very differently interpreted. The failure of the Senate to approve the Treaty of Versailles is often attributed to such immediate and contingent factors as the bitter personal hostility between Wilson and Henry Cabot Lodge or the effects of the president's declining health, particularly the severe stroke he suffered in October 1919. In this reading, not much of substance divided Wilson and Lodge, and so it should have been quite possible to find a compromise that would easily have gained the necessary two-thirds majority in the Senate. In the revisionist interpretation of American policy, which will be considered more extensively in the next chapter, the narrowness of the difference between Wilson and his Republican opponents also reduces the significance of the decision. "The fight over the League of Nations was in reality a conflict over tactics, or the means of implementing a strategic program," William Appleman Williams wrote in a highly influential book. U.S. foreign policy in the 1920s manifested "a broad program of conscious involvement in world affairs for well-defined objectives."[164] On the other hand, the decision has been seen as having more profound causes and more significant consequences. "The American people," the historian Alexander De Conde writes, "were not ready to assume the responsibilities that Wilson's system of collective security offered. They chose, instead, to retreat into another era of isolationism."[165]

Those who see contingent factors as crucial stress the extent of support for the League of Nations, both among public opinion and in the Senate. Before direct polling, surveys of the positions of the hundreds of newspapers published across the country were the best measure of public opinion. Such surveys in the spring and early summer of 1919 showed large majorities in favor of the League of Nations in some form, with no more than 20 percent firmly opposed to membership. Similarly, only sixteen of the ninety-six senators were "irreconcilables" who unreservedly opposed entry into the League of Nations, and a few of these favored other forms of international commitment.[166]

Nevertheless, the two-thirds majority in the Senate that would have brought the United States into the League of Nations was never achieved. This was because of the reservations that were presented in late October 1919 by Lodge, now the leader of the Republican majority. In votes in November, a resolution approving the treaty with the Lodge reservations was defeated by a combination of Democrats and irreconcilables, whereupon the treaty without the reservations was defeated by an almost unanimous Republican vote supplemented by a few Democratic defectors. Outside pressure and reluctance within the Senate to make a separate peace with Germany led to reconsideration of the matter. On the final vote, in March 1920, the Treaty with the Lodge reservations secured a majority that was only seven short of the necessary two-thirds. This was because about half of the Democratic senators were now prepared to accept the reservations, but the remainder, at Wilson's behest, joined the irreconcilables in blocking approval.[167] "The Supreme Infanticide," the historian Thomas A. Bailey calls it: "With his own sickly hands, Wilson slew his own brain child—or the one to which he had contributed so much."[168]

There is little question that the United States would have joined the League of Nations had Wilson been less intransigent. But before we conclude that this was an occasion on which the course of history was determined by such contingent factors as the collapse of the president's health or the peculiarities of his psychology, we need to consider how significant the issue was between Wilson's position and that of the Senate majority—and also why it proved to be impossible to secure approval of the treaty without the Lodge reservations.

The principal bone of contention in the debate over the League was the undertaking under Article 10 of the Covenant to "preserve as against external aggression the territorial integrity and existing political independence of all Members of the League." By contrast, one of the Lodge reservations declared that "the United States assumes no obligation to preserve the territorial integrity or political independence of any other country . . . under the provisions of Article 10, or to employ the military or naval forces of the United States under any article of the treaty for any purpose, unless in any particular case the Congress, which, under the Constitution, has the sole power to declare war or authorize the employment of the military or naval forces of the United States, shall by act or joint resolution so provide."[169]

It is not difficult to see why Wilson found this reservation unacceptable. He envisaged the League of Nations not as a mere forum for diplomatic interchange—the "debating society" of which he spoke contemptuously—but as a body on which all nations could rely for their security. The skepticism with which this project was regarded in other countries even by those well disposed to it had been brought home to him in Paris. The sense of insecurity that underpinned the reliance on armaments and alliances had found expression in the demands, particularly by the French, that the Covenant should contain a formal guarantee and binding obligation. The formulation in Article 10, designed to avoid constitutional objections in the United States, was the absolute minimum that could hope to satisfy such demands. Like other forms of deterrent, the system of collective security that Wilson saw the League of Nations as creating depended on credibility. This would be fatally undermined if the United States repudiated any obligation, let alone commitment, to collaborate in responses to acts of aggression. As his biographer, William C. Widenor, acknowledges, Lodge's reservation was incompatible with "the theory on which collective security was based."[170] In Wilson's words, it would "exempt the United States from all responsibility for the preservation of peace" and constitute a "nullification" of the treaty.[171]

Nor is there reason to believe that a fitter president in a more accommodating mood would have been able to find a satisfactory compromise on this issue. There certainly were attempts at compromise, both in the summer of 1919, before Wilson went on his speaking tour in the country, and in January 1920, when there was a "bipartisan conference" of leading senators. In August, those Republican senators most favorable to the League were endeavoring to formulate some "mild reservations" intended to make possible speedy ratification of the treaty, and Democratic senators, too, were increasingly inclining toward a compromise. However, these Republican "mild reservationists" were not numerous enough to produce the requisite two-thirds majority and could only hope to attract party colleagues by formulating reservations that would substantially alter—rather than merely clarify—the Covenant.[172] Similarly, in the bipartisan conference, Lodge ultimately refused to accept any change to the wording of his reservation on Article 10.[173] In 1919–20, there was no possibility of securing an American commitment of future action firm enough to make the League of Nations the credible system of global collective security that Wilson projected.

This was, of course, partly because Wilson's opponents did not see such a system as practicable or even desirable. Lodge, Root, and other leading Republicans were not opposed in principle to an active American role in world politics; on the contrary, they had been advocating this for decades. In 1914–17 they had been much readier than Wilson to envisage intervention in the war on the Allied side, and they were prepared after the war to commit the country to do likewise in the future. "If it is necessary for the security of western Europe that we should agree to go to the support say of France if attacked, let us agree to do that particular thing plainly," Root wrote in a public letter to Lodge. "But let us not wrap up such a purpose in a vague universal obligation, under the impression that it really does not mean anything [is] likely to happen."[174] The former secretary of state Philander C. Knox (R–Pa.), an "irreconcilable" over the League, proposed "a new American doctrine," that "if a situation should arise in which any power or *combination* of powers should, directly or indirectly, menace the freedom and peace of Europe, the United States . . . would consult with other powers affected with a view to concerted action for the removal of such menace." Knox, like Lodge, favored the security treaty with France that Wilson had signed in Paris as part of the price for French concessions over the Rhineland and the Saar.[175]

This has led several historians to conclude that the battle in the Senate "was not primarily a debate between isolationists and internationalists" but "rather a contest between the champions of a potentially strong system of collective security and a group who favored a more limited commitment."[176] However, this was only part of the picture, and also one that diminished over time. The bilateral treaty guaranteeing French security was never even reported out of the Foreign Relations Committee. Although Lodge blamed this treaty's fate on Wilson's subordination of it to the League, there was little effective political pressure on behalf of it. This was hardly surprising given the negative reaction to the treaty, both within the American delegation and in American press comment, when Wilson agreed to it in Paris.[177] Whatever the merits of a more "realistic" version of internationalism, it faced political obstacles at home that Wilson's approach sought to bypass. A commitment limited to the countries with which the United States had fought the war would not only run into the traditional aversion to the European system of power politics and to "entangling alliances" but also face the antagonism of Americans whose sympathies did not lie with England and France.

Above all, it became clear as the debate developed that the objections to Article 10 focused much less on the geographical scope of the obligations it contained than on the degree of their definiteness. The Senate's determination to preserve unimpaired the freedom of action of a future Congress was clearly incompatible with a reliable commitment to the security of any other country, and the reluctance to accept constraints on the nation's sovereign rights in any respect militated against all forms of international undertaking. Moreover, on these basic points, it seems that the Senate represented the sentiments of most Americans. By April 1920, Lodge felt it necessary to explain to Lord Bryce, a staunch advocate of the League and of Anglo-American cooperation, that "the protracted debate on the League both inside and outside the Senate has wrought a great change in public opinion and the feeling is growing constantly stronger against the United States involving itself in the quarrels of Europe at all."[178] The presidential election campaign later in the year confirmed the accuracy of Lodge's judgment. The Republican candidate, Warren Harding, began by equivocating over the League, but by October he was declaring that he did not want to "clarify" the obligations of membership but to "turn my back" on them: "It is not interpretation, but rejection, that I am seeking. My position is that the proposed league strikes a deadly blow at our constitutional integrity and surrenders to a dangerous extent our independence of action." The Democratic candidate, James M. Cox, began by firmly endorsing Wilson's position but later stated his support for reservations, especially with regard to obligations under Article 10. Notwithstanding this, he and his loyally Wilsonian running mate, Franklin D. Roosevelt, were buried by one of the biggest landslides in American electoral history.[179]

In a sense, therefore, the failure of the United States to join the League of Nations *did* reflect the persistence of isolationism. It may well have been that principled adherence to the perceived wisdom of Washington and Jefferson as advocated by Borah and Hiram Johnson was a minority position. But this did not mean that Americans were prepared to pay the price of assuming a responsibility for world order. Most, apparently, did not see this as a sufficiently important national interest to justify significant costs. Although this has often been attributed to innocent illusions resulting from the nation's long experience of "free security," it can be seen as a reasonable assessment of the balance between the costs and the benefits of commitment as these were portrayed in the course of the debate.[180]

Critics pointed to three main types of cost that joining the League would entail. The first was the risk of involvement in overseas conflicts in which the United States had no direct interest—the Balkans were often mentioned in this connection. The second was the constraints on America's own freedom of action—even, Wilson's opponents claimed, with regard to such domestic matters as immigration but certainly in the surrender of sovereignty that commitment to collective action in international affairs inevitably entailed. This led to the third cost, which was to the moral standing of American policy if the United States were to be obliged to take positions on foreign situations that were contrary to the nation's principles and sentiments. It was in this last connection that the attacks on the provisions of the peace treaty, especially with respect to Shantung and to a lesser extent Ireland, were pertinent.

Naturally, Wilson sought to downplay these costs. He insisted that immigration, naturalization, and the tariff would remain domestic questions, unaffected by membership of the League. Even with regard to international affairs, the League could act only with the approval of all members of the Council, including the United States—"we have an absolute veto on the thing, unless we are parties to the dispute." Moreover, if there were to be trouble in the Balkans or Central Europe, the League would not call upon American forces to deal with it: "If you want to put out a fire in Utah, you don't send to Oklahoma for the fire engine." In any case, the primary sanction for enforcement was not armed force but "something much more terrible than war—absolute boycott of the nation." In addition to its devastating moral effect, such a punishment would be crippling economically because "with the exception of the United States, there is not a country in the world that could live without imports." He admitted that the treaty provisions on Shantung were not as he would have wished but argued that rejecting the agreement would do China no good—unless America was prepared to go to war with Britain and France as well as Japan over the issue.[181]

Indeed, a major benefit of League membership, Wilson argued, was that it would enhance the influence of the United States in world affairs. For one thing, the nation would gain the right to intervene in situations in which it had no direct interest. "At present we have to mind our own business," he declared, but under Article 11 of the Covenant "we can force a nation on the other side of the globe to bring to that bar of mankind any wrong that is afoot in that part of the world." While minimizing the costs that League membership would entail, Wilson still declared that the United States was being offered "the leadership of the world" and thereby the opportunity to "fulfill her destiny."[182] This destiny, as Wilson portrayed it, had two inter-related aspects. The first was "the emancipation of people throughout the world" through the universalization of the principle that "all just government rests upon the consent of the governed."[183] The second was the establishment of international peace. The United States was uniquely able to bring this about, not only because of its "overwhelming force" and command of "some of the most important resources of the world" but also because of "the absolutely unquestioning confidence of the peoples of the world in the people of America." Given that "the counsels of the United States will be the prevailing counsels of the League," the issue was, "Shall we keep the primacy of the world, or shall we abandon it?"[184]

The debate was not conducted entirely at this abstract, ideological level. "If you want to talk business, I can talk business," Wilson declared. He portrayed the consequences of not joining the League in dire terms. Without the ratification of the peace treaty and the extension of American credits, the war-torn nations of Europe would not provide a market for American exports. Moreover, if America disappointed the hopes that were invested in her, Wilson prophesied that the goodwill with which she was regarded abroad would be replaced by antagonism. One consequence would be that "by every device possible foreign markets will be closed to you." Nor would it be only the nation's economic interests that would suffer. "If we must stand apart and be the hostile rivals of the rest of the world," he warned, "we must be physically ready for anything to come." The United States would have to become a great military state in a way that would not only raise taxes and check social reform but also be incompatible with its domestic liberties and open, democratic system of government.[185]

Above all, Wilson predicted that "within another generation, there will be another world war" if the League of Nations did not prevent it by concerted action. He detailed the appalling costs of the war in both money and lives to all the belligerents and warned that the development of weaponry was such that the great guns with which the Germans had bombarded Paris "were toys as compared with what would be used in the next war." As the only great power not "exhausted" by the recent conflict, the United States would bear the brunt: "The next war would have to be paid for in American blood and American money."[186] The League of Nations provided "the only possible guarantee against war"—not an absolute guarantee but one that Wilson repeatedly described as "a 98 per cent insurance."[187] That assurance depended on the commitment made in Article 10, which had to be universal and to include providing security to the vulnerable new nations established by the peace treaty, because "if we don't take care of the weak nations of the world, there will be war."[188]

In the end, none of these arguments, either individually or collectively, was sufficiently persuasive to develop the imperative public sentiment in favor of the Treaty and the League that Wilson was seeking—indeed, as we have seen, the tide of opinion flowed the other way. Not many seem to have been attracted by the opportunity to promote American values through assuming the role of global leadership.[189] The League mandate for Armenia that Wilson had agreed to was overwhelmingly rejected by the Senate in June 1920, notwithstanding the ardent championship of the Armenian cause by Lodge and other Republicans during the war.[190]

Nor can the president's somewhat apocalyptic warnings of the consequences for America's prosperity or domestic liberty of remaining out of the League have won many converts. They were, after all, hard to reconcile with the picture he presented of America's strong position in the world. As well as the economic self-sufficiency that gave it a unique capacity to survive without imports, he drew attention to the nation's enhanced financial strength. His claim that going it alone would necessitate constructing "a garrison state" was rather undermined by his own dismissal of the possibility of an attack on North America: "Who has an arm long enough, who has an audacity great enough to try to take a single inch of American territory or to seek to interfere for one moment with the political independence of the United States?"[191]

Emphasizing the unique economic strength and physical security of the United States certainly buttressed Wilson's argument that "the peace of the world cannot be established without America." But it tended to weaken the reverse proposition, that "the peace and good will of the world are necessary to America." The very terms in which the president argued that it had become "impossible for the United States to play a lone hand" suggested that the assumption of overseas commitments would be an act of philanthropy as much as self-interest: "We are tied into the rest of the world by kinship, by sympathy, by interest in every great enterprise of human affairs. . . . Our assistance is essential to the establishment of normal conditions throughout the world."[192] Not surprisingly, Wilson's opponents also stressed the scale of American power in rejecting the argument that the costs of remaining outside the League would be greater than those entailed by joining it. "We hear the timid cry that America will be isolated," Lodge observed. "Have no fear. The United States cannot be isolated. The world needs us too much. We have never turned a deaf ear to the cry of suffering humanity and we never shall but we must do it in our own way, freely and without constraint from abroad."[193]

The argument that failed, therefore, was that active and strenuous involvement in world politics, with the costs that this was likely to entail, was a matter of necessity rather than choice. After all, Wilson himself had implied the opposite when he warned European governments that an American commitment was conditional on the kind of settlement that was made. He had done this in his January 1917 address to the Senate, and he did it again in the run up to the peace conference. "If the future had nothing for us but a new attempt to keep the world at a right poise by a balance of power, the United States would take no interest," he warned an audience in Manchester, England, in December 1918.[194]

Of course, the basic proposition that America's own peace and security depended on the establishment of a peaceful world order could be seen as having been demonstrated by its failure to avoid participation in the European war. As Wilson reminded his audiences, that was what the country had "chiefly desired." But in explaining why the United States had nonetheless entered the war, Wilson did not argue that the country had been driven into the war by such a clear national interest as the need to protect its territory or prosperity. On the contrary, he stressed that "America was not directly attacked" and that "we did not send men three thousand miles away to defend our own territory." It was because "we found the currents of humanity too strong for us" and came to recognize that "an obligation of duty rested upon us" that the United States had gone to war. It was for "the salvation of mankind everywhere" that "thousands of our gallant youth lie buried in France," the price of "the noblest errand that troops ever went on."[195] As historians have recognized, the crusading idealism to which Wilson was appealing had been overdrawn by 1919–20.[196]

Between 1917 and 1919, the United States exercised an influence on world politics commensurate with the scale of its relative power in the international system. It determined the outcome of the European war. By mobilizing its financial and military strength, it brought about the defeat of Germany, something surely beyond the capabilities of that country's other, exhausted, opponents. The armistice that ended the conflict was based on the acceptance by all of the terms and principles earlier proclaimed by the American president, who was widely expected to be the dominant figure at the peace conference—a prospect welcomed by many in Europe and across the world who had invested their hopes in his ability to establish a new international order, at once peaceful and liberal.[197] From the American point of view, Wilson's program represented a strategy for ensuring the nation's own security and prosperity in an era when wars could be, like trade, global.

The preeminence of America's potential power was a long-term phenomenon, antedating World War I as well as long outlasting it. Likewise, Wilson's broad claim that the nation's own interests required a liberal and peaceful world order was to shape the thinking of American policymakers for the remainder of the twentieth century and beyond. Yet the exercise of American power proved extremely short-lived. The product of war and of determination to defeat the enemy, it did not survive the end of hostilities. As we have seen, Wilson's influence over the postwar settlement was much diminished by the very limited extent to which he could use America's financial resources or potential military strength as bargaining counters in the negotiations. This signaled the withdrawal of the United States from effective involvement in world politics, a process confirmed and dramatized by the failure to join the League of Nations.

The abruptness of both the advance and the retreat indicates that America's course cannot be adequately explained by long-term factors such as the sheer scale of its potential power or a steadily held strategic goal. In fact, as we have seen, Wilson's actions and statements with regard to the European war were shaped by a series of different objectives: initially, to minimize its effects on America's domestic life; then, to avoid American involvement without abandoning opposition to the use of submarines against noncombatant vessels; then, once the United States was a belligerent, to win the war; and, finally, to vindicate American intervention by establishing the League of Nations in a form that plausibly would prevent the recurrence of all-out modern warfare between great powers. These successive objectives are best understood as responses to immediate circumstances and to the effects of these upon American opinion.

If one looks for the broader factors shaping these responses, one must start by recognizing the role of contingency and of the actions of other countries, particularly Germany. If the Germans had never employed submarines against merchant vessels, the course of events would have been very different. The United States would almost certainly not have become a belligerent. Nor is it likely that in 1916–17 Wilson would have made the commitment to participate in a postwar league of nations or have sought so energetically to end the war and to shape the peace.

Of all the decisions that the American government made, therefore, the most momentous was its unyielding stand against submarine warfare. This stand cannot be plausibly explained by economic interest or anxiety about the nation's security. The country's exports to Europe were indeed an important national interest, but they did not need to be protected from submarine attacks by the U.S. government, as the Allies had ample physical means as well as incentive to sustain the trade by themselves. The belief that a German victory in Europe would impair the security of the United States itself was certainly articulated by some Americans, but it was held only by people strongly committed to the Allied cause; the great majority, including the president, remained confident that geography and the nation's own power would keep it safe from attack whatever the outcome of the war. In any case, the German submarine campaign was not seen as a serious threat to the Allies in the spring of 1917, let alone 1915.

The emotion that underlay the implicit threat of war after the sinking of the *Lusitania* was not fear but outrage—a compound of moral indignation and a fierce desire to uphold the rights of American citizens. These emotions were certainly heightened by the pro-Allied sympathies of many of those best placed to express their views through forums that could influence both wider opinion and policy. For the most part, the strength of this pro-Allied feeling testified to the salience of an involvement with Europe that was not the product of economic interest or strategic concerns but derived from the sense of participation in a shared culture, reinforced in some cases by personal or family relationships. As the initial shock of the *Lusitania* sinking faded, however, the militancy it stimulated was more than balanced by the deep reluctance of most Americans to become involved in the European conflict.

It was this desire to keep out of the war that led, paradoxically, to the first break with the time-honored policy of non-entanglement in European politics. For it was in an attempt to remove the danger of involvement by bringing about an early end to the war that Wilson made his commitment to participate in a postwar league of nations. Such a league, in combination with the kind of settlement he called for, would, the president argued, also preserve the country from the danger of involvement in future wars. For a neutral power to seek to force the embattled combatants to yield to its wishes over when and how the war should be ended was an ambitious objective. Wilson's apparent belief that it could be achieved reflected his confidence not only in the hard power constituted by the Allies' growing financial dependence on the United States but also the soft power represented by the appeal of his position to war-weary people in all the belligerent nations.

Wilson's confidence was almost certainly misplaced, but it was Germany's launching of an unrestricted submarine campaign that changed the course of

American policy. The sinking of American ships, following on the Zimmermann note, was generally seen as an attack on the nation itself, an assault that honor demanded be resisted and punished. Yet it remained the case that the issue at stake, the right of Americans to travel safely in the German war zone, seemed to many disproportionate to the costs and sacrifices of a major foreign war. So it was natural for Wilson to maintain that the nation was fighting for much more—for a new international order in which there would be no more such wars and in which America's values of freedom and democracy would prevail across the world.

This ambitious goal was, however, the consequence rather than the cause of the decision to go to war, and during the period of American belligerency it was subordinated to the immediate objective of victory over the German government. This objective affected the content as well as the timing of Wilson's amplifications of his peace program during the period of American belligerency. Although this process involved some accommodation of Allied interests, it remained quite autonomous, and one of Wilson's principal purposes throughout was to maintain and develop domestic support not only for the war but also for an active American role in world affairs thereafter. But in relation to the world beyond the nation's borders, the unilateralism of the policy and the ambitiousness of the program again reflected great confidence in the extent of American power, both material and moral. This confidence proved excessive, not least because, after the defeat of the enemy, Americans were not prepared to meet the various sorts of costs that strenuous efforts to influence developments on other continents would entail.

Two general conclusions may be drawn from this story. The first is that few Americans at this time believed that the nation's core interests of security and prosperity required the achievement of any particular foreign policy objectives. The second is that Wilson's policymaking reflected an assumption that the United States possessed great power in the world, should it choose to exercise it. Public debate at the time showed that this confidence was shared by most of the political and opinion-forming classes and apparently by Americans generally. The combination of this sense of power with the lack of a foreign policy agenda arising out of clear and compelling national interests helps to explain the pattern of advance and retreat reminiscent of that over imperialism twenty years earlier.

This pattern also reflected the extent to which American policy was the subject of internal debate, the natural outcome of a situation in which what the United States was reasonably thought to have the potential capacity to do in world politics so greatly exceeded what it clearly needed to do to protect its own narrow national interests. Which of these two realities people emphasized largely determined the position they took over participation in the League of Nations.

Although that issue was effectively settled in a practical way in 1920, this did not mean that a consensus had been reached about the extent to which the United States ought, or needed, to play an active and extensive role in world politics. As the debate over this continued, the question of how necessary, and how wise, American intervention in World War I had been was to remain central to it for the next three decades—and beyond.

3

A RESTRAINED SUPERPOWER, 1920–1938

If the degree of America's potential power in world politics had not been widely recognized before 1914, after World War I it was obvious to all. The nation had demonstrated the capacity to raise an enormous army rapidly and to transport it across an ocean, while its naval building program had created a fleet equal in strength to the British, at least in terms of capital ships. Indeed, the United States was the only belligerent whose relative power was enhanced by the conflict—in that sense, the only victor.

The most significant aspect of this was America's financial and economic preeminence. By 1919, it had become a net creditor on its international private account to the tune of $8.5 billion—leaving aside the over $10 billion intergovernmental loans it was owed. The outflow of capital (and also the inflow of gold) was further stimulated by the healthy positive trade balances the United States enjoyed throughout the 1920s. As the country built up large gold reserves, New York supplanted London as the world's principal financial center. The status of the pound sterling as the determinant of the international gold standard was more and more displaced by the U.S. gold-dollar system—a process that culminated in Germany's inclusion within this system in 1924.[1]

The war had also had sharply contrasting effects on the productive capacities of the American economy and those of the other belligerent countries. A particularly striking illustration of this is that in 1920, U.S. crude steel production was twice as large as that of the United Kingdom, Germany, France, Russia, Japan, and Italy *combined*. Such a scale of difference was bound to be reduced as the devastated economies of Europe (including Russia) recovered, but America's own boom in the 1920s was such that in 1928 its share of the world's total output of manufactures was almost 40 percent, more than that of the six other major powers combined.[2] Along with the proportional scale of its output, the nation's share of world trade rose from 12.9 percent in 1913 to 17.3 percent in 1928, and the United States overtook the United Kingdom to become the world's greatest trading nation.[3]

As international historians recognize, all of this made the United States "the real potential hegemon of the post-World War I era."[4] Yet over the next two decades the country did not play such a role. This was not because other powers combined to balance its great power and limit its influence; on the contrary, the pressure from outside was for the United States to increase its involvement and expand the definition of its interests. The constraints on the exercise of America's great potential power were not external but internal.

The Character of U.S. Foreign Policy in the 1920s

Nothing better illustrates the connection between debates over U.S. foreign policy and interpretations of its history than the way the character of U.S. policy in the 1920s became a historiographical battleground. The contending interpretations arose out of opposing views about the desirability of America's global role, each of which was justified by a different explanation of how it came about. Just because the nation's overseas involvement and commitments seemed to shrink rather than to grow in the interwar years, this period played a crucial part in both the competing narratives.

To the "realist" school that was dominant in the 1940s and 1950s, the retreat in the interwar period represented a mistaken and ultimately disastrous attempt to avoid the responsibilities that came with great power status and also a failure to recognize the altered and expanded requirements of national security. The fruits of this "return to isolationism" were the collapse of the international economy after 1929 and the sequence of aggressions by Japan, Italy, and Nazi Germany in the 1930s that culminated in World War II. The costs of these catastrophes constituted a learning process, one that finally taught Americans that the United States needed to build and maintain a stable international order for the sake of its own prosperity and security. In this account, the nation's global role was essentially forced on it by external realities rather than representing a choice made for internally generated reasons.

This was the proposition challenged by the "revisionist" historiography that arose in the 1960s and 1970s, the era of the Vietnam War. According to William

Appleman Williams and his disciples, it was not inescapable external threats to the nation's security that led to the great expansion of its diplomatic and military commitments and its involvement in the politics of other countries, but an internally generated drive to create an "Open Door world" into which American exports, investments, and indeed values could freely expand. This drive arose from the need (or, in some versions, the perceived need) for such overseas expansion if the capitalist system was to produce the rising prosperity necessary for its own political stability at home.[5] However, since such a need would be a permanent rather than episodic one, this interpretation was bound to see the consequent policy as continuous. If at some point the United States adopted a passive and uninvolved posture in international affairs, this would imply that overseas economic expansion had not been seen as either so vital or so dependent on government support as the thesis maintains. So it is not surprising that Williams strongly challenged the view that the United States withdrew from active participation in world politics after 1919. Portraying the fight over the League of Nations as "a conflict over tactics," Williams argued that the Republican administrations of the 1920s were as committed as Wilson to "the Open Door Policy as the strategy of the United States in foreign affairs." The idea that the United States at this time reverted to "isolationism" was a "legend."[6]

Notwithstanding these starkly different interpretations, there seems now to be little disagreement among historians over the general character of U.S. policy in the 1920s. The picture they present suggests that each of the warring schools highlighted one aspect while ignoring or downplaying others. As has been widely recognized, the revisionists had a point in challenging the notion of "a return to isolationism"—indeed, it may well be that it is in regard to the 1920s that they have had their greatest impact on mainstream historiography. Policymakers in the Republican administrations of 1921–33 undoubtedly sought to exert influence beyond the Western Hemisphere. Their proclaimed objective was a peaceful and stable world order, and the more active and thoughtful of them, notably Charles Evans Hughes and Herbert Hoover, also had clear and distinctive ideas about how such a world order could be established. The key was their faith in the benign political effects of rising prosperity and their confidence that such prosperity would result from unhampered international trade and investment. "The dominating fact of this last century," Hoover declared, "has been economic development. And it continues today as the force which dominates the whole spiritual, social and political life of our country and the world."[7] Material progress, in this view, brought moral progress. International relations would become a law-governed arena in which conflicts would be resolved by the processes of diplomacy and judicial arbitration rather than military force. This would facilitate the reduction of armaments, which would itself contribute to increasing prosperity by avoiding the waste of resources and cutting the burden of taxation. As a concomitant of this process, economic incentives and penalties would be the major means by which a state's actions might be influenced from the outside. Such inducements and sanctions might well require that the behavior of private economic interests be coordinated with government policy, and to this end investment banks were requested to submit proposals for foreign loans to the State Department in advance.[8]

Such assumptions and purposes lay behind the major foreign policy initiatives of the Republican era. The first and the most publicly notable of these was the Washington conference of 1921–22, convened by Hughes in response to congressional and popular pressure for arms reduction. The secretary of state opened proceedings with a dramatic call not only for a ten-year halt in the construction of capital ships by the major powers but also for the scrapping of over sixty existing or authorized vessels. After lengthy negotiations, the upshot was a series of agreements dealing with both naval disarmament and the delicate political situation in the Far East. A Five-Power Treaty established a ratio in battleship tonnage between the United States, Britain, Japan, France, and Italy. In the Four-Power Treaty, the United States, Britain, Japan, and France agreed mutually to respect each other's insular possessions in the Pacific and to confer in case of any dispute between them or any outside threat to their possessions; this treaty superseded the bilateral Anglo-Japanese alliance, which American policymakers had long disliked. In the Nine-Power Treaty, other European colonial nations joined the big five powers in pledging formal respect for Chinese sovereignty and territorial integrity and the principle of the Open Door. This pact involved no substantial changes in the existing rights and privileges of the signatory powers, but in 1928 the United States granted China tariff autonomy on a most-favored-nation basis, thereby becoming the first power to yield some of its rights under the treaties that had earlier been forced on China.

With respect to the Western Hemisphere, too, pressure from anti-imperialists in Congress reinforced the inclination to reduce the role of force in international relations. Republican policymakers sought to maintain in other ways a stability that would serve the nation's strategic and economic interests. The U.S. troops that had been in the Dominican Republic and Nicaragua since the Wilson administration were withdrawn in 1924–25. Although the outbreak of a civil war led to the Marines' return to Nicaragua in 1926, American efforts were concentrated on finding local means to keep order in the small states of the Caribbean region that remained the nation's preeminent hegemonic sphere. More generally, the United States made greater efforts to establish pan-Americanism on a consensual basis; it participated in 41 out of 44 conferences involving nations of the Western Hemisphere between 1921 and 1933, in contrast to its participation in only 23 out of the 50 such conferences held between 1889 and 1921.[9]

None of these activities constituted direct participation in the politics of Europe, still the location of most of the world's other major powers as well as the traditional focus of the principle of non-involvement. That principle had been reiterated by the "irreconcilable" opponents of the League of Nations, and their effective victory in 1919–20 gave it renewed authority. But this did not prevent the United States playing a significantly greater role in European affairs in the 1920s than it had done before World War I. In the realm of international finance, the Federal Reserve Bank of New York under Benjamin Strong took the lead in efforts to restore a stable system of currency exchange, pressing Britain to return to the Gold Standard in 1925.[10]

A more direct involvement in European politics came when American policymakers sought a resolution of the conflict arising from the large payments demanded from Germany by the Reparations Commission set up under the Treaty of Versailles. In December 1922, Hughes warned against the application of sanctions to extract reparations and expressed America's readiness to participate in an apolitical solution based on an experts' study of Germany's capacity to pay. He pressed this proposal on the reluctant French after the Germans' passive resistance to France's military occupation of the Rhineland in 1923 had produced an impasse. The "expert" committee set up under the chairmanship of the Chicago banker Charles G. Dawes produced a plan, a key feature of which was an international loan to Germany. The loan was managed by the J.P. Morgan bank, which made it conditional on France's withdrawal from the Ruhr and renunciation of the sanctions written into the Treaty of Versailles. More broadly, the argument that U.S. investors would only invest in German loan obligations and French bonds if there were a political settlement was repeatedly employed, explicitly by Morgan's and informally by Hughes, to secure the acceptance by Germany, and particularly by France, of the Dawes Plan and subsequently to reinforce the multilateral diplomacy that led to the signing by Britain, France, and Germany of the Locarno Treaties in 1925. This guaranteed Germany's western boundary and paved the way for its admission to the League of Nations. Taken together, the Dawes Plan and Locarno have recently been described as the "real" settlement following World War I and have been seen as establishing "a Euro-Atlantic peace system whose *de facto* pre-eminent power was the United States."[11]

The Washington treaties and the contribution to European stabilization were the major steps taken by the Republican administrations to promote world order, but there were also lesser ones. Over the course of the decade, a closer relationship with the League of Nations was cautiously and tentatively developed. It began with officials from various executive departments sitting as "observers" on some of the League's specialist agencies. Invitations to attend the proceedings of the League Council on the same basis were also accepted occasionally, although not as a matter of course, and the United States participated in the preparations for the Disarmament Conference that finally convened under League auspices in February 1932. Most significantly, Henry L. Stimson, as secretary of state, sought to align U.S. policy with that of the League over the Japanese military action in Manchuria and China in 1931–32. For the first time, an American official (Prentiss Gilbert) participated formally when the Council discussed the matter, and Stimson indicated that the United States would not obstruct any embargo. Such a strong sanction did not win favor in either Geneva or Washington, but President Hoover did approve what became known as the Stimson Doctrine, a declaration that the United States would not "recognize any situation, treaty, or agreement" brought about through the use of force.[12]

All of this amply justifies one historian's observation that "in the 1920s the United States was more profoundly engaged in international matters than in any peacetime era in its history."[13] In keeping with this, the instrumentalities for exercising power in the world developed. By the end of World War I, there had been a fivefold increase since 1898 in the personnel of the State Department in Washington and in the number of diplomatic secretaries abroad. The Rogers Act of 1924 created the United States Foreign Service by merging the diplomatic and consular services. The act established entry examinations and a merit system of promotion for the new professional body and also created a Foreign Service School. Although the conscript army that had been raised during the war was demobilized afterwards, at around 140,000 the U.S. Army's overall manpower remained more than 50 percent greater than it had been before the war—and the officer corps was three times as large. Following the naval-building program embarked on in 1916, the U.S. Navy had become one of the two largest in the world, its equality with the British Navy in terms of capital ships recognized and perpetuated in the 1922 Five-Power Treaty. In 1926 an act of Congress established the Army Air Corps, which had over 1,100 front-line aircraft by 1933. In the interwar years, the proportion of the GNP devoted to the army and navy was double what it had been between 1899 and 1916.[14]

However, at 1.7 percent, this remained a very low figure by later standards. In other and more immediately relevant ways, too, Americans showed that they were unwilling to pay a significant price for exercising influence in the world. Thus, the contribution of the United States to the economic recovery and political stabilization of Europe fell far short of what many informed Americans as well as European leaders believed to be both necessary and possible. Although some additional credits were provided to European governments in the immediate aftermath of the Armistice, both the Treasury Department and Congress firmly ruled out further government lending to aid postwar reconstruction. Various proposals from leading Wall Street bankers for some government-supported financial consortium to help finance European recovery were firmly squashed by the Wilson administration; a petition from forty-seven prominent lawyers, bankers, and economists in January 1920 received a polite brush-off from the White House. In January 1922, Hoover saw it as "the most unlikely event on the economic earth" that "the United States, as a government, [would] again engage in any governmental loans" to European countries. Hughes made it publicly clear a little later that "the needed capital, if it is to be supplied at all, must be furnished by private organizations." And, although the administration collaborated with and encouraged private bankers over the funding for the Dawes Plan, it firmly resisted their demands in the later 1920s for some sort of government protection for loans made to Germany.[15]

The United States refused to take part in international conferences on European reconstruction in 1920 and 1922. A major reason for this was the determination to avoid accepting the link that Britain and France repeatedly sought to make between the scale of their financial demands on Germany and the extent of their obligations to the United States. Clearly, the most direct and effective manner in which the United States could have contributed to the stabilization of Europe would have been by adopting a more generous position with respect to the large loans it had made to its co-belligerents during the war. Although some business leaders and diplomats urged the cancellation or reduction of these war debts, policymakers adamantly refused to countenance this. Committed to reducing taxes, the Republican administrations were not disposed to relieve foreign debtors at the expense of American taxpayers, and Congress was even more resistant to doing this. It was recognized that the war debts constituted a potential source of diplomatic leverage, but this was exploited only in a very limited way, through some readiness to make concessions over rates of interest and periods of repayment in bilateral funding agreements. Moreover, a threat to restrict further private credits was employed to pressure France, in particular, to accept the obligations of such a settlement.[16]

Another area in which domestic interests overrode foreign policy desiderata was tariff policy. Both the Fordney-McCumber Act of 1922 and the Hawley-Smoot Act of 1930 raised rates, disregarding the possible effects of this on the ability of European nations to gain the access to the huge American market that could have stimulated their own economies and eased the burden of repaying and servicing their war debts.[17] But the protection of American businesses and their workers was a higher priority for Congress, and one not seriously challenged by the executive. As Warren Harding explained to a correspondent, the governing principle of U.S. policy was to "assert a helpful influence abroad without sacrificing anything of importance to our own people."[18]

The reluctance to make sacrifices for the sake of achieving foreign policy objectives was manifested in nonmonetary respects as well. Those loyal Wilsonians who continued to hope that the nation would in some way join the League of Nations found the tide of opinion continuing to run against them after 1920. Warren Harding categorically rejected any connection with the League after he entered the White House, and this position was firmly upheld by his Republican successors, Calvin Coolidge and Herbert Hoover. The Democratic Party's commitment to League membership was progressively weakened in the party's 1924 and 1928 platforms. Leading internationalists came to focus on participation in the World Court as a lesser step, but the hostility to the League presented a problem for this proposal also. When the administration sent a treaty of adherence to the World Court to the Senate in 1923, it attached a reservation stressing that this would bring no legal connection with the League. Nevertheless, the Senate insisted on adding a further reservation that, on any dispute in which the United States had an interest, the Court should not entertain "any request" for even an advisory opinion without American consent. Unsurprisingly, the existing members of the Court found this unacceptable.

All of this might be seen as part of the backlash against Wilsonian "internationalism," drawing strength from the bitter emotions that had been aroused in the partisan battles of 1918–20. But the unwillingness to make any commitment that carried the least risk of war or limited America's freedom of action applied also to the initiatives of the Republican administrations. Thus the Four-Power Treaty of 1921 met opposition in the Senate and achieved approval by a narrow majority only with a reservation making it clear that it involved "no commitment to armed force, no alliance, no obligation to join in any defense."

The extreme wariness about anything approximating an "entangling alliance" was manifested in the Coolidge administration's response to the proposal by the French premier, Aristide Briand, in 1927 of a bilateral "Pact of Perpetual Friendship" in which France and the United States would renounce war between themselves. Briand had been encouraged to make this proposal by a Columbia University professor, James T. Shotwell. Shotwell, a former member of the Inquiry and a leading advocate of League membership, had become a supporter of the campaign for the outlawry of war that had developed considerable popular and political support in the United States since its launch in 1921. At the suggestion of William Borah, now chairman of the Senate Foreign Relations Committee, Secretary of State Frank B. Kellogg sidestepped Briand's suggestion for a bilateral treaty by proposing a multinational pact in which all nations would renounce war "as an instrument of national policy" and seek to solve their disputes "by pacific means." In August 1928, such a pact was signed in Paris by the representatives of fifteen states; a further thirty-one later adhered to it. But, at Kellogg's insistence, the pact contained no provisions for its enforcement and thus no obligation on the United States to take any particular action if a nation violated it. The Senate approved the treaty overwhelmingly, but only after adding riders reasserting the right of self-defense and the Monroe Doctrine.

The refusal to undertake binding commitments can be linked with the unilateralist tradition in American foreign policy and the deep-seated instinct that the nation should not compromise its freedom to choose its own course in any future circumstances. At least equally important, however, was the determination to avoid any possibility of entanglement in a foreign war. Thus, in the Manchuria crisis, Hoover was quite ready to cooperate with the League of Nations but adamantly opposed to imposing economic sanctions on Japan on the grounds that they "would be provocative and lead to war."[19]

The explanatory task with respect to U.S. foreign policy in the 1920s is thus twofold. We need to find reasons both for the increase in the extent of the nation's involvement in world politics and also for the limits of that involvement, in particular the unwillingness to pay any significant price—even in terms of such nonmaterial values as unfettered freedom of action in the future—to achieve foreign policy objectives.

The Role of Security Concerns and Economic Interests

Strategic considerations played at most a minor part in expanding the scope of involvement in the 1920s. There was some concern, particularly in naval circles, that an aggressive Japan might menace American interests in the western Pacific and East Asia. Countering this potential threat was one of the objectives of American diplomacy at the Washington conference of 1921–22, reflected in all three of the subsequent treaties, particularly the Four-Power Treaty that superseded the Anglo-Japanese alliance. But policymakers, the military, and the general public shared a confidence that the nation could protect its vital interests unaided and irrespective of political developments in Europe and Asia. As we have seen, the specter of a transoceanic invasion that preparedness advocates had conjured up in 1914–15 had never gained much credence; after the war, it faded altogether. No one in the 1920s sought to suggest that any European country had the capacity to threaten the continental coastlines, challenge the Monroe Doctrine, or endanger the Panama Canal. This sense of security was underpinned by a commitment to maintaining America's defense capabilities. Notwithstanding the push to reach international disarmament agreements, politicians were determined to maintain the comparative strength of the navy. This was reflected in the introduction of technical advances, including the development of naval aviation, and also in the hard bargaining manifested at the Geneva naval disarmament conference of 1927. After the failure there to reach an agreement with the British over cruisers, Congress authorized the building of fifteen new cruisers and an aircraft carrier— dismaying peace advocates by doing so in the immediate aftermath of approving the Kellogg-Briand Pact. However, that admirals seeking larger appropriations chose to play up the danger of a war with Britain over trade issues was itself a striking demonstration of the benignity of the strategic environment at this time.[20]

If historians generally agree in discounting strategic concerns as an explanation for the greater involvement of the United States in world politics in the 1920s, the same is far from true of economic interests. On the contrary, revisionists of the Williams school see the expansion of American policy as driven by "a belief in the vital connection between domestic prosperity and the control of external markets, sources of raw materials, and investment opportunities."[21] In their view, this belief produced a commitment not only to the promotion of these specific material interests but also to the broad goals of establishing the norms of marketplace capitalism and the Open Door principle across the world and countering the threats posed to these by revolutionary nationalism and communism.

There were certainly cases where the U.S. government acted to promote American economic interests overseas. But in some of the most notable examples, the prime impulse was neither a desire to maintain the profits of particular American businesses nor a general commitment to the principle of the Open Door. Rather, it was a concern with the availability of raw materials seen as important for the nation's economic and security interests. This was true of rubber, of which the United States, lacking a domestic supply, consumed about 75 percent of global imports. Two-thirds of the rubber traded internationally came from areas under the control of Great Britain, which in 1922 enacted the Stevenson Plan, imposing a system of compulsory production and export controls. With demand rising as automobile production soared, this led to a fivefold increase in rubber prices over three years. Both the administration, with Hoover in the lead, and Congress sought new sources of supply, but most American rubber company executives, having plantations in British areas, showed little interest. However, Harvey Firestone was an exception, and the U.S. government strenuously promoted and assisted his establishment of plantations in Liberia.[22]

An even more vital resource was petroleum, needed by the navy as well as by the economy generally. Here there was less dependence on imports. Indeed, in 1918, U.S. companies accounted for 70 to 80 percent of world production, supplying the great bulk of the oil that had carried the Allies to victory in the war. But in the immediate postwar years there was widespread anxiety about the depletion of continental reserves at a time when the only American foreign operations in production were in Mexico and Romania. The known resources in the rest of the world were under the control of foreign companies with close links to their own national governments. Anglo-Dutch Shell had a monopoly in the Netherlands East Indies, while Britain and France divided oil activity in the Middle East, Romania, and Russia between themselves in the San Remo Resolution of 1920. In 1921 Hughes and Hoover encouraged American oil executives to fight for control of overseas reserves, particularly in the Middle East. Pressure from Washington, which included retaliatory action against Shell's interests in the United States, succeeded in gaining access for U.S. corporations in the East Indies and to the former Ottoman Empire. As a result, American oil firms participated in the Turkish Petroleum Company established by the Red Line Agreement of 1928. This company's effective monopoly over almost all the oil-producing areas of the Middle East hardly accorded with the principle of the Open Door, though the U.S. government continued to pay lip service to this—particularly after the discovery of ample domestic reserves in the mid-1920s assuaged the fears of an impending shortage.[23]

As for the potential threat of revolutionary nationalism to America's overseas economic interests, the prime example in the 1920s was Mexico, where an animating dynamic of the revolution that had begun in 1913 was anger at the extent to which the country's land and mineral resources had been appropriated by foreign interests, mostly American. The Mexican constitution of 1917 reinstated the Civil Law principle that subsoil rights belonged to the state, leaving uncertain the legal basis of concessions already granted to U.S. oil and mining corporations, which were also now subjected to higher taxation. In response, these interests helped orchestrate a vocal public and congressional campaign for military intervention, making much of the revolution's attacks also on the Catholic church. This campaign was firmly resisted, first by Wilson (whose previous experiences with military incursions into Mexico had left him with a vivid sense of their perils) and then by his Republican successors. Not only would military intervention in Mexico be a much more expensive and hazardous enterprise than it was in small Caribbean and Central American countries, but it would also have conflicted both with the broader objective of improving relations with Latin America and with other U.S. interests in Mexico itself—particularly those of investment bankers who were not averse to higher taxes on the oil companies if these would enable Mexico to pay its debts to American bondholders. Nevertheless, the U.S. government did employ nonmilitary forms of pressure to uphold the rights of American property holders, not only a series of protest notes but also the restriction of loans and the withholding of diplomatic recognition. Mexico's need for development loans gave it a strong incentive to compromise and also gave Wall Street bankers a crucial role. The Morgan partner Thomas Lamont brokered an agreement in 1923, and another Morgan partner, Dwight Morrow, as U.S. Ambassador to Mexico, brought about both a final settlement in 1928 and a vast improvement in bilateral relations overall.[24]

The U.S. government did take some steps to advance the nation's overseas economic interests more generally. Fearing revived European competition in markets where American businesses had made inroads during the war, Congress passed the Webb-Pomerene Act in 1918 and the Edge Act in 1919. These allowed, respectively, exporters and banks to enter into combinations, exempt from antitrust laws, to facilitate foreign trade. Under Hoover, the Department of Commerce encouraged such trade associations and became a clearinghouse of information for American businesses, establishing branches in many foreign cities. Yet government support for overseas business activity was neither unequivocal nor, apparently, of any great practical significance. Hoover, like other officials, feared that branch factories abroad represented an export of jobs and deplored loans to German municipalities as unproductive.[25] The U.S. government's efforts to induce American banks and businesses to invest in China rather than Japan were unsuccessful.[26] Nor does the Edge Act seem to have been very efficacious. It did little to stimulate overseas investments in the early 1920s when there was a domestic economic recession and financial and political uncertainty in Europe.

When these broader conditions changed during the economic boom of 1922–29, private lending abroad rose by more than 50 percent. Merchandise exports also rose by 37 percent in the same period, with motor vehicles contributing almost 10 percent of the total by 1929.[27] This might suggest that the influence of economic interest on U.S. foreign policy is to be looked for less in specific measures to promote overseas business activity directly than in the extent to which they shaped measures that pursued broad policy objectives. The role played by the United States in helping to establish financial and political stability in Europe represented the most striking advance on the nation's prewar stance, and this commitment can be seen as reflecting the importance of transatlantic economic ties. Europe was still America's most important overseas market, absorbing around half of its exports and an increasing proportion of its capital outflows.

Yet the difficulty of attributing the expanded scope of American foreign policy to a concern with overseas economic interests is that those interests made no larger contribution to national prosperity in the 1920s than they had done earlier. Indeed, with respect to exports, the reverse was the case. The ratio of exports to gross national product (in current dollars) during 1922–29 was 5.3 percent, whereas from 1869 to 1913 it had been 6.8 percent. The ratio of exports to national income was 6.3 percent in 1928, the same as in 1909 and below the 8 percent of 1899. This was a much smaller ratio than in other major industrial countries, such as Britain (20.3%), Germany (16.6%), and France (22.9%). A regional analysis further weakens any purported link between the changing shape of American foreign policy and overseas markets. It was in respect to Europe that there was significantly greater diplomatic engagement in the 1920s than before, but that continent's share of American exports had declined from 75 percent to 50 percent between 1900 and 1920 and was further reduced during the course of the subsequent decade.

Capital outflows, on the other hand, did increase greatly in the 1920s. The total of direct investments abroad rose from $2.7 billion in 1914 to $7.6 billion in 1929, as corporations such as Ford, RCA, Eastman Kodak, Standard Oil, DuPont, United Fruit, and International Harvester expanded their overseas operations. Portfolio overseas investment increased even more, from $862 million in 1914 to $7.8 billion in 1929. Moreover, investments, unlike exports, were increasingly directed to Europe. That continent's share of America's overseas portfolio investment (excluding the war debts) more than doubled between 1914 and 1929 (from 20.7 percent to 42.6 percent). Yet, when viewed in proportional terms, the figures for foreign investment, like those for merchandise exports, appear less impressive. The net capital outflow in the 1920s represented around 3 percent of gross capital formation in these years and no more than 0.5 percent of GNP. By contrast, the amount of British capital flowing into foreign investment between 1870 and 1913 had averaged almost half of that country's domestic capital formation.[28]

The Expansive Effects of Power

America's material interests overseas, then, were only marginally more important to the nation as a whole after World War I than they had been before. On the other hand, America's power, relative to that of other states, had been greatly enhanced. In view of the assumption of some Realist theorists that states in the international system are incessantly engaged in a struggle for power and also with regard to claims that "the U.S. rise to world power" demonstrates that "American foreign policy works," it is worth observing that the nation's new status was not the product of deliberate policy.[29] As the historian Melvyn Leffler points out, New York's emergence as the world's financial center "had more to do with the impact of the war on London than with any concrete measures taken by Washington."[30] Likewise, the preeminence of the United States in production, world trade, and global capital investment did not represent the accomplishment of some governmental project. America's remarkable economic growth was the product of the country's abundant resources and the efforts of millions of Americans who were overwhelmingly motivated by a desire to raise their own and their families' standard of living rather than by the pursuit of national glory or a concern to enhance America's standing among the powers.

Yet if America's superpower status had not been produced by its foreign policy, it nonetheless profoundly affected the context in which that policy was made. Most directly, it enabled the nation to exert a greater influence with less effort or sacrifice to itself. This was clearest with respect to monetary resources. Despite their relative modesty in relation to domestic investment, the foreign loans floated in the United States between 1919 and 1929 amounted to more than that provided by all other capital-exporting nations combined.[31] As we have seen, the conditionality of such loans gave the U.S. government potent diplomatic leverage across the globe, with Mexico and Europe constituting particularly notable instances. Exercising influence abroad through financial means could bring benefits rather than costs. In extending gold credits to other central banks to facilitate the stabilization of their currencies, Benjamin Strong was minimizing the possibility that the huge stocks of gold in Federal Reserve vaults would lead to domestic inflation.[32]

(Incidentally, the disproportion between the cost and the impact of U.S. actions helps to explain the divergent characterizations of American foreign policy in the 1920s. Those who portray the country as "isolationist" focus on the unwillingness to pay any significant price to achieve foreign policy objectives. On the other hand, international historians, highlighting the crucial impact of the limited actions that the United States did undertake, can see it as exercising an "informal hegemony" over Europe.)[33]

Moreover, the obvious potential of American power could have an effect on the behavior of other states without the United States doing much more than making its policy and preferences known. There is direct evidence of this in the case of the United Kingdom. As we have seen, the idea of an Anglo-American partnership in world affairs had gained influential adherents on both sides of the ocean before World War I, and the continued rise of America's power (together with the decline of Britain's own) increased the attractiveness of the vision to British statesmen. In pursuit of it, they were ready to accommodate British policy to that of the United States. Just as Lloyd George and Robert Cecil had worked with Wilson to establish the League of Nations out of a belief that the "greatest guarantee" of a "settled peace" was "a good understanding with the United States," so London gave up its bilateral alliance with Japan in 1920–21 for the sake of what Foreign Office officials called a "mutual alliance with America" in the Far East that could affect the whole range of "world politics, which are dominated by our relations with the United States as constituting the prime factor in the maintenance of order and peace throughout the world." In 1925, Foreign Secretary Austen Chamberlain emphasized to his officials the need to "avoid the dangers which must arise to our international relations from the growing agitation in America" over the Stevenson rubber scheme.[34] French leaders, too, despite manifold disappointments in their quest for an American underwriting of their security objectives, continued to court the United States out of the recognition that the scale of its resources gave it a unique capacity to help resolve the reparations tangle. Even Raymond Poincaré, opposed as he was to any reduction of Germany's obligations at the expense of French bondholders, compromised on the issue as Prime Minister when he feared that the United States might retract the proposal for an experts' inquiry and withdraw further from European affairs.[35]

As this example illustrates, these concessive moves not only demonstrated the influence of America's potential power but also served as an inducement to increased U.S. involvement. If the hegemony of the United States over western Europe after World War II may be seen as "empire by invitation," the invitation was of long standing.[36] The "invitation" was accompanied and supplemented by exhortation. Private citizens in Britain and other European countries as well as government officials repeatedly urged that America's great power brought with it a much increased responsibility for the welfare and stability of the international order as a whole.

Given the general American suspicion of European diplomacy and concern not to be entangled by its "intrigues," such pleas would have had little effect had not many Americans felt the same way. As we have seen, the argument that the nation's growth brought with it an obligation to play a much larger role in international affairs had been current since the late nineteenth century, resonating strongly in the upper-class East Coast circles where many had long desired closer Anglo-American relations in particular.

It was from this milieu that the Council on Foreign Relations emerged. Incorporated under New York state law in 1921, the organization grew in part out of meetings that members of the Inquiry had held in Paris during the peace conference, often with their British counterparts. Another strand was a group of New York lawyers and bankers who had formed "a species of dinner club" in 1918 to discuss world affairs under the leadership of Elihu Root. Launching its well-funded journal *Foreign Affairs* in 1922, the Council soon became the heart of what critics saw as an "Eastern establishment," many of whose members moved in and out of government positions over the course of the next half-century at least. Although there was considerable diversity both in their positions on particular issues and in their views on the general character of international relations, members of the Council were united by a desire that the United States should become more fully involved. Career Foreign Service officers, particularly those who had entered the State Department before the Rogers Act, mostly shared this social background and outlook.[37]

If the sociological profile of this strong source of pressure toward greater involvement is clear, the explanation for it is inevitably more a matter of interpretation and therefore merits somewhat fuller consideration. For many analysts, foreign policy attitudes simply reflected economic interests. As the political scientist Jeff Frieden argues, "Internationally oriented sectors could be expected to support an extension of American diplomatic commitments abroad, both specifically to safeguard their investments and more generally to provide an international environment conducive to foreign economic growth." This expectation receives confirmation in the prominence of Wall Street bankers and lawyers among those who supported American entry into the League of Nations, U.S. financing of European reconstruction, and international monetary and financial cooperation. "Financial interests, import-export groups and large manufacturers with foreign markets tended to be more internationally oriented" than "the average businessman," Joan Hoff Wilson observes.[38]

Yet there are good reasons for thinking that matters were not as simple as this. As we have seen, the upper echelons of East Coast society had developed transatlantic ties that went well beyond the economic. Most had spent time in Europe, and many had developed personal relationships with individuals there, in some cases through family connections resulting from marriage. There was a strong sense of cultural connection as well as ethnic identification with countries, especially Great Britain, that were seen as part of the same civilization. It is surely unlikely that an equal level of economic interest in an area of the world not linked to these Americans in such nonmaterial ways would have generated similar concern or willingness to provide resources to help it achieve prosperity and political stability.

Nor should the fact that those who favored greater commitment commonly stressed the degree of economic self-interest involved when they made the case for it publicly be taken as transparent evidence of their own motivation. Robert Schulzinger's observation about Foreign Service officers might well have a wider application: "Privately, among themselves, diplomats rejected the notion that foreign commerce was the sole purpose of foreign policy, but they were worried by the fact that a portion of the American public maintained this principle. Thus their advocacy of trade expansion helped them to gain popular respect for their profession."[39]

The complexity of the factors that might lead to a desire to expand the scope of U.S. foreign policy can perhaps best be illuminated by considering an individual case. No one made greater efforts in the 1920s to increase America's involvement in European matters than Alanson Houghton, successively ambassador to Germany (1922–25) and the United Kingdom (1925–29). A political appointment, Houghton was a successful businessman who had built the Corning Glass

Works, which he had inherited, into a major enterprise that did indeed trade internationally. Just as relevant, however, may have been his family background and life history. After education at a New England prep school and Harvard, he spent two years in Europe, taking postgraduate courses in Göttingen, Berlin, and Paris. From an old-stock New England family (his mother, a Bigelow, was a true Boston Brahmin), he was a devout Episcopalian, a paternalistic employer, and an active philanthropist. Inspired it seems by patriotic idealism, he entered politics in 1918 and won election as a Republican congressman. During the campaign, he informed voters that after the war America had to be prepared to "take its place among nations as a world power—THE WORLD POWER." In a speech at the Metropolitan Club in New York before taking up his post in Berlin, he stressed that the United States had a "conscious duty" to help rebuild European civilization: "we Americans must do our part" and do it "now." He expanded on this theme in another address a little later: "The American people must understand their responsibility and their opportunity. God has given us the power to render a vast service to humanity. No such opportunity ever has come to any nation in two thousand years. . . . The idea of isolation must be dismissed. The sentiment and the sense of responsibility for building a better world civilization must be cultivated."[40] Houghton was not appealing to the traditional idea that America had a providential ideological mission so much as to the belief, deeply instilled through the Protestant churches and educational establishments his class were nurtured in, that power, like privilege, brought responsibility.

That this idea was more than a rationalization of material interests is indicated by the kind of people who advocated greater international commitment as well as by the manner in which they did so. Businessmen, whether exporters or not, were not particularly prominent among those pressing for closer ties with the League of Nations and adherence to the World Court. Opponents, who complained that internationalists were claiming to speak for "all the women, all the teachers, and all the preachers," pointed to the role of organizations like the League of Women Voters and the Federal Council of Churches in these campaigns. America should not continue "shirking international responsibilities and obligations," the FCC's Commission on International Justice and Goodwill argued, but should cooperate with the World Court, assist in international economic reconstruction, and lead the way toward further arms reduction. And it was not only in religious circles that the issue was typically couched in ethical terms. It was America's "moral place" and "moral duty" to stand for "ideals of international justice," Shotwell urged in the pages of *Parents Magazine* in 1929: "We have duties to perform in the community of nations as well as in the community of individuals."[41]

The scale of the nation's power was what made the responsibility so great. Many stressed, as Theodore Roosevelt had done, that whatever the United States did or failed to do would be highly consequential. Wilsonian internationalists continued to argue that the whole nature of international relations in the future depended on it. Similarly, most took it for granted that if the United States did participate in efforts to establish international peace and justice, it would direct and shape them. According to the Reverend Charles C. Morrison, editor of the *Christian Century*, the country was "foreordained to leadership in a world-embracing crusade to abolish war." The enormous power of the United States "will really tip the balances finally toward peace or toward war," Frederick Libby of the National Council for the Limitation of Armaments insisted, "Only America can lead."[42]

The argument that the unique scale of America's power brought a special responsibility was frequently voiced by policymakers, too, both in public and in private. When Hughes came to give official backing to the participation of American experts in the Dawes Plan, he was swayed by the realization that *only* American action could forestall an escalation of the Franco-German crisis that could have disastrous consequences for the future stability of Europe. President Calvin Coolidge himself stated that "the one great duty that stands out requires us to use our enormous powers to trim the balance of the world." As Coolidge's successor, Hoover, asserted in 1929, the "colossal power of the United States overshadows scores of freedom-loving nations and thus makes concomitant American leadership in world affairs indispensable."[43]

Explaining the Limits of Commitment

Despite such sentiments, the actions of the United States in the 1920s fell far short of the measure of its responsibilities to the international system as these were viewed by many at the time and have been judged to be since. America failed to take over the "hegemonic" role in international finance and commerce that Britain no longer had the power to fulfill.[44] The priority for the Federal Reserve of domestic considerations was demonstrated when it raised interest rates in 1928 to check the stock market boom, causing an inward flow of both gold and funds that destabilized the delicate three-way international balance of reparation transfers, war debt servicing, and American loans to Germany established by the Dawes Plan. As the international financial crisis deepened, Hoover did initiate a one-year moratorium on debt and reparation payments in June 1931, but the United States refused to cancel the war debts, increased rather than reduced its tariffs, and declined to extend government loans to hard-pressed nations in Latin America. Nor was the United States prepared to do more on the political front. When the peaceful, stable order embodied in the Washington treaties and Kellogg-Briand Pact was challenged by Japan's military action in 1931, the American response, as we have seen, did not go beyond verbal protest.

Somewhat paradoxically, the limits to America's involvement may be seen as further confirmation that the primary impetus came from a consciousness of the nation's unique capacity to influence overseas developments rather than from a perceived need to achieve goals of direct importance to the United States itself. In the first place, a general sense of international responsibility did not give as clear a focus to policy as the pursuit of a more specific national interest would have done. Consequently, the direction action should take was in question as much as the desirability of acting at all. This made it more difficult for policymakers to muster support in Congress, especially in the Senate, which remained determined to assert its prerogatives in the post-Wilson era. After Congress firmly asserted control over debt repayments in 1921, Hughes frequently stressed to audiences and interlocutors that under the American Constitution both the war debts issue and possible security commitments were outside "the province of the executive."[45]

Borah and the other senators who blocked adherence to the World Court or greater cooperation with the League of Nations did not lack a sense of America's power. On the contrary, they tended to exaggerate it, as when they suggested that the war debts could be used as leverage to compel a change in British and French policy. The anti-imperialist "peace progressives" in the Senate were not, as recent scholarship has emphasized, "isolationists" with no interest in international affairs.[46] Their dissent was less about the degree of America's involvement than over the form such involvement should take. With respect to Europe, the central issue was their deep hostility to the Versailles settlement and their sympathy with Germany and the Soviet Union. Underlying this was a broader animus against British and French imperialism and those seen as its allies in Wall Street and among the Eastern establishment.

This sentiment resonated well beyond the Senate. In the 1920s, as the historian Charles DeBenedetti shows, it divided the peace movement. The campaign for the outlawry of war, which Borah sponsored, was devised and portrayed as an alternative to the League of Nations and the World Court. It was the brainchild of a Chicago attorney, Salmon O. Levinson—an early sign that Chicago would become the center of opposition to the form of internationalism identified with New York. One of Outlawry's most energetic proponents, the former Bull Moose Progressive Raymond Robins, saw the World Court battle as an opportunity "to win a final victory over the British Americans and European Internationalists among our citizenship."[47] Contrasting attitudes to Britain and its global role remained central to divisions over foreign policy in this period.[48]

This fundamental cleavage between entrenched positions was by no means the only obstacle to strenuous action in pursuit of a clear objective. Another was the shifting and unpredictable attitudes of the general public to foreign situations; the official reaction to France's occupation of the Ruhr was muted when Hughes discovered, to his surprise, that many Americans sympathized with it. Nor were policymakers themselves always united. This mattered more because of a decision-making process that was, in Leffler's words, "complex, cumbersome, and decentralized."[49] Under Hoover's assertive leadership, the Commerce Department not only set its own priorities regardless of State Department preferences but also insisted on an input into most policy areas.[50] On financial matters, the Treasury and the Federal Reserve Bank of New York were also independent players. Thus, negotiations over a debt settlement with France in the late 1920s found Strong and Treasury Secretary Andrew Mellon pitted against Hoover, whose insistence on a tough line prevailed.[51]

Such disagreements, whether within the administration and Congress or among interested members of the public, reflected the variety of considerations, perspectives, and prejudices that shaped people's views. Some policymakers recognized that these differences might have been overridden by the general perception of a clearly defined and reasonably specific national interest. Hughes explained to a British audience in 1924 why he thought that it was peculiarly difficult to achieve this in the United States:

> You are conscious of certain definite British interests; the problems of Empire are never absent from the thought of your statesman. With other European nations, there are national interests clearly perceived, often strongly supported by a keen racial consciousness. . . . As a nation we are relatively disinterested, the very fact of that disinterestedness which may excite your appeal gives opportunity with us for the most acute divisions of sentiment among a people drawn from many races and countries who are still bound by ties of sentiment and interest to many lands.

This, Hughes argued, was the basic problem, not the division of authority between executive and legislature: "When American interests are directly involved and clearly perceived by our people, we are capable of unity of sentiment and action, and in such a case our constitutional methods are no hindrance to efficiency, as we showed in the Great War." However, "our capacity for governmental action of a sustained character depends upon a predominant sentiment which brings the authorities of government into unison of effort."[52] Such a sentiment required the establishment of a reasonably direct connection between a national interest generally agreed to be of real importance on the one hand and the achievement of a particular foreign policy objective on the other.

The consciousness of America's great power added to the difficulty of making such a connection with respect to the core national interests of security and prosperity. With the nation's security generally seen as entailing only the safety of North America and the maintenance of the Monroe Doctrine, few doubted that the United States could achieve these objectives through its own strength regardless of developments in Europe or Asia. In reviews of the international situation conducted in the middle and late 1920s, army and navy analysts never perceived a threat to American strategic interests from Germany despite extensive information gathered by the Military Intelligence Division about German technical violations of the Treaty of Versailles. In 1926, Kellogg emphasized "the peculiarly fortunate situation" of the United States, able because of its "geographical isolation from those areas of the world where conflicting territorial or political issues have led to the maintenance of large standing armies" to reduce its land forces to a "regular army of about 118,000."[53]

With respect to the importance of overseas developments to the nation's economic well-being, the situation is less straightforward. Those who urged action to assist European reconstruction commonly argued, like George W. Wickersham in 1922, that "until we have a reorganized, a sound, a normal condition of affairs in Europe . . . we shall not have normal healthy times at home." "It is idle to say that we are not interested in these problems," Hughes stated as he proposed American participation in an "expert" commission to resolve the reparations dispute, "for we are deeply interested from an economic standpoint, as our credits and markets are involved." Now that the world had become "little more than a great neighborhood," Coolidge told the Chicago Commercial Club, "our common sense must tell us, if our self-interest did not, that our prosperity, our advancement, our portion of good fortune, must largely depend upon the share that shall be allocated to our neighbors."[54]

Yet such statements fell far short of showing that a commitment to European recovery after the war, or to world order more generally, was believed by policymakers to be vital for America's own prosperity. In the first place, other reasons for action were always presented in addition to economic self-interest. Thus, in the sentence quoted above, Hughes saw the United States as interested in Europe's well-being also "from a humanitarian standpoint, as the heart of the American people goes out to those who are in distress." In recommending American membership of the World Court, Coolidge made the case that "stability, tranquility and international justice" were important to the United States not in terms of economic interest but as a means of maintaining the nation's republican independence from militarism and alliances.[55]

Indeed, the expansion of export markets does not seem to have been regarded as an important policy objective, or even particularly desirable. Noting that the United States was recovering from the sharp recession of 1920–21 even as the European situation was still deteriorating, Hoover argued the country could "reestablish its material prosperity and comfort without European trade." Not only did policymakers not view exports as vital, they also saw dangers in their over-expansion. "A foreign trade that is too large in proportion to domestic production," Secretary of Commerce Robert P. Lamont warned in April 1929, "involves a dependence that means risk."

The prioritizing of the domestic market was only strengthened by the depression that started later that year. It was expressed and reinforced by the raising of tariff rates in the Smoot-Hawley Act of 1930. "The most striking feature of America's rise to the position of foremost industrial nation in the world is the creation of our immense domestic market," Smoot observed. Hoover signed the tariff bill reluctantly, but he retained his belief that "we can make a very large measure of recovery irrespective of foreign influence." With the fall in world demand, exports declined as a proportion of GNP, and there was little apparent interest among American businessmen in measures to promote them. "A major reason why foreign policy initiatives were circumscribed in the years 1930 to 1932," Leffler concludes in his thorough study, "was because State and Commerce Department officials realized that there was little support for such actions in the business community." Indeed, the preoccupation with economic recovery added to the difficulty of taking strenuous measures in any area of foreign policy. Following the Japanese military action in Shanghai in early 1932, Admiral Mark L. Bristol, president of the General Board of the Navy, emphasized that "the United States should put its own house in order without worrying about other nations unless we can help ourselves by helping others. . . . I don't believe the financial or economic conditions of other countries have as much to do with our economic depression as do our home circumstances."[56]

Bristol's comment indicated that many Americans regarded a commitment to a stable world order as a luxury that might be affordable when times were good but not as a vital interest that had to be maintained continuously. This is what one might expect of a commitment that was the product of a consciousness of capability and a sense of responsibility rather than one rooted in a concern with protecting North America from the danger of external attack or with maintaining Americans' own standard of living. Indeed, contrary to the premise of the Open Door interpretation, a brutally materialist approach to understanding American foreign policy does more to explain its limited nature in this period than the extent to which the scope of its involvement, and even its commitments, broadened.

The Apogee of Isolationism

That "the phenomenon known as isolationism became a major force in America in the mid-1930s" is a commonplace.[57] However, as a description of American attitudes to foreign policy, "isolationism" is as problematic a term as it is inescapable. It began as an epithet coined by its opponents, those desiring active support for Europe's revolutionary liberalism in the mid-nineteenth century.[58] As we have seen, "the end of isolation" had been much heralded at the turn of the century and during World War I by those advocating greater participation in world politics.[59] Isolationism has remained a staple of American debate ever since, generally retaining a negative connotation. Yet some historians and commentators have questioned its existence, at least as an influence on U.S. policy. Others see it as a "default position" to which Americans revert when not provoked by some direct assault on their interests.

These controversies tend to revolve around the meaning of the term. Those who argue that the United States has never been isolationist point particularly to the importance of foreign commerce throughout its history as well as the extent to which Americans have traveled and engaged with the people of other countries in a whole variety of ways. None of this, however, violated the guidance the nation's first president had set forth in his Farewell Address, a sacred text for isolationists. "The great rule of conduct for us, in regard to foreign nations," Washington had declared, "is, in extending our commercial relations, to have with them as little political connection as possible."[60]

By the 1930s, isolationism in this sense had developed into a fully fledged doctrine of American foreign policy, comparable to the Monroe Doctrine or to "containment" during the Cold War. Like these, it was advocated in terms of both the nation's strategic interests and its ideals. With respect to the first, the argument was that America's security from attack could not be enhanced, and could only be diminished, by alliances with other countries or involvement in foreign wars. The ocean barriers together with the nation's potential military strength protected it from the danger of attack, which was in any event very remote. The United States did not need to "become alarmed about the ups and downs of European conflicts, intrigues, aggressions, and wars," the historian Charles Beard argued, "until some formidable European power comes into the western Atlantic, breathing the fire of aggression and conquest. And this peril is slight at worst."[61] As for the nation's overseas economic interests, these were not sufficiently important to the nation as a whole to be worth the costs of a war. It followed that those economic activities that could involve the nation in a foreign conflict should be restricted, though as we shall see there were significant differences of opinion about exactly where the line in this regard needed to be drawn.

Isolationists did not repudiate the nation's historic mission to promote its ideals in the world. But they called for adherence to the traditional conception of this mission as essentially demonstrative—to provide mankind with the example of a successful polity based on the principles of freedom and self-government. In doing so, they argued that recent history had shown what was wrong about seeking to promote these values through an active exercise of power. In the first place, such an enterprise was doomed to failure because it overestimated America's capacity to re-shape other societies and reform practices that were deeply rooted in history. The turbulence and conflicts of the post–Versailles world showed how futile had been Wilson's ambition of establishing a new world order. Europe in particular was, in Beard's words, "encrusted in the blood-rust of fifty centuries." More broadly, Americans should recognize "that the United States, either alone or in coalition, did not possess the power to force peace on Europe and Asia, to assure the establishment of democratic and pacific governments there, or to provide the social and economic underwriting necessary to the perdurance of such governments."[62] The wartime experience had also confirmed for many the traditional republican belief that involvement in power politics was incompatible with the maintenance of a free society at home. This was common ground for people at both ends of the domestic political spectrum. Whereas liberals had been appalled by the suppression of civil liberties during the war and the subsequent Red Scare, anti-statist business conservatives wanted no repetition of the extension of government control over the economy and the sharp rise in taxes.

The structure of this position has been an element in American debate over foreign policy throughout the nation's history. It can be traced back not only to Washington's Farewell Address but also to John Quincy Adams's much-cited speech of July 4, 1821, opposing demands that the United States act in support of the Greeks then fighting against Ottoman rule, in which he declared that America was "the well-wisher to the freedom of all" but "the champion and vindicator only of her own."[63] It was widely accepted through the nineteenth century and strongly reaffirmed, as we have seen, by those most intransigently opposed to membership of the League of Nations in 1919–20. The case for it has also been restated by some commentators, and the occasional politician, in more recent decades, particularly during the Vietnam War and following the end of the Cold War.[64] But there is no doubt that the mid-1930s represented its twentieth-century apogee in terms of both its full articulation as a doctrine and its influence on U.S. policy.

However, it is much easier to characterize isolationism as a doctrine than to find consistent isolationists. Analysts of 1930s isolationism have seen it as composed of two conceptually distinct and not always easily compatible elements—unilateralism and pacifism. Unilateralism was the strand that could invoke Washington's authority. It could reasonably be presented as a basic feature of the nation's traditional approach to foreign policy, and strict adherence to it marked the "irreconcilable" opponents of the League of Nations. One of these, Senator William Borah, elaborated this position when he addressed the internationally inclined Council on Foreign Relations in January 1934:

> In matters of trade and commerce we have never been isolationists and never will be. In matters of finance, unfortunately, we have not been isolationist and never will be. When earthquake and famine, or whatever brings human suffering, visit any part of the human race, we have not been isolationists, and never will be. . . . But in all matters political, in all commitments of any nature or kind, which encroach in the slightest upon the free and unembarrassed action of our people, or which circumscribe their discretion and judgment, we have been free, we have been independent, we have been isolationist.

The other strand in 1930s isolationism was pacifism, the determination to avoid involvement in another war. This was a more novel element, the product of recent experience. Of course, a deep desire to avoid any repetition of the horrors of the Great War was felt also in other countries, particularly France and Britain, and by Americans who never endorsed isolationism. What distinguished the isolationist position was the belief that achieving this goal did not necessarily depend on there not being another major international war because, if one were to occur, the United States could still keep out of it at an acceptable cost.[65]

Even in the 1930s, endorsement of the full isolationist position was both limited in extent and fragile in nature. The different elements of the isolationist case enjoyed very different levels of support. Widely shared was the implicit confidence that the nation's security would not be endangered whatever the outcome of wars on other continents. As we have seen, this assumption had been challenged by some publicists early in the century and during World War I. But by the 1920s the challenge had faded, and the traditional view of the nation's security requirements had become firmly reestablished. The structure of the armed forces as well as their war planning reflected the premise that their mission was simply to protect the North American homeland and the country's overseas possessions. On the extent of the latter interest and the best means of defending it, the army and the navy tended to disagree, but as the historian Maurice Matloff points out, the war planning of both services was based on "the strategic concept . . . of defending against any foreign threat, the continental United States and its interests by the United States alone."[66] There was no perceptible anxiety among politicians or the general public about the nation's capacity to raise and equip the forces needed to achieve these objectives, notwithstanding the sharp disagreements over specific requirements that were particularly evident in debates over naval appropriations. Nor, in this era when the United States was itself by far the world's largest source of oil, did anyone argue that the country had overseas economic interests important enough to justify significant foreign policy commitments or the risk of involvement in war.

Indeed, there was general agreement, at least until the late 1930s, that avoiding involvement in a major overseas war should be the supreme goal of U.S. foreign policy, trumping all others. However, this goal did not necessarily lead to support for the isolationist position. As we have seen, it had been a central part of Wilson's case for participation in a league of nations that the only realistic way to ensure that the United States did not get caught up in a conflict like World War I was to prevent such wars occurring in the first place. In a sense, "never again" had been common ground in the debate over the League. The case for making the commitment set out in Article 10 of the Covenant was that it would make it much less likely that there would ever be another conflict like the one that had just ended; the case against was that the commitment would make it impossible to stay out of any such war.

Wilson and his supporters had lost the argument in 1919–20, and the issue of League membership had more or less disappeared from serious political debate soon after. But, as we have seen, neither the determination to avoid any risk of involvement in an overseas war nor the general acceptance of a narrow view of the nation's security requirements had prevented the United States from making efforts to promote world order during the 1920s. Cautiously and with great respect for the domestic political constraints, policymakers had sought to exercise influence abroad through diplomacy and the leverage provided by the nation's great financial and economic power. In practice, few Americans adhered to the strict isolationist position that the United States had no interest in political developments on other continents. Actions to affect such developments in ways favorable to American interests and values had enjoyed general support, provided they involved little cost and no risk of war. Moreover, many both at home and abroad argued that, given the scale of the nation's power, it had a responsibility to do more to promote international peace and world order. U.S. policy was thus balanced between conflicting pressures—those leading it to assume a larger role in world politics and those restraining it. In the early and middle 1930s, the restraining pressures grew stronger, but the impulses to action remained, if in weaker form, and they grew much stronger at the end of the decade.

Legislating Neutrality

Both the existence of conflicting pressures and the greater strength of the restraining ones were demonstrated in the process that led to what is usually seen as the most concrete manifestation of American isolationism in this period, the neutrality laws passed by Congress between 1935 and 1937. Just because access to America's enormous resources was a major source of power to other states in time of war, these laws had large international consequences, as foreign statesmen emphasized. Neville Chamberlain, for example, told Treasury Secretary Henry Morgenthau in March 1937 that "the greatest single contribution which the United States could make at the present moment to the preservation of world peace would be the amendment of the existing neutrality legislation." In constraining and reducing America's potential capacity to influence events overseas, the legislation represented a signal example of self-restraint in the exercise of power. It is also a striking case of a significant policy formulated more in Congress than by the executive branch. This has the advantage for the historian of giving greater transparency to the various considerations, interests, and prejudices whose complex interplay produced the outcome.[67]

Somewhat ironically, it was internationalists sympathetic to the League of Nations who had first proposed the abandonment or modification of the traditional policy of asserting the legal rights of neutral states and their citizens during war. They did so because they desired to prevent the United States from obstructing or deterring the League's imposition of economic sanctions under Article XVI on any state that resorted to war in violation of the Covenant. Accordingly, Representative Theodore E. Burton (R–Oh.), president of the American Peace Society, introduced a resolution in December 1927 to embargo the export of arms to a nation that resorted to war in violation of a treaty obligation to settle disputes by peaceful means. This was too close an identification with the League to win widespread support, with President Coolidge among those stressing the difficulty of clearly identifying an aggressor when conflicts broke out. Burton then amended his proposal to make the embargo apply to all belligerents upon the outbreak of war, but in this form it failed to overcome strong opposition from the munitions industry, the American Legion, and the War and Navy Departments.[68]

However, the Kellogg-Briand Pact of 1928 was seen by supporters of collective security as providing a new basis for the desired change in America's neutrality policy. In early 1929 a resolution was introduced by Senator Arthur Capper (R–Kans.) authorizing the President to embargo the export of arms to any nation violating the Kellogg pact. Over the next few years, this proposal in one form or another gained the support of most prominent internationalists, including

Henry Stimson and Franklin D. Roosevelt. In advocating the modification of the nation's traditional insistence on the rights of a neutral in time of conflict, Stimson, whose earliest political mentor had been Theodore Roosevelt, reiterated the argument that both TR and Wilson had made that the world had become too interconnected for non-involvement to be any longer a viable option: "The day is gone when the spread of a conflagration is easily confined to any continent or hemisphere." This, in Stimson's view, meant that the United States had a vital stake in forestalling war by upholding treaties such as the Nine-Power and Kellogg-Briand pacts. If the president received congressional authority to impose an arms embargo at his discretion, it would "give encouragement and momentum to the struggle for world peace and against the use of force."[69]

It was the Manchurian crisis that had led Stimson to reemphasize the argument that isolation was not a real option, and this was only the first example of the way in which the debate over neutrality was shaped by events overseas. As it became clear that Italy and Germany as well as Japan were ready to challenge the status quo by force, the question of what, if anything, the United States was prepared to do to maintain international order became inescapable in a way that it had not been in the relatively benign world environment of the 1920s. In the early 1930s, Stimson was by no means the only one who wanted the United States to act in a way that would help the League of Nations to be effective. His successor as secretary of state, Cordell Hull, also favored giving the president discretionary authority to impose an embargo on arms exports to particular countries. However, this approach failed to gain the requisite political and congressional support. There were two main objections to it. One was that it involved taking sides in European conflicts. The traditional aversion to doing this gained strength not only from a predisposition on the part of many, including some influential senators, against any policy that aligned the United States with the British Empire but also from a wider feeling that the Versailles settlement was both unjust and inherently unstable. (In the mid-1930s, this view was endorsed even by an Anglophile liberal like Walter Lippmann.) The second, and for most ordinary Americans the greater, objection to discretionary and potentially discriminatory trade restrictions was that they might lead to the country becoming involved in another war.[70]

Neither of these objections applied, however, to a mandatory embargo on all munitions exports to any country involved in a conflict. This proposal was energetically promoted by those in the peace movement who saw armaments and the arms trade as themselves a major cause of war. The active opposition of the munitions lobby to earlier proposals for a discriminatory embargo had fueled hostility to the "merchants of death," as they were described in journalistic exposés in 1934.[71] This agitation led the Senate to set up an investigation of the industry under Senator Gerald P. Nye (R–N.D.). As a newspaper editor, Nye had earlier supported the Non-Partisan League, a radical agrarian movement that strongly opposed intervention in World War I, and his committee's attention soon focused particularly on that period. Among the revelations of the hearings was that the profits of the DuPont corporation had increased by a factor of 160 between 1914 and 1916 and that in the latter year it paid dividends equal to the par value of its stock. The loans by J.P. Morgan & Co. that financed Allied purchases were also highlighted, which was particularly damaging politically at a time when the practices of Wall Street were widely held to have been responsible for the 1929 Crash and the subsequent depression. Committee members argued that the scale and one-sided nature of this trade was the basic cause of the German submarine campaign and hence of American involvement in the war. As Senator Homer T. Bone (D–Wash.) put it, "For the sake of profits, for dollars to protect the loans of certain commercial interests in this country, 50,000 boys now lie buried in France."[72]

The Italian attack on Ethiopia provided a quite different kind of impetus to the process of neutrality revision. Although this did not take place until October 1935, the situation had been very tense since a clash in December 1934 and was an important part of the context in which the first Neutrality Act was passed. The looming threat of war spurred both those who retained some faith in collective security and those who sought greater protection against the risk of involvement more urgently to seek some modification of the traditional policy. The former favored granting the president authority to impose a discriminatory arms embargo at his discretion, and this was the measure that the administration initially proposed. But the tide of opinion, even within peace organizations like the National Council for the Prevention of War, was against this, favoring instead an impartial, mandatory ban on all arms exports. Roosevelt quickly yielded and signed an act that imposed such a ban during foreign wars but also granted the president discretionary authority to implement other measures, including warning Americans against travel on ships belonging to belligerent nations. When Italy launched its full-scale invasion of Ethiopia, the administration immediately activated these provisions and also called for a "moral embargo" on all trade in contraband materials, including, importantly, oil. These measures, which were clearly discriminatory in practice (since Ethiopia owned no transatlantic liners and imported little from the United States), were designed to harmonize with any League of Nations sanctions, though the administration was careful to keep its distance from that organization's deliberations.[73]

The arms embargo provision of the 1935 act, passed hurriedly at the tail end of the congressional session, ran for only six months, so in 1936 there was need for a reconsideration of the whole question of neutrality policy. This led to an extensive congressional and public debate in the next year and a half over the provisions of a more permanent law. By this time, with the Spanish Civil War in progress and Hitler's Germany openly rearming, the prospect of another European war in the near future was evident. Polls also showed that an overwhelming majority of Americans felt that policy should be directed toward keeping the United States out of such a war rather than trying to prevent it.[74] They thus implicitly rejected the argument that the country had become too inextricably connected to the outside world to escape involvement in major conflicts. Rather than seeing World War I as proof of this proposition, they assumed that the country could have avoided participation at an acceptable cost.

Indeed, American intervention was looked back on with increasing disfavor as it became ever harder to argue that the outcome had justified the sacrifices. Public opinion polls in 1937 revealed that two-thirds of Americans had come to view entry into the war as a mistake, and few now argued the contrary.[75] Determining what it would take to keep the country out of such a war in the future naturally entailed consideration of the causes of U.S. intervention in 1917. The centrality of this historical question to immediate policy issues led to the publication of several articles and books on the subject, including a Book of the Month Club bestseller, Walter Millis's *Road to War* (1935). In addition to official records, such studies could draw on the many documents from the archives of corporations and banks brought to light by the hearings and reports of the Nye Committee.

The Nye Committee had concentrated its attention on the role of munitions manufacturers and bankers in causing the war trade with the Allies to grow so greatly. This focus was reflected in the Neutrality Act of 1936, which extended the mandatory arms embargo and other restrictions of the 1935 act and added to them a prohibition of loans to belligerent governments. However, historical accounts and the Nye Committee's own inquiry had made it clear that the economic factors that entangled the country in World War I went beyond the sale of munitions or the supposed stake in the Allies' success of those who had lent them money. It was pointed out that the great growth in exports had pulled the entire American economy out of a recession in 1914–15 and by 1916 had created a boom. Charles Beard and others cited letters from Secretary of the Treasury William G. McAdoo and Lansing to Wilson in 1915 to show that it was in order to protect the prosperity of the nation as a whole that the administration had permitted the extension of credits, and then loans, to the Allies. Recognition that the problem went beyond the profits and influence of special interests led Nye to conclude that "a complete embargo on all trade is the only absolute insurance against the United States being drawn into another prolonged major war between great powers."[76] The key strategic importance in the Ethiopian war of American oil exports to Italy (which tripled despite the administration's exhortations) further indicated the broader requirements of true non-involvement.

With the inclusion of an impartial arms embargo and ban on loans largely taken for granted by 1936, the debate over neutrality legislation came to focus on the form that further trade restrictions should take. On this issue, there was a wide spectrum of opinion. At one extreme was Charles Beard, who saw the search for export markets as at all times bound to lead to imperialism and war. Stressing the extent of the nation's economic self-sufficiency, he urged that even in peacetime foreign trade should be subject to government control and reduced to the level required to secure necessary raw materials and "foreign commodities of peculiar distinction." At the other extreme were those, like Senator Hiram Johnson (R–Calif.) and Edwin Borchard of the Yale Law School, who denied the need for any limitations on commerce apart from the arms embargo. They argued that American involvement in World War I had been the product not of the insistence on the nation's neutral rights vis-à-vis Germany but of the failure to uphold them in the face of Britain's violations of international law. Both of these positions reflected wider agendas and attitudes than a simple desire to protect the United States from involvement in a foreign war at an acceptable cost. Beard sought a fundamental change in the nation's economic system, "a direct antithesis of the historic policy which has eventuated in the present economic calamity" of the depression, and one that would produce a more equal distribution of wealth and income. An animus against the British Empire and the League of Nations underlay the arguments of Johnson and Borchard.[77]

Neither of these positions commanded majority support. Beard's, indeed, was an eccentric one in terms of mainstream opinion, notwithstanding his illusion in 1933–34 that the new Roosevelt administration shared his vision of a planned, self-contained economy.[78] Critics argued that, in stressing that less than 10 percent of American production was exported, Beard was "using statistics to obscure the realities." Walter Lippmann claimed that "to reduce American agriculture to a self-contained market would . . . call for reducing the productive acreage by 40,000,000 acres of average land or by 60–70,000,000 acres of poor land," and that in 1928 "two and a half million families were dependent upon industrial production for export."[79] Whatever the validity of such calculations at a time when the depression had reduced the proportion of American production exported to a historic low (around 3 percent), it was evident that the interests involved still had far too much political influence to be so completely overridden.[80] Indeed, some organizations and journals representing exporters vociferously opposed any restrictions on wartime trade, arguing that they would cause America to lose overseas markets in peacetime too as other countries switched to more secure sources of supply. Italian-Americans, indignant at the way the 1935 act had been employed during the Ethiopian war, were also vocal in support of traditional neutrality.[81]

Nevertheless, the perception that the upholding of neutral rights during World War I had attached the nation's prestige to interests that were not worth the cost of defending them had become widespread by this time, even among those who were by no means isolationists. Allen W. Dulles and the editor of *Foreign Affairs*, Hamilton Fish Armstrong, for example, warned that "no neutrality legislation can give us the advantages of an isolation which does not exist," but they agreed that "the treatment which our trade or even our citizens may receive from belligerents, even if lawless, is not in itself an adequate reason for the United States to abandon neutrality." They therefore approved of measures to "restrict the actions of our citizens in time of war, so that they do not unnecessarily engage the honor, prestige or interests of the nation as a whole." Against these arguments, the interests of exporters could not prevail, as even business journals recognized. "If we face the choice of profits or peace," Roosevelt roundly declared, "the Nation will answer—must answer—'we choose peace.'"[82]

Between the extreme positions, a consensus emerged that there should be a law that effectively guarded against a repeat of the World War I experience without causing unnecessary damage to the nation's economic interests. A variety of measures to secure this objective were considered. An absolute embargo on trade with belligerents was proposed but gained little support. The idea of imposing quotas limiting trade to peacetime levels arose during the Ethiopian war and briefly won the endorsement of the administration, but the practical difficulties of implementing it soon became apparent. The simplest approach was a declaration that all commerce with belligerents should be at the trader's own risk, but for many this did not go far enough. Bernard Baruch was the first to suggest that the risk of involvement through loans and maritime incidents could be eliminated by what he called "cash-and-carry"—"We will sell to any belligerent anything except lethal weapons, but the terms are '*cash on the barrel-head and come and get it.*'" The 1937 act, which made mandatory upon the outbreak of a foreign war the imposition of an arms embargo and the prohibition of loans and travel on belligerent ships, also included this cash-and-carry provision for designated goods other than arms, on a discretionary basis and for a two-year period.[83]

Cash-and-carry was widely seen as benefiting Britain and France in any conflict with the Axis Powers. This had been an attractive feature of the idea to many, including President Roosevelt. Conversely, the same perception inflamed attacks on the proposal by Senators Borah and Johnson, who denounced it as a cowardly and dishonorable scheme to gain the profits of trade without assuming the concomitant risks and dangers. "What sort of government is this and what sort of men are we," asked Johnson, "to accept a formula which will enable us to sell goods and then hide?" Borah also pointed out that in the Pacific cash-and-carry would operate to the advantage of Japan in any war with China. The upshot was that, somewhat paradoxically, two of the six Senate votes against what was the acme of the legislative measures to keep the United States out of a foreign war were cast by the Senators who had ever since their "irreconcilable" opposition to the League of Nations been seen as the prime spokesmen of isolationism.[84]

The Complexities of American Opinion

What can we discern from all this about the extent to which Americans in these years endorsed isolationism? In the first place, it needs to be stressed that support for the neutrality laws by no means always implied a readiness to give up, or even to reduce, American influence on international affairs. As we have seen, the earliest and some of the most consistent advocates of neutrality revision were people who wished to align U.S. policy with any action by the League of Nations. Beyond this, one did not have to be a committed isolationist to think that the defense of neutral rights had provided an unsatisfactory basis for U.S. policy during World War I—one that both represented an inadequate appraisal of the national interest and effectively passed the decision for war or peace to Germany.

This last view seems to have been shared by President Roosevelt himself. He said more than once in 1935 that he now believed that Bryan had been right twenty years earlier in opposing Wilson's stand on submarine warfare. Although some historians have taken this as showing that FDR "had concluded that intervention in the world war had been a mistake," this inference is unwarranted. The writings of men like Lippmann, Dulles, and Armstrong showed that it was quite possible to believe both that American intervention had been right and that the defense of neutral rights had provided an inadequate justification for it. Roosevelt clearly favored modification of the traditional interpretation of neutrality, and indeed it was he who had first suggested to Nye that his committee investigate this issue. But what he wanted was freedom from the obligation to base policy rigidly on the defense of legal rights; throughout the legislative process the administration sought to maximize presidential discretion to respond flexibly to the varying circumstances of particular cases. In other private statements at this time, FDR made it clear how far he was from sharing a truly isolationist perspective. Thus, in a letter to Colonel House in 1935, he condemned "the very large and perhaps increasing school of thought which holds that we can and should withdraw wholly within ourselves" and who "imagine that if the civilization of Europe is about to destroy itself through internal strife, it might just as well go ahead and do it and that the United States can stand idly by."[85]

Nevertheless, Roosevelt committed himself to the avoidance of war as his supreme foreign policy objective. "We are not isolationists," he declared in 1936, "except insofar as we seek to isolate ourselves completely from war." There is little question that most Americans agreed that this should be the dominant foreign policy objective. Few at this time challenged the assumption that the United States could stay out of conflicts in Europe or Asia because, whatever the outcome of such conflicts, America's truly vital interests would not be affected. Geography and the scale of American power would ensure the nation's security in any case, as Roosevelt himself implied when he declared, "Of all the Nations in the world today we are in many ways most singularly blessed. Our closest neighbors are good neighbors. If there are remoter Nations that wish us not good but ill, they know that we are strong; they know that we can and will defend ourselves and defend our neighborhood."[86]

Confidence that the nation's core interests could not be threatened from without led many to conclude that the danger of involvement in war came from within—from political leaders responsive to special interests, foreign influence, or simply a desire to pursue some ambitious foreign policy agenda. This lay behind the movement for a constitutional amendment requiring a national referendum before war was declared (except in case of invasion). A Gallup poll in October 1937 registered 73 percent approval of this proposal, and a bill to this effect, sponsored by Representative Louis Ludlow (D–Ind.), lost in the House of Representatives in January 1938 only by the narrow margin of 188 votes to 209.[87]

Although the simple division between an untrustworthy elite and a pacific populace posited by Ludlow and his supporters represented an inadequate and distorted view of American opinion, it is true that the degree of detachment from events overseas prescribed by isolationist doctrine was attained in practice by few politically aware citizens and by no policymakers. The belief that the United States had a serious interest in world order and a responsibility to do more to promote it persisted in informed circles. As before, this outlook was particularly well represented among the northeastern upper middle class. The Council on Foreign Relations and its journal *Foreign Affairs* made some effort to provide a forum for a variety of views, but the preponderant perspective was anti-isolationist. The same was true of most East Coast metropolitan newspapers and of officials in the State Department and Foreign Service. Even though the concern to ensure that the United States did not become involved in war increasingly took priority with the spokesmen of the organized peace movement, there also remained some support for the League of Nations and collective security within its ranks. Thus a writer in *Christian Century* argued in March 1937 that "we have a moral obligation to exert our influence to the limit in protection of peoples in danger; we have an ethical responsibility to help preserve the peace of the world."[88]

Beyond this, foreign conflicts stimulated a wider engagement with international affairs, and often a desire to influence their outcome. Many Americans emphatically took sides in the wars of the 1930s. Their feelings arose from ethnic ties, ideological commitments, moral judgments, or some combination of these. Thus, African-Americans felt strongly about Ethiopia, a country that held a special place in biblical lore and was one of the few in Africa that had not succumbed to European colonialism. After the Italian attack, they organized mass rallies, raised funds, boycotted Italian-American businesses, and even, in small numbers, volunteered to fight. By contrast, as we have seen, Italian-Americans generally backed Italy, while Mussolini's aggression was condemned in most other public comment, especially by those who favored the League of Nations. The Spanish Civil War that began in July 1936 aroused strong partisanship more widely, the American Catholic hierarchy vocally defending Franco's rebellion while liberals and the left passionately supported the Republican Loyalists, some hundreds going so far as to join the Abraham Lincoln Brigade (which suffered heavy casualties).

An obvious but significant fact about the mobilizations of opinion over these conflicts is that they were directed not simply to arousing sympathy and support for a foreign cause but also to affecting U.S. policy. With Ethiopia, the issue was whether more (or less) should be done to obstruct the Italian war effort. Over Spain, the controversy revolved around the policy of denying arms to both sides, which was instituted as a moral embargo at the start of the conflict and enforced by act of Congress in January 1937. As it became clear that this policy, upheld by Britain and France but flagrantly disregarded by Italy and Germany, was aiding Franco, demands grew for its repeal. The difficulty all Americans had in adhering to strict isolationism was illustrated when Senator Nye himself proposed that the export of arms (on a cash-and-carry basis) be permitted to the Loyalists but not the rebels. Underlying all these arguments was the assumption that the terms of access to America's resources would have a crucial effect on the outcome of overseas wars. Rather than underestimating the nation's potential power, many were inclined to exaggerate it. Thus, in proposing the ban on loans in 1936, Representative Frank Kloeb argued that governments would hesitate to engage in war if they knew beforehand that American financial resources would be closed to them.[89]

Insofar as the differences of opinion over the Ethiopian and Spanish wars reflected ethnic loyalties or religious ties, they illustrated the potential threat that foreign conflicts could pose to the domestic harmony of a society with diverse national origins. For Wilson in 1914, as we have seen, this had been a powerful reason for the United States to adopt a strictly neutral stance toward the European war and for Americans to strive to be "impartial in thought as well as in action." In 1937, Walter Lippmann saw it as still explaining the particular determination to avoid entanglement in European affairs. "Because political action in Europe divides the nation at home, the instinctive feeling of almost all Americans is to keep Europe at arm's length," he wrote. "What they really fear is not the costs of intervention in the quarrels of Europe but the intrusion of European quarrels into American affairs." By contrast, Lippmann observed, "we can confront the Asiatic peoples and the Latin Americans with a secure sense of national unity."[90]

Certainly, there was a more united reaction to the Sino-Japanese war that began in July 1937. From the beginning of the conflict, polls showed that those with an opinion overwhelmingly favored China, and this sentiment widened and deepened as Americans were shocked by the ferocious nature of the Japanese attack in the Yangtze valley and the Rape of Nanjing. Taking advantage of the fact that war had not been formally declared, the president did not invoke the Neutrality Act but simply warned that Americans shipping arms to the belligerents did so at their own risk. Not only did China have greater need of foreign arms than Japan, but cash-and-carry, in Roosevelt's words, worked "all wrong in the Pacific," where Japan possessed both greater financial resources and command of the sea. As the conflict developed into full-scale war, there were vocal demands for the invocation of the Neutrality Act, but those making them felt it necessary to argue that doing this would hurt Japan as much as China, and the administration's line retained broad public approval. The policy involved no significant cost or risk of involvement in war, but still the response to the fighting in China showed that the Achilles heel of isolationism was the difficulty Americans had in retaining a strictly impartial attitude to foreign conflicts or viewing them as morally neutral. The strong partisan emotions such conflicts could arouse represented a potential Trojan horse within "Fortress America."[91]

FDR's Approach

President Roosevelt took this opportunity openly to challenge the premises of isolationism. In fact, he had always done so implicitly, as when, in signing the 1935 Neutrality Act, he had observed that the mandatory arms embargo "might drag us into war instead of keeping us out."[92] In October 1937, in a speech in the isolationist stronghold of Chicago, he more strongly emphasized that "we cannot insure ourselves against the disastrous effects of war and the dangers of involvement" because "there is a solidarity and interdependence about the modern world, both technically and morally, which makes it impossible for any nation completely to isolate itself from economic and political upheavals in the rest of the world." Making clear though not explicit references to the Japanese attack on China and foreign states' involvement in the Spanish Civil War, he spoke of the "vast numbers of women and children" who were "being ruthlessly murdered with bombs from the air," and quoted a prophecy that the spread of such violence across the world would endanger the whole fabric of civilization—"every book and picture and harmony, every treasure garnered through two millenniums." Observing that "the overwhelming majority of the peoples and nations of the world today want to live in peace," he declared that "the peace-loving nations must make a concerted effort in opposition to those violations of treaties and those ignorings of humane instincts which today are creating a state of international anarchy and instability from which there is no escape through mere isolation or neutrality." Above all, "the will for peace on the part of peace-loving nations must express itself to the end that nations that may be tempted to violate their agreements and the rights of others will desist from such a course." The president gave no indication as to how this was to be done, apart from a vague reference to the use of a quarantine to protect the health of a community against an epidemic of physical disease. But he emphasized that it was "a matter of vital interest and concern to the people of the United States that the sanctity of international treaties and the maintenance of international morality be restored."[93]

The speech was an unequivocal rejection of the isolationist argument that, however conflict-ridden the outside world became, the United States could avoid involvement in war through unilateral measures of self-restraint. "I verily believe," Roosevelt wrote shortly afterwards to Colonel House, "that as time goes on we can slowly but surely make people realize that war will be a greater danger to us if we close all the doors and windows than if we go out in the street and use our influence to curb the riot."[94] FDR's choice of correspondent was appropriate because he was essentially reiterating Wilson's argument that the United States had a vital interest in the existence of a world governed by law and international norms rather than by the unrestrained operation of power politics.

In fact, Roosevelt had never really strayed from the Wilsonian vision of world order. When, as a candidate for the presidency in 1932, he stated that he no longer favored League membership, it had been on the grounds that "the League of Nations today is not the League conceived by Woodrow Wilson." It had become "a mere meeting place for the political discussion of strictly European national difficulties," and its "principal members" had shown no disposition to reduce expenditures on armaments; joining it "would not serve the highest purpose of the prevention of war and a settlement of international difficulties in accordance with fundamental American ideals." In his first year in the White House, speaking at the Woodrow Wilson Foundation, Roosevelt described the League more kindly as "a prop in the world peace structure" but still shifted the focus to other aspects of Wilson's program, particularly disarmament.[95]

These specific invocations of Wilson's League and legacy each had a political purpose—in the first case, to check the campaign against FDR's nomination by the fiercely anti-League William Randolph Hearst, and in the second to reassure the Wilsonian faithful that he had not betrayed them. However, a liberal, law-governed world order, in which nations shunned armed conflict and international commerce flourished, remained the basic foreign policy goal of the Roosevelt administration, just as it had been for the Republican policymakers of the 1920s. Initially, this goal was completely subordinated to the overriding objective of lifting America out of the catastrophic depression, as Roosevelt's torpedoing of the London economic conference in 1933 dramatically demonstrated. But after the passage of the Reciprocal Trade Agreements Act in 1934, Cordell Hull, who was particularly committed to the economic aspect of the Wilsonian program, energetically sought to reduce tariff barriers generally through extension of the most-favored nation principle. Roosevelt may have been more concerned with using the act to expand U.S. exports through bilateral agreements, but when in the mid-1930s he sought to refocus the nation's attention on the darkening world scene, he did so in Wilsonian terms. Not only did he describe the objective as the "observance of international treaties and law," "liberal trade policies," and the limitation of armaments, he also stressed that "peace is jeopardized by the few and not the many." It was clear, he stated in January 1936, "that autocracy in world affairs endangers peace and that such threats do not spring from those Nations devoted to the democratic ideal." A year later, he observed that "in oligarchies, militarism has leapt forward, while in those Nations which have retained democracy, militarism has waned."[96]

As the basis for active American participation in world politics, the Wilsonian approach had problems both internally and externally. With regard to domestic opinion, it suffered from the disillusionment with the results of American intervention in World War I. In retrospect, Wilson's aspirations were widely viewed as unrealistic; he had underestimated how difficult it was to induce other countries to change the ways they governed themselves and conducted foreign policy. The United States lacked the capacity to do so. It also lacked sufficient motivation. The goal of a new world order was not only excessively ambitious; it was also insufficiently imperative to justify actions that involved significant cost or risk. The whole nature of U.S. policy since the League debate had demonstrated that, and it was confirmed when Roosevelt quickly indicated that his reference to "quarantine" had not implied an immediate readiness to join in imposing collective sanctions on the states whose behavior he had criticized in such emphatic terms. His caution in this respect was of a piece with the administration's consistent refusal to become actively involved in the East Asian situation, whether through cooperation with the League powers, unilateral measures, or even acceptance of a Chinese invitation to mediate the conflict. Stanley K. Hornbeck, the long-serving and influential chief of the Far Eastern Division of the State Department, provided an explanation of this stance when he observed in 1933 that "the United States has not much to lose" from Japanese aggression in China: "The principles of our Far Eastern policy and our ideals with regard to world peace may be further scratched and dented . . . and our trade prospects may be somewhat further impaired; but from the point of view of material interests there is nothing there that is vital to us."[97]

The resulting combination of a commitment to exacting standards of international behavior and unwillingness to take any action that could conceivably risk war made it difficult to establish the cooperation with other "peace-loving nations" that Roosevelt had spoken of. The key relationship here was with Great Britain, with which Roosevelt and his aides developed a much closer connection in private than they ever admitted to publicly. But the perspective of an empire with very tangible worldwide interests and highly conscious of limited resources was, not surprisingly, very different from that of a nation as self-sufficient, powerful, and secure as the United States. The Realpolitik calculations and compromises that British statesmen felt obliged to make were seen by Americans at all levels as demonstrating Old World cynicism and lack of moral fiber. An early example of this was the abortive Hoare-Laval pact of 1935 to grant Italy a substantial part of Ethiopia in order to end the war there and hopefully realign Mussolini with Britain and France against Germany. Perceived as a clear betrayal of the League of Nations, which had condemned Italian aggression, this plan proved unacceptable to British public opinion in the event, but Roosevelt nonetheless saw it as an "outrageous proceeding" that would confirm American suspicion of European diplomacy. Following the ineffectual response to Manchuria, it caused him to abandon the aspiration to make it possible for the United States to cooperate with sanctions imposed by the League.

The president still hoped, however, to find some basis for action on the international front that would be acceptable to American opinion. This lay behind the proposal he advanced in various forms between 1936 and 1938 for an international conference to set out the fundamentals of world peace, including reduction of armaments and equality of economic opportunity for all peoples. He apparently believed that this initiative would both develop domestic support for cooperation with states that endorsed American principles and help to reduce tensions in Europe. In January 1938, Roosevelt privately suggested to the British government that he call such a conference, but he received a discouraging reply. His approach cut across Prime Minister Neville Chamberlain's plan to avert war by reaching separate agreements with Britain's potential antagonists. Like other British statesmen of his generation, Chamberlain had painful memories of how vain had been the effort in 1919 to gain the support of American power by going along with a universal, principled, approach to international peace.[98] The lesson he had drawn from this and later experience was, as he wrote to his sister, that "it is always best and safest to count on *nothing* from the Americans except words."[99]

This remark did, indeed, express Chamberlain's general view but, ironically, it was made on an occasion when he hoped that the Americans would do more. This was in December 1937 after a naval gunboat, USS *Panay*, had been sunk on the Yangtze by Japanese warplanes. Two people aboard had been killed and some thirty wounded. Although the preponderant public reaction indicated that fear of involvement in war was now stronger than the desire to retaliate against a deliberate attack, Roosevelt told the cabinet that he wanted to do something to control Japan. He spoke of means short of war, such as economic sanctions and the possibility of an Anglo-American naval blockade running from the Aleutians to Singapore. In the end, the upshot was no more than private presidential assurances to the British ambassador and informal, noncommittal talks in London between naval staff officers. But, as the leading student of Anglo-American relations in these years puts it, these showed that Roosevelt "was inclined increasingly towards carefully defined co-operation with the British."[100]

The practice of the Roosevelt administration, then, was hardly in accordance with Borah's ideal of unilateral independence, let alone the complete detachment from extra-continental politics advocated by Beard. Indeed, it would seem that U.S. foreign policy in the 1930s was less different from that of the 1920s than is often suggested. In both decades, American statesmen sought a peaceful and liberal world order; in neither were they prepared to undertake actions or commitments that involved significant cost or any risk of war. It is true that U.S. diplomacy in the 1920s could boast more significant accomplishments—the Washington treaties, the Dawes Plan, even the Kellogg-Briand pact. But we need to take account of the context. The external environment was much more amenable to the American program in the 1920s than in the 1930s, especially with respect to the governments of Japan and Germany. The basic parameters of U.S. policy remained the same, and if there was some diminution in the energy put into positive initiatives, this trend had been discernible since the mid-1920s.[101]

Both the degree of continuity between administrations of different parties and the ways in which American attitudes were affected by changes in the world environment throw light on the basic factors shaping U.S. foreign policy. Throughout the period from 1921 to 1937 there was no foreign policy objective for which the United States was prepared to deploy anything like its full potential power in international affairs. The scope of American hegemony remained limited to the Caribbean and Central America, where it was uncontested by other powers. Insofar as there were internally generated pressures to influence political developments on other continents, these were weak and diffuse. Those who traded or invested abroad rarely sought official backing, and they could not rely on receiving it when they did. Sympathy for embattled countries or causes overseas led some to urge that American power be brought to bear on their behalf, but on no occasion did such advocates gain enough adherents to produce significant action. More broadly, it was generally accepted that a peaceful, law-governed world was desirable, but successive presidents judged that strenuous actions to promote this goal would not secure the necessary political support. This was partly because the consensus on general principles often broke down when it came to applying these in particular circumstances. The sharp differences over cooperation with the League of Nations or the justice of the status quo in Europe illustrated this. The chief reason, though, was that the nation's interest in building such a world order was not seen by the majority of Americans as sufficiently great to justify actions entailing substantial costs or the risk of war.

There were in principle two different reasons for taking this view. One was that the nation's core interests were not seriously dependent on the nature of the world environment. The other was that that environment was already sufficiently accommodating to American interests for no positive action to be required. As the darkening international scene from the mid-1930s made it progressively more difficult to sustain the latter view, the significance of this distinction emerged. Those who responded by redoubling their efforts to keep the United States out of any foreign war were driven to articulate and defend the first position. But those who felt that, in one way or another, the nature of the world beyond its borders was of great importance to the United States were led to challenge such "isolationism."

4

LESSENING RESTRAINT, 1938–1941

Between the fall of 1938 and December 1941, the restraints on the exercise of America's potential influence in world politics were enormously weakened. The United States adopted policies that made serious demands on the nation's financial and productive resources and that carried a high risk of involvement in a world war. President Franklin Roosevelt took the lead in this process and in doing so stressed the vital nature of the nation's interest in political developments on other continents. By 1941, the administration had implicitly committed itself to the defeat of Germany. This position had gained sufficient domestic support to sustain a course of action that has fairly been described as a form of "undeclared war," but the United States did not take the further step to full-scale belligerency until the direct Japanese attack on America's own territory and armed forces at Pearl Harbor.[1]

The impetus for this move away from anything that could be called "isolationism" clearly came from the course of events abroad. Hitler had broken the terms of the Versailles treaty by his military occupation of the Rhineland in 1936 and incorporation of Austria into the Reich two years later, but it was his demand for the cession of Czechoslovakia's Sudetenland in September 1938 that brought Europe to the brink of another full-scale war, an outcome only precariously and controversially averted by the Munich agreement. 1939 saw the German takeover of the rest of Czechoslovakia in March, the Nazi-Soviet pact in August, and the declaration of war on Germany by Britain and France in September in response to Hitler's attack on Poland. More dramatic still was the German blitzkrieg in the

spring and early summer of 1940. After Denmark, Norway, and the Low Countries had been overrun, France fell in late June, raising the real possibility—never
seriously envisaged in 1917—that Britain too would be defeated, leaving Nazi
Germany in control of the whole of western and central Europe. Japan took
advantage of the consequent weakness of the European imperial powers to push
into French Indochina and threaten the British and Dutch colonies in Southeast
Asia and the East Indies. The initial success of Hitler's attack on the Soviet Union
in June 1941 raised the prospect of the whole Eurasian continent coming under
the domination of the Axis Powers.

Why did these external developments so weaken the potent constraints on
American involvement in foreign wars? The answer to this question is often
seen as entirely unproblematic. According to a commonly stated view, it was
because a victory for the Axis Powers was perceived as posing a grave threat
to the most vital national interest of homeland security that the United States
took action to prevent such an outcome. "The great body of Americans came
to understand that their most fundamental interest, national self-preservation,
was at stake in the course of world politics," Robert Osgood writes. "It was
national self-interest in its lowest common denominator, self-preservation,
that brought the nation to the point of wanting an Allied victory more than
it feared involvement in war." Melvyn Leffler sees policy as driven by the conviction that "the physical safety of the United States required that Hitler be
defeated before he had the capacity to assimilate the resources of Europe,
acquire bases in Northwest Africa, take over the British fleet, or gain sustained
access to the petroleum of the Caucasus and the Near East or the breadbasket of
the Ukraine." For Realist political scientists, this was an occasion on which "systemic pressures" effectively determined policy; Roosevelt "felt that the United
States had no choice but to intervene as a balancer of last resort to forestall the
Nazi threat to the Western Hemisphere."[2]

Public statements of administration officials at the time lend support to
this view. For example, in a Fireside Chat in December 1940, Roosevelt warned
that "if Great Britain goes down, the Axis powers will control the continents of
Europe, Asia, Africa, Australasia, and the high seas—and they will be in a position to bring enormous military and naval resources against this hemisphere." In
another radio talk in September 1941, the president amplified the point:

> If the world outside of the Americas falls under Axis domination, the
> shipbuilding facilities which the Axis powers would then possess in
> all of Europe, in the British Isles, and in the Far East would be much
> greater than all the shipbuilding facilities and potentialities of all the
> Americas—not only greater, but two or three times greater—enough to

win. Even if the United States threw all its resources into such a situation, seeking to double and even redouble the size of our Navy, the Axis powers, in control of the rest of the world, would have the manpower and the physical resources to outbuild us several times over.

Nor was it only a matter of capabilities; the intentions of the Axis Powers, too, could hardly have been more threatening: "The Nazi masters of Germany have made it clear that they intend not only to dominate all life and thought in their own country, but also to enslave the whole of Europe, and then to use the resources of Europe to dominate the rest of the world." If they won control of the seas, "the way can obviously become clear for their next step—domination of the United States—domination of the Western Hemisphere by force of arms."[3]

Yet in the context in which these speeches were given, there was a striking disjunction between Roosevelt's portrayal of the threat and the actions that he advocated and took. In December 1940, Britain and her dominions were fighting a lonely war, with no ally save an embattled Greece (which had been attacked by Italy two months earlier). Although the Battle of Britain in the late summer of 1940 had averted the immediate danger of a cross-Channel invasion, a thorough assessment by the U.S. Chief of Naval Operations in November concluded not only that "the British Empire lacks the manpower and the material means to master Germany" but also that "it is not at all sure that the British Isles can hold out." Yet, in his broadcast, Roosevelt emphasized that "our national policy is not directed toward war" and that his audience could "nail any talk about sending armies to Europe as deliberate untruth."[4] Britain's position deteriorated further in the early months of 1941, with military defeats in Greece, North Africa, and Crete and, most worrying of all, heavy shipping losses to the U-boat campaign. Prime Minister Winston Churchill, whose whole strategy rested on eventual U.S. entry into the war, feared in May that "we are being left to our fate."[5] The German attack on Russia in June took the immediate pressure off Britain, but the rapid eastward advance of the Wehrmacht's divisions suggested that Hitler might soon gain another, even larger, conquest. American military planners concluded unequivocally in early September that "if our European enemies are to be defeated, it will be necessary for the United States to enter the war, and to employ a part of its armed forces offensively in the Eastern Atlantic and in Europe or Africa."[6] But the only move that Roosevelt made at this time, even as he asserted that an Axis victory would place the United States in mortal danger, was one that he had been hesitating over for months—instituting U.S. naval escorts for merchant shipping convoys in the western Atlantic.

It took the Japanese attack on Hawaii in December to bring the United States into the war as a full-scale belligerent. By then, it could well be argued that it was evident that Hitler's attempt to overcome Russia had not succeeded and thus that there was no longer any real possibility of his being able to bring the resources of a conquered continent to bear upon the United States.[7] Whatever danger of this there had been, it had been averted before the United States had made more than a marginal contribution to the fight against the Axis Powers. (A mere 1 percent of the munitions used by Britain, the Commonwealth and Empire in 1941 were provided under Lend-Lease.)[8] In a paradoxical way, the thesis that the United States was impelled into action by the perception of a clear threat to its very survival constitutes *too strong* an explanation to account for the actual course of American policy in 1940–41.

The most obvious reason for the gap between what the American military advised was necessary if Hitler was to be defeated and what was actually done is the state of public and congressional opinion. Of course, the administration was not the passive servant of such opinion. Roosevelt had firm ideas of his own about what the nation's policy should be, and he took full advantage of the president's unique ability to influence public attitudes. Moreover, he was quite ready to do things that were concealed from (or occasionally misrepresented to) the public when he felt that the national interest demanded it. As we have seen, relations with the British had long been closer in private than was acknowledged in public, and from 1940 they developed into what was aptly described by Robert Sherwood as a "common-law alliance." The informal contacts between the armed forces that been initiated in 1938 culminated in secret staff talks in Washington in the spring of 1941 in which a joint strategy was worked out for a war that the United States was not officially fighting.[9]

Nevertheless, the president was clearly both conscious of the limited extent to which he could shape opinion and extremely concerned to secure public and political backing for any major steps he took. When working on his speeches, Sherwood reports, FDR "would look up at the portrait of Woodrow Wilson over the mantelpiece. The tragedy of Wilson was always somewhere within the rim of his consciousness. . . . There was no motivating force in all of Roosevelt's wartime political policy stronger than the determination to prevent repetition of the same mistakes."[10] The most obvious of these mistakes was Wilson's commitment of the nation to a policy that it was not, in the end, willing to support. Like Wilson in 1918–20, Roosevelt faced an articulate opposition to his foreign policy both in Congress and in the arena of public opinion. Indeed, these years witnessed perhaps the most intensive debate over American policy and strategy in the nation's history. The president's portrayals of the threat that an Axis victory would pose to the United States, and his arguments about the best way to counter it, were part of that debate, and they were vigorously disputed by many. Roosevelt closely monitored the effect of this debate on public attitudes, taking much account of the White House mail after his broadcasts and also, after the summer of 1940, receiving poll data direct from (and also suggesting questions to) Hadley Cantril, head of the Office of Public Opinion Research at Princeton University.[11]

Although, as we shall see, the poll data from this period reveals some complexities, the broad picture is clear. The basic shape of the course that the United States followed accorded with the wishes of the majority of the American people. They supported aid to the countries fighting the Axis, and from the summer of 1940 an increasing number saw this as more important than keeping out of war. On the other hand, only a minority favored doing more than this. The proportion of Americans favoring direct entry into the war fluctuated between 15 and 20 percent through the latter part of 1940, rose to over 20 percent in the summer of 1941 (with a high of 24 percent in June), but fell back to 17 percent in late October 1941.[12]

Explaining the behavior of the United States as a nation-state in this period thus requires an assessment of the factors shaping public opinion as well as an examination of the concerns and calculations of policymakers. A constant in the attitudes of most Americans was the strong desire not to be involved in another foreign war, together with a belief that defending the American homeland itself from attack was the overriding national interest and, for many, the only justification for the costs and sacrifices of a major war. Advocates of a more active involvement in overseas conflicts generally recognized these features of public opinion, which gave them a strong incentive to argue their case in terms of national security. They began doing this before the European war broke out, at a time when the prospect of an Axis-dominated Europe seemed very remote to most observers, including the nation's military leaders and, it would seem, even FDR himself. The shock of Hitler's victories in the early summer of 1940, particularly the fall of France, immediately gave rise to fears that the Western Hemisphere itself might be attacked. This produced a national consensus in favor of a defense build-up, but the provision of aid to the nations still fighting the Axis Powers remained more controversial. Actions to assist Britain, in particular, did come to enjoy majority support over the next eighteen months, but the evidence suggests that the reasons for this were complex. That it cannot be accounted for simply by fears for America's own physical safety is suggested both by the way the debate developed and the nature of the division over the issue. Nor does concern with the economic interests of either the nation as a whole or sections within it provide a sufficient explanation. Those who favored strong action against the Axis Powers even at the risk of war were motivated by a complex variety of emotions and considerations. Security and economic anxieties undoubtedly played a part, but so did moral and ideological convictions, identification with Britain, and a concern with the future status and influence of the United States in world affairs.

What gave all these impulses and anxieties much greater force after the fall of France was the realization that only if the United States threw its weight into the scales could Hitler be defeated. Recognition of the potentialities of the nation's great power gave many a sense of grave responsibility, and it also imbued Americans generally, including policymakers, with an underlying confidence that the nation could prevail in international conflicts—provided it was prepared to make the necessary effort.

The Erosion of Neutrality

As we have seen, there was more than one reason why in the interwar period the United States did not play a role in world politics commensurate with its potential power. The most fundamental were the determination to avoid all possibility of involvement in a foreign war and the general reluctance to pay any sort of cost for the achievement of foreign policy objectives. But in addition there was uncertainty and division over what the policy objectives should be. The broad goal of a peaceful, law-governed world order was uncontentious, but there was less agreement or clarity, even among those who would have liked the United States to do more, about how this could best be promoted. At least since the days of Theodore Roosevelt, most of those who wanted the United States to play a larger role on the world stage had envisaged doing so in cooperation with Britain, and World War I had seen Americans fighting side by side with the British and the French. But the partnership, never complete, had not survived the Paris Peace Conference. Many informed Americans doubted the legitimacy and viability of the Versailles settlement and remained distrustful of what they saw as the narrowly nationalist or imperialist character of French and British policy. Senior figures in the State Department, such as Sumner Welles, were among those who believed that the key to world peace and stability was that all nations should have open and equal access to raw materials and other resources and that the United States should press for this independently while remaining detached from the political conflicts of the European powers.[13]

In the late 1930s this ambivalence and uncertainty gradually dissipated as both U.S. policy and majority public opinion firmly sided with the western democracies against the Axis Powers. This was a reaction to the actions of Nazi Germany, at home as well as abroad. The American press had reported on Nazi mistreatment of the Jews since the regime came to power in 1933, and there had been a move to boycott the 1936 Olympic Games in Berlin. But the atrocities of Kristallnacht in November 1938 provoked a new level of outrage. "I myself could scarcely believe that such things could occur in a twentieth-century civilization," observed Roosevelt. The American ambassador to Berlin was recalled for "consultations" and never returned to his post. Roosevelt had already been appalled by Hitler's behavior during the Czech crisis in September.[14] The impact of Munich and Kristallnacht on American public opinion is evident in the polls conducted by Gallup and *Fortune* magazine. While 62 percent of Americans were neutral toward Germany in October 1937, by November 1938 a majority (61 percent) said that they would support a movement to stop buying German goods, and in the following February 69 percent favored extending all aid short of war to England and France if they became involved in a conflict with the Axis Powers.[15]

The change of attitude found reflection in American policy. Roosevelt's earlier attitude to appeasement has been variously interpreted by historians, but it seems clear that he had hoped that peace might be preserved in Europe through diplomacy, even if he was more equivocal and reserved about Neville Chamberlain's attempt to conciliate the dictators through specific concessions than about the open and general international agreements advocated by Sumner Welles. In the aftermath of the Munich settlement, he evidently concluded that Hitler was a "wild man" whose word could not be trusted and whose limitless ambitions could only be checked by being firmly resisted by superior power. He now sought to encourage and assist Britain and France to take a stronger line, though initially more in private than in public. Persuaded by a number of reports that it was their inferiority to Germany in air power that had led the western democracies to back down in the Czech crisis, Roosevelt began in October 1938 to make strenuous efforts to increase U.S. aircraft production massively, calling initially for the establishment of eight new government-owned plants and a target of fifteen thousand planes a year. In the same month, he approved a French mission to the United States to discuss purchases of American planes and their possible assembly in Canada where the neutrality law would not apply in wartime. He also sent a private message to the British prime minister through an intermediary that, insofar as the president was able to achieve it, he would have "the industrial resources of the American nation behind him in the event of war with the dictatorships." In March 1939, at the administration's urging, a bill was introduced in the Senate to amend the neutrality law by repealing the arms embargo in a time of war and placing all trade with belligerents on a cash-and-carry basis (which would, of course, favor the Atlantic powers in any European conflict).[16]

What caused this change of policy? The most common explanation is that Roosevelt had become convinced that, if left unchecked, Hitler's Germany would pose a direct threat to the physical security of the United States itself. This interpretation may partly reflect a tendency to attribute all significant steps in foreign policy to the needs of national security, but it also finds support in some of the president's own statements and actions. At a meeting with his civilian and military defense chiefs on November 14, 1938, Roosevelt stated that "for the first time since the Holy Alliance in 1818 the United States now faced the possibility of an attack on the Atlantic side in both the Northern and Southern Hemispheres." In a press conference the following day, the president claimed that "any possible attack has been brought infinitely closer than it was five years or twenty years or fifty years ago," arguing that "one of the reasons is the development in aircraft." He also talked of the vulnerability of Latin American countries to subversion and of the narrowness of the Atlantic between west Africa and the bulge of Brazil.[17]

However, there are problems with this explanation of the change in U.S. policy after Munich. One is the weakness of the link between Munich and any enhanced threat to the United States, and a second is the nature of the measures Roosevelt wanted to take. Leaving aside the practical difficulties of a transatlantic attack, it was obvious that Germany would be unable to engage in any such enterprise without defeating France and Britain first. But the president's private comments at the time indicate that he did not anticipate such an eventuality. During the crisis, he had talked about the strategy that Britain and France should follow in a war with Germany in a manner that displayed confidence that they would prevail. The Munich agreement had not significantly altered the material balance of power, and Roosevelt still seems to have seen the western democracies as essentially stronger than the Axis Powers. The measures he took were designed to strengthen their will at least as much as their air forces. "What the British need today," he wrote in February 1939, "is a good stiff grog, inducing not only the desire to save civilization but the continued belief that they can do it."[18]

It was not the probable outcome of a European war that Munich had cast in a new light but rather Hitler's refusal to respect basic international norms. As the president explained to a radio audience at the time, good relations among nations required "certain fundamental reciprocal obligations" and "a deliberate and conscious will that such political changes as changing needs require shall be made peacefully." From the Führer's behavior during the Czech crisis, Roosevelt had drawn the conclusion that the Nazi regime was too insatiably aggressive and untrustworthy ever to be incorporated into a stable, norm-governed European order. It was because he believed that such an order was important to the United States, rather than because he feared for the physical safety of North America, that he strove energetically to deploy American power in support of the effort to contain and resist Germany.[19]

Confirmation of this is provided by the action Roosevelt sought to take. Shortly after Munich, he said that he would request a substantial increase in defense spending. In an interview, he indicated that this was for the purpose of home defense, but the program he set forth belied this.[20] The only measure that he showed any real interest in was an enormous increase in American aircraft production. This led to a sharp confrontation with the nation's military chiefs, who wanted a balanced build-up of defense capabilities. "What are we going to do with fifteen thousand planes?" the Army Chief of Staff, General Malin Craig, asked. "Who you going to fight, what you going to do with them, with three thousand miles of ocean?" As the service participants at the conference on November 14 came to recognize, the answer was implicit in the president's failure to propose a training program for pilots or ground crew. In the words of the Official History, "the airplanes were, in his mind, principally destined not for the U.S. Army Air Corps but for direct purchase by the air forces of Great Britain and France." As Roosevelt put it, "When I write to foreign countries I must have something to back up my words. Had we this summer 5,000 planes and the capacity immediately to produce 10,000 per year, even though I might have had to ask Congress for authority to sell or lend them to the countries in Europe, Hitler would not have dared to take the stand he did."[21] "New barracks in Wyoming" would not have the same effect. The president followed up by insisting, over the strong objections of the Chief of the Air Corps, that the French mission be allowed to inspect and purchase the latest types of American aircraft, including the Douglas DB-7 bomber.[22]

This permission was intended to be kept secret, but in his State of the Union Address in January 1939, Roosevelt openly made a general case for adopting "methods short of war, but stronger and more effective than mere words, of bringing home to aggressor governments the aggregate sentiments of our own people." He did so on grounds much broader than the requirements of self-defense: "There comes a time in the affairs of men, when they must prepare to defend, not their homes alone, but the tenets of faith and humanity on which their churches, their governments and their very civilization are founded. The defense of religion, of democracy and of good faith among nations is all the same fight. To save one we must now make up our minds to save all."[23] In stressing that American values were at stake, and the importance of a norm-governed international order, Roosevelt was essentially reviving Wilson's arguments for involvement in European conflicts.

However, later in the month, Roosevelt again justified his policy in terms of self-defense. This was after the crash of a Douglas bomber with a French official on board had revealed that a foreign country had been granted access to America's most advanced military technology, and the chief of the Air Staff had told the Senate Military Affairs Committee that this was "at the direction of the Treasury Department." To explain why this was so, FDR invited members of the Committee to the White House for a confidential meeting. "What is the first line of defense in the United States?" he began by asking. For the Pacific, he described that first line of defense as "a series of islands, with the hope that through the

Navy and the Army and the airplanes we can keep the Japanese—let us be quite frank—from dominating the entire Pacific Ocean and prevent us from having access to the west coast of South America." On the Atlantic side, America's first line of defense was "the continued independent existence of a very large group of nations." This was threatened by the Axis Powers, who were seeking "world domination" and would move on Africa and the Western Hemisphere if they conquered Europe. Therefore, "the foreign policy of the United States" was to do everything possible "to maintain the independence of these other nations by sending them all they can pay for on the barrelhead, to these about forty or fifty now independent nations of the world." He named twenty such nations, mostly small states in Europe. By including countries like Latvia and Greece in "the first line of defense" of the United States, Roosevelt was implying that U.S. security depended not so much on the distribution of world power as on the nature of international relations. When one of the senators, violating the confidentiality of the meeting, told the press that the president had said that "America's frontier lay on the Rhine," Roosevelt angrily denounced this at a press conference as a "deliberate lie." In "a simple statement" of his policy, he summarized it as "against any entangling alliances, obviously," "the maintenance of world trade for everybody," the reduction or limitation of armaments, and "the peaceful maintenance of political, economic and social independence of all nations in the world."[24]

Although there were some differences between the statements Roosevelt made at this time in confidential meetings with his military officials and senators and those he made in public, he always fended off any suggestion that the United States was repeating the experience of World War I. "About the last thing that this country should do is ever to send an army to Europe again," he assured the Military Affairs Committee. He knew that it was widely believed that the United States had been inveigled into war in 1917 by some combination of Allied propaganda, the financial links between Wall Street and London, and the Anglophile sympathies of Wilson and his advisers. (In an October 1939 poll, 34 percent attributed the nation's entry to "propaganda and selfish interests.") Although Roosevelt unequivocally declared his hostility to "the dictator nations," he was clearly nervous about admitting to a particularly close relationship or cooperative action with Britain and France. As late as April 1940, he ventured at a press conference to say no more than:

> We believe that the British Empire, to a certain extent, has stood more nearly for the democratic way of life and has been less trouble to us than some of these newfangled countries that believe in Naziism and Bolshevism, et cetera and, on the whole, Canada has been a pretty good

neighbor to us and we have never had any threat against us by Bermuda and Jamaica or by any of the Windward or Leeward Islands.[25]

This domestic context shaped the way in which the administration made the case for revising the neutrality legislation in a way that allowed Britain and France access to America's great productive resources. The motif was that this would serve America's own national interest. In a long letter to Senate leaders, Secretary of State Cordell Hull wrote that the proposed revisions, including repeal of the arms embargo, were "intended to aid in keeping the United States from being involved in war." The argument here was that the best way to secure this goal was by forestalling a war in Europe and that the Axis Powers were most likely to be deterred from starting one by the knowledge that their opponents would have the backing of America's economic might. At a crucial meeting with Senate leaders, Roosevelt reviewed the various messages he had sent European leaders urging peace, concluding "I've fired my last shot. I think I ought to have another round in my belt."[26]

Beyond this, however, the president maintained that America's own security, in the most basic sense, was at stake. In the first place, he warned that the Nazis might win a quick victory in Europe and obtain control of the British and French fleets, leaving the United States and the whole New World on the defensive "in our own back yard." In a conference with House leaders in the White House, FDR said that "in case of war there was at least [an] even chance that Germans and Italians might win":

> In that case their first act would be either to seize the British Navy or put it out of action. Then they would establish trade relations with Latin America, put instructors in the armies, etc. . . . in a very short time we would find ourselves surrounded by hostile states. . . . Further, the Japanese, who "always like to play with the big boys" would probably go into a hard and fast alliance. The combined German and Italian Navies were about the equal of ours and the Japanese was about eighty per cent of ours. Therefore, the temptation to them would always be to try another quick war with us, if we got rough about their South American penetration.[27]

To the press, Roosevelt raised the specter of an air attack on the United States itself. Existing bombers, he admitted, "cannot hop directly across our three thousand miles [of ocean] but they can do it in three hops, middle Europe, Cape Verde, Brazil, Yucatan and Tampico. I think I am a lot safer on the Hudson River than I would be if I were in Kansas. . . . It would take planes based at Yucatan, modern bombing planes, about an hour and fifty minutes to smash up New Orleans."[28]

Roosevelt was by no means alone in raising such fears. As the first witness at the Senate Foreign Relations Committee's hearings on the proposed revision to the neutrality legislation, Henry Stimson contended that the arms embargo facilitated an outcome of a European war that would "make the United States the next victim of attack." Opponents of isolationism in public debate had been arguing along the same lines for some time. Former State Department official Livingston Hartley, in a 1937 book calling for a more active foreign policy "in order to halt the Third Reich and place an insurmountable barrier in the path of German hegemony over Europe or German victory over the British Empire," portrayed the threat of a military attack on the North American continent in the most vivid terms. Foreseeing a joint assault by "the Tokyo-Berlin Alliance," Hartley envisaged the following scenario: "The last days of free America might see our government grimly 'carrying on' from Topeka, while the German headquarters in Texas and the Japanese General commanding the Michigan front coordinated the offensives of their polyglot armies of subject peoples." In a more measured way, Walter Lippmann argued that "the first line of defense against European aggression in this hemisphere has in the past been the European balance of power and British maritime supremacy" and that "if Great Britain and France fall before the menace which confronts them in Europe . . . we shall have become for the first time in our history insecure and vulnerable."[29]

It is not surprising that those seeking to counter isolationism made the case for aid to Britain and France in such terms. Arguments about the need to defend democracy or international order carried too many echoes of the way Wilson and others had justified intervention in 1917. In the fall of 1939, 68 percent of Americans still thought that intervention had been a mistake, according to polls. Calling for a research program to establish the "things for which we propose to fight," Edward M. Earle of Princeton's Institute for Advanced Study observed that "it is doubtful if generalized terms like 'rights' and 'defense' and 'honor' and 'international law' will move the United States to warlike action." Quoting *The Federalist*, Earle noted that, by contrast, "safety from external danger is the most powerful dictator of national conduct." Stressing the need for a policy on which the country could unite, Lippmann argued that "in the last analysis it is the preservation of this invulnerable security that Americans are primarily interested in, and not in the China trade, not in any quixotic desire to uphold treaties that the Europeans and the Asiatics are breaking or abandoning, not in their ideological sympathy, not in cultural or ancestral memories and certainly not in any imperial ambition of their own." To many, only the need to defend oneself from attack could override moral objections to participation in power politics. As Roosevelt wrote in his public message to Hitler (and Mussolini) in April 1939, "Nothing can persuade the peoples of the earth that any governing power has any right or need to inflict the consequences of war on its own or any other people save in the cause of self-evident home defense."[30]

The actions of Congress suggest that the looming war in Europe was much more widely seen as having implications for defense preparations than for foreign policy. To the surprise of some, Roosevelt's request for an almost doubling of military and naval appropriations was approved by both houses in the spring of 1939 by comfortable majorities. On the other hand, despite the desperate pleas of Roosevelt and Hull, the attempt to secure a revision of the neutrality law that would repeal the arms embargo failed in the summer. It is true that this failure was due in large part to domestic politics, in that the bill was defeated by a combination of Republicans and the conservative Democrats whom the president had attempted to "purge" in the 1938 primaries. But that such considerations weighed so heavily was itself a sign that the nation's safety was not seen to be at stake. And the public support for relaxation of the arms embargo was much less strong and steady than that for rearmament. Throughout 1939, 80 to 90 percent recorded their approval of enlarging America's armed forces, and over two-thirds declared themselves willing to pay higher taxes for this purpose. The picture regarding neutrality was much less clear-cut. The support for selling war materials to England and France if they were in a conflict with Germany and Italy declined from its high point at the beginning of the year. By April only 57 percent favored repealing the arms embargo, and in August polls a majority registered approval of the rejection of the measure by Congress.[31]

The implication of the difference between the strong and almost unanimous support for rearmament and the lesser and wavering approval of neutrality revision was that many had not been persuaded that American security depended on the maintenance of Roosevelt's "front line." If the United States built up its own army, navy, and especially air force, it could protect North America, and probably the whole Western Hemisphere, from attack.[32] Not surprisingly, opponents of neutrality revision made this argument in emphatic terms. In an article in *Foreign Affairs* in April 1939, the respected military analyst Hanson W. Baldwin concluded that, with the increases in America's armed forces currently being approved by Congress, "any invasion of our borders in force, even by a combination of Powers, becomes virtually impossible in the foreseeable future."[33] In resisting demands for greater anti-aircraft protection of the homeland, the recently appointed Army chief of staff George C. Marshall assured Congress that air attacks on American cities "would not be practicable unless we permitted the establishment of air bases in close proximity to the United States"—which the military had no intention of doing.[34]

This confidence was essentially unaffected by the outbreak of the European war in September 1939. Following this vindication of his predictions, which had been confidently dismissed by Borah a few weeks earlier, Roosevelt called Congress into special session to reconsider a revision of the neutrality law. Although he was moved to do so by reports from Europe that Britain and France attached great importance to repeal of the arms embargo, he did not present the measure as one to aid the Allies. He justified it as a return to international law and "reenactment of the historic and traditional American policy." "From a purely material point of view," this would increase employment by enabling American businesses to export finished products rather than just the materials that could be made into weapons by others. Emphasizing that "our acts must be guided by one single, hard-headed thought—keeping America out of war," the president recommended a continuing ban on loans and credits to belligerents, the exclusion of American citizens and ships from combat zones, and the prior transfer of title on all exports to nations at war. When combined with such measures, "by the repeal of the embargo the United States will more probably remain at peace than if the law remains as it stands today." This claim seems to have rested on the implicit premise that the nation was too deeply involved with Europe to remain indifferent to the outcome of the conflict. The president alluded to this connection in his peroration: "our policy must be to appreciate in the deepest sense the true American interest. Rightly considered, this interest is not selfish. Destiny first made us, with our sister nations on this Hemisphere, joint heirs of European culture. Fate seems now to compel us to assume the task of helping to maintain in the Western world a citadel wherein that civilization may be kept alive."[35]

In the sharp debate that followed Roosevelt's speech, the closeness and inescapability of the link between Europe and America was questioned. Herbert Hoover expatiated on the different history and political character of the two continents. The ex-president drew on the authority of his own experience in describing the "hell's brew of malign spirits" that condemned Europe to ceaseless power politics and bred utopian ideologies. He also vigorously disputed the idea that the security of the United States depended on the outcome of the European war. After such an exhausting conflict, the victor was not going to "attack 130,000,000 people 3000 miles overseas, who have a capacity of 10,000,000 soldiers and 25,000 aircraft." In the Senate, opponents of the president's proposals like Henry Cabot Lodge Jr. (R–Mass.) and Hiram Johnson stressed the same point. If Hitler were so foolish as to attempt an invasion, Johnson declared, "we could stand on our shores, with our airplanes and carriers, and a vastly superior navy, and laugh at his efforts." In a Study Group of the Council on Foreign Relations on the defense of the Western Hemisphere, it was recognized that "no one believes that an actual military threat to this country exists, even if Britain and France were to be conquered by Germany."[36]

The main argument of those who wanted to stand by the existing legislation was that repeal of the arms embargo would represent a departure from neutrality that would tie the United States to the Allied cause and thereby lead, sooner or later, to involvement in the war. "There is no middle ground," Senator Arthur Vandenberg (R–Mich.) insisted. "We are either *all the way in* or *all the way out*" (emphasis in original). To Borah, talk of returning to the nation's historic stance or keeping out of war was camouflage; the cash-and-carry scheme was born of "the desire to break down the traditional foreign policy of the United States and to associate ourselves in practically everything of importance that comes up in Europe in which Great Britain is deeply interested."[37]

Borah's characteristic hyperbole and inveterate Anglophobia should not obscure the fact that he was basically right. As with the administration, support for the repeal of the arms embargo in Congress and among the general public derived from a desire to help Britain and France in their fight against Nazi Germany. In self-conscious contrast to Wilson, Roosevelt had at the outset of the war declared that "this nation will remain a neutral nation, but I cannot ask that every American remain neutral in thought as well. . . . Even a neutral cannot be asked to close his mind or his conscience." Opinion polls in September and October showed that over 80 percent favored an Allied victory; a similar proportion held Germany, particularly Hitler, responsible for the war.

Concomitantly, more saw the conflict as one of democracy versus dictatorship than as a simple power struggle. This was the theme emphasized in the campaign for repeal of the arms embargo. As part of that campaign, the State Department encouraged and supported the formation of the Non-Partisan Committee for Peace through Revision of the Neutrality Act. Funded in part by Henry Luce, publisher of *Life* and *Time*, the group quickly established local units in thirty states. It was headed by William Allen White, a well-known and widely respected Republican newspaper editor from Kansas. In a nationwide broadcast, White asserted that the war "is not a contest of imperialist nations struggling for place and power. It is a clash of ideologies. . . . These European democracies are carrying our banner, fighting the American battle." By the end of October, polls reported 62 percent as supporting the repeal of the arms embargo, and a similar proportion saying that "we should do everything possible to help England and France win except to go to war ourselves."[38]

Buoyed by such sentiment, repeal of the arms embargo secured congressional approval in early November by votes of 55 to 24 in the Senate and 243 to 172 in the House of Representatives. "As Americans," said Representative John McCormack of Massachusetts, who had supported the embargo in the spring, "we should put our country in a position where the results of our law do not help the anti-God forces of the world and do not penalize those that stand for the existence and permanence of religion, of Christianity, and of democracy." But the new legislation also contained the other provisions that Roosevelt had called for. American ships were forbidden to enter any area designated by the president as a combat zone, and the prohibitions on loans to the belligerents or travel on their ships were maintained. All trade with the nations at war in Europe was to be on a cash-and-carry basis.[39]

Repeal of the arms embargo was hailed by Neville Chamberlain as "a momentous event" that "reopens for the Allies the doors of the greatest storehouse of supplies in the world." No doubt for morale reasons, and perhaps also because, like Vandenberg, he saw it as the first step on a path, the prime minister greatly exaggerated the practical effect of the new legislation. Access to the storehouse was much narrowed by the cash-and-carry provision, reinforced by the 1934 Johnson Act that prohibited loans to governments that had defaulted on their World War I debts. Concerned to husband their gold and dollar reserves for a long war, the British Treasury treated America as "a limited marginal source of war supplies" and spent most of its restricted dollar budget on purchases of food and raw materials rather than armaments or aircraft.[40] The ironic upshot was that, although both the administration and the great majority of Americans were more explicitly and unequivocally pro-Allied than had been the case in World War I, in practice America's productive power weighed much less in the European balance of forces in 1939–40 than it had in 1915–17. The United States had abandoned any pretense of neutrality but, in ensuring that its modified stance still involved no cost and carried no risk of war, it continued to severely constrain its ability to influence world politics.

The Impact of the Fall of France

"I was a sort of—who was the fellow? John the Baptist—'voice crying in the wilderness' all last summer," Franklin Roosevelt remarked in late May 1940. The president's post-Munich suggestions that the Axis Powers might defeat Britain and France had been widely discounted. In polls following the outbreak of war, between 65 and 80 percent said they expected an Allied victory. Nor was this only popular opinion. Few informed Americans would have dissented from Senator Lodge's assessment in October 1939 that "the chances of England and France being defeated are slim indeed" and that "the choice seems to be between a defeat of Germany on the one hand and a stalemate on the other." In early March 1940, the Chief of Naval Operations, Admiral Harold Stark, sent the president "an estimate of the foreign situation as it exists today" in which he concluded that "a successful attack by either belligerent on the fortified Western Front is considered highly improbable."[41] The events of the next few months dramatically changed the picture. In May 1940, the number expecting an Allied victory had dropped to 55 percent, and polls in July showed rather more Americans (35–40%) now anticipating an Axis victory than a British one (30–32%).[42]

This transformation of the European situation induced not only shock but also some alarm. Perhaps as a concomitant of pro-Allied sentiment as well as because of the warnings of Roosevelt and others, from the beginning of the war a majority had told pollsters that they believed a victorious Germany would turn on the United States. In a *Fortune* poll in January 1940, for example, 61 percent thought that if Germany won a decisive victory over France and England, she would be a threat to the United States, and 42 percent had seen this in terms of an actual military invasion.[43] As the German offensive began in the spring, the president portrayed the danger in stark terms to an off-the-record press conference:

> I think every man, woman and child ought to ask themselves the question, "What is going to happen to the United States if dictatorship wins in Europe and the Far East?" In other words, what would be the logical steps taken by that kind of victorious cause? ... When Napoleon started out, he had no idea of dominating all of Europe, when Alexander started out from Macedonia, he did not think he was going to conquer Persia. The thing grows.... If you or I were Hitler, isn't it just common sense to say that, having conquered Europe and destroyed the British Fleet and the French Army, and having no opposition, . . . Why leave an entire continent, North, Central and South America, absolutely all alone?

Roosevelt spoke again of the feasibility of bombing raids on the American heartland via the Cape Verde islands and bases in Brazil. To the Congress a month later, he cited the speed of aircraft as the reason why the oceans no longer provided the "reasonably adequate defensive barriers" that they had in the days of sailing ships. In a Fireside Chat, he also raised the specter of a "Fifth Column that betrays a nation unprepared for treachery."[44]

At the same time, the president emphasized America's existing and potential military strength. The danger he portrayed was not that of invasion and conquest but of the consequences for the nation's way of life of becoming "a lone island in a world dominated by the philosophy of force." As France was falling, he told the graduating class of the University of Virginia that "such an island represents ... the nightmare of a people lodged in prison, handcuffed, hungry, and fed through the bars from day to day by the contemptuous, unpitying masters of other continents." To avert this danger, Roosevelt declared his intention to pursue "two obvious and simultaneous courses: we will extend to the opponents of force the material resources of this nation" and "at the same time" build up the nation's own defenses.[45]

The adoption of this two-pronged program constituted the transformative effect of Hitler's 1940 victories on U.S. policy. But the political process proved resistant to the president's emphasis on the first element. There was a strong consensus behind greater military preparedness. A poll in July 1940 found 75 percent of respondents willing to pay "considerably more taxes now" to meet the costs of national defense and 69 percent favoring the drafting of men to serve in the armed services.[46] Congress responded to this public mood with virtually unanimous votes in favor of greater defense spending. In the month of May alone appropriations were massively increased twice, on each occasion by more than the administration had requested, and by the end of the year they had increased fivefold. In September, the Selective Service Act, establishing the first peacetime draft in the nation's history, passed both houses with large majorities.[47] That the anti-militarist strain in interwar isolationism had largely disappeared was also shown by the manifesto of the America First Committee on its formation in September. This called for the building of "an impregnable defense" and declared that "no foreign power, nor group of powers, can successfully attack a *prepared* America."

However, the formation of America First also showed that aid to the nations fighting the Axis enjoyed much less emphatic and unanimous support than military preparedness. As France had been reeling in May, there had been no question of Roosevelt's acceding to Premier Paul Reynaud's desperate appeal for military equipment or at least some declaration that the United States "could not permit the defeat of France and England." The urgent pleas of the new British prime minister, Winston Churchill, for aircraft and over-age destroyers were responded to only partially and belatedly. Engaged in their own build-up, the American military resisted sending supplies to France or Britain; "if we were required to mobilize after having released guns necessary for this mobilization and were found to be short in artillery material," an Army Staff officer observed, "everyone who was a party to the deal might hope to be found hanging from a lamp post." Admiral Stark adamantly opposed giving the British the old destroyers. In June, Congress passed the Walsh Amendment, which made the transfer of any equipment conditional on certification by the relevant service chief that it was "not essential to the defense of the United States."[48] Although opinion polls on the subject fluctuated as events unfolded and the question was differently phrased, they consistently revealed substantial popular opposition to the sale or transfer of aircraft and other supplies if this would delay America's own defense program. That program continued to obstruct efforts to aid Britain through the fall, as the president and Secretary of the Treasury Morgenthau engaged in a sort of tug-of-war with the defense establishment over how much of America's munitions production should be allocated to the Allies.[49]

Given the speed and unpredictability with which the European situation changed in the summer of 1940, it is not surprising that there was uncertainty and some oscillation, both in government circles and more broadly, about what the United States should do. Nevertheless, the broad character of the nation's response carried certain implications. One was that the emphasis that opponents of isolation had for some time placed on the threat of direct attack by a victorious Axis had been more effective in undermining confidence in the security provided by geography than in inducing a sense of vital dependence on the fate of other countries. There may, indeed, have been something counterproductive about the way in which, for example, the recently returned Ambassador to France, William C. Bullitt, called for greater aid to Britain in a widely publicized speech in Philadelphia. "Do we want to see Hitler in Independence Hall making fun of the Liberty Bell?" he demanded. "I am certain that, if Great Britain is defeated, the attack will come."[50] Such rhetoric can only have contributed to the nervousness over homeland security that had led naturally to the concentration on hemispheric defense that governed military planning at this time. Such planning envisaged taking over the possessions of the defeated allies in the Western Hemisphere and a preemptive intervention in Brazil. But it was not defeatist. An assessment by the Joint Planning Committee prepared for the Joint Board (the predecessor of the Joint Chiefs of Staff) in January 1941 stated flatly that "the United States can safeguard the North American continent and probably the Western Hemisphere, whether allied with Britain or not."[51]

That this task was not only clearly the first priority but also the only one for which the nation was prepared to make an all-out effort was implied by the provision in the Selective Service Act that confined the service of those drafted to American possessions and the Western Hemisphere. In calling for additional defense spending in July, the president assured Congress that "we will not use our arms in a war of aggression; we will not send our men to take part in European wars." The Democratic Party platform on which Roosevelt ran for an unprecedented third term contained the firm commitment: "We will not participate in foreign wars, and we will not send our army, naval or air forces to fight in foreign lands outside of the Americas, except in case of attack." A surge in the polls by the Republican challenger Wendell Willkie during October coincided with his increasing exploitation of fears that Roosevelt's reelection would lead to the draftees being sent to Europe to fight. Following pleas by Democratic bosses, Roosevelt responded by giving "you mothers and fathers" the emphatic assurance that "your boys are not going to be sent into any foreign wars. They are going into training to form a force so strong that, by its very existence, it will keep the threat of war far away from our shores."[52]

This context made it natural to present moves to assist Britain under the rubric of continental defense. Even before the war, the scope of this concept had been widened to "hemisphere" defense. In December 1938, Cordell Hull's efforts to promote the principle of collective security on a pan-American basis produced the Declaration of Lima in which the nations of the New World affirmed their "continental solidarity" and agreed to consult in the event of a threat to any of them from outside the hemisphere. Shortly thereafter, the U.S. Army War College was asked to study how to protect Brazil from Axis machinations; its secret report called for the creation of a Hemisphere Defense Force equipped to conduct operations in Latin America.[53] When the European war broke out, the United States obtained the agreement of the Latin American countries to the Declaration of Panama, which proclaimed a "neutrality zone" extending three hundred miles into the Atlantic. This was to be patrolled by the U.S. Navy, and belligerent warships were to be excluded from it (with the exception of the waters around Canada and European possessions in the New World). The zone was very much Roosevelt's own idea and, as he made clear to the British on more than one occasion, it was intended to help the Allies by releasing the Royal Navy for duties elsewhere.[54] When the transfer of the old destroyers was at last agreed (during the Battle of Britain), Roosevelt described it as "an epochal and far-reaching act of preparation for continental defense in face of grave danger" because in exchange the British had been persuaded to grant the United States ninety-nine-year leases for naval and air bases on British possessions in the Caribbean and western Atlantic.[55] In 1941, the boundaries of "the Western Hemisphere" were gradually pushed forward, ostensibly to provide greater protection but also as a form of aid to the Allies. Thus, in response to British appeals at a difficult time in the Battle of the Atlantic, Roosevelt widened the Neutrality Zone to the twenty-fifth meridian in April, thereby incorporating Greenland. In May, the president was apparently contemplating a preemptive military expedition to the Azores, or even Dakar, but the idea was opposed by the army (who would have preferred to strengthen hemispheric defense by establishing bases in northeastern Brazil). In July, naval patrolling was extended as far east as Iceland, to which a marine brigade was dispatched.[56]

Of more lasting consequence was the revision of the premises of military planning to include the configuration of power beyond the Western Hemisphere among the requirements of America's own national security. A key document in this process was Admiral Stark's famous "Plan Dog" memorandum of November 1940, in which he observed that "a very strong pillar of the defense structure of the Americas has, for many years, been the balance of power existing in Europe. The collapse of Great Britain or the destruction or surrender of the British Fleet will destroy this balance and will free European military power for possible encroachment in this hemisphere." As the historian Mark Stoler points out in a study of American military planning, Stark had "departed sharply from past estimates by openly linking, for the first time, U.S. security to the European balance of power and the continuation of that balance to British fortunes."

This official adoption of what had been a staple argument of Anglophile internationalists for decades was not the product of a consensual expert judgment arrived at through an autonomous process of objective strategic analysis. Indeed, the senior Army planner, General Stanley D. Embick, had favored "noninvolvement in Europe, withdrawal in the Far East, rapprochement with Japan, and an emphasis on continental defense." But, as Stoler writes, "the planners were forced to come to grips with . . . a White House-directed policy, supported by the public, of aid to and collaboration with London." Thereafter, consideration of strategic alternatives took place within this framework. Stark himself had been a friend of FDR's since World War I and had been selected by the president to be head of the navy over several of his seniors. The thrust of his memorandum was that the best strategy would be "an eventual strong offensive in the Atlantic as an ally of the British, and a defensive in the Pacific." This meant opposing Churchill's strong pressure for a U.S. naval squadron to be sent to Singapore; to secure a coordination of strategy, Stark recommended the secret staff talks with the British that took place in January and where the priority of the war against Germany was agreed.[57]

Of far greater immediate significance than this secret contingency planning was Lend-Lease, Roosevelt's ingenious response to the problem epitomized by the U.K. ambassador's (probably apocryphal) comment to American reporters: "Well boys, Britain's broke; it's your money we want."[58] In arguing that the country needed to become "the great arsenal of democracy," the president insisted that "this is not a matter of sentiment or of controversial personal opinion. It is a matter of realistic, practical military policy, based on the advice of our military experts." As quoted earlier, he pictured the victorious Axis controlling all the non-American continents and then turning on the United States. The legislation authorizing the president to transfer war materials to any country whose defense he deemed "vital" to America's own security was entitled "an Act Further to Promote the Defense of the United States." In their congressional testimony in support of it, administration spokesmen developed this theme. If Britain were defeated and lost control of the seas, Hull asserted, "Germany could easily cross the Atlantic—especially the South Atlantic." Henry Stimson and Frank Knox, anti-isolationist Republicans who had been appointed secretary of war and the navy, respectively, in June 1940, argued that America's own physical safety depended on Britain's survival, speaking specifically of the danger of air attacks and of naval inferiority in the Atlantic. "The only thing

I am sure of," Knox declared, "is that if England is defeated and destroyed, we will be attacked."[59]

These propositions were strongly contested both by isolationist congressmen like Hamilton Fish (R–N.Y.) and by some of those who testified. Former Ambassador to Britain Joseph P. Kennedy questioned the idea that if Germany won, the United States would have to become "an armed camp." "It seems to me that an air force can work pretty well on this continent," he argued. "And it is probably not as expensive as all the other things are." Charles Lindbergh, speaking with the authority of his fame as an aviator, endorsed this assessment, arguing that, contrary to the claims of Roosevelt and others, the development of air power had enhanced rather than diminished the protection afforded by the oceans. He cited the unsuccessful operations of the British navy in the Norwegian campaign as evidence that opposition from the air made it "more difficult than ever before for a navy to approach a hostile shore." An American air force of "about 10,000 thoroughly modern planes plus reserves," he estimated, working in conjunction with the U.S. Navy, "would make it practically impossible for a foreign navy to do serious damage or to land an expeditionary force of any size on our coasts." As for air attacks on the American homeland, Lindbergh admitted that bombing raids from across the ocean might be technically feasible, but since they would involve heavy costs and losses and bring little military benefit, it was hardly surprising that "not a single squadron of transoceanic bombing planes exists anywhere in the world today." In sum, Lindbergh concluded, "aviation has added to America's security against Europe and to Europe's security against America."[60]

The Lend-Lease bill was approved by the House of Representatives in early February by 260 votes to 165. A month later a slightly revised version was enacted by majorities of 60–31 in the Senate and 317–71 in the House. Polls during the period when the bill was under discussion recorded more than 55 percent in favor of its passage and less than half that number against it.[61]

Explaining the Move toward Involvement

The Issue of Security

Given the way that the Lend-Lease bill had been presented and advocated, the majorities favoring it in Congress and public opinion polls might be taken to show that most people had been persuaded that America's own security was at stake—that the country's safety was vitally dependent on Britain's survival and the balance of power in Europe. However, this is not how Henry Luce, for one, saw it at the time. In his famous essay on "the American Century," which appeared during the Lend-Lease debate, Luce began by declaring that "we are *in* the war" and then asked,

> how did we get in? We got in on the basis of defense. Even that very word, defense, has been full of deceit and self-deceit. To the average American the plain meaning of the word defense is defense of American territory. Is our national policy today limited to the defense of the American homeland by whatever means may seem wise? It is not. . . . If the entire rest of the world came under the domination of evil tyrants, it is quite possible to imagine that this country could make itself such a tough nut to crack that not all the tyrants in the world would care to come against us. No man can say that that picture of America as an impregnable armed camp is false. No man can honestly say that as a pure matter of defense—defense of our homeland—it is necessary to get into or be in this war.

In truth, Luce maintained, "we are *not* in a war to defend American territory. We are in a war to defend and even to promote, encourage and incite so-called democratic principles throughout the world."[62]

It is not necessary to share Luce's confidence in America's commitment to its historic ideological mission in order to agree with his view that it was not the requirements of the nation's own physical safety that had led the United States to become so involved in the fight against Nazi Germany. There are several reasons for such skepticism. In the first place, authoritative commentators dismissed the more alarmist scenarios. Hanson W. Baldwin, the military correspondent of the *New York Times*, published a book-length study of the nation's defense requirements in April 1941 in which he not only dismissed "the bogey of invasion" but also maintained that the United States had the capacity to protect the Western Hemisphere from any attack.[63] Baldwin's views were much cited by anti-interventionists, with whom he privately sympathized, but his basic claim about the defensibility of North America was accepted even by scholars who argued that the maintenance of a balance of power in Europe was a vital strategic interest for the United States.[64]

At the level of popular opinion, there was a decline of 12 percentage points between December 1940 and May 1941 in the proportion who said they thought America's future safety depended on Britain winning the war.[65] The developing campaign of America First may have been partly responsible for this, as may growing confidence in the nation's military preparedness. However, the main influence was probably the course of events. The widespread fear in the summer of 1940 of an Axis attack across the Atlantic had not been based on careful consideration of its technical feasibility but was a product of the shock created by the sudden German victories in Europe—as was shown by the emphasis placed on the threat from "fifth columnists."[66] Subsequent developments were somewhat more reassuring. In particular, Hitler's failure to mount an invasion across the twenty-odd miles of the English Channel seemed to demonstrate that three thousand miles of ocean remained a formidable barrier (as Hull acknowledged in his Lend-Lease testimony). The British ambassador reported to the Foreign Office in November 1940 that "public opinion is still inclined to live in complacency derived from the failure of Hitler's attempt at invasion of Britain this autumn, while nothing has happened on the international front to revive American anxiety about its own security."[67] Later events further diminished the sense of danger. Assistant Secretary of State Adolf Berle concluded in May 1941 that "the fact that the *Bismarck* was sunk (substantially) by air power, seems to make it plain that if there is anything like an adequate air force, a naval invasion of the Western Hemisphere is out of the question."[68]

Yet at the same time there was a substantial increase in the majority saying that it was more important to help England than to keep out of the war; during 1941 there was not only the public endorsement of Lend-Lease but also increasing support for the use of the U.S. Navy to protect Allied convoys in the Atlantic.[69] These divergent trends suggest that the desire to throw America's weight into the scales against the Axis was driven by factors other than anxiety over America's own safety. Breakdowns of the division of opinion over such issues as Lend-Lease and convoying tend to confirm that the degree to which people cared about the outcome of the European conflict was a crucial variable. Had the argument been simply over the means by which America's military security could be best maintained, it might have reflected differences of temperament (degrees of sanguinity) and of knowledge. Temperamental differences are impossible to re-capture but may perhaps be assumed to be fairly randomly distributed. Polls indicated that somewhat more "well-informed" than "uninformed" people favored Lend-Lease, but the difference between regions was far more striking. Whereas over 75 percent in the South favored "the President's Lend-Lease bill," in the East Central region (Ohio, Indiana, Illinois, and Michigan) only around 40 percent did so.[70] In this case, the size of the difference no doubt owed something to party loyalty, but this factor would have been less salient in most of the other polls in the neutrality period which consistently showed much greater readiness in the South than in the rest of the country to take risks, or even enter the war, on behalf of the Allies.[71] This surely reflected the stronger and more unanimous pro-Allied feelings in the region rather than any greater anxiety over America's own safety.

The nature of the Lend-Lease debate itself suggested that the division was rooted in attitudes toward the European war rather than views on the relative merits of rival military strategies. Thus, after Lindbergh had presented his analysis of the strategic implications of aviation to the House Committee, Luther A. Johnson of Texas, who led for the Democratic majority in the hearings, repeatedly pressed him on the question, "Which side do you want to see win?" Lindbergh replied that he would "prefer to see neither side win" and felt that "it would be better for us, and for every nation in Europe, to have this war end without a conclusive victory." Similarly, although Navy Secretary Knox opened his testimony before the Senate Foreign Relations Committee by declaring that "my entire statement today can be considered a refutation of the argument Colonel Lindbergh made," he did not in fact discuss the impact of air power on America's defensive position, answering questions on such subjects by saying that "my technical knowledge is limited." It was "Colonel Lindbergh's idea that it might be possible now to effect a stable negotiated peace between Great Britain and Germany" that Knox attacked, denouncing it as "a wild fancy" and insisting that "the question to decide is, would we rather see Europe dominated by a democratic system, or would we rather see Europe dominated by a Hitler system?"[72]

Leading figures on both sides of the debate recognized the salience of the strongly pro-British, anti-Hitler feelings in the country. Lend-Lease passed, Vandenberg lamented in his diary, "because it wore the popular label of an aid-to-England bill."[73] Lindbergh's strictly neutral attitude to the European war was exceptional among those who opposed the measure. Even Mrs. Robert E. Wood, wife of America First's national chairman, participated in benefits for the British War Relief Society. Recognizing that, as Representative Edith Rogers (R–Mass.) put it, "it is the overwhelming sentiment of the country to aid Great Britain," most did not oppose such aid in principle but criticized the powers granted to the president under the legislation and suggested that this would enable him to lead the country into war.[74]

That this was thought to be a damaging charge reflected the fact that most Americans continued to oppose full-scale belligerency. To some extent, this might be attributed to wishful thinking that the British would be able, as Churchill promised, to "finish the job" if "given the tools." The loss of confidence in the Allies' prospects in the summer of 1940 proved to be short-lived. By mid-September 1940, over 60 percent were again professing confidence in an Allied victory, and the proportion fluctuated between 50 percent and 78 percent over the course of the next fifteen months.[75] Yet it cannot be assumed that there would have been more support for entering the war if the British situation had been more realistically perceived. When, in the weeks following the fall of France, there had been widespread pessimism in Washington about Britain's chances of survival, the effect had been to check the provision of aid rather than to accelerate it.[76] There was also at that time a slight but perceptible dip in the proportion anticipating that they, personally, would be affected by a German victory.[77] Some people, it would seem, reacted to that prospect's becoming a more real one by appraising its effects with less alarm.[78] At another very critical point in Britain's struggle for survival in May 1941, when pollsters asked whether people would favor going to war if the president said he was "certain" that Britain would otherwise be defeated, only about 50 percent answered in the affirmative. In July 1941 almost a third (31 percent) said that the United States should go to war only if it was invaded.[79]

All this indicated the double-edged nature of military security as the rationale for American foreign policy. On the one hand, protecting the American homeland from attack possessed a unique status as something that was almost universally agreed to be of supreme importance and hence to justify whatever sacrifices were required to achieve it. On the other hand, given the country's advantageous geographical position, comparative self-sufficiency and confidence in its capacity to defend itself unaided, justifying policy in terms of this goal tended to circumscribe the scope and scale of power projection.

An "Open-Door World" and Other Economic Concerns

Yet, while not taking the final step, the United States in 1941 followed a course of action that clearly involved not only significant costs but also a real risk of involvement in a major foreign war. If it was not the perceived threat to America's own physical security that led it to do this, how is it to be explained? Some historians have offered an equally clear-cut, but quite different, answer to the question. "Strategic defense was not the primary factor underlying the American decision to intervene in the epic contest," Patrick J. Hearden writes. "American leaders were primarily concerned about the menace that a triumphant Germany would present to the free enterprise system in the United States. . . . Convinced that capitalism could not function within the framework of only one country, they chose to fight to keep foreign markets open for surplus American commodities and thereby to preserve entrepreneurial freedom in the United States."[80]

In support of this interpretation are many public and private statements by administration leaders and others suggesting that a German victory would have far-reaching consequences on American economic life. Export markets were vital for the nation's prosperity, Roosevelt stressed, because "we do not eat all the food we can produce, we do not burn all the oil we can pump, we do not use all the goods we can manufacture." The president asserted that a victorious Hitler would be able to use this dependence to establish "an economic stranglehold" on the nations of the Western Hemisphere. "The American laborer would have to compete with slave labor in the rest of the world," which meant that "wages and hours would be fixed by Hitler," while "the American farmer would get for his products exactly what Hitler wanted to give."[81] A fuller version of this prospect was provided by Douglas Miller, who had served as U.S. commercial attaché in Berlin from 1925 to 1939. In *You Can't Do Business with Hitler*, published in June 1941, Miller drew on his own experience in arguing that the Nazis would always insist that international trade be conducted through a government-controlled barter system that they would manipulate to their own advantage. Through this method, a victorious Germany would be able both to exert a paramount influence in Latin American countries, whose economies were dependent on the export of agricultural goods to Europe, and to deprive American producers of vital markets. "The slave labor of the greater part of the world" would enable Hitler's regime to "quote prices with which American firms could never compete." To meet the challenge of this centrally directed economic power, the United States itself would have to move toward a "planned economy and a system of State Socialism."[82] Similar (if generally less elaborated) fears about the effects of a German victory on American economic interests were expressed by, among others, Cordell Hull, Sumner Welles, Secretary of Commerce Jesse Jones, Will Clayton (a large cotton broker), the bankers Thomas W. Lamont and W. H. Schubart, the business journals *Barron's* and *Fortune*, the Bureau of Foreign and Domestic Commerce, the National Foreign Trade Council, the columnists Walter Lippmann and Dorothy Thompson, and the historian Allan Nevins.[83]

These statements, however, were made in the context of the wider public debate over American policy in these years. All those who made them also offered other reasons why the United States ought to throw its weight into the scales against Hitler. Even Douglas Miller devoted almost as much attention to the strategic threat a victorious Germany would pose as to the economic one.[84] So why should we regard the economic arguments as the key explanation for administration policy and the support it enjoyed?

Two kinds of answer have been offered to this question. The first is that warnings about the consequences for America's political economy of a Nazi-dominated Europe were a genuine indication of policymakers' real concerns because, unlike the fears expressed over the nation's military security, they were rational and well-founded. But were they? Certainly, the claims were energetically contested at the time. Anti-interventionists questioned how far trade patterns would be affected by an Axis victory. Robert E. Wood, chairman of both Sears Roebuck and America First, observed that "when two nations or two continents each have things the other needs, trade eventually results regardless of the feelings each may have for the other." Senator Robert A. Taft (R–Oh.) was another who saw no reason why the United States would not be able to trade as well with a victorious Germany as it was then doing with Japan, also "a totalitarian nation."[85]

This might seem too cavalier a dismissal of the effect of the Nazis' use of various mechanisms to restrict and direct international transactions. The proportion of U.S. exports going to Germany had declined from 8.4 percent to 3.5 percent between 1933 and 1938. However, this was only slightly more than the decline in these years of the proportion of U.S. exports going to France (7.2% to 4.3%), and the dollar value of the trade with Germany remained steady, with the balance substantially in the U.S. favor. Likewise, American manufacturers' investments in Germany increased by 50 percent between 1929 and 1940, while those in France declined by the same proportion over the same period. Nor had the political restrictions in this period been all on one side. With the ending of a commercial treaty in 1934, Germany lost its most-favored-nation status, and in 1936 and 1939 the United States imposed countervailing duties, initially in retaliation for Nazi trading practices but also in response to such actions as the takeover of Czechoslovakia.[86]

In any case, it was not clear that, in the hypothesized division of the world into two spheres, the balance of advantage would lie with the one controlled by the Nazis. That "slave labor" would provide all the industries in a Nazi-controlled Europe with a new and decisive competitive advantage over their American counterparts was surely an unwarranted assumption. As Harvard economist Brooks Emeny pointed out, the scale of America's industrial capacity and the size of its market would give the United States "important bargaining power" in any eventuality. The Research Division of America First drew on a Brookings Institution study to argue that a Nazi Europe would be extremely vulnerable to United States pressure.[87] In any case, exports to countries outside North America constituted less than 3 percent of the gross national product in the 1930s (and even before the Depression, during the 1920s, only about 4.4 percent).[88] This is not to say that such trade, which did of course absorb a much higher proportion of the output of particular goods and commodities (about a third of America's cotton went to Europe in the 1930s), could have been lightly written off.[89] But the low aggregate level of dependence on overseas markets does make somewhat implausible the claim that an Axis victory would have compelled the United States to change the whole nature of its economic system.

There was, however, one limitation to America's self-sufficiency that could be seen as having serious strategic as well as economic significance. As war threatened, concern rose about the availability in case of need of strategic minerals such as chromium, manganese, tungsten, and bauxite, and a stockpiling program was instituted.[90] Some interventionists placed great emphasis on the nation's vulnerability in this respect. To Spykman, it was the key reason why North America would not be defensible in the long run if a hostile power controlled the Old World. After an extensive analysis of the statistics for 1937, he concluded that "encirclement and blockade of the Western Hemisphere would make it exceedingly difficult for the United States to maintain a war industry adequate for defense." The loss of southern South America (which he anticipated) would be decisive: "Without the tin and the tungsten of Bolivia, the copper of Chile, and the tungsten, wool, and tanning products of the Argentine, our war industries would be seriously crippled even if we could produce in northern Brazil the materials which now come from the tropical zones of Asia and Africa. The quarter-sphere does not contain the power potential necessary for an adequate system of defense against the complete encirclement which would then prevail."[91]

However, this pessimistic view was neither generally accepted nor, in fact, correct. At the time, many emphasized the extent to which the American continents were self-sufficient and the potentialities of stockpiling, substitution, and the development of synthetic materials.[92] *Fortune* magazine in December 1940 pointed out that the development of synthetic rubber removed the fear that Japan, by taking over Southeast Asia, could cripple America's economy and war-making capacity.[93] Administration officials professed confidence about the ability of the United States to survive the loss of raw materials from other continents—Roosevelt, on one occasion, remarked that newspaper columnists who expressed anxieties on this score "don't know a damn thing about it."[94] Spykman's assumption that, in the event of war, domestic production of minerals would be unable to keep pace with increased demand did not accord with the experience of World War I, when, as the prices for ferro-alloys such as manganese and chromite more than tripled, domestic production rose to meet a much higher proportion of the nation's needs.[95] In a recent, very thorough examination of the situation with respect to the eleven most important strategic materials, the political scientist Robert J. Art concludes that "in terms of his own argument and data, Spykman was wrong": "Through a variety of measures—substitution, synthetic production, conservation, recycling, and imports from sources within the quarter sphere—the United States could have acquired what it needed."[96] And with respect to one material vital to modern war-making, the New World was much better placed than the Old World. The Western Hemisphere in 1938 produced 77 percent of the world's oil—almost all of it from the "quarter-sphere" of North and Central America—and over 60 percent from the United States itself.[97]

A second approach to explaining U.S. policy in economic terms focuses on sectional interests rather than national ones. In the most thorough presentation of this argument, Peter Trubowitz locates support for aid to the Allies in the urban Northeast and the South, attributing it to the interests of international bankers and export-oriented manufacturers in the former region and the dependence on cotton exports to Europe in the latter. By contrast, he argues, the agrarian West was more concerned about protecting the home market than exporting and consequently was a bastion of isolationism. This division is linked with that over tariff policy, where the Reciprocal Trade Agreements Act of 1934 is seen as the beginning of a historic shift, reflecting the growing interest of northeastern business in export markets and of banks and corporations in overseas investments.[98]

That positions on the tariff have throughout American history reflected sectional economic interests is almost axiomatic, and on the surface it seems plausible to assume that this would also be true of attitudes to foreign policy. In broad terms, favoring free trade does seem to have been associated with support for a more active involvement in world politics. (In this period, no one embodied this connection better than Cordell Hull.) As we have seen, Wall Street bankers and lawyers had been working for the adoption of an "internationalist" approach at least since the time of World War I. People from this background had been influential, both in public office and behind the scenes, from the time of Elihu Root, and Stimson's accession to the cabinet in 1940 symbolized the centrality and bipartisan character of this "establishment."

The longstanding nature of this viewpoint should, however, caution us against attributing it simply to economic interests. In World War I, as we have seen, the prevalence of passionate pro-Allied sentiment among the East Coast upper middle class extended well beyond Wall Street. This sentiment also predated the European loans and investments by U.S. banks and corporations that are seen as explaining their position in the interwar period.[99] Similarly, it is questionable whether the South's uniquely strong support for aid to the Allies can be explained simply by a concern with cotton exports, given the high proportion of Southerners who traced their ancestry to the British Isles and the virtual absence of other European ethnic groups.[100]

Nor is the correlation between economic interest and foreign policy position consistently firm. It is argued that capital-intensive, export-oriented businesses were internationalist, whereas labor-intensive manufacturing industry producing for the home market was protectionist and isolationist.[101] One careful student of America First, Justus D. Doenecke, notes that the organization's financial support came disproportionately from the manufacturing sector (rather than finance or communications), family-owned firms, and "agriculture-based enterprises, such as meat-packing." It is no doubt true, as Doenecke writes, that these conservative businessmen feared that "war would accelerate higher taxes and promote industrial unionism," but their economic interests were not entirely confined to the domestic market.[102] Food processing, for example, was a sector of the economy with significant export sales. The Ford Motor Company had substantial overseas investments as well, which did not stop Henry Ford from being a supporter of America First. At a more general level, too, sectional differences on foreign policy did not correlate very well with economic interest; wheat farmers in the western

states had long been more attuned to world markets than had many manufacturers in the Northeast.

Finally, whatever merit the economic interpretation may have with regard
to the *division* over aid to the Allies, its focus on long-term structural developments cannot explain the sharp *decline* in the political strength of isolationism
between the mid-1930s and Pearl Harbor. In February 1937, 95 percent of those
polled said that the United States should not take part "if another war like the
World War develops in Europe," but by November 1941, 68 percent that it was
"more important" that Germany be defeated than that the United States keep
out of war.[103] Notwithstanding regional differences—which were larger in congressional voting figures than in public opinion polls—this was a nationwide
phenomenon. The adoption of a more interventionist foreign policy was the
result not of a shift in the sectional political balance but of a movement of
opinion. The change was in the minds of Americans, not in their economic
interests.

This being so, the question becomes how far economic considerations helped
to produce this change of opinion. Clearly, warnings that the future of the American economy depended on the outcome of the war were designed to affect public
opinion. "A great deal has been and is being written about fighting the Nazis or
dealing with them," Douglas Miller wrote in the preface to his book (dated May
12, 1941). "But there is one group in America which has not been adequately
brought face to face with the facts. I mean American business men."[104] Roosevelt expatiated on the dire economic consequences of an Axis victory in the
radio address in which he announced his proclamation of "an unlimited national
emergency." The president's emphasis on the economic dimension, which was
comparatively novel, may have reflected a wish to broaden the terms of the debate
from a concentration upon the likelihood and practicality of a direct military
attack on the United States.

It is impossible to gauge with any precision the impact of these various arguments on public opinion. The president's radio address of May 27, 1941, was
followed by a slight increase in the proportion of people who said that helping
England was more important than keeping out of the war, but there is no way
of knowing how far this was due to the impression made by his portrayal of
the economic consequences of a German victory.[105] Data from polls addressing
the issue more directly are confusing and difficult to interpret. A survey in the
winter of 1939–40 indicated that, of the 61 percent believing that a victorious
Germany would be a threat to the United States, only 14 percent thought it would
be a "commercial and economic threat," compared to 42 percent who saw it as a
"military threat."[106] But a similar survey in June 1940 found that 74 percent now
thought that, if Germany won the war, she would "interfere seriously with our

vital interests in foreign trade," a much higher proportion than the 45 percent who expected her to "actually attack us on our own territory as soon as possible."[107] That the striking discrepancy between these two polls may have been largely due to the different order in which the questions were asked is a reminder that ordinary Americans may not have distinguished between the various aspects of the perceived threat as clearly as subsequent analysts would like. More illuminating, perhaps, was "the *Fortune* Forum of Executive Opinion" in the summer of 1940. In response to the question, "If Hitler wins, do you think American business will have to be reorganized in a manner resembling the totalitarians?" only 14 percent of the fifteen thousand executives polled responded affirmatively, 48 percent said no, and 35 percent said only in the field of foreign trade.[108] This survey, made at the time when expectations of a German victory were at their highest, hardly suggests that fear among the American business community as a whole for the future of their own free enterprise system was a decisive factor in generating support for a more interventionist foreign policy. In 1940–41, neither the U.S. Chamber of Commerce nor the National Association of Manufacturers took a direct position on foreign policy issues, as they were to do in later years.[109]

In fact, the desire to throw America's weight into the struggle against the Axis seems to have stemmed from a variety of concerns and emotions, as Spykman recognized even as he strove to establish U.S. policy on a more strictly geopolitical conception of the national interest: "Some asked participation because they were pro-British; others because they believed that, in a period of ideological warfare, we had a moral obligation to support the people whose social and political structure most closely resembled our own. Many insisted that we should become belligerents in the war because only in that manner could we make good our failure of 1920 and present the post-war world with a system of collective security and durable peace."[110] To these "idealistic considerations," as Spykman termed them, should no doubt be added concern about how secure or prosperous the United States would be in a world dominated by the Axis. But there is no reason to elevate any one of these concerns into the decisive, all-important explanation for the policy that was followed.

The Effects of a Sense of Power

An often overlooked feature of the debate of 1940–41 is that both sides accused the other of a lack of confidence in American power. Roosevelt regarded isolationism as "a species of defeatism." "Shall we now," he asked in his May 27 address, "with all our potential strength, hesitate to take every single measure necessary to maintain our American liberties?" Lindbergh responded that "the real defeatist in America is the man who says that this Nation cannot survive alone."[111] This exchange brought out clearly that the debate was not about different means to the same end so much as about the end that should be pursued. Few really feared that the United States would not be able to "survive alone." But many felt that, given its great potential power, the nation could, and should, strive to achieve more than this.

As we have seen, an assumption that the United States was intrinsically the most powerful country in the world had been pervasive in the nation's culture since at least the turn of the century. This confidence shaped the response to the fall of France, underlying and outlasting the immediate panic that this dramatic event induced in some quarters. As the Nazi blitzkrieg swept through the Low Countries and into France, *Life* observed that "the German victories brought shock and deep fear to the United States, but they brought also a consciousness of national strength. The old nations of Europe may fall before the conqueror but the young, strong giant of the West will meet any challenge that Adolf Hitler dares to make."[112]

Indeed, many anticipated that the war would make the United States more powerful than ever before. "I have been saying to myself and other people," Berle recorded in his diary in September 1940, "that the only possible effect of this war would be that the United States would emerge with an imperial power greater than the world had ever seen."[113] It was, of course, the basic premise of Henry Luce's "American Century" essay that the United States now had the potential to be "a dominant power in the world."[114] "In looking into the future, it is clear that it is America's policy which will give the first answer to what kind of world is to come out of the war," a Council on Foreign Relations memorandum observed in September 1941. "The United States is growing enormously in strength and power; the other nations are rapidly exhausting themselves; the disproportion between their resources and America's is constantly widening." The memorandum derived from one of the "War and Peace Studies" that the Council, in informal liaison with the State Department, had been sponsoring since September 1939. The premise of this enterprise, in which various international issues were addressed, was that the war presented the United States with a "grand opportunity" to become "the premier power in the world."[115] "We have now about 90 per cent of the gold in the world," Douglas Miller observed. "No matter what we intend to do, it will be important for the rest of the world."[116]

This perception that the nation's behavior would have global consequences induced in many a sense of moral responsibility. Henry Luce, the missionary's son, declared roundly that "as the most powerful and vital nation in the world . . . America is responsible, to herself as well as to history, for the world-environment in which she lives."[117] This sense of responsibility was greatly enhanced by the events of 1940. Whether or not Hitler's domination of Europe really posed a threat to the safety of North America, few informed observers could doubt that it had produced a situation in which the outcome of the war would depend on what the United States did—or failed to do. Given the values perceived to be at stake in the conflict, many were morally troubled by the consequences of inaction. As the columnist Dorothy Thompson put it, "you cannot say that you believe in freedom and democracy and then help to destroy it somewhere else."[118] In December 1940 Stimson described isolationists as "people who have no morals in international affairs."[119] This moral issue was keenly felt by many liberals, including some who had adopted a pacifistic, non-interventionist position a few years earlier. This movement of opinion was promoted by the passionate advocacy of the theologian Reinhold Niebuhr. "If we should define the present struggle in Europe as merely a clash between rival imperialisms," Niebuhr told the Senate Foreign Relations Committee, "it would merely mean that a strange combination of cynicism and abstract idealism had so corrupted the common-sense moral insights of a people that we could no longer distinguish between right and wrong."[120]

Niebuhr saw the Lend-Lease bill as justified by "the obligations which we owe to the community of nations as one of the nations which may be regarded as an inheritor and custodian of the standards of justice of western civilization."[121] The birthplace of that civilization, of course, was Europe, and the shock of Hitler's victories in 1940 seems to have brought home to many the involvement they felt with the continent from which the great majority of Americans or their forebears had come. Some changed their foreign policy views as a result. Among the most notable converts from isolationism at this time was Frank Knox, a former Republican vice-presidential candidate. Knox's newspaper, the *Chicago Daily News*, saw the fall of France as "nothing short of a disaster for the values we cherish."[122] Britain's peril moved Knox greatly. "The type of civilization that has developed in the United Kingdom has conditioned the development of American civilization," he told the Senate Foreign Relations Committee in 1941. "From a cultural standpoint it would be a calamity for us if British life were uprooted and replaced by a Nazi growth."[123] The salience of this sense of a common western civilization is often overlooked, but its importance may be gauged through an imaginary counterfactual. If Europe had been inhabited by peoples with whom they had no cultural connection (say, Hindus or Muslims), would Americans have felt their interests to have been so involved in the outcome of a war like that of 1939–41, even had the "objective" strategic and economic realities been exactly the same?

No segment of American society felt this cultural connection with Europe more strongly than the upper middle class WASPs of the East Coast. They had also been bred into the ethic that power brings responsibility, and as we have seen, many had long favored a much more active American role in world affairs. So it is not surprising that the most prominent and active advocates of all-out aid to the allies or even intervention were from this milieu.[124] While publicly playing up the threat to America's physical security, they clearly believed that the world's most powerful nation should have broader concerns. "The fundamental question," Lewis W. Douglas wrote to James B. Conant in October 1940, was "whether or not the American people will support a public policy resting upon the assumption of our world responsibilities."[125] Douglas and Conant were members of the "Century Group," founded in the summer of 1940 to promote American involvement in the war, as was the Episcopalian bishop Henry W. Hobson, who argued that "as children of God we, 'members one of another', have a world-wide responsibility for the well-being and rights of man."[126]

Many members of the Century Group were Anglophiles who had long sought to strengthen Anglo-American ties through such organizations as the English-Speaking Union.[127] Associated with this sentiment was the belief that British power had played a crucial and benign role in world affairs. In November 1939, Dean Acheson argued that "the economic and political system of the Nineteenth Century, which throughout the world produced an amazing increase in the production of wealth and population," had rested on British financial and naval power. With the decline of these, it was incumbent upon the United States to assume "some responsibility for making possible a world of order." Britain's desperate plight in 1940 seemed to people who interpreted history in this way to be the prompt for the United States to take over the role that Britain had played. In October, the longtime internationalist Norman H. Davis observed that the British would not be strong enough to hold their empire together after the war: "We shall in effect be the heirs of the Empire, and it is up to us to preserve its vital parts."[128]

Such views appealed to many in policymaking circles and the media, but they also aroused hostility in others. The private as well as the public writings of supporters of America First manifested a deep distrust of the Anglophile influence on American opinion, and suspicion that the United States was being manipulated into upholding the British Empire.[129] Nor did everyone see the issues of the European war in the same way. Lindbergh was not the only isolationist who feared the effects of a victory for either side in the European war. Several argued that continuing the war until Hitler was defeated would leave a devastated Europe prey to communism.[130] Taft, for example, declared that "the victory of communism in the world would be far more dangerous to the United States than the victory of fascism."[131] There were even some who thought the United States should align itself with Japan rather than China in the Far East.[132] Views about the requirements of American security were refracted through, and shaped by, particular ideological perspectives and views of foreign conflicts.

The variety of attitudes cannot be encompassed by a simple division between pro-British interventionists and neutralist isolationists. The belief that the United States should have more ambitious goals than simple survival or home-land defense could be inspired by a quite independent nationalism. Adolf Berle, for example, had been deeply distrustful of British policy since the Paris Peace Conference. "In the World War we came so into the English camp that we became virtually an adjunct to the British war machine," he noted in his diary in October 1940. "This time it seems to me that the thing should be the other way around." Berle predicted that the United States would be "the inevitable economic center of the regime which will emerge." Henry Luce insisted, "Stop the Nazi propa-ganda about fighting somebody else's war. We fight no wars except our wars." Americans must "exert upon the world the full impact of our influence, for such purposes as we see fit and by such means as we see fit." Such aspirations neces-sitated, of course, the frustration of Nazi ambitions. "If any one power dominates Asia, Europe and Africa," a General Staff officer wrote in his diary, "our country will ultimately become a second class power even if we gain South America and the whole of North America."[133]

A sense of the nation's power not only influenced the views and attitudes of many individual Americans; it was also reflected in the conduct of U.S. policy. This was true of both the setting of goals and the assessment of how these goals could be achieved. Whatever visions of a postwar world might be entertained by the study groups of the Council of Foreign Relations and others, the immediate objective was the defeat of the Axis Powers. Even though this was not explic-itly and openly declared to be the aim of U.S. policy before Pearl Harbor, it clearly became so during the course of 1940. At the time of the Welles Mission to Europe in February, the administration seems to have looked quite favorably on the possibility of a negotiated peace, but by December Roosevelt declared that such an outcome "would be no peace at all" but "only an armistice": "The expe-rience of the past two years has proven beyond doubt that no nation can appease the Nazis. No man can tame a tiger into a kitten by stroking it."[134] In other words, as the war situation deteriorated, U.S. objectives became more ambitious. In 1941, the purposes of American policy were set out in a way that was clearly premised on the defeat of the Axis. "Freedom means the supremacy of human rights everywhere," Roosevelt declared in his "Four Freedoms" address of Janu-ary 1941. "To that high concept there can be no end save victory." The Atlantic Charter, issued jointly with Churchill in August 1941, was explicitly about the principles that should govern the world "after the final destruction of the Nazi tyranny."[135]

It is true that, as an Army planner complained, it remained "more or less nebulous" how far the government was going "to commit itself with reference to the defeat of the Axis powers." In his November 1940 memorandum, Admiral Stark had concluded that, in order to secure victory over Germany, "the United States, in addition to sending naval assistance, would also need to send large air and land forces to Europe or Africa, or both, and to participate strongly in this land offensive." As Stark noted, the scenario was premised on Britain's retention of "geographical positions from which successful land action can later be launched"; keeping the British Isles out of enemy hands might not be vital to the defense of the Western Hemisphere, but it was essential if American military power was to be projected to Europe.[136]

The president was not willing to accept the logic of Stark's analysis. He clearly judged it politically impossible to declare war and send U.S. forces to Europe. But this did not cause him to lessen his commitment to the defeat of the Axis. Rather, he suggested that the objective could be achieved by transforming the United States into "the great arsenal of democracy." He expressed great confidence both in the scale of the country's industrial might and in its potentially determining effect on the outcome of the conflict. "With our national resources, our productive capacity, and the genius of our people for mass production, we will help Britain to outstrip the Axis powers in munitions of war," he told Congress. Privately, he assured Stimson "that the reservoir of munitions power available to the United States and her friends is sufficiently superior to that available to the Axis powers to insure defeat of the latter." In July 1941, Roosevelt asked the War and Navy departments for a report on "the overall production requirements required to defeat our potential enemies."[137]

The report produced two months later outlined a three-phase program of operations to achieve its "strategic objective," the "total defeat of Germany."[138] This "Victory Program" is not, as some have argued, proof that by this time Roosevelt had decided that the United States needed to enter the war as a full-scale belligerent. On whether or not that was the case, historians who have made thorough studies of the available evidence have come to different conclusions.[139] When he received the planners' report, the president indicated to Stimson his displeasure at the suggestion that "we must invade and crush Germany," and so the Victory Program remained, in the words of the official War Department history, "a hypothesis without real influence."[140] The true significance of such planning and of the broader commitment at this time to the goal of defeating the Axis Powers was the implicit confidence in American power that it reflected. The military leadership might have had doubts about the nation's will to fight, but they had a high estimation of its potential capabilities if it did. Pessimistically assuming that "Germany will occupy Russian territory west of the general line; White Sea, Moscow, Volga River (all inclusive) by July 1, 1942, and that militarily, Russia will be substantially impotent subsequent to that date," the staff officers who drew up the September 1941 study still envisaged that a preponderantly American force could successfully invade the continent of Europe and defeat Germany—provided that the United States made the urgent, all-out effort that they called for.[141]

Confidence in America's power also underlay the handling of relations with Japan in 1941. Following Hitler's victories in the summer of 1940, it was clear that France and Holland were quite unable to defend their colonies in Southeast Asia, and that Britain was only marginally better placed in this respect. In these circumstances, Washington began to bring American power to bear to contain Japanese expansion. The main U.S. fleet was stationed at Pearl Harbor in Hawaii, and export embargoes were imposed on aviation fuel and, when Japanese forces advanced into the northern part of Indochina, extended to all scrap metal. The Tripartite Pact between Japan, Germany, and Italy in September 1940 confirmed Roosevelt and his advisers in their view that the conflicts in Europe and Asia were parts of the same "world war" between dictatorship and democracy.[142] But the demands of some cabinet members for a total oil embargo and a greater naval presence in the western Pacific were rejected for many months. The resistance was led by Hull, who had a much larger role in formulating policy in this area than over the European war, and by the navy, which held firmly to the view Stark had developed in his memorandum that the United States should aim to avoid conflict with Japan and concentrate on the war against Germany.

Roosevelt adhered to this position until July 1941, when Japan, seeing the Soviet Union's preoccupation with Hitler's assault as an opportunity, moved into southern Indochina. Japanese assets in the United States were then frozen, subjecting all their American purchases to a system of licensing. As implemented, this became a total embargo, including on all oil. This was recognized as creating a critical situation for Japan, a country engaged in a demanding war in China and without petroleum resources of its own. Japanese officials in Washington were warned that an attack on the Netherlands East Indies, another source of oil, would in all probability mean war with the United States. At the same time, the creation of a full-scale Philippine army was announced, with General Douglas MacArthur called out of retirement to head it. In an attempt to get the embargo lifted, Japan entered negotiations with the United States, but Hull, who conducted these, made it clear that an agreement would be possible only if Japan accepted four principles of international conduct—principles that would, Hull indicated, entail a complete Japanese withdrawal from China. This was unacceptable in Tokyo, especially to army leaders, who saw it as representing a return to "Little Japan before the Manchurian incident." Seeing war with the United States as inevitable, the Japanese planned the surprise attack on Pearl Harbor as a preemptive strike. Before carrying it out, they proposed an interim agreement by which they would withdraw from southern Indochina in return for a lifting of the oil embargo and the suspension of American aid to China. After showing interest in some such modus vivendi, Hull and Roosevelt rejected the idea and insisted on Hull's original terms for a settlement.[143]

This was the course of events that has led Roosevelt's critics to accuse him of using a "back door to war"—taking advantage of the strongly anti-Japanese sentiment of the American people to bring them into the full-scale belligerency against Germany that he wanted but did not think he could gain public support for by direct means. This interpretation, without its hostile slant, has recently been endorsed by some political scientists who are perhaps predisposed to see policy as the product of rational strategic calculations.[144] It is, however, hard to reconcile with the record of the complex internal deliberations and diplomatic negotiations in the fall of 1941.[145] From this, it seems that the administration still sought to hold Japan in check through a policy of deterrence rather than to provoke a war. But it became harder to avoid war once this required the two sides to reach some sort of agreement because neither could modify its position on China sufficiently to make them reconcilable. Although the United States had not given China much practical support in the early years of the Sino-Japanese conflict, by 1941 with the extension of Lend-Lease aid to China (not to mention the official encouragement of Colonel Claire Chennault's Flying Tigers) a quasi-alliance had developed, bolstered by the well-placed and vocal "China lobby." More fundamentally, the United States had consistently refused to recognize the legitimacy of actions violating China's political independence and territorial integrity. To accept the continued presence of Japanese troops in that country, let alone submit to the demand that U.S. aid to China be suspended, would represent a retreat. Neither Roosevelt nor Hull was prepared to engage in this sort of "appeasement," even as part of a temporary accommodation to buy time.[146]

Conscious of the great imbalance in the two countries' power resources, many Americans believed that Japan could be compelled to accept American terms. "The noose is around Japan's neck at last," a writer in *PM* magazine declared when the oil embargo was imposed. "For a time it may bluster and retaliate, but in the end it can only whimper and capitulate."[147] Similar confidence was expressed by some policymakers. History showed, Stimson claimed, "that when the United States indicates by clear language and bold actions that she intends to carry out a clear and affirmative policy in the Far East, Japan will yield to that policy even though it conflicts with her own Asiatic policy and conceived interests."[148] Such confidence in the deterrent effect of American power was reinforced by the new B-17 heavy bombers; from July 1941, half of those being produced were sent to the Philippines, and there was talk in Washington of how this might make it possible to bomb the home islands of Japan itself as well as bases in Formosa and amphibious forces.[149]

However, in late November signals intelligence and other evidence indicated that deterrence had failed and that the Japanese were preparing a military offensive to the south. It was in this context that Roosevelt abandoned any interest in a modus vivendi and also assured the British that, in the event of an attack on their or the Dutch colonies, "we should obviously all be together."[150] He thus confirmed the premise that had underlain the conduct of relations with Japan since the imposition of the oil embargo. Whether or not it was the end they had actively sought (and it was probably not), American policymakers had shown themselves quite willing to run the risk of fighting a major war on two fronts. This was striking evidence of their basic confidence in the scale of American capabilities.

Looked at in detail, the course that the United States followed in this period was the product of a series of decisions by the president and his advisers (who themselves had significantly different outlooks) in response to unpredictable and dramatic overseas developments in the context of deeply felt divisions in American public opinion. But regarded more broadly, the behavior of the United States as an actor on the stage of world politics may be seen to reflect a coherent, rational, and consistent view of the national interest, one based on a scaled assessment of the costs and benefits of various outcomes.

From this point of view, full-scale participation in a world war was an extremely large cost, to be avoided if at all possible. The only benefit generally seen as sufficiently important to justify such a cost was safeguarding the territory of the United States itself. "The nation will offer the lives of its sons only for national defense," and "to the man in the street, national defense means defense against attack, and attack is identified with invasion," Spykman observed regretfully.[151] This explains why so much of the internal debate focused on the safety of North America, even in the late 1930s when the posited threats to that safety were too far-fetched to gain much credibility. Hitler's unexpected victories in 1940 greatly increased anxiety about the possibility of an attack on the Western Hemisphere and led to the ready acceptance of the cost of a substantial military build-up. As a proportion of GNP, defense spending rose from 1.4 percent in 1939 to 11.2 percent in 1941, and the American army grew from less than 190,000 men to a million and a half.[152] But the option of preempting any attack through a full-scale military offensive against the threat, although advocated by some, was not generally judged to be worth the cost. Most did not see such a preemptive move as vital for America's safety, either because they did not believe that the Axis Powers would ever be in a position to launch an attack on the United States itself or because they had confidence in the nation's ability to defend itself unaided, or for both reasons. In these circumstances, the issue, as Henry Luce observed, was "not primarily one of necessity and survival. It is a question of choice and calculation. The true questions are: Do we *want* to be in this war? Do we *prefer* to be in it?"[153]

The answer to Luce's question that was implicit in the actions that the United States took was "yes, to a significant, but limited, extent." The nation *did* become involved in the war—by unequivocally taking sides, by mobilizing its productive resources to aid the belligerents it favored, and by taking other actions, in both the Atlantic and Pacific theaters, which ran a high risk that the powers it was seeking to defeat or contain would view the United States as a belligerent and act accordingly. The costs of such actions were judged to be outweighed by the decisive effects it was hoped that they would have on the outcome of the conflict. That outcome mattered because it would determine, in quite fundamental ways, the nature of the world in which the United States would have to live. The interests at stake were at least as much moral, ideological, and power-political as strategic or economic. It is not possible to weigh the relative importance of these various considerations, and to attempt to do so is to try to impose upon history a neatness it did not have for, as we have seen, people's assessment of the security and economic consequences of a Nazi victory were inflected by other values. It is better and truer to say simply that most politically engaged Americans, including those in Congress as well as the administration, very much did not want to live in a world in which a victorious and unchecked Hitler dominated the whole of Europe. The belief that the actions of the United States would determine the outcome of the conflict derived partly from a perception of the limited capacities of the other states fighting the Axis and partly from a great confidence in the potential effectiveness of American power—even if this was not deployed and brought to bear in the form of full-scale military intervention.

From a wider perspective, it had taken a quite exceptional crisis in world politics to induce the United States, for a second time, to exercise something approaching its full power in an effort to achieve foreign policy objectives. In 1941, two aggressive military empires, in loose association with each other, were already in control of the most productive parts of Europe and East Asia and were continuing to expand their dominion in an apparently limitless way. That it took so much to overcome the reluctance to pay the price of exercising power that had so limited America's influence in the interwar years owed much to the powerful reaction against intervention in World War I and the costs that that had entailed. But it had also been due to the difficulty of demonstrating that truly important national interests were dependent on the achievement of foreign policy objectives. It remained to be seen whether Americans would be persuaded that they were in more normal circumstances than those of 1940–41. Even after Pearl Harbor, it was by no means certain that the abandonment of "isolationism" would be durable.

5

FULL-SCALE INVOLVEMENT, 1941–1945

The attack on the American fleet in Pearl Harbor ended debate about participation in the war. The declaration of war on Japan was passed by Congress quickly and with virtual unanimity, in contrast to the passionate debate and significant dissent in both houses over entry into World War I.[1] The America First Committee was dissolved. Given the bitter divisions over earlier measures, it is not surprising that Roosevelt's response to Pearl Harbor, according to the testimony of those close to him, included a considerable measure of relief.[2] It was a Japanese attack to the south, on the colonies of the European empires, that had been anticipated. Although the president had indicated, both to the Japanese and to the British, that the United States would respond to such a move with war, administration officials recognized that fulfilling this commitment would be politically difficult.[3]

The relief that Pearl Harbor induced in Roosevelt, Churchill, and others also shows that they did not fear that the United States would be drawn into an exclusively Pacific war, neglecting or downplaying its contribution to the struggle against the more formidable enemy in Europe. It is true that on the day after the attack the president asked Congress for a declaration of war only on Japan, resisting strong pressure from Stimson and others to add Germany and Italy. But in his subsequent radio address, FDR went further than ever (and well beyond the truth) in linking the three "gangster" nations, claiming that the U.S. government knew that "Germany and Japan are conducting their military and naval operations in accordance with a joint plan" and that "for weeks Germany has been telling Japan that if Japan did not attack the United States, Japan would not share in dividing the spoils with Germany when peace came." The president's delay in asking for a declaration of war with Germany was probably due not only to the misgivings about opinion "in some quarters of the public" that he expressed to the British ambassador but also to intelligence from intercepted messages that Hitler would take the initiative, which the Führer and Mussolini duly did on December 11.[4] This undoubtedly made things easier for Roosevelt, but the suggestion that otherwise the United States would have been trapped in a war only against the secondary threat is highly implausible. A survey in late December showed that most Americans shared the government's sense of strategic priorities; almost 60 percent identified Germany as the main enemy, only 32 percent Japan.[5]

Once in the war, the United States demonstrated the extraordinary scale of its economic and military strength, and the geopolitical implications of this. Its role in determining the outcome of this world war was even greater than it had been in the previous one three decades earlier. The maintenance of public support for the devotion of so many material and human resources to what remained a foreign war was made easier by the nature of America's contribution to the fight against the Axis Powers. An emphasis on maximizing the nation's productivity and on the use of air and naval power limited the toll of casualties. At the same time, innovative techniques and the employment of previously under-used labor power generated a degree of economic growth that enabled the domestic standard of living to rise even as the huge demands of war were being met.

More significant in the long run was the emergence of a political and popular consensus that the United States should take the lead after the war in establishing a peaceful international order. Contrary to a common belief, this consensus was not the direct product of the Pearl Harbor attack. Rather, it was the result of a broad and sustained exercise in public persuasion, led by the president but widely supported by a variety of politicians, institutions, and interest groups. The perceived lessons of history were central to these persuasive efforts, but the evidence suggests that it was not so much the Pearl Harbor attack in itself that discredited "isolationism" as the fact that the United States had now been drawn into a major foreign war twice in a generation. There were, however, two strands within the new "internationalist" consensus—a revived Wilsonianism, especially in Congress and public opinion, and a more Realpolitik emphasis on the fundamental role of hard power in international politics. The Roosevelt administration's postwar planning contained elements of both, which bequeathed an ambiguous legacy to its successors.

Wielding Global Power

The Scale of the War Effort

Both the exceptional dimensions and the particular nature of America's potential international power were demonstrated during World War II. The nation's armed forces grew to over twelve million by 1945—only those of the Soviet Union were larger. To some extent, this expansion had started before Pearl Harbor, largely as a result of the Selective Service Act of 1940; the army, which had numbered only 188,000 in 1939, had become 1.5 million strong by December 1941. A year later, it had grown to 5.4 million; by March 1945, to 8.1 million. (These figures include the Army Air Force.) The navy and Marine Corps had more than doubled their July 1940 size by the time of Pearl Harbor and increased almost tenfold thereafter. From these new recruits were drawn the great majority of the men who formed the land, sea, and air forces that fought a major war on two fronts—or three, if the skies above Germany and Japan are distinguished from the battlegrounds of the Pacific and those in North Africa and Europe.[6]

Impressive though these numbers were, manpower constituted a quite inadequate measure of the nation's military and naval might, as it was in the amount and quality of their weaponry and equipment that its forces were most superior to those of their enemies. Astonishingly, the United States built 8,812 major naval vessels between 1941 and 1945, dwarfing Britain's figure of 951 and Japan's of only 538. In retrospect, there was an almost pathetic naiveté about the Japanese idea that the surprise attack on Pearl Harbor might disable the American Pacific fleet. They were unlucky that the fleet's aircraft carriers were away from port at the time for various reasons, but the veteran battle-ships they sank (only two of which were beyond repair) would in any case have been too slow to participate in the naval battles of the Pacific war, which were to be dominated by fast carrier striking forces. In the fierce fighting of 1942, both the Japanese and the Americans lost four fleet aircraft carriers. By the end of 1943, however, the U.S. Navy had acquired fourteen new fast car-riers (including seven light carriers) and the Japanese none. The one-sided battles that destroyed the Imperial Japanese Navy in 1944 had really been won in the shipyards of Brooklyn and of Newport News and Norfolk, Virginia. Of at least equal importance to the outcome of the war as warships were the merchant ships that maintained Britain's lifeline across the U-boat–infested Atlantic and carried vital supplies to North Russian ports, and also the landing craft and ships that made possible the amphibious invasions central to both the Pacific war and Anglo-American operations in Europe. In response to all these demands, the performance of American shipbuilding was beyond previ-ous imaginings. More than 5,000 merchant ships, totaling 39 million gross tons, were launched in the course of the war, and also nearly 90,000 landing ships and landing craft.[7]

In the production of military equipment and aircraft the United States did not out-distance its allies and its enemies to quite the same extent; indeed, such was the increase in the Soviet output of tanks that by 1944 it was significantly larger than America's. Overall, however, the United States was in a league of its own as a manufacturer of munitions. Thus, its production of 306,180 military aircraft in 1941–45 compared with figures of 137,271 for the Soviet Union, 108,560 for Britain, 99,339 for Germany, and 69,888 for Japan. Nor do the sheer numbers reveal the advanced character of American warplanes, many of which were unmatched by anything produced by the Axis Powers. Unlike those of the other belligerents, the U.S. Army was completely mechanized; the infantry and artillery as well as the armored units were motorized. This was made possible by the prewar size of the domestic automobile industry and the availability of a large number of drivers and mechanics. During 1944, America produced 600,000 purpose-built army trucks; Germany made 88,000. It has been estimated that for every American soldier in the Pacific war there were four tons of supplies, for every Japanese soldier a mere two pounds. Finally, of course, the United States was the only country to develop the uncertain potential of nuclear weapons, making and then using in the summer of 1945 both an enriched uranium and a plutonium atomic bomb.[8]

In dollar terms, U.S. arms production in 1943 constituted 60 percent of the Allied total. By no means all of this ended up in the hands of American service-men. Under Lend-Lease, the United States supplied Britain with almost a quar-ter of its munitions as well as large quantities of machinery. The Soviet Union received much less in the way of weapons but was provided with hundreds of thousands of trucks and jeeps—it is estimated that by 1945 more than half of all the vehicles in the Red Army were of American origin. It was not only America's manufacturing industry that contributed so mightily to the joint war effort but also its agriculture and natural resources. Agricultural production, particularly of meat, expanded greatly, with a tenth of the food being exported, chiefly to the United Kingdom (43%) and the Soviet Union (28%).[9]

By far the most crucial resource for military combat, whether on land, on sea, or in the air was oil. The Axis Powers controlled only a small fraction of the world's petroleum production, and attempts to acquire more shaped the strategy of both Japan and Germany. The Allies were much more favorably placed because the chief source of oil at this time was the Western Hemisphere. The United States itself produced 63 percent of the world's petroleum in 1940, and the proportion rose slightly during the war even as global output almost doubled. However, uti-lization of this asset for military purposes required transporting oil to the fronts and increasing the quantity and quality of the high-octane fuel used by aircraft.

In meeting the first problem, a 1,380-mile-long pipeline was constructed from Texas to Pennsylvania, and tanker tonnage was built up to 11.4 million tons by 1945, compared to 2.5 million tons in 1941 (much of which had been sunk). By 1944 the United States was refining 90 percent of the Allies' aviation fuel and to a higher octane-value than that used by the Luftwaffe. In the end, two-thirds of all Lend-Lease supplies consisted of oil. "This is a war of engines and octanes," Stalin declared as he proposed a toast at the Tehran Conference in 1943. "I drink to the American auto industry and the American oil industry."[10]

Most basically, the enormous material contribution of the United States to the defeat of the Axis reflected the size of the American economy. But it also depended on more specific factors—rapid economic growth, organizational and technological innovation, and the devotion to the war effort of a high proportion of the nation's production. In money terms, GNP more than doubled between 1940 and 1944, from $100 billion to $210 billion; in real terms (allowing for inflation) it rose 60 percent. Manufacturing output in 1945 was twice as large as it had been in 1941. Such a large expansion was only possible because there was still a good deal of slack in the economy at the beginning of the European war. Despite eleven million people joining the armed forces between 1940 and 1944, the total number of people in civilian employment increased by over six million. This made it possible for the United States to increase substantially the amount of labor devoted to producing munitions without significantly reducing that engaged in other sectors (except possibly agricultural and household workers).[11]

The effectiveness of this larger labor force was enhanced by a growth in the productivity of labor and capital, which it has been estimated contributed about 24 percent of the increased output. This was partly the result of investment in bold new manufacturing techniques, the most famous of which is rightly the mass production of "Liberty ships" by Henry J. Kaiser through a radically new system of ship-building. Whereas at the start of the program, ships took 1.4 million man-hours and 355 days to build, by 1943 this had been reduced to under 500,000 man-hours and an average of 41 days. Mass production had been pioneered, of course, by the motor industry, which switched entirely after the United States entered the war from making cars to manufacturing vehicles, ordnance, and equipment for America's new armies. The assembly-line technique was adapted to the production of bombers, most notably at a huge new Ford plant called Willow Run. By 1944 each American aircraft worker was producing more than twice his German counterpart, four times the output of a Japanese worker. In the economy as a whole, between 1940 and 1945 productivity per worker-hour increased by 21 percent.[12]

World War II outranked all other foreign wars in America's history in terms of the proportion of the nation's resources that were devoted to it. From 1941 to

1945, an average of 32 percent of GNP was spent on the military, compared to 10.5 percent in the 1917–18 period, 10.4 percent in the Korean War (1950–53), and 7.7 percent in the Vietnam War (1964–72). In the peak years, 1943 and 1944, direct expenditure on the armed forces absorbed 36 to 38 percent of GNP, and a broader measure of "national security outlays" rose as high as 42 percent.[13]

The scale of the war effort led to the development of new institutions and instrumentalities for its direction and conduct. To combat the traditional problem of service independence and rivalry and also to facilitate coordination of military planning with the British, the Joint Chiefs of Staff (JCS) was created in January 1942, and a few months later Admiral William D. Leahy, as the president's chief of staff, joined the Army, Navy, and Air Force chiefs on this body. The military's growing importance in Washington was symbolized by the giant Pentagon building across the Potomac, into which it moved in 1942. That year, too, the Office of Strategic Services grew out of Colonel William D. Donovan's Office of the Coordinator of Information (OCI). The precursor of the Central Intelligence Agency, the OSS at its peak employed thirteen thousand people, including both scholarly analysts in Washington and nine thousand agents overseas. Over the course of the war, a plethora of other agencies were created to organize production, mobilize opinion at home and abroad, run Lend-Lease, conduct economic warfare, and handle relief programs in liberated areas. To run these agencies and manage the war effort, the government drew on the world of private business, particularly New York law firms and banks. Whereas the civilian employees of the federal government had constituted only 1 percent of the national labor force in 1938, by 1945 the proportion had risen to 5 percent.[14]

This massive commitment to a foreign war was impressively successful. In the summer of 1942, following Japan's sweeping victories in Southeast Asia and the German advances in the southern USSR and north Africa, the Axis Powers dominated one-third of the world's population and mineral resources. The complete unraveling of this position within the next three years was very largely the product of American power. This was obviously the case in the Pacific war, where a combination of amphibious advances by Nimitz's and MacArthur's forces across the islands of the Central and South Pacific, the virtual annihilation of Japan's merchant shipping by American submarines, and eventually the devastating air raids on its cities had brought the island empire to its knees even before the atomic bombs delivered the coup de grâce. In the European war, by far the largest and most prolonged land fighting was, of course, on the eastern front, and this accounted for more than half the total losses of the German army, in both casualties and prisoners. Yet it has been estimated that even in 1943, when the overwhelming majority of Germany's troops and tanks were deployed against the Red Army, more than half of its war production was directed against the western powers, not so much on land as in the battle of the Atlantic and attempts to counter the increasingly effective strategic bombing campaign. This proportion naturally increased in 1944 after D-Day and the opening of a major front in France. Taking into account also the importance of Lend-Lease aid to both the British and Russian war efforts, it seems safe to conclude that the actions of the United States determined the outcome of the European war also.[15]

Sustaining Public Support

In the event, then, the effectiveness of America's war effort served to vindicate Roosevelt's earlier confidence in the nation's ability to shape events overseas, provided that its potential power was mobilized and clearly focused. But experience had taught him the difficulty of achieving such mobilization and focus, and he certainly had not taken it for granted that the Pearl Harbor attack would inspire Americans with a willingness to make the wholehearted commitment and accept the inevitable costs that full-scale war required and entailed. From the beginning, he exhorted his countrymen to greater efforts in his public addresses and press conferences, and the concern to build and retain domestic support helped to shape the nature of America's war effort and also affected both strategy and diplomacy.

After Pearl Harbor as before, Roosevelt evinced implicit faith that America's vast industrial strength could determine the outcome of the conflict. "Victory," he explained in January 1942, was "a task, not only of shooting and fighting, but an even more urgent one of working and producing," because "the superiority of the United Nations in munitions and ships must be overwhelming—so overwhelming that the Axis Nations can never hope to catch up with it." He was confident that this could be achieved because, whereas "Germany, Italy and Japan are very close to their maximum output of planes, guns, tanks, and ships, the United Nations are not—especially the United States of America." As he had since 1938, he set very ambitious targets, calling for 60,000 aircraft in 1942 and 125,000 more in 1943, 120,000 tanks in the same period, 55,000 antiaircraft guns and 16 million deadweight tons of merchant shipping. Like Wilson before him, he evidently believed that the shadow of American power could itself have an effect, expressing the hope "that all these figures which I have given will become common knowledge in Germany and Japan."[16]

When Roosevelt had first called for the United States to become "the great arsenal of democracy," he had presented it as an alternative to "sending an American Expeditionary Force outside our own borders," and students of wartime strategy have concluded that he continued to see this role as the nation's "proper contribution to victory," thus "leaving most of the battle fighting to others while

Americans toiled on the production lines."[17] After Republicans in Congress attacked the size of the planned army, the Victory Program's target of a ground force of 215 divisions was cut back in 1942–43 to ninety; Stalingrad had ended the fear of a Russian collapse, and great hopes were pinned on the recently launched strategic bombing campaign. This reduced the number of men who needed to be drafted under the Selective Service Act. Although the initial exemption for married men was repealed in December 1942, few fathers were conscripted, and other exemptions, such as those for most agricultural workers, remained in place. Long-range bombing crews, where the death rate was high, were all volunteers. In the end, 18 percent of American families contributed at least one member to the armed forces; a high proportion in comparison with the nation's other foreign wars, but much lower than the other major combatants. The contrast was even greater with respect to casualties. A total of 405,399 American service personnel lost their lives, 291,557 in battle. For the Soviet Union, the comparable figure is variously estimated between 9 and 13 million, for Germany up to 5.5 million, for Japan 2.1 million, and even the British figure of 383,800 represented about three times the proportion of the country's 1939 population as the American figure did for the United States.[18]

However, Roosevelt's call for "a crushing superiority of equipment" also brought the war home, demanding greater effort and sacrifice from the whole nation, not only those who entered the armed services. Stressing that "there is one thought for us at home to keep uppermost—the fulfillment of our special task of production," the president sought in the aftermath of Pearl Harbor to sustain an aroused patriotism across all sections and classes: "It is not a sacrifice for the industrialist or the wage earner, the farmer or the shopkeeper, the trainman or the doctor, to pay more taxes, to buy more bonds, to forego extra profits, to work longer or harder at the task for which he is best fitted. Rather it is a privilege."[19] At this time it was anticipated in Washington that, as in other countries, the war would impose great hardships on the civilian population.[20]

This expectation proved much too pessimistic, and in the event the burdens the war imposed on most ordinary Americans were outweighed by the benefits it brought. There was, indeed, a great increase in taxes; whereas only four million paid any federal income tax in 1941, 42.6 million were doing so by 1945.[21] In addition, some consumer items, notably meat, butter, coffee, tires, and gasoline, were subject to rationing. But with so many more people in paying jobs and the good wages produced by a tight labor market, the great majority of households were better off than before. Notwithstanding the huge output of munitions and the export of goods under Lend-Lease, the American economy proved able to meet the consequent rise in domestic civilian demand. As calculated by the Commerce Department, real consumption per head did drop slightly in 1942 but then rose to a new peak in 1944. With an abundance of meat, fowl, and eggs, Americans were eating more protein than ever before. This experience was quite unique among the countries at war. Personal consumption shrank in the course of the war by 22 percent in Britain, nearly 20 percent in Germany, and 26 percent in Japan, while in the Soviet Union food output fell by two-thirds and many starved to death.[22]

But if hardship and deprivation might have undermined support for the war, their absence could also make it difficult to achieve the necessary degree of commitment to what remained essentially a distant war. The same dilemma applied to portrayals of the state of the conflict. On the one hand, the need to generate a sense of urgency could induce the government to play up the danger of defeat or of a direct attack on the Western Hemisphere. The Office of Civilian Defense ran articles on "What to Do in an Air Raid" in newspapers not only in the East Coast cities but also in small towns as far inland as Nebraska. It was vital, Archibald MacLeish, head of the Office of Facts and Figures, wrote in April 1942, to make people realize that "we *can* be defeated," that "America *can* lose," and that "It *Can* Happen Here!" In this vein, FDR sought to name the conflict "the war for survival." But one of his advisers warned that this term might seem "somewhat defeatist," and it was at least likely to strengthen the desire to keep most of the army at home, a course favored by more than a third (36 percent) of those polled in March 1942. At this time, with the Japanese surging ahead in Asia, the war was going badly, but the turn of the tide created a different sort of morale problem.[23] "Overconfidence and complacency are among our deadliest enemies," Roosevelt warned in January 1944, as he pointed out that after Allied victories in Russia, north Africa, and the Atlantic, war production had fallen off the previous summer. A few weeks earlier, he had observed to Harold Ickes that "it really would be a good thing for us if a few German bombs could be dropped over here."[24]

It was no accident that the president referred to *German* bombs. Bombs had been dropped on Hawaii, of course, but by the Japanese, and this presented continuous problems for sustaining public and political support for the "Hitler-first" strategy. The initial success in persuading people that Germany was the main enemy came under pressure with the sweeping Japanese advance in early 1942, and in particular the press coverage of the desperate and heroic stand of the American and Filipino forces on Bataan. Polls now showed a more than two to one majority in favor of directing the country's main efforts toward beating Japan, a sentiment unsurprisingly held on the west coast particularly strongly. It was to counter demands for a Pacific-oriented war as well out of a desire to offer some relief to the Russians that Roosevelt insisted on a ground operation against the European Axis in 1942, overcoming the strong opposition of Marshall and the other joint chiefs to the north African offensive that was eventually launched in November. Even after this was underway, a poll in February 1943 found a majority of 53 to 34 percent identifying Japan rather than Germany as "our chief enemy," although opinion about which theater most resources should be devoted to fluctuated in response to external events.[25] Underlying these oscillations was the fact that, whereas Germany was generally recognized to be the more powerful foe, the animus toward Japan was more intense and universal. Asked "Which country do you think we can get along with better after the war?" in the early summer of 1943, 67 percent said Germany and only 8 percent Japan. "The enemy whom the American people really hated," Stimson explained to Churchill, "was Japan which had dealt them a foul blow." But there was more to it than the desire to avenge Pearl Harbor, including clearly a strong racial element.[26]

Moreover, there had always been less division of opinion over the Asian conflict than the European one. To many, that the fight in the Pacific was an almost exclusively American one, not involving significant collaboration with European powers, made it the ideologically purer cause as well as the more patriotic. The Asian ally, China, seen as a victim rather than a practitioner of power politics, was almost universally popular. By contrast, there was widespread suspicion that Britain was mostly concerned with the preservation of her empire, and fear that a Soviet triumph over Germany would lead to the spread of a communism that many, especially conservative Republicans, found even more obnoxious and threatening than fascism.

Concern that such suspicions and fears should not weaken support for the war against Germany helped to shape both American diplomacy and Roosevelt's public statements. Distrust of British imperialism had always been the chief impediment to close Anglo-American relations, and it was principally for this reason that Roosevelt persistently urged a highly resistant Churchill to smooth the path toward Indian independence or at least self-government. Likewise, unlike Britain, the United States firmly resisted Moscow's demands in 1941–42 that the western powers sign a treaty recognizing the Soviet Union's June 1941 boundaries (which incorporated the Baltic states, territories gained from Finland and Romania, and the eastern part of Poland seized under the Nazi-Soviet pact). In explaining their refusal to accept this proposal to the Russians, Roosevelt and his emissaries stressed the bad impression such an agreement would make on American public opinion, where the general suspicion of big-power carve-ups at the expense of small nations would be reinforced by the particularly intense feelings of Polish-Americans and other east European ethnic groups. The American position softened thereafter, in the face of the desire for Soviet cooperation after the war as well as during it, awareness that it would hardly be possible to force the Red Army out of positions it had occupied, and an increasing recognition by U.S. officials that there was a case for the revision of the advanced Polish frontier of 1939. But the reversion to the "Curzon line" of 1919 was not formally agreed upon until the Yalta conference of February 1945, Roosevelt having evaded making any public commitment on postwar boundaries at the Tehran Conference in late 1943 by stressing to Stalin the likely effects of doing so on his reelection prospects in 1944.[27]

The desire to "sanitize" America's allies ideologically was also apparent in the image of the Soviet Union that became widely current in the war years. Reports and commentary, especially in "internationalist" media and literature, emphasized that it was traditional Russian patriotism rather than communist fervor that was inspiring the fight against the German invader; the dissolution of the Comintern in 1943 was regarded as highly significant, and much was made of the regime's increasing toleration of religion. Roosevelt reassured the press in March 1944 that the Russians were "friendly people" who "haven't got any crazy ideas of conquest and so forth."[28]

The president's consciousness of both the heterogeneous character of the Grand Alliance and the potentially divisive effects at home of a too precisely defined ideological commitment was reflected in the way he presented the issues at stake in the war. Fascism as a doctrine was not identified as the enemy in the way that communism would be in the Cold War, and even the general link that Roosevelt had made in the 1930s between international aggression and nondemocratic regimes was now somewhat downplayed.[29] Rather, the president stressed that the nation was fighting to uphold the most basic legal and moral norms, several times describing the foe as "international gangsterism." After Pearl Harbor, Americans faced "a long war against crafty and powerful bandits." As the historian Emily Rosenberg has pointed out, such language, especially in association with the "treachery" of the Japanese attack, evoked the powerful national myths of Indian-fighting and outlaw-subduing on the frontier. Roosevelt plucked the chords of other consensual values by charging that the Nazis had a "plan for enforcing their new, pagan religion all over the world—a plan by which the Holy Bible and the Cross of Mercy would be replaced by *Mein Kampf* and the swastika and the naked sword," and later by describing the need after the war to restrain "any other nation which seeks to violate the Tenth Commandment—'Thou shalt not covet.'" This portrayal of the conflict in terms of a pervasive cultural myth and a generally accepted moral code no doubt arose from FDR's instinct about how best to appeal to the emotions of ordinary Americans, but it was also a way of side-stepping more controversial issues.[30]

There was in any case strong pressure for national unity behind the war effort. This did not lead to coalition government and the suspension of elections, as it did in Britain; the ordinary processes of domestic politics and party conflict continued, with the administration having to face both critical commentary in the media and opposition in Congress to many of its measures and proposals. But the furthest the "peace bloc" went was to express a readiness to consider a peace on the basis of the status quo "if the German Army overthrew Hitler." There was no equivalent of the armed resistance to the draft or the outright antiwar electoral campaigns of World War I. But on that earlier occasion, too, mainstream politicians of both parties and the overwhelming majority of newspapers had rallied behind the war effort. It had been with respect to the postwar settlement and the nation's future policy that serious and deep divisions had arisen and support for a continuing commitment had eroded.[31]

The Discrediting of "Isolationism"

Pearl Harbor is the prime exhibit in the argument of those who see America's adoption of a world role as something forced on a reluctant nation by external developments. In popular media, it is remembered as "the moment that changed Americans from a nation of provincial innocents, not only ignorant of the great world but proud of their ignorance, into a nation that would often have to bear the burdens of rescuing that world."[32] Historians, too, have seen the surprise attack as teaching Americans the need for a broader conception of national security because it "undermined as perhaps nothing else could have the cherished notion that America was secure from foreign threat."[33] Much cited in this connection is the later remark of the staunch anti-interventionist Senator Arthur Vandenberg that his "convictions regarding international co-operation and collective security for peace took firm form on the afternoon of the Pearl Harbor attack. That day ended isolationism for any realist."[34]

Vandenberg's immediate reaction, however, did not register the Damascene effect he later claimed that "that day" had had. On December 11, 1941, just after Germany and Italy had declared war on the United States, the senator wrote in his private diary: "The interventionist says today—as the president virtually did in his address to the nation—'See! This proves we were right and this war was *sure* to involve us.' The non-interventionist says (and I say)—'See! We have insisted that this course would lead to war and it has done exactly that.'" This was a common reaction of anti-interventionists to the Japanese attack. "This continuous putting pins in rattlesnakes," remarked Herbert Hoover, "has finally got this country bitten." "Our principles were right," the America First Committee declared. "Had they been followed, war could have been avoided."[35]

This response reveals two ways in which the idea that the long-term character of U.S. foreign policy was transformed by Pearl Harbor is misleading. In the first place, it reminds us that the United States had abandoned "isolationism" and the strategy of unilateral continental defense ("Fortress America") *before* December 1941. As we have seen, by that time it had been intervening in a major way in overseas conflicts for at least eighteen months through its aid to the countries fighting Hitler and the sanctions imposed on Japan. Moreover, the purpose of such intervention had not been only to avert a perceived immediate threat to the nation's own security. As far as the administration and influential circles outside it were concerned, defeating the Axis nations was preliminary to the achievement of ambitious postwar goals. Roosevelt himself had made this clear in his January 1941 "Four Freedoms" address and the Atlantic Charter. Even before the fall of France, Secretary of State Cordell Hull had also publicly stressed "the vital need of throwing the weight of our country's moral and material influence in the direction of creating a stable and enduring world order under law."[36]

Behind the scenes, more detailed preparatory work was undertaken. As early as December 1939, a committee was established in the State Department "to survey the basic principles which should underlie a desirable world order" and "to determine policies which should be pursued by the United States in furtherance of the establishment of such a world order." In this enterprise, the State Department unofficially drew on the personnel and resources of the Council on Foreign Relations. By December 1941, this "War and Peace Studies" project had prepared some 250 memoranda on the historical background of the war, what the United States should do in the immediate future, and what the postwar world should look like. These memoranda were prepared by "study groups" in which serving military officers and government officials participated along with scholars, businessmen, journalists, and other publicists and commentators. As one of the participants in this process wrote to another in September 1941, the planning was based on the assumption "that Germany will be defeated and that England with participation on the part of the United States will win the war by a clear and uncompromising victory enabling us to disarm the enemy."[37]

The Council on Foreign Relations was by no means the only organization with ties to the government that was engaged before Pearl Harbor in systematic thinking about the long-term goals of American foreign policy. As early as 1937 Professor Edward M. Earle of Princeton's Institute of Advanced Study had sought funding for a "research seminar" that would seek to produce a comprehensive "grand strategy for the United States" and in the meantime generate new ideas for "key people in the government services." This seminar attracted several notable scholars, some of whom were to become pioneers in the field of strategic studies. The scope and scale of such activities grew greatly after the outbreak of the European war and particularly after the fall of France. The Carnegie and Rockefeller foundations funded research into the role the United States should play with regard to the postwar settlement. Earle directed much of this work, and his own ties with Washington were strengthened in July 1941 when William Donovan called on him to help organize and staff the Research and Analysis Division of the OCI. All this activity took place before Pearl Harbor.[38]

Second, the initial response of anti-interventionists to Pearl Harbor shows that the Japanese attack did not automatically create a consensus behind an "internationalist" approach to America's national security and role in the world. The Council on Foreign Relations, reporting on the views expressed by its twelve regional committees of American leaders, concluded in 1942 that "Pearl Harbor changed no one's thinking very much."[39] Vandenberg's diary entry implicitly referred back to his warning that there was "no middle ground" between being "all the way in" the war and "all the way out."[40] Pearl Harbor could be seen as exposing the illusion that the United States might be able to employ its power to determine the outcome of the conflict without paying the full price for doing so. In principle, this could have led to the conclusion that the commitment had not been worth the ultimate cost. This had been the case in the aftermath of World War I and would be later regarding Vietnam.

In short, the "lessons" of Pearl Harbor were not self-evident; as with most historical events, the implications of the Japanese attack depended on the way it was interpreted.[41] Rather than seeing it as the basic cause of America's adoption of a globalist foreign policy, it is better viewed as an episode, albeit a major one, in the long-running debate over how far, and in what ways, the circumstances of the twentieth century required or obliged the United States to define its vital interests and responsibilities more widely than it had done in the past—and to pay the necessary price for achieving these more ambitious goals. It was within the framework of that debate that the long-term significance of Pearl Harbor was interpreted at the time and has been since.[42]

Roosevelt himself lost no time in relating Pearl Harbor to the broader issues of national strategy and policy that had been the subject of such intense debate beforehand. "We have learned a terrible lesson," he told the nation two days after the attack. As the president portrayed it, this lesson had several aspects. The first was the inadequacy of a strategy of a continental defense: "We have learned that our ocean-girt hemisphere is not immune from severe attack—that we cannot measure our safety in terms of miles on any map any more." Lest some of his listeners doubted whether Hawaii was properly part of the United States itself, he warned that "the attack at Pearl Harbor can be repeated at any one of many points, points in both oceans and along both coast lines and against all the rest of the hemisphere." Second, Roosevelt drew the moral that "there is no such thing as security for any Nation—or any individual—in a world ruled by the principles of gangsterism." This he took as vindication of his administration's actions since the fall of France: "Our policy rested on the fundamental truth that the defense of any country resisting Hitler or Japan was in the long run the defense of our own country." This implied adopting a less unilateralist course. Thus, the United States was now engaged in a collaborative effort "with other free peoples . . . to maintain our right to live among our world neighbors in freedom and in common decency, without fear of assault."[43]

These points were reiterated and developed tirelessly in the next few years, not only by members of the administration but also by commentators and scholars seeking to promote a wider conception of the nation's security requirements, both among the general public and in the thinking of the military. The least controversial proposition was the need for a broader geographical definition of the nation's defense zone. As early as November 1939, Dean Acheson had maintained that "with a nation, as with a boxer, one of the greatest assurances of safety is to add reach to power" and that the United States needed to develop "a navy and air force adequate to secure us in both oceans simultaneously and with striking power sufficient to reach to the other side of one of them." The natural inclination to strike back at the Japanese after Pearl Harbor made this a propitious time to drive home the case for, in Roosevelt's words, "carrying the war to the enemy in distant lands and distant waters—as far away as possible from our own home grounds." "Those who still think in terms of the days of sailing ships," the president declared, "advise us to pull our warships and our planes and our merchant ships into our own home waters and concentrate solely on last-ditch defense." Before the war, such adherents of an illusory isolationism had "wanted the American eagle to imitate the tactics of the ostrich. Now, many of those same people, afraid that we may be sticking our necks out, want our national bird to be turned into a turtle. But we prefer to retain the eagle as it is—flying high and striking hard."[44]

As in World War I, the transoceanic projection of American power could easily be justified by the immediate objective of defeating the enemy. But this time it also led, as it had not on the previous occasion, to a re-formulation of defense strategy in the long term. Belligerency advanced the process that had begun with Stark's November 1940 memorandum by which military planners moved beyond the traditional conception of continental or hemispheric defense. In a report completed in November 1943, the Joint Chiefs of Staff argued that the "direct defense" of the United States and its possessions required encircling the Western Hemisphere with a ring of outlying bases. In the Pacific this ring had to include the Aleutians, the Philippines, and the islands that the Japanese had held as mandates under the League of Nations. In the Atlantic, the minimum requirements were bases in the Azores or Canary Islands, Iceland and Greenland. In pressing the case for this wider strategic frontier, the Army Air Force Chief, General H. H. Arnold pointed to the dangers posed by technological developments in weaponry and aircraft range: "We must meet such attack as far from our own borders as possible to insure against any part of the United States mainland being visited by a sudden devastation beyond any 'Pearl Harbor' experience or our present power of imagination to conceive." The potential threat to American security was so grave that it should override "avoidable restrictions upon our ability to base and operate military aircraft in and over certain territories under foreign sovereignty."[45]

As Arnold intimated, such "defense in depth" modulated the traditional unilateralism of America's military planning by implying that the United States needed to establish security relationships with other countries. Walter Lippmann developed this point in *U.S. Foreign Policy: Shield of the Republic* (1943): "The strategic defenses of the United States are not at the three-mile limit in American waters, but extend across both oceans and to all the trans-oceanic lands from which an attack by sea or by air can be launched. . . . In the new age of air power it extends beyond the coast line to the lands where there are airdromes from which planes can take off." As Lippmann described them, the ramifications of this were far-reaching. The fall of France in 1940 had "opened up the threat, in the event of a German victory in Europe, of a sea-borne and air-borne invasion of South America," thus demonstrating that "France is a member of the great defensive system in which the American republics live." The Netherlands and Belgium constituted "outer bastions" of both France and Britain, while Denmark and Norway were also members of the Atlantic Community. Thus Lippmann saw the defense of most of western Europe as vital for America's own physical safety.[46]

The need to guard the gateways to America's ocean frontiers was not the only reason why Lippmann saw a commitment to the independence of countries on other continents as necessary for America's own security. He also argued that the nation had a vital interest in maintaining a balance of power in Eurasia because otherwise it could be outmatched in a global contest. He presented this case in simple terms:

> The area of American defensive commitment is not quite 40 per cent of the land surface of the earth. But it contains a little less than 25 per cent of the population of the earth. The Old World contains 75 per cent of mankind living on 60 per cent of the land of this globe. Thus it is evident that the potential military strength of the Old World is enormously greater than that of the New World. When we look more closely at the facts of power the disparity is even greater. The only arsenal of the New World is in North America. . . . The Old World, on the other hand, comprises the military states of Britain, Russia, Germany, France, Japan, Italy, and China—all of them arsenals or potential arsenals and each of them with a population used to war and the carrying of arms.

Lippmann concluded "that the New World cannot afford to be isolated against the combined forces of the Old World, and that it must, therefore, find in the Old World dependable friends."[47]

Lippmann's book sold half a million copies, was condensed in *Reader's Digest*, and was published by the *Ladies' Home Journal* in the form of seven pages of cartoon strips.[48] But, while it was perhaps the most widely circulated attack on the "mirages" underlying prewar "isolationism," it was by no means the only one. The most thorough and sophisticated presentation of the "realist" perspective was Spykman's *America's Strategy in World Politics* (1942). Although written as a contribution to the pre–Pearl Harbor debate, this work stressed that the dependence of America's security on a balance of power in Europe or Eurasia would outlast the current conflict just as it had long predated it. As we have seen, it was not so much the nation's safety from direct attack that Spykman saw as being at stake as its "power position in the world." He wrote, "The outcome of the Second World War will determine whether the United States is to remain a great power with a voice in the affairs of the Old World, or become merely a buffer state between the mighty empires of Germany and Japan." Discounting the role of "moral values" in the conduct of foreign policy, Spykman offered "an analysis of the position of our country in terms of geography and power politics."[49]

Spykman's book was the harbinger of what became something of a vogue for geopolitics. To some extent, this arose from the assumption that the thinking of German geopoliticians, particularly Karl Haushofer, had shaped the policies of the Third Reich. Spykman was careful to distance himself from their approach, emphasizing that peace and security should be the aim of national policy, rather than "expansion and aggrandizement of power," but the association seems only to have added to the authority accorded the ideas and axioms of the British geographer Halford Mackinder, who was universally acknowledged as the founding father of this "science." Mackinder's 1919 work *Democratic Ideals and Reality* was re-published in New York in 1942 with an introduction in which Earle hailed the author as "one of the truly outstanding students of strategy." Earle highlighted Mackinder's insistence that "the World-Island" of Europe, Asia, and Africa constituted "the true center of gravity of world power, the Western Hemisphere being only an island of lesser proportions, lesser manpower, and lesser natural resources." Like Roosevelt in his September 1941 Fireside Chat, Mackinder had argued that "if the Great Continent, the whole World-Island or a large part of it, were . . . to become a single and united base of sea-power," the other "insular bases" (Great Britain and the United States) would be "outbuilt as regards ships and outmanned as regards seamen."[50]

Mackinder's terminology became widely current. Thus, in introducing Spykman's *The Geography of the Peace*, posthumously published in 1944, Frederick

Sherwood Dunn, director of the Yale Institute of International Studies, observed that the "principal lesson" was the need to prevent "the rimlands of Europe and Asia" from being controlled by "a single power or combination of powers hostile to the United States." Should that be allowed to happen, "the resulting encirclement would put us in a position of grave peril, regardless of the size of our army and navy." Dunn, along with Earle, William T. R. Fox, Grayson Kirk, Arnold Wolfers, and others, was one of the authors of a Brookings Institution study in 1945 that concluded that postwar "security policy" should be based on the premise that the United States would not be able to withstand attack from an adversary who had subdued the whole of Europe or Eurasia.[51]

As we have seen, the argument that, to be secure, the United States needed allies, or at least friendly nations, beyond the Western Hemisphere was not a new one. That the safety of North America from external attack depended on British command of the Atlantic and a balance of power in Europe had been argued by Mahan, Lewis Einstein, and others before World War I. During that conflict, it had been among the reasons given for favoring the Allied cause, and it had figured in the campaign for preparedness in 1914–16. In the assault on "isolationism" that developed in the late 1930s, and particularly after the fall of France, this view of the foundations of American security had been energetically propounded by supporters of aid to the Allies from the president down. It may well have helped to generate the necessary political and public support for a departure from neutrality that carried a real risk of war, but it had not created the consensus necessary to sustain full-scale belligerency—or even the sort of postwar commitment that Wilson had made in 1916. Many of those who had been skeptical about the claim that America's security was truly dependent on what happened on other continents had seen the interventionist actions of 1940–41 as likely to lead to war. Why should they have been persuaded by the Pearl Harbor attack that the nation now needed to adopt a long-term policy involving potentially costly commitments?

The manner in which the case for a wider definition of America's security requirements had been made may help to answer this question. As we have seen, the contrary assessments of the strategic implications of aviation advanced by anti-interventionists like Lindbergh and Hanson Baldwin had not been engaged at the technical level. Nor, with the exception of Spykman's analysis of the availability of strategic and critical materials, had the military relevance of the relative populations and resources of the Old and New Worlds ever been spelled out. Much more commonly, the argument had rested on an interpretation of history. "The kind of isolation which we enjoyed until 1914 and which we rightly cherish today as an ideal, was the product, not of geography, but of great statesmanship," Lippmann wrote as Hitler's armies advanced on Paris. Recognizing that oceans were "not a barrier" but "a highway," the leaders of the young republic had insulated the United States from the powers of continental Europe through the Louisiana Purchase and the "joint and parallel policy" with Great Britain of the Monroe Doctrine. Subsequent presidents had implicitly realized that "the security of the Atlantic Ocean is and always has been the most fundamental American interest" and that this had depended on "British command of the seas." This version of history, forcefully propounded by Lippmann in a series of featured articles in Henry Luce's *Life* magazine in 1940–41, was presented at book length by Forrest Davis in *The Atlantic System* (1941). Edward M. Earle adopted the same mode of argument but extended the scope of concerns attributed to past American statesmen, particularly "the Fathers of this nation": "Almost from the beginning it was recognized that our security depended not merely upon relative geographical remoteness, but equally upon the European balance of power, the maintenance of the British navy, and the existence of a universal concept of international order."[52]

A key part of this narrative was a revised explanation of U.S. entry into World War I. Earle had led the way here. In articles published during the "phony war" of 1939–40, he argued that the real reason for intervention had been to prevent a German victory that would have left the United States "in a precarious strategic position."[53] As France fell, Lippmann sought to give this interpretation greater authority by citing his own experience at the time: "America entered the World War because Germany's declaration of unlimited submarine warfare threatened to blockade and starve the Allies and to destroy British sea power. I venture to say this categorically and on the basis of direct personal knowledge of what determined President Wilson's decision." When the Lend-Lease Act was passed, Lippmann observed that "for the second time in 23 years the American people have intervened in a war towards which they had meant to be neutral." The reason, he argued, was the same in both cases: "We intervened the first time when, and only when, a victorious Germany was threatening to conquer Britain and to become the master of the other shore of the Atlantic Ocean; . . . we are intervening a second time at a similar point in the war and for exactly the same fundamental reason."[54]

That the United States had entered World War I to prevent a German victory was now argued by others besides Lippmann. No further evidence about the thinking of Wilson and others at the time was offered, but instead some writers asserted that this is what American leaders *must* been concerned about, given the situation.[55] Such claims suggested that the dynamics of the international power system shaped the behavior of statesmen in a way they did not avow and may not even have been fully conscious of. This reading of history became axiomatic among interventionists and later policymakers.[56]

This view implied that the realm of foreign policy choice was limited. If the United States was compelled always to maintain the balance of power in the Old World, its actions would be determined by external developments. By precipitating the nation into full-scale belligerency, Pearl Harbor could be seen as confirming that there was no escaping this geopolitical logic. The argument *from* history had been validated *by* history. After Pearl Harbor, only some 20 percent of Americans continued to believe that intervention in World War I had been a mistake.[57] Thereafter, policymakers, commentators, and historians commonly took the very fact that the United States had intervened in both world wars as demonstrating that the nation had a vital interest in maintaining the European balance of power.[58]

However, it was not necessary to hold this geopolitical conception of the nation's security requirements in order to conclude that experience had shown that it was no longer possible for the United States to avoid involvement in major overseas wars. As we have seen, Wilson had had no perceptible anxieties about the safety of the North American continent when he had declared in 1916 that the impact of the European war on the United States had shown that "we are participants, whether we would or not, in the life of the world" and that "what affects mankind is inevitably our affair as well as the affair of the nations of Europe and of Asia." The only way that the United States could continue to enjoy the benefits of peace, Wilson had argued, was by exercising its great potential strength in international affairs to prevent wars from arising in the first place. In campaigning for ratification of the Treaty of Versailles in 1919, he had predicted "with absolute certainty that, within another generation, there will be another world war if the nations of the world—if the League of Nations—does [*sic*] not prevent it by concerted action." He had also warned that such a war would be fought with "methods of destruction inconceivable" and that the United States would inevitably be involved.[59]

These prophecies were frequently recalled as events seemed to fulfill them. To those who had never abandoned the Wilsonian faith, the collapse of the international order in the 1930s served to confirm it. When Hitler took over Czechoslovakia in March 1939, Clark M. Eichelberger of the League of Nations Association (LNA) observed that "if, as many people say, the World War has finally been lost, it was lost twenty years ago in the United States Senate."[60] At this time, others drew the contrary lesson—that the failure of the League of Nations to preserve the peace showed the unrealistic nature of Wilson's scheme and confirmed the wisdom of not having taken part in it. But the deepening involvement of the United States itself in the European war after 1940 provided Wilsonian internationalists with more ammunition. "The American people are now paying the price of two decades of international irresponsibility," former LNA director

James Shotwell declared in June 1941. After the United States became a belliger-ent, the lesson was driven home relentlessly. "Do you want another bloody, ruin-ous war in 25 years? Did the U.S. Senate in 1919 unwittingly vote for Pearl Har-bor?" demanded a booklet distributed by the hundred thousand in 1943. A full-page advertisement in the *New York Times* blamed "the long depression, Hitler in Germany, the League failure, the war, Pearl Harbor, our hundreds of expended billions, our dying and our dead" on American rejection of the League. In 1944, the rehabilitation of the twenty-eighth president and his ideas reached a climax. *Look* magazine published a pictorial biography with the subtitle "The Unforget-table Figure Who Has Returned to Haunt Us," while Darryl F. Zanuck in Holly-wood portrayed the former president as a humane hero with prophetic vision in the Technicolor blockbuster *Wilson*. Although the unprecedentedly large budget (even exceeding that for *Gone With the Wind*) was not recouped by box office receipts, the movie won five Oscars and was seen by millions of Americans.[61]

Zanuck's film was part of the extraordinarily energetic and multi-faceted campaign during the war years to build public support for participation in a postwar international organization. Not surprisingly, the lead was taken by peo-ple who had long been active in such organizations as the League of Nations Association, the Foreign Policy Association, and the Council on Foreign Rela-tions. The Council had created regional committees on foreign relations as early as 1938, to be made up of "leading individuals" in cities across the country. Most of the members were businessmen and professionals, but trade union and farm leaders were also represented together with some congressmen, columnists, and others in the media. During the war, these bodies became active proponents of the view that, in the words of the St. Paul-Minneapolis committee, "America has a responsibility for world organization which it cannot discharge alone, but only in concert with the international community." Likewise, the Federal Council of Churches in America, which had been another redoubt of pro-League sentiment in the interwar years, was quick to redouble its commitment in the more propi-tious climate, establishing a Commission on a Just and Durable Peace under the energetic chairmanship of John Foster Dulles as early as December 1940.[62]

But such longstanding centers of support were far from the only ones engaged in mustering support for "internationalism" during the war years. Importantly, the cause generated an exceptional breadth of support among the commonly divided churches of the country. "If there was ever a consensus moment in Amer-ican religious politics," Andrew Preston notes in his authoritative study of the influence of religion on attitudes to foreign policy, "it was over the need for a fed-eral world order." A "World Order Sunday" in October 1943 attracted the support even of conservative Southern Presbyterians and Baptists. Catholic bishops and organizations, too, became strong proponents of international organization, as did many representatives of Judaism. Established social organizations and interest groups also became involved in the campaign. In 1943–44, local veterans' groups, women's clubs, labor unions, and business associations passed resolutions supporting participation in a postwar international organization. The U.S. Chamber of Commerce conducted a referendum among its members in which 1,829 favored American entry into a world body possessing the power to use force in the maintenance of peace, with only 71 dissenting.[63]

Several of the organizations most prominent in this campaign drew their membership overwhelmingly from well-educated professional and business people, mostly from the northeastern part of the country. Their activities were financed by foundations, particularly the Carnegie Corporation, as well as by wealthy individuals. The Carnegie and Rockefeller foundations also funded scholars and academic enterprises engaged in research directed toward providing the intellectual basis for a more ambitious engagement with world politics, and the Carnegie Endowment promoted bipartisan political support for the cause by helping to finance a speaking tour by eight teams of congressmen in the summer of 1943. Following the Moscow Declaration of November 1943 in which the administration, together with the Soviet Union, Britain, and China, committed itself to the creation of an international organization to maintain peace, the State Department embarked on an extensive public relations campaign under the direction of the new undersecretary of state, Edward Stettinius. The plan for an international organization that emerged from the Dumbarton Oaks conference in the summer of 1944 was publicized very widely not only through printed material but also by informal, off-the-record briefings for representatives of pressure groups, speaking tours across the country by State Department teams that included high officers as well as staff members, and the participation of officials in panel discussions on the radio.[64]

In view of all this, it is hard to dispute the observation of the historian Inderjeet Parmar that, in the contest over what "lessons" should be drawn from Pearl Harbor and other events, "the power to win attention for one interpretation rather than another was unequally distributed."[65] But it would be wrong to attribute the emergence of a political and public consensus that the United States should play a leading part in world affairs after the war solely to the activities and social power of an economic and political elite. After all, the people and organizations leading the campaign had been in favor of a much more active involvement in world politics for decades but had been frustrated by the unwillingness of Congress and the general public to meet the costs of a more strenuous policy. Both the increased intensity and focus of their own efforts during the war years and the greater receptivity to their message of people across the country (and, relatedly, of politicians) can be attributed only to the impact of events.

But the question is, what events and experience had caused people to be receptive to arguments that they should change their views? As noted above, it was not simply Pearl Harbor. Four months after that attack, the Republican National Committee balked at a resolution proposed by Wendell Willkie committing the party to the acceptance of "just and reasonable international responsibilities" after the war. The pollster Hadley Cantril warned the Democratic party, as it prepared for the congressional elections, that there had been no "profound conversion or change of conviction among pre-Pearl Harbor isolationists." And many of these figures were reelected in 1942 (when the Republicans made gains) after some of the most prominent of them had easily beaten off primary challenges by Willkie-supported internationalists.[66]

Over the next two years, however, internationalism gained support among congressional Republicans, a development reflected in the party's policy declarations. Vandenberg's famous conversion, as his son acknowledges, "evolved slowly," and it reflected more than led a general movement of public opinion. Polls show that this wider movement was itself not abrupt but gathered momentum over the whole length of the war. In 1937, only 26 percent said that the United States should have joined the League in 1919. By the summer of 1941, pollsters found a more or less even division between those who held this view and favored participation in a postwar league and those still opposed. A year later, after the United States had itself been at war for six months, 59 percent of respondents favored joining a new league of nations and only 22 percent were opposed, with the remainder having no opinion. In July 1944, the proportion favoring participation in a new organization "to take the place of the old League of Nations" had risen to 72 percent and by April 1945 to 81 percent.[67]

It was not the sudden shock of Pearl Harbor that changed attitudes so much as the recurrence of world war and the involvement in it of the United States, with all that that brought in terms of conscription, casualties, taxes, and the disruption of ordinary life. The form that the change took also suggests that it was not primarily prompted by a new sense of vulnerability. It is true that in September 1943, the suggestion that the United States and Great Britain should "make a permanent military alliance" and "agree to come to each other's defense immediately if the other is attacked at any future time" was favored by a margin of 61 to 25 percent and that a small plurality (39% to 37%) even favored a similar arrangement with Russia. But these were significantly smaller majorities than the one in favor of a revived league of nations.

In short, events seemed to have vindicated the most basic argument of internationalists since Wilson—that the United States could not hope to avoid involvement in major overseas wars and therefore had a vital interest in preventing such conflicts from arising. In his initial reaction, Vandenberg had challenged the presentation of Pearl Harbor as an unprovoked attack, arguing that it vindicated the non-interventionists' warning that the course the United States had followed was bound to lead to war. At the same time, however, he had acknowledged the strength of the president's argument that "this war was *sure* to involve us," conceding that "perhaps, in a sense, we are *both* right." In both the "realist" and "Wilsonian" versions of the anti-isolationist case, the clinching argument had become that "twice within a generation" the United States had been dragged into a major foreign war. An implication of this is that explaining U.S. intervention in World War I, that fraught and much-debated issue, must remain central to any explanation of America's ultimate assumption of a global role.[68]

What Kind of Internationalism?

The repudiation of "isolationism" did not in itself establish a very specific policy agenda. With events having seemingly discredited the idea that the United States could avoid involvement in major overseas conflicts, by May 1944 four out of five Americans thought that the country should "take an active part in world affairs after the war" rather than "stay out."[69] Yet this was less of a novelty than is implied by those who portray Pearl Harbor as transformative. In 1918–19, too, the great majority of politicians and commentators had favored continued participation in world affairs. Initially, it was a partisan division over *how* the nation could best preserve its peace and security through international action, rather than a positive commitment to traditional isolationism, that had led to the failure of the Senate to approve the Treaty of Versailles and kept the United States out of the League of Nations. Thereafter, the support for future involvement had waned in the face of the costs it might entail. This comparatively recent history was very much in the minds of Roosevelt and Secretary of State Cordell Hull as they thought about the postwar world and the role that the United States should play in it. To a State Department committee planning postwar policy, Cordell Hull stressed that it was of the "utmost importance to have the support of American public opinion."[70]

This contributed to the early focus on economic and financial questions as the commitment to an open market system that underlay the American approach to these was less domestically controversial than political ties with other countries.[71] But this focus also reflected the role of the executive departments in developing a program for the postwar world, a role which was much larger than it had been under Wilson. The State Department had little input into high-policy decisions during the war; strategy and relations with the allies were determined in the White House, where the president consulted with the military chiefs and a few trusted associates—of which Hull was rarely one. Instead, the Department devoted much of its attention to postwar planning, establishing a series of committees and subcommittees that gathered the views of outside figures, most of them associated with the Council on Foreign Relations, as well as those of serving and former government officials. The dominant perspective in these deliberations, that of Hull himself and of his chief lieutenants such as Sumner Welles and Adolf Berle, was essentially Wilsonian, though modified by responses to the Versailles treaty and the events of the interwar years.[72]

The chief effect of these later experiences had been greatly to increase the emphasis placed on economic factors and the goal of an open, multilateral system of international trade and exchange. "The establishment of a system of international trade which would make it possible for each country to have access to world markets and resources would reduce incentives to military aggression," a State Department memo argued in 1944. Perceiving Japan and Germany as lacking an internal natural resource base to sustain their dense urban populations, officials attributed the aggressiveness of these countries to their exclusion from overseas trading opportunities by established European empires. More generally, the rise of militaristic regimes was linked to the collapse of the international economy in the early 1930s. This viewpoint was epitomized in the aphorism "If goods can't cross borders, soldiers will."[73]

Cordell Hull had long been committed to the reduction of trade barriers and the elimination of discriminatory ones. He had been primarily responsible for the 1934 Reciprocal Trade Agreements Act, which gave the president authority to negotiate the reciprocal lowering of tariffs with other countries. In the bilateral treaties made under this legislation, the State Department insisted on the application of the most-favored nation principle—that is, that no other trading partner would enjoy more (or less) advantageous terms than the United States. To Hull and his associates, the chief problem was the system of imperial preference established by Britain and her dominions at Ottawa in 1932. The dismantling of this protected trading bloc was a major U.S. policy objective and became one of the principal sources of tension in Anglo-American relations. Churchill had succeeded in qualifying the commitment of the two nations in the Atlantic Charter to promote equal access to the trade and raw materials of the world by the insertion of the phrase "with due respect for their existing obligations." But in the Mutual Aid Agreement of February 1942, "agreed action . . . directed to . . . the elimination of all forms of discriminatory treatment in international commerce" was included as "the consideration" for Lend-Lease, although the British had stonewalled on agreeing to this until Roosevelt assured them that it did not entail "a commitment in advance that Empire preference will be abolished." The State Department continued to press both the president and the British for such a commitment through the rest of the war and into the postwar period.[74]

The British, represented in these negotiations by John Maynard Keynes, viewed the belief that the elimination of trade barriers would in itself produce stable prosperity for all countries as naïve. In seeking a broader approach, they gained support from the Treasury Department, which recognized that international trade had been stifled in the 1930s not only by high tariffs, quotas, and bilateral arrangements but also by competitive devaluations and exchange restrictions. Through further bilateral negotiations in which the Americans were very conscious of having the upper hand, a scheme emerged for overcoming these problems by the creation of two new international institutions—a fund from which countries having difficulties with payments could obtain the currency they needed but that would also monitor and limit changes in exchange rates and a bank that would make or (more commonly) underwrite long-term loans for reconstruction and development. Membership of the fund would be conditional on a commitment to free currency convertibility and nondiscriminatory trade practices. The International Monetary Fund and World Bank were duly established by the Bretton Woods Conference of July 1944, which was attended by representatives of forty-four countries, including the Soviet Union. No one doubted that its unique financial strength would enable the United States to play the leading role in both institutions for the foreseeable future.[75]

As contemporary commentators noted, there was greater clarity and consistency in the drive to establish a multilateral economic order than in other aspects of Washington's postwar planning. Whereas the American approach to political and military problems was "vague," the British *Economist* observed in 1942, American politicians dwelt "at much greater length, and in much greater detail, on the side of postwar economic collaboration."[76] This might be taken to show that the expansion of the nation's foreign policy goals was primarily the product of economic concerns, particularly a desire to open the world to penetration by American goods and capital. Those who advance this interpretation can certainly point to many statements by policymakers and businessmen stressing the need for export markets to absorb America's increased production and avert a postwar depression. Thus, in a speech in Detroit, Secretary of the Treasury Henry Morgenthau argued that currency stabilization would protect American automobile manufacturers from the danger that devaluation of the pound or the franc would make their cars too expensive for prospective customers in Britain or France. Morgenthau's deputy Harry Dexter White, the chief architect of the Bretton Woods system, pointed out that the IMF would make available to other countries the dollars they would need to buy American goods. Addressing broader issues in congressional testimony, Assistant Secretary of State Dean

Acheson conceded that "if you wish to control the entire trade and income of the United States, which means the life of the people, you could probably fix it so that everything produced here would be consumed here." But, if Americans wished to preserve their accustomed economic freedoms, "we cannot have full employment and prosperity in the United States without the foreign markets."[77]

Before taking such statements as revealing the fundamental explanation for American policy, as the historian William Appleman Williams influentially did, we need to recognize that they were made by officials as they were seeking to gain political support for their policy.[78] They naturally received such support from those sectors of the domestic economy with significant overseas interests. Export-oriented industries such as oil, automobiles, cotton, and others formed a lobbying group, the Business and Industry Committee for Bretton Woods, Inc. But the policy was not shaped by private interests. For example, although Wall Street bankers favored the proposal for a World Bank, they strongly opposed the plan for an International Monetary Fund because they feared that it would eliminate the role that private bankers had historically played in preventing governments from pursuing inflationary policies. The IMF would not only provide member states with an alternative source of credit but would also permit them to impose restrictions on the transfer of capital. The opposition of the American Bankers' Association to the plan had strong backing from the *New York Times* and the *Wall Street Journal*.[79]

Indeed, those who designed the Bretton Woods system saw it as a New Deal–style project to subordinate private interests to public purposes—as Morgenthau would put it in 1946, "to move the financial center of the world from London and Wall Street to the United States Treasury." The public purpose was the achievement of a prosperity that extended beyond the United States itself and thus established the essential basis for international peace. Rather than arising from existing societal pressures, the new system involved significant changes in America's political economy. The shift of financial power from the private sphere to public authorities was institutionalized by making the American executive directors of the IMF accountable to an interdepartmental government committee.[80]

Likewise, the goal of freeing up international trade required Congress to yield some of its traditional prerogatives to the executive by granting the president authority to negotiate tariff levels with other nations—initially through renewals and extensions of the Reciprocal Trade Agreements Act in 1943 and 1945. The subsequent relaxation of the protectionism that had historically characterized America's own tariff policy was made politically easier by the devastating effects of the war on the economies of the nation's commercial rivals. In 1945, when the United States held two-thirds of the world's gold reserves and produced almost half of the world's manufactured goods, American businesses did not have much reason to fear foreign competitors in either overseas markets or the domestic one.[81] Yet protectionist sentiment remained strong in Congress, as was indicated by the requirement that no tariff reduction should seriously injure a domestic industry. Nor did concern with overseas markets necessarily lead to an "internationalist" approach. The restrictions imposed by Congress on the use of Lend-Lease supplies and the insistence that they cease when the war ended both derived support from exporters who saw Britain as a commercial rival.[82]

The liberalization of American trade policy and the establishment of international financial institutions was a concomitant of the repudiation of isolationism. In the policymaking process, diplomatic objectives shaped economic ones, rather than the other way around. And it was on this basis that congressional approval was secured. "It is desirable to continue in existence this tested and sound instrument of international cooperation," the House Ways and Means Committee majority declared of the Reciprocal Trade agreements program in 1943, "in the interest both of unity in the war effort [and] of a secure peace thereafter." In his testimony on the Bretton Woods agreements, White claimed that those who voted against them would be as "indicted" by history as those who had prevented the United States from joining the League of Nations had been. This parallel evidently did much to produce the overwhelming majorities in both houses by which the new institutions were approved in the summer of 1945.[83]

In the minds of the postwar planners, the economic and political aspects of their program were interconnected in more than one way. On the one hand, a multilateral trading system would provide the basis for international peace. On the other, peace would promote prosperity by reducing wasteful expenditure on armaments.[84] Most Americans had long seen the reduction of armaments as an essential ingredient of a peaceful world order, and it had been declared as a goal by Taft, Wilson, and the Republican administrations of the 1920s. Roosevelt himself, who showed much more interest in the political than the economic aspects of postwar planning, had continued to lay great emphasis on this goal even as he retreated from his commitment to the League of Nations. "The elimination of costly armaments is still the keystone—for the security of all little nations and for economic solvency," the president told Berle as the latter was developing plans for the postwar world. "Don't forget what I discovered—that over ninety percent of all national deficits from 1921 to 1939 were caused by payments for past, present and future wars."[85]

As Wilson's program had recognized, the reduction of armaments was unlikely to be achieved unless there was an alternative form of security on which states could rely. FDR, however, initially resisted the idea of recreating anything like the League of Nations, insisting on altering a British draft of the Atlantic Charter that implied this was intended. No doubt the president wanted to avoid giving

his isolationist critics another chance to fight a battle they had won, but his attitude also seems to have reflected his own judgment that in practice the League
of Nations had made the democracies less rather than more willing to forcefully
uphold international order. His emphasis on the greater urgency of disarming the
aggressors accorded with his long-expressed view that "the threat to world peace"
came from countries led by regimes that sought territorial expansion through
the use of force. Like other criminals, these "gangsters" had to be repressed by
the law-abiding majority and prevented from behaving this way in the future.
"Surely by unanimous action in driving out the outlaws and keeping them under
heel forever," Roosevelt declared in 1943, "we can attain a freedom from fear of
violence." He insisted that Germany, Italy, and Japan "must be disarmed and kept
disarmed" after the war; "if we do not pull the fangs of the predatory animals
of this world, they will multiply and grow in strength—and they will be at our
throats again once more in a short generation."[86]

If the desire for peace was less universal than Wilson's project had implicitly
assumed, the establishment of a law-governed world would require some mechanism of enforcement. From at least 1941, Roosevelt looked to the creation after
the war of "an international police force," proposing at the Atlantic conference
that the United States and Britain should constitute such a force. Meeting with
Soviet Foreign Minister Vyacheslav Molotov in 1942, the president suggested that
the Soviet Union, and possibly China too, should also "act as the policemen of the
world" and enforce disarmament on other nations by inspection. He conceded
that "other nations might eventually be accepted progressively at various times
among the guarantors of peace" but insisted that reviving the League of Nations
"would be impractical."[87]

FDR was by no means the only erstwhile follower of Wilson who had come
to believe that the League of Nations had embodied unrealistic assumptions. In
a bestselling book cowritten with a retired diplomat, Herbert Hoover suggested
that a future international organization should limit itself to the peaceful settlement of disputes and the development of international law but not have the power
to impose economic or military sanctions. The enforcement of peace should be
organized more regionally, though in the immediate postwar period, "the victorious Powers must maintain order in the world by military force" and determine
the terms of the settlement. In his two widely circulated wartime books, Walter
Lippmann made a more explicit and thoroughgoing attack on Wilson's approach
and principles. Wilson's program, Lippmann argued, had rested on the illusory
premise that an association like the League of Nations could "*replace* the ordinary
instruments of international life" and provide the conditions for general disarmament: "While a universal society can reinsure national and regional security,
it is not a substitute for solid frontiers, adequate and rationally planned armed

force, strategic position, alliances among natural and necessary allies." History had proved that the League of Nations "could enforce the peace only if the league were led by a strong combination of powers resolved to enforce the peace." In the present circumstances, "combined action by America, Britain, and Russia is . . . the only condition under which it is possible even to begin to establish any wider order of security." Consequently, "the formation of this nuclear alliance must in our thinking and in our action take precedence over all other considerations."[88]

Roosevelt, too, clearly saw the continuation of the wartime alliance as crucial for the establishment of a peaceful world afterwards. His idea of the "Four Policemen" was a step in this direction in that it won Stalin's immediate approval and was later endorsed by Churchill (with only a caveat about the inclusion of China among the policemen). However, the conception was not only crude but also vague, in particular leaving open the question of how far there should be a joint condominium and how far a division of the world into separate spheres of influence. The ambiguity reflected Roosevelt's reading of American public opinion. As he indicated on several occasions, he did not believe that it would be politically possible for the United States to assume responsibility for the enforcement of peace, at least by ground forces, beyond the Western Hemisphere, yet he also did not wish to circumscribe the scope of the nation's interests. The Kremlin presumably envisaged spheres of influence, as initially did Churchill who, while speaking favorably in general terms of an international organization, proposed in the spring of 1943 that the primary responsibility for maintaining order should rest with regional councils.[89]

Although some in Washington, notably Sumner Welles and initially Roosevelt himself, favored an element of regionalism in the structure of a postwar security organization, the regional approach met strong opposition in the State Department. In the long run, Isaiah Bowman warned, this was likely to lead to a situation in which "region will be arrayed against region." Hull himself feared that a regional structure would lead to spheres of influence in which great powers would dominate their smaller neighbors and might establish "closed trade areas or discriminatory systems." The secretary of state was not only an unreconstructed Wilsonian himself but also very attentive to attitudes in Congress, and his judgment that only through the establishment of a worldwide system could support be mustered for the assumption of responsibilities beyond the Western Hemisphere no doubt helped to dissuade Roosevelt from including a regional dimension in the plans for a new international organization.[90]

As these plans took firmer shape in the summer of 1943, they represented a melding of the "Four Policemen" concept and a revival of the League of Nations. In a draft "Charter of the United Nations" produced in the State Department, the organization would be open to all nations, but peacekeeping authority would be vested in a council composed of the four great powers and three other members elected for annual terms. The council was to establish a system of armament regulations (to be policed through inspections), with due consideration given to the special responsibilities for security of the permanent members. At a foreign ministers' conference in Moscow in October, Hull secured agreement to a joint declaration that the four nations recognized "the necessity of establishing at the earliest practicable date a general international organization, based on the principle of the sovereign equality of all peace-loving states, and open to membership by all such states, large and small, for the maintenance of international peace and security." Reporting to Congress, where both houses had recently passed resolutions favoring American membership of an international peacekeeping body, Hull interpreted the declaration as meaning that "there will no longer be need for spheres of influence, for balance of power, or any other of the special arrangements through which, in the unhappy past, the nations strove to safeguard their security or to promote their interests."[91]

Wilson's program, as we have seen, had evolved as an attempt to legitimate American participation in a system of collective security without compromising the nation's traditional anti-imperialist values. The eighteen months following the Moscow conference demonstrated the continuing difficulty of achieving this balancing act. As the signers of the Moscow Declaration were about to meet at Dumbarton Oaks, Washington, to draw up a charter for the United Nations, the Republican presidential candidate, Thomas E. Dewey, charged that they were planning "to subject the nations of the world, great and small, permanently to the coercive power of the four nations holding this conference"; such a four-power alliance would be "immoral" and "the rankest form of imperialism." Hull fiercely rebutted this accusation and managed, by reaching an agreement with Dewey's foreign policy adviser, John Foster Dulles, to prevent the issue from figuring in the 1944 election campaign. But the Dumbarton Oaks conference itself did little to dispel suspicions that the new organization would be unable to subject the great powers to its authority when the Soviet Union insisted that a permanent member of the Security Council should be able to veto the consideration of any matter, including disputes in which it was itself involved.[92]

More broadly, leading senators, notably Vandenberg, had insisted that American participation in an international organization should be conditional on the nature of the peace settlement. This was potentially problematic in that America's major allies showed few signs of having abandoned power politics. The failure of the Red Army to offer any relief to the Warsaw uprising against the Germans in August–October 1944 seemed to offer brutal evidence of Stalin's determination to dominate postwar Poland. In October, Churchill and Stalin agreed on their respective degrees of interest in the various Balkan countries. Greece was assigned to the British sphere and in December UK troops sent there "to restore order" came into conflict with the communist-led resistance movement. This action, interpreted as an attempt to restore the monarchy, aroused fierce criticism in the American press, prompting the administration to leak a purported warning to the British that "the American people are in a mood where the actions of their Allies can precipitate them into wholehearted cooperation for the maintenance of the peace of Europe or bring about a wave of disillusionment which will make the isolationism of the nineteen-twenties pale by comparison." Public opinion polls showed significant declines in the numbers expressing confidence that Britain and Russia would cooperate with the United States after the war.[93]

Policymakers attempted in various ways to reduce the conflict between domestic political realities and international ones. In the first place, they sought to find policy positions that would accommodate both. Thus, they recognized that the Russians' desire to establish a defensive buffer zone to their west was natural and legitimate and also that this might well require some qualification of the right to untrammeled self-determination on the part of their neighbors. Willingness to accept an extension of the borders of the Soviet Union itself was a part of this; it was in this context that FDR had remarked to the British Foreign Secretary Anthony Eden that "as far as Poland is concerned, the important thing is to set it up in a way that will help maintain the peace of the world." More broadly, State Department officials thought that it would be reasonable for the Soviet Union to exercise the kind of role in eastern Europe that the United States did in the Western Hemisphere; the United States should not oppose the Russians' establishment of a "Monroe Doctrine" in their security zone. But this was seen as very different from total domination. "There should be some basis of adjustment whereby the safety and international interest of the USSR will be assured without their claiming to dictate the method of life, cultural development and type of civilization to be enjoyed by these countries," Berle wrote in 1942. It was also seen as important that the Soviet sphere of influence should be "open" rather than "closed," with no restrictions imposed on normal trade, cultural exchange, or travel.[94]

Roosevelt also sought to soften the conflict between domestic opinion and his allies' policies by bringing it into the open in attempts to moderate attitudes on both sides. Thus, on issues ranging from India and Greece in the British case to Poland and the form of voting in the United Nations in the Soviet one, he urged Churchill and Stalin to respect American sentiment in order to sustain public and congressional support for international cooperation.[95] Conversely, the president told Congress and the American people that "perfectionism, no less than isolationism or imperialism or power politics, may obstruct the paths to international peace," recalling that "in our disillusionment after the last war we preferred international anarchy to international cooperation with Nations that did not see and think exactly as we did. We gave up the hope of gradually achieving a better peace because we had not the courage to fulfill our responsibilities in an admittedly imperfect world. We must not let that happen again, or we shall follow the same tragic road again—the road to a third world war."[96]

Another, less candid way to address the problem was to say somewhat different things to the two audiences. One historian has suggested that the president engaged in this practice to the extent that there was a "considerable gap between Roosevelt's *foreign* foreign policy and his *domestic* foreign policy." Thus it has been observed that, in messages to Churchill and Stalin, FDR seemed to express tacit approval of their agreement over the Balkans, and that at Yalta he and Churchill accepted that the Soviet Union should have a large say over the composition of the government of liberated Poland. This is contrasted with the president's report to Congress after the conference in which he discounted "queer ideas of . . . 'spheres of influence,'" insisting that "the three most powerful Nations have agreed that the political and economic problems of any area liberated from Nazi conquest, or of any former Axis satellite, are a joint responsibility of all three Governments" and that these countries would be helped "to solve their own problems through firmly established democratic processes." If there was an ambiguity about American policy, particularly with respect to eastern Europe, this was partly due to the persistent difference between the president's outlook and that of the State Department. To Roosevelt, the continuing cooperation of the major victor powers remained the key to the maintenance of peace in the postwar period, all the more so as he seems to have envisaged the chief potential threat to that peace as an attempt by the defeated nations to reassert themselves and challenge the outcome of the war as Germany had the Versailles settlement. For Hull and his officials, the overriding goal was the establishment of a global order based on liberal principles.[97]

Ultimately, most Americans, including those in government as well as members of Congress and the wider public, believed that conflicts between America's goals and those of other countries could be resolved largely on American terms. This assumption rested on confidence in the potential diplomatic leverage provided by the nation's economic strength. During the war, the control of resources, especially food and oil, enabled pressure to be brought on neutral countries not to aid the enemy. General George V. Strong, chief of Army Intelligence, observed that Lend-Lease gave the United States the ability to "dictate, if necessary, to any or all of the other three United Nations, forcing them to accept our leadership by threatening to divert the flow of American materials to other more cooperative nations." As the tide of war turned, there was greater readiness to use Lend-Lease as a diplomatic tool, as when Hull hinted to the Russians that if China were not to be included among the signatories of the Four-Power Declaration, some of the supplies currently being sent to the Soviet Union might be diverted to China instead. The potential efficacy of economic diplomacy was seen as extending beyond Lend-Lease. Thus Hull believed that Britain could be compelled to abandon its Imperial Preference system if postwar economic aid was made conditional upon its doing so. Similarly, the State Department hoped to induce de Gaulle to adopt liberal economic policies by offering to rearm France with American weapons. Averell Harriman, as U.S. Ambassador in Moscow, advised that economic assistance to the countries of eastern Europe could "help keep them from following the Communist philosophy" after the war.

America's economic strength was also seen as giving it the upper hand in relations with the Soviet Union. After Stalin indicated in 1943 that he would like to import substantial quantities of railroad and industrial equipment from the United States after the war, Harriman raised the possibility of a postwar loan to facilitate this in the hope that it would provide diplomatic leverage. In the disagreements that arose over voting in the United Nations the following year, Harriman and Hull were confident that the Russians' interest in good relations with the United States would lead them to back down in the end. Similarly, Harriman and others suggested that Soviet behavior in eastern Europe could be moderated if the possibility of postwar aid were linked to it, and this was the approach adopted after Molotov requested a $6 billion reconstruction loan in January 1945. "I think it's very important," Roosevelt told Stettinius and Morgenthau, "that we hold this back until we get what we want." After Roosevelt's death, Harriman advised the new president that the Russians did not want to break with the United States "since they needed our help in order to reduce the burden of reconstruction." Truman responded that he believed "we should be able to get 85 per cent" of what we wanted in disagreements with the Soviets because they "needed us more than we needed them."[98]

America's move to full-scale belligerency was taken to be a lasting turning point by those who had long wanted the nation to play a much more active role in international affairs and had been confident that the scale of its power gave it the capacity to exercise great influence across the globe. Washington had become "the newly-created World Capital on the Potomac," the *New Republic* observed in January 1942, as it claimed that "world leadership" was the "American destiny."[99] No longer would the nation be content with hegemony in the Western Hemisphere; as Roosevelt warned Stalin in 1944, "There is in this global war literally no question, either military or political, in which the United States is not interested." The scale and scope of America's war effort seemed to show that such an unbounded definition of its sphere of influence was not unrealistic. The nation had developed many of the instrumentalities and institutions, and also the informed and experienced civilian and military leadership, that would enable it to play a much more active and extensive role in world politics than it had before the war. Its potential capability to shape the postwar international order was little more in question than was its desire to do so.[100]

What remained in doubt was the nation's readiness to devote resources to the achievement of foreign policy goals. Those officials who, in the era of Lend-Lease, anticipated using economic assistance as a form of diplomatic leverage in the future were discounting the difficulty of securing congressional authority for foreign loans. Roosevelt himself, scarred by his earlier experience, clearly remained doubtful whether political support would be forthcoming for costly overseas enterprises, particularly those involving the use of land forces. At Tehran, he told Stalin that it would take "a terrible crisis such as at present" before Congress would agree to send troops back to Europe, observing "that if the Japanese had not attacked the United States he doubted very much if it would have been possible to send any American forces to Europe." In the planning for the United Nations, he told the State Department that he did not want there to be any obligation to send troops to Europe after the war, indicating that the principal American contribution to the preservation of world peace should be made by naval and air forces operating in the Western Hemisphere and the Pacific Ocean. He and his political advisors were apparently impressed by a survey showing that only 11 percent of the public saw international cooperation for a lasting peace as the chief postwar worry, whereas 80 percent expected it to be domestic economic problems. This was the form of isolationism that Roosevelt feared—not so much a principled adherence to traditional neutrality as a lack of real concern with foreign affairs and resistance to paying the price of involvement.[101]

Hitherto, only an attack on the United States or a perceived threat to the physical safety of North America had produced the political support necessary for a really substantial exercise of American power. In the absence of such a sense of threat, there had indeed been public and congressional interest in overseas situations, and some desire to affect their outcome, but it had been impossible to achieve a policy consensus sufficiently broad and deep to sustain a costly enterprise. This had been partly because of internal differences of opinion, whether rooted in ideology, ethnicity, or economic interest, but it had also reflected the general popular assumption that only the requirements of self-defense justified war or commitments involving the risk of war. So it is not surprising that in public debate those advocating a commitment to international order argued that it was necessary for America's own basic security.[102]

The experiences of World War II, from Pearl Harbor to the atomic bomb, *did* persuade most Americans that a greater investment needed to be made in the country's own armed forces and that these forces should adopt a more extended defensive posture. But the very effectiveness of the war effort and the even greater confidence in the scale of the country's power that it engendered in some ways worked against the argument that America's own security depended upon the establishment of an ordered world. The tendency, by government officials as well as politicians like Vandenberg, to make participation in an international organization conditional on the nature of the peace settlement, implied that a peaceful world order was, in the last analysis, a desirable goal rather than an absolutely necessary one. In that context, it could not be taken for granted at the end of World War II that the United States would be willing to undertake and sustain the costly foreign policy commitments that in peacetime it had always previously abjured.

6

ASSUMING "THE RESPONSIBILITIES OF POWER," 1945–1952

Before 1945, both the importance of foreign affairs in American life and the nation's impact on world politics had differed dramatically in peace and in war. For most of the time, the experience of the great majority of Americans and the focus of the nation's politics had been notably inward-looking and self-contained. Of course, some commentators, interest groups, and elected politicians had articulated wide-ranging and ambitious foreign policy aspirations. But the concrete actions of the U.S. government had been circumscribed in their scope and much constrained by a reluctance to incur significant costs. By contrast, for the five or six years in the twentieth century during which it had been engaged in full-scale war, the country had mobilized its unparalleled resources and projected its power across the oceans effectively enough to defeat formidable enemies in relatively short order. However, the costs of these efforts in terms of casualties, money, and the disruption of normal life had only been borne because they were viewed as essentially temporary.

The discrediting of "isolationism" in public discourse did not in itself alter this mindset. Historians have differed over the extent to which Franklin D. Roosevelt remained Wilson's heir, but the two were alike in promoting what might be called "low-cost internationalism." It may be going too far to say, as some scholars do, that the Bretton Woods system and the United Nations, like the League of Nations, were envisaged as a form of world order that "could run itself" almost "automatically"; it was always expected that Washington would play a "leadership" role in these institutions.[1] But, like Wilson, Roosevelt had suggested that this need not in the long term involve substantial overseas military or financial commitments.

In the event, of course, the United States was to assume just such commitments in the postwar era as it took forceful steps to shape the course of events on other continents. Some see this development as a natural and inevitable consequence of the scale of the nation's relative power. America's "post-1945 outward thrust could come as no surprise to those familiar with the history of international politics," Paul Kennedy writes. "With the traditional Great Powers fading away, it steadily moved into the vacuum which their going created; having become number one, it could no longer contain itself within its own shores, or even its own hemisphere." Certainly, there was no question about America's uniquely powerful position at the end of the war. Following its own wartime growth and the devastation that had been wrought in all of the other industrialized countries, the United States was producing a third of total global output and half of the world's manufactured goods. Its GNP was more than three times that of the Soviet Union and almost five times that of Britain. It possessed almost two-thirds of the world's gold reserves, three-fourths of its invested capital, and half of world shipping. The war also left the United States with a military strength that no other country could match in its range and striking power, including by far the world's largest navy, sole possession of the atomic bomb, and a worldwide network of overseas bases, airfields, and communication stations.[2]

The possession of such abundant power resources undoubtedly gave the United States the means to exert great influence across the globe. But it did not make it inevitable that it would develop and make use of this capacity. After all, America's share of world manufacturing output had been only slightly less (40%) in the 1920s, and it inevitably declined from its 1945 peak as other countries recovered from the effects of the war.[3] America's economic preeminence following World War I had not inspired an "outward thrust" or a greater readiness to become involved in overseas political conflicts. Indeed, the experience of the interwar years had left policymakers wary of the extent to which the American people would be prepared to pay the price of exercising effective power abroad, and such skepticism was reinforced by the overpowering public and bipartisan congressional demand at the end of World War II for the swift demobilization of American forces (accompanied by some riots at overseas military bases). A few years later, General George Marshall, serving as secretary of defense, bitterly recalled watching "people rush back to their civilian jobs and leave the tanks to rot in the Pacific and the military strength that was built up to fade away."[4]

When Marshall made this remark in 1950, American troops were fighting Chinese and North Korean forces in Korea. In the intervening period, the United States had provided 26 billion dollars to aid European recovery (through immediate postwar relief as well as the Marshall Plan), a sum that was the equivalent of 10 percent of one year's GDP. Military spending in 1947–50 fluctuated around 5 percent of GNP, an unprecedented amount for peacetime (in 1934–39, it had averaged only 1.3%), and by the fiscal year 1950 the total security budget (including foreign aid and atomic energy research) was more than 7 percent of GNP. Under the impact of the Korean War, it climbed much further until in 1952–54 it was absorbing as much as 15 percent of GNP (and nearly 70% of all federal spending). By then, the United States had not only committed itself by treaty to the defense of eleven European countries and Japan but had also stationed forces in these countries on a long-term basis.[5] This enormous expansion both of American commitments and of the proportion of the nation's resources regularly devoted to the achievement of foreign policy objectives clearly requires an explanation that goes beyond assumptions about how great powers naturally behave.

Overseas developments, mostly not anticipated in 1945, were crucial—particularly, the extent to which European recovery would be impeded by shortage of dollars, Britain's inability to sustain its role in the Near and Middle East, and the hostile and apparently expansionary nature of Soviet policy. But the way such developments were perceived, interpreted, and responded to reflected internal influences on U.S. policy that were already in place as the country emerged from the war.

The broadest and most fundamental of these was the general belief that the United States had to play a much larger role in world affairs than it ever had before. The argument that had long been advanced by proponents of more active involvement—that the possession of great power brought with it a responsibility that went beyond the protection and promotion of narrow national interests—had gained wide acceptance in political circles. Even those wary of expensive overseas commitments, notably Senator Robert Taft, did not challenge this basic premise. The new president, Harry S Truman, had long internalized it, having lamented as early as 1939 that isolationists like Lindbergh were keeping the country from accepting "its responsibilities as a great power." In closing the conference that established the United Nations, Truman echoed Wilson in combining reaffirmation of the nation's traditional anti-imperialist principles with insistence that the growth of its power demanded increased involvement. Great states had "no right to dominate the world," he declared, but it *was* "the duty of these powerful nations to assume the responsibility for leadership toward a world of peace." The "great 'musts' for your generation," George C. Marshall told the graduating class at Princeton in February 1947, are "the development of a sense of responsibility for world order and security, the development of a sense of [the] overwhelming importance of this country's acts, the failures to act, in relation to world order and security." "We must act with the consciousness that our responsibility is to interests which are broader than our immediate American interests," Marshall's successor as secretary of state, Dean Acheson, explained to the press a few years later. "We must operate in a pattern of responsibility which is greater than our own interests."[6]

Acheson, the son of an Episcopal bishop, may have been particularly imbued with the ethic that power brought obligations.[7] But in the belief that the growth of America's power entailed a broadening of its responsibilities, he and Marshall were representative of the department they headed. Joseph M. Jones, a lawyer who had joined the department in 1942, recalled its state of mind at the end of the war:

> Educated or professionally active in the interwar period, its members were acutely conscious each day of the role the United States could be playing to assure greater prosperity at home and help prevent a new war, and yet they had almost invariably seen United States action fall far short of the need. . . . Throughout these years of restraint the State Department staff had nevertheless been in ferment, a largely unculti-vated but fertile source of ideas, pushing, ever-pushing toward more effective policy, toward greater United States assumption of world responsibility commensurate with its power.[8]

The professional military also drew on a reading of the recent past in making the case for a larger defense establishment in the postwar world. This would not only deter "prospective enemies," army planners argued, but would also enable aggression to be nipped in the bud by "powerful offensive action"; "if the law-abiding nations had been able to take this attitude when Japan first invaded Man-churia, they might have discouraged subsequent adventures in aggression on the part of Italy and Germany." To Marshall, the "emasculation of the Army" in the 1920s and 1930s had led directly to "the tragedy of war." Anticipating a simi-lar postwar reaction, Marshall had pressured his colleagues to trim their force projections to what it might be realistic to expect Congress to fund. He himself attached overriding importance to universal military training (UMT), an Army goal since World War I; propelled by the wartime chief of staff's determination and enormous prestige, such a program was endorsed by both Roosevelt and Truman in 1945. But this did not prevent the navy and the Army Air Force from demanding much larger peacetime force levels and expensive new weapons sys-tems, for which they lobbied aggressively (and competitively) in Congress as well as in the executive branch.

More generally, the military sought to retain as much as possible of the wartime enhancement both of its capacity to project power overseas and of its influence in Washington. Abroad, this entailed the maintenance of a system of overseas bases ranging from Okinawa to Iceland and wide-ranging air transit and landing rights across the globe. At home, the military's continuing involvement with policy formation was effected first through the establishment of the State-War-Navy Coordinating Committee in late 1944. In 1945 the National War College was set up where mid-career army, navy, and Foreign Service officers would study together. Less formally, the process was advanced by the appointment of military officers, notably George Marshall and Walter Bedell Smith, to senior positions in the State Department. It was institutionalized by the National Security Act of 1947, which gave the Joint Chiefs of Staff formal recognition and their own staff, brought all the services within a single Department of Defense, established the Central Intelligence Agency, and created a National Security Council on which the new secretary of defense would serve alongside the secretary of state.[9]

Advocates of a larger defense establishment drew on, and fostered, the second impulse for a more strenuous involvement in world politics—fear for America's own security. On the face of it, such fear was a paradoxical concomitant of the nation's acknowledged preeminence as a great power. It was justified in several ways, not all of which were consistent with each other. One was that technological developments in warfare—particularly atomic weapons and rocket-fired missiles such as the V-2s that Germany had unleashed on London in the last year of the war—raised the nightmare prospect of a swift, unstoppable, and devastating attack on North America itself. "War may descend upon us by thousands of robots passing unannounced across our shorelines," General H. H. Arnold, chief of the Army Air Force, warned in his end-of-war report. Arnold's report led to an article in *Life* magazine, vividly illustrated with pictures of "a great shower of enemy rockets" delivering atomic bombs on "13 key American cities": "the destruction caused by the bombs would be so swift and terrible that the war might well be decided in 36 hours." "Our geographical security is now gone—gone with the advent of the robot bomb, the rocket, aircraft carriers, and modern airborne armies," President Truman told Congress in October 1945. "The surest guarantee that no nation will dare again to attack us is to remain strong in the only kind of strength an aggressor can understand—military power."[10]

Truman's speech was a call for Congress to establish a permanent program of military training for all fit, young American men. The capacity to mobilize large ground forces swiftly that this program was designed to produce might have been thought irrelevant to a war of rockets and atomic bombs. In his report, Arnold argued that, since there appeared to be "insurmountable difficulties in an active defense" against such aerial attacks, the only real security lay in the development of an offensive capability that would make it "apparent to a potential aggressor that an attack on the United States would be immediately followed by an immensely devastating air-atomic attack on him." This point was, indeed, made by some of the opponents of universal military training. Truman sought to preempt this objection by arguing that conventional forces were still needed "to protect our shores" and "to move forward and direct the bomb against the enemy's own territory."

In fact, policymakers were very conscious how few atomic bombs the United States possessed and how difficult it would be to deliver them over great distances. The kind of future war that government officials and other proponents of preparedness envisaged at this time was a repeat of World War II, but on an even greater scale. It would be another "total war," preparedness for which required not only large and balanced military forces, an efficient and comprehensive intelligence service, and the stockpiling of critical materials but also the support and direction of scientific research (especially in the field of atomic energy) and a means of mobilizing the nation's productive capacities and focusing all its energies on the war effort. In the public arena, efforts were made to counter the impression that the atomic bomb was an "absolute" weapon, rendering all other forms of warfare obsolete or redundant. It was pointed out that the bombs dropped on Hiroshima and Nagasaki had not destroyed those cities entirely and, indeed, had been no more destructive than the incendiary raids on Tokyo and other centers earlier. In a book based on the deliberations of a Council on Foreign Relations study group, Hanson Baldwin stressed not only that the existing number of bombs was limited but also that the expense and difficulty of manufacturing them and the shortage of some of the necessary raw materials would limit the supply in the near future and always "prevent real mass production of the atomic bomb." The next war might begin in the air, Marshall told Congress, but it would end up "in the mud and on the ground."[11]

Part of the case for UMT was that the United States would no longer have the time for preparation that it had had in the two world wars. This was seen as a somewhat paradoxical consequence of its preeminent power. As "top dog" now, General of Army Air Forces Carl Spaatz told Congress, the United States would be the "No. 1 target" of potential aggressors.[12] Nor, it was argued, did America's great strength mean that it could be complacent about its own security. It would still be vulnerable if a single power obtained mastery of the Old World. Given the configuration of forces as the war ended, only the Soviet Union, possibly aligned with a revived Germany, could conceivably achieve control of the whole of Eurasia. The possibility that it might follow the same path as Nazi Germany in pursuit of "world domination" was already being voiced by some military planners in 1945 and added an edge to the intense debate in Washington about Moscow's postwar intentions.[13]

These sentiments of responsibility and of apprehension about America's future security, each institutionally embedded within the government and commonly articulated in political discourse, served to create a predisposition toward a forward, proactive response to the evolving international scene. But there also remained countervailing restraints on the expansion of overseas commitments. The most basic of these was the continuing public and political reluctance to devote resources in peacetime to the achievement of foreign policy objectives. A poll in late October 1945 found only 7 percent who identified world peace as the number one problem facing the country, far less than were most concerned with jobs or labor conflict.[14] The pressure for rapid demobilization that Marshall so deplored led Truman to announce an accelerated rate of discharge in September 1945. By June 1947, the U.S. armed forces had shrunk from approximately 12 million at the end of the war to 1.5 million; the number of ground divisions from ninety-seven to a mere twelve, all under strength and most committed to occupation duties. Although public opinion polls showed majorities of 60 to 75 percent in favor of universal military training, the measure failed to pass Congress in 1945–46—and continued to do so when the administration revived the proposal in 1947, 1948, and 1951–52.[15]

The resistance to financial costs was almost as great as it was to human ones. Congress insisted that Lend-Lease aid terminate as soon as military operations did, explicitly forbidding its use for postwar relief or reconstruction.[16] Despite the prosperity brought by wartime government spending, the U.S. Chamber of Commerce and the National Association of Manufacturers called in 1945 for an end to high taxes and deficit spending. Confident that the accumulated savings of consumers and the pent-up need for durable goods and housing would create strong domestic demand from the private sector, businessmen saw inflation rather than depression as the postwar economic problem. This was also the view of most of the administration's economic advisers, and Truman, himself no Keynesian, was determined to balance the budget and reduce the swollen national debt. Congress was an obstacle to achieving these goals through taxation, not only refusing the president's requests for increases but also cutting taxes in 1945 and 1948 (on the latter occasion over Truman's veto).[17]

The resistance to creating the instrumentalities for exercising power overseas drew strength from ideology as well as from immediate material interests. The traditional belief that involvement in power politics was incompatible with republican liberty ran deep. Opponents of UMT and a large peacetime national security establishment from both ends of the political spectrum invoked the specter of a "garrison state" in which every aspect of life came under government control. In the case of anti–New Deal conservatives, such Jeffersonian anxieties were reinforced by the anti-collectivist critique of Friedrich Hayek, whose *The*

Road to Serfdom (1944) became a Book of the Month Club selection. Anti-statism formed the central ideological thrust of the Republican Party, which gained control of both houses of Congress in 1946.[18]

In assailing the New Deal, Republicans portrayed it as un-American Socialism and the administration as "soft on communism." Some extreme opponents of the New Deal, such as the Hearst press and the American Liberty League, had used such language from the beginning, but it gained more political traction in the late 1930s when the American Communist Party sought to participate in a "popular front against fascism" and avowed Communists became prominent in the vigorous union organizing drives of the militant Congress of Industrial Organization (CIO). The closeness of the CIO leadership to the Democratic Party was highlighted by the Republicans in the 1944 election. The partisan incentive for doing so arose from the depth of most Americans' antipathy to communism. A Gallup poll in 1939 found that a majority, if forced to choose, would prefer fascism to communism, and another in May 1941 reported that 71 percent supported outlawing the Communist Party. The Catholic hierarchy and Catholic publications crusaded relentlessly against the atheistic creed, while the American Legion and business organizations portrayed its followers as constantly working to subvert both the nation's strength and individual property rights. In 1946, the U.S. Chamber of Commerce distributed two hundred thousand copies of a pamphlet entitled *Communist Infiltration in the United States*; accusing their Democratic opponents of sympathy with communism helped many Republican candidates, most notably Richard Nixon, gain election to Congress that year.[19]

Various as these viewpoints, pressures, and interests were, beneath them all lay a high sense of America's power and what it could potentially achieve. For, although the scale of American power resources did not in itself generate a will to meet the costs of deploying them strenuously, it did create a confident state of mind. This was expressed in different idioms—patriotic, idealistic, and hard-nosed. "Every American faces himself and his countrymen with a new confidence, a new sense of power," the *New York Herald Tribune* observed in August 1945. "We cannot, if we would, shut our eyes to the fact that ours is the supreme position. The Great Republic has come into its own; it stands first among the peoples of the earth." To Archibald MacLeish, the country now had "the abundant means to bring our boldest dreams to pass—to create for ourselves whatever world we have the courage to desire." "Let us not forget," the veteran Washington hand Bernard Baruch advised the new president, Harry Truman, "that it is on the productive capacity of America that all countries must rely for the comforts—even the necessities—that a modern world will demand. We have the mass production and the know-how. Without us the rest of the world cannot recuperate; it cannot rebuild, feed, house or clothe itself."[20]

The Commitment to Western Europe

As World War II came to its rather sudden end in 1945, the United States as a major victor power was inevitably heavily involved in dealing with its aftermath. The nation's armed forces were still spread across Europe and the western Pacific, and they were committed to the occupation and governance of Japan and of a zone in Germany until there were peace treaties with the former enemy countries. At the Potsdam meeting of the big three allied powers in the summer of 1945, a council of foreign ministers was established to draw up such treaties and propose settlements of other territorial questions in Europe. This body, which came to include the French foreign minister and to deal also with issues arising from the occupation of Germany, had several meetings over the next few years in which disputes quickly arose, especially between the Soviet Union and the western powers. It was not until January 1947 that treaties were signed with Italy and the east European countries that had joined in Germany's attack on the Soviet Union (Romania, Bulgaria, Hungary, and Finland). In Asia, there was uncertainty about how and by whom the territories that Japan had occupied would be governed. In China, Chiang Kai-shek's Kuomintang and the Communists were competing for control of them, while it had been agreed at Yalta that the Soviet Union should gain rights in Manchuria as well as the acquisition from Japan of southern Sakhalin and the Kuriles. Korea, about which there had been some talk of a four-power trusteeship, ended up occupied by Soviet forces in the north and by an American command south of the 38th parallel. In Southeast Asia, the restoration of European imperial authority was resisted by nationalist movements in French Indochina and the Netherlands East Indies. The United States avoided direct involvement in these conflicts by giving the responsibility for arranging the surrender of Japanese troops in this area to the British, but its evident power and tradition of anticolonialism led some nationalist leaders, notably Ho Chi Minh in Vietnam, to appeal to it for support.

The broad goals of American policymakers as they addressed these and other international issues remained as they had been at least since Wilson's time— the establishment of peaceful stability and the promotion of American values. Although it remained a fundamental assumption that ultimately these two goals were harmonious—in that democracy, civil liberties and an "open door" for trade and investment were seen as conducive to the establishment of world order—in particular situations they were often in conflict. This was most significantly the case in eastern Europe, where the Soviet Union's determination to install friendly governments in its neighboring countries came at the expense of free elections and civil liberties in Poland, Romania, Bulgaria, and eventually Hungary (though not Finland). It is true that, as some scholars emphasize, the

United States came to accept this situation, recognizing communist-dominated governments in Poland in May 1945 and in Romania and Bulgaria in December. But these concessions came after confrontation and at a considerable cost to the good relationship with the major wartime ally that Roosevelt and others had seen as crucial to postwar peace and stability. Opinion polls following the acrimony and deadlock at the London Foreign Ministers' conference in September 1945 showed a ten-point drop (to 32%) in those expecting Russia to "co-operate with us in world affairs." Republicans in Congress and elsewhere denounced the "betrayal of the small nations of the world in the making of the peace." Even those policymakers most sympathetic to Soviet security concerns, such as Secretary of State James F. Byrnes and Charles E. Bohlen in the State Department, were shocked by the flagrant manner in which the Kremlin flouted the principles set out in the Yalta Declaration on Liberated Europe. Others, both in the State Department and in the military, already saw the Soviet Union as an ideologically driven power, perhaps even, like Hitler, intent on "world domination."[21]

In early 1946, the American attitude toward Russia hardened. The precipitants for this were Truman's negative reaction to the concessions Byrnes had made in Moscow in December 1945, a public address by Stalin reasserting the validity of communist ideology, and the impact in Washington of the "Long Telegram" from George F. Kennan in the Moscow embassy. After attributing the Kremlin's antagonism to the West to the nature and needs of the regime and as therefore impervious to any form of appeasement, Kennan predicted that the Soviet Union would pursue a cautiously expansionist policy, both openly and through covert subversion. American opposition to the spread of communism was not new. In China, for example, the United States had sought to strengthen Chiang Kai-shek's Nationalist government against Mao Tse-tung's Communists by equipping and training its army, airlifting troops to Manchuria after the Japanese surrender, and sending fifty thousand U.S. marines to guard strategic sites. But 1946 witnessed more overt and forceful opposition to what were seen as Soviet expansionary moves. In March, the United States publicly demanded that the Russians promptly fulfill a commitment to withdraw their forces from wartime positions in northern Iran and encouraged Tehran to take the issue to the Security Council. In August, when Moscow requested a revision of the Montreux Convention to allow for joint Turkish-Soviet defense of the Dardanelles, Washington not only strongly encouraged Ankara to resist this request but also dispatched a naval task force, including the latest aircraft carrier, to the eastern Mediterranean, shortly thereafter announcing that the navy would maintain a permanent presence in that sea.[22]

Both the Iranian and Turkish crises gave rise to loose talk of war in the press. But U.S. policymakers were confident that the Soviet Union did not want war and would back down if firmly resisted—as, indeed, it did in these cases. The handling of these incidents, therefore, did not involve the commitment of significant resources to the achievement of foreign policy objectives, either immediately or in the long term. Where preventing communist expansion would require such a commitment, American actions were constrained by this consideration. In China, where the position of Chiang Kai-shek's government was perceived to be shaky, even if the totality and speed of its collapse in 1948–49 was not anticipated, the administration limited its intervention to Marshall's unsuccessful efforts in 1946 to establish a coalition government including the Communists, and to limited economic aid to Chiang's regime thereafter.[23]

It was only with respect to western Europe that steps involving significant costs and commitments were taken in the immediate postwar years. This line of policy originated before what by 1947 was being called the Cold War had really begun, and not in response to any actions by the Soviet Union.[24] Detailing the economic devastation of Europe to a Senate committee in June 1945, Dean Acheson (never guilty of understatement to such audiences) compared the situation to that following the Muslim conquests of the eighth century from which "it took Europe a thousand years to get back to where it had come from before." Acheson, at this time assistant secretary of state, was testifying in support of the Bretton Woods agreements, but it soon became evident that the problem was both too great and too urgent to be left to the embryonic IMF and World Bank. Immediate relief was supplied by the United Nations Relief and Rehabilitation Agency (UNRRA), to which the United States contributed almost three billion dollars between 1943 and 1947 (three-quarters of the agency's funding). But the distribution of aid to the Russian satellites by this international agency came in for sharp congressional criticism. Loans from the Export-Import Bank, on the other hand, could be targeted to serve the purposes of U.S. foreign policy, and in the summer of 1945 Congress increased this body's assets more than threefold. This did not, however, meet the needs of Britain following the end of Lend-Lease. With its exports reduced to a third of their prewar level, the country lacked the dollars to pay for needed American supplies. In response to aggrieved British pleas and after imposing some conditions, the administration agreed to a $3.75 billion loan on terms better than those currently being offered by the Export-Import Bank.[25]

In continental Europe, the situation after the war was even more desperate than in the uninvaded British Isles. In April 1945, Assistant Secretary of War John J. McCloy, who like Acheson was to be an influential policymaker in the new administration, reported to Truman on conditions there: "There is a complete economic, social and political collapse going on in Central Europe, the extent of which is unparalleled in history unless one goes back to the collapse of the

Roman Empire and even that may not have been as great an economic upheaval." An Anglo-American study by economists concluded in June 1945 that "unless immediate and drastic steps are taken, there will occur in northwest Europe and the Mediterranean next winter a coal famine of such severity as to destroy all semblance of law and order, and thus delay any chance of reasonable stability." It was clear that this situation could be alleviated only by a resuscitation of German coal production, and in July 1945 Truman directed General Dwight Eisenhower, as commander of American forces in Europe, to make the export of twenty-five million tons of coal from western Germany by April 1946 his number one priority (after the protection of U.S. troops). The military governor of the American zone, General Lucius Clay, pointed out that "the successful mining of coal means some restoration of the German economy" and that this required importing food, clothing, and machinery. To avoid adding to the burden on American taxpayers, the United States insisted at the Potsdam Conference that paying for such imports should be a "first charge" on all German exports. Soviet Foreign Minister Molotov protested that this would be at the expense of the reparations agreed to at Yalta.[26]

In this way, the concern to restore the economy of western Europe had a negative effect on Soviet-American relations even before the end of the Pacific war. At Potsdam, the Russians reluctantly agreed to a compromise by which the victors would take reparations primarily from the zones they occupied, with the Soviet Union also receiving from the Anglo-American zones 25 percent "of such industrial capital equipment as is unnecessary for the German peace economy," part of it in exchange for food and other commodities from their zone. However, in May 1946 Clay suspended all reparation payments from the U.S. zone in an attempt to pressure the Russians (and the French) to implement a common import-export program for the whole of Germany. The motivation for this move, and for the subsequent merging of the British and American zones, was the desire to revive the German economy so that it could not only deal with the problems of reconstruction and the settlement of refugees from the east without continual support from the American taxpayer but also contribute to the recovery of western Europe as a whole. The consequent resistance to Soviet demands for reparations from current production was central to the impasse over the German settlement at the Moscow conference of foreign ministers in the spring of 1947.[27]

"The patient is sinking while the doctors deliberate," Marshall observed in his report to the nation after the Moscow conference. The harsh winter of 1946–47 accentuated the shortages of fuel and food in Europe. "Millions of people in the cities are slowly starving," Undersecretary of State William L. Clayton reported after a tour of the continent. The situation was particularly bad in Germany, where there had been food riots while Marshall was in Moscow and where industrial production was about a quarter of what it had been before the war. This was a product of the disagreements, within Washington as well as among the allies, over such questions as the future of the Ruhr and the restrictions that should be imposed on German industry. In March 1947, former president Hoover, sent to investigate conditions after the Republican victory in the 1946 congressional elections, called for the rehabilitation of the German economy to stabilize western Europe and reduce the burden on American taxpayers. Although output had recovered better in other European countries during 1946, it was still below 1938 levels. Moreover, this recovery had been dependent on the import of food, fuel, and other commodities from North America, 80 percent of which had been paid for by various forms of U.S. aid. But with UNRRA due to expire in March 1947 and the Anglo-American loan being drawn on at a rate that would exhaust it by 1948, European governments were foreseeing a reduction of 50 percent in total imports and an 80 percent decline in imports from the United States; in Britain and France food rations were being cut.[28]

This looming "dollar gap" was the precipitant of Marshall's public offer in June 1947 of "friendly aid" in the drafting of "a European program" for recovery and of "later support" for it. In form, the offer was to the whole continent, but the Soviet withdrawal from the negotiations over the formulation of an agreed European response was neither unanticipated nor undesired by most in Washington.[29] It nonetheless contributed to the hardening division of both Germany and Europe and the increasingly open conflict between the Soviet Union and the West. The formation of the Cominform in September 1947 was followed by the brutal imposition of communist rule in Poland, Bulgaria, and Hungary and of bilateral trade agreements and security pacts between east European countries and the Soviet Union. When the communists seized power in Czechoslovakia, it gave rise to a war scare in March 1948. Meanwhile, the three western zones of Germany were being consolidated to prepare the way for the establishment of a west German state. After the introduction of a reformed currency and its extension to West Berlin, the Soviet Union cut off overland access to the city. Although the subsequent airlift preserved the western position in the city without the use of force, policymakers and public alike now shared the sense of a conflict that bore the potential of full-scale war.

Marshall's June 1947 speech was the prelude to a substantial commitment of American resources to the stabilization of western Europe. Truman told congressional leaders in September that France, Italy, and Austria needed "interim aid" while a comprehensive program was being developed, and a special session of Congress approved the grant of over five hundred million dollars for this purpose a few weeks later. In December 1947, Truman requested 6.8 billion dollars for the first fifteen months of the European Recovery Program and seventeen billion dollars for the first four years. Although the president later observed that seventeen billion dollars amounted to only 5 percent of the costs of World War II and 3 percent of national income in 1948, it was a huge sum in comparison with the peacetime federal budgets of the 1930s. After Congress had trimmed the request a little, nearly thirteen billion dollars, mostly in the form of grants, were devoted to European recovery over the next four years. This amounted to an average of 1.2 percent of GNP, and 2.3 percent in 1948–49.[30]

Nor was it only money that the United States committed. As early as September 1946, Secretary of State Byrnes had pledged that American troops would remain in Germany until all occupying forces were withdrawn. Implementing the policy of building a prosperous, integrated, Atlantic-oriented western Europe ratcheted up this military commitment over the next few years. The French in particular were unwilling to agree to the reconstruction of German industry without an assurance that the Americans would help defend the Rhine frontier, while the British, too, sought a firm U.S. commitment to aid militarily in the case of aggression in Europe. Following the Czech crisis in March 1948, Truman reiterated that the United States would "keep our occupation forces in Germany until the peace is secure in Europe." A few months later, the Joint Chiefs of Staff agreed that these forces should stand and fight in the event of a Soviet offensive rather than, as existing war plans envisaged, evacuating the continent and relying on strategic airpower in the initial stages of a conflict. Neither this nor the promise of military supplies to the signatories of the Brussels mutual-defense pact of March 1948 (Britain, France, and the Benelux countries) satisfied the Europeans; they wanted a formal treaty binding the United States to the protection of their security. The recognition in Washington that only this would make possible German participation in an association of west European democracies led to the North Atlantic treaty of April 1949. From the American perspective, as the *New York Times* observed, this involved making "promises not even dreamed of by Woodrow Wilson." It constituted a much more unequivocal breach of the time-honored injunction against "entangling alliances" than the League of Nations would have been or than the United Nations Charter was. It was also a long-term commitment (initially twenty years) that carried the potential of involving the United States in a major war.[31]

The Spurs to Action

In the four years after V-E Day, then, the United States had undertaken overseas financial and military commitments of a different order of magnitude to any previously made in peacetime. The basic purpose of these actions was to establish a stable order in western Europe in which the individual countries could enjoy freedom from both internal and external coercion. Seeking to explain why such unprecedented costs and risks were assumed in pursuit of this goal involves addressing two related questions: What were perceived to be the threats to its achievement, and why was it seen to be so important a national interest? If only because these commitments required congressional approval, answering such questions necessitates considering not only the thinking of policymakers in the administration but also the sources of the wider political and public support for them.

By far the most often voiced threat was the spread of communism. This was the specter that those seeking action to promote economic recovery in Europe commonly evoked. Thus General Clay, pleading for a relaxation of the restrictions on German production, observed that there was little choice "between becoming a communist on 1,500 calories [a day] and a believer in democracy on 1,000 calories." Clay at this time still believed in the possibility of cooperation with the Soviet Union and firmly rejected the analysis of the Kremlin's policy advanced by Kennan in his Long Telegram. The desire to stifle communism in postwar Europe predated the Cold War and was not simply a product of fears that local communist parties would be instruments through which the Soviet Union might come to dominate the whole continent. It was an aspect, if a central one, of a broader desire for the establishment of those "stable, democratic and friendly governments" that Truman as early as May 1945 had declared to be essential for "the future permanent peace of Europe." This goal could be undermined by social unrest and political anarchy, or a revanchist German nationalism, as much as by communism. To all these threats, economic prosperity was seen as the antidote.[32]

Peace and stability in Europe had become a major goal of U.S. foreign policy under Woodrow Wilson. Despite the failure to join the League of Nations, it remained so during the 1920s. And, as some historians have pointed out, the views of policymakers then about how the goal could best be achieved—by integrating German productive power within a wider, interdependent economy—were broadly similar to those of their successors in the Truman administration.[33] Efforts had been made, notably through the Dawes Plan and the encouragement of the Locarno process, to promote this objective. But the United States had not been prepared then to undertake costly commitments or to make any sacrifices for the sake of achieving it. Even the Wilson administration had insisted on the repayment of the war debts and had judged it politically impossible to proffer further economic aid from public funds. For its Republican successors, reducing the burden on American taxpayers and maintaining tariffs to protect American producers clearly took priority over foreign policy objectives.

However, as we have seen, a significant segment of American opinion, not least among the Eastern establishment centered in New York, had thought that the

United States should make a more substantial contribution to Europe's economic recovery from World War I—as well as to its future peace through participation in the League of Nations. Greater American involvement had also been desired by many Europeans; in 1919 British and French statesmen wanted a security guarantee and postwar reconstruction aid, while the Germans in the 1920s sought U.S. support of their efforts to reduce reparations and revise the terms of the Versailles treaty. The disappointment of such hopes shows that European pressure for American commitments after World War II is not sufficient to explain them; not all "invitations" are accepted.[34]

But these elements of continuity do broaden the context in which the later commitments should be understood. Their assumption represented a shift in the balance of opinion within the United States rather than a completely new development. Thus, when a committee was formed in 1947 to develop support for the Marshall Plan, many of its members were not only veterans of the Committee to Defend America by Aiding the Allies in 1940–41 but had been engaged in the promotion of internationalism ever since the campaign for the League of Nations.[35] Within policymaking circles, it had long been accepted that peace and stability in Europe mattered to the United States; what had changed was, to some extent, the importance attached to this interest and, to a greater extent, assessments of how much the United States needed to do to secure it.

Without doubt, differences between the two postwar situations help to explain the shift. Europe after World War I had not been so dependent on imports from North America for the means of existence and of production as it was after 1945, and so the dollar gap had been neither so large nor so consequential. Nor had the geopolitical capabilities of the west European empires been as debilitated as they were after World War II; indeed, on both sides of the Atlantic it had been assumed that even under the League of Nations Britain and France would retain the primary responsibility for order not only in Europe but also in much of the rest of the world outside the Western Hemisphere. The diminution and consequent retreat of British power after World War II played a very direct part in expanding the scope of U.S. involvement and commitments. Even before the end of the war, American diplomats were warning of the weakening position of the British Empire in the Middle East and arguing that it was "in the strategic interests of the United States . . . to protect the vital communications of the Empire between Europe and the Far East." Such thinking lay behind the actions of the United States in the Iranian and Turkish crises of 1946, but it was the decisions of the British government in February 1947 to withdraw their troops from Greece and to terminate military aid to Turkey that precipitated the first substantial and sustained intervention in the politics of the region. "The reins of world leadership are fast slipping from Britain's competent but now very weak hands," William

Clayton noted. With reports indicating that without outside support the Greek government would be unable to resist the communist-led insurgency, it was quickly agreed within the administration that the United States should accede to Britain's request that it take over the responsibility.[36]

Congress would have to approve the substantial economic and military aid thought necessary. This obstacle had been the greatest constraint on action in the interwar period, and it was not easily overcome in this case either. Committed to tax cuts, spending reductions, and smaller government, the recently victorious Republicans had already slashed three billion dollars from Truman's budget for the fiscal year 1948 and would be strongly resistant to any increase in foreign aid. Moreover, at this time many, both in Congress and the wider public, still felt that any action in the international arena would only be legitimate if taken under the auspices of the United Nations. As we have seen, the role of the British military in internal Greek politics had been widely regarded as an instance of reactionary imperialism when Churchill had first sent troops to Athens in 1944. Suspicions that London was once again maneuvering to get the United States "to pull British chestnuts out of the fire" were voiced in the initial unenthusiastic response to Marshall's briefing on the proposed action at a White House meeting with congressional leaders.[37]

It was at this point that Dean Acheson, then undersecretary of state, made what was by all accounts a crucial intervention. Recollecting that "no time was left for measured appraisal," he presented the consequences of failure to act in apocalyptic terms. "Like apples in a barrel infected by one rotten one, the corruption of Greece would infect Iran and all to the east," he warned. "A highly possible Soviet breakthrough might open three continents to Soviet penetration." As in 1939, when he had sought to muster support for aid to the Allies, Acheson raised the prospect that the whole world beyond the Western Hemisphere might fall under the domination of forces hostile to freedom. As then, he argued that if the United States were to suffer "internment on this continent," the American way of life could not survive.[38]

Acheson's presentation evidently impressed the congressional leaders, and Vandenberg advised Truman to stress this broader context when he requested Congress for aid to Greece and Turkey. In his address on March 12, 1947, the president did so in a way that not only followed Acheson in predicting that the effects of not aiding Greece and Turkey would be "far reaching to the West as well as to the East" but also presented the issue in terms of a worldwide ideological contest. Since "totalitarian regimes imposed on free peoples, by direct or indirect aggression, undermine the foundations of international peace and hence the security of the United States," Truman declared in what became known as his "Doctrine," "I believe that it must be the policy of the United States to support free peoples who are resisting attempted subjugation by armed minorities or by outside pressures." Congress approved $400 million in economic and military aid to Greece and Turkey by margins of 67 to 23 in the Senate and 287 to 107 in the House of Representatives.[39]

So, although policymakers' concern with the recovery and stability of western Europe had preceded the Cold War, that conflict became the principal way in which they sought to muster political support for measures to address the continent's problems. This process had first manifested itself with the so-called British Loan. Despite the administration's rather exaggerated claims about how the loan's conditions would open up new export opportunities for American business in the sterling area, it initially fared badly in public opinion polls and encountered stiff opposition in Congress on both political and economic grounds. Approval seemed unlikely until the confrontation with Russia over Iran in March 1946 awakened concern about the future orientation of British policy. "The British people and their way of life form the last barrier in Europe against Communism, and we must help them hold that line," former Ambassador Joseph P. Kennedy observed in a widely quoted statement. When the loan won Senate approval in May, conservative Republicans provided the crucial margin for defeating what would have been a wrecking amendment.[40]

It was a similar story with the Marshall Plan. As in the case of aid to Greece and Turkey, Marshall initially appealed to the sense of the obligations of power that he had urged on the Princeton graduating class earlier that year. "It is logical," he said in making the proposal, "that the United States should do whatever it is able to do to assist in the return of normal economic health in the world, without which there can be no political stability and no assured peace. Our policy is directed not against any country or doctrine but against hunger, poverty, desperation, and chaos." Requesting Congress for interim aid in November 1947, Truman struck a similar note: "The American people . . . are learning that great responsibility goes with great power." But even before the special session opened, commentators noted that "the Marshall Plan appears to draw its greatest strength now not from any special feeling that other peoples should be helped for their own sake, but only as a demonstration against the spread of communism." With Gallup polls reporting that the aid proposal enjoyed greater popular support if its purpose was stated to be to "keep these countries from going communist" rather than "to improve conditions and help get business going" or "to be spent for goods to be bought in this country," the Marshall Plan was increasingly presented as a weapon in the Cold War.[41] "It is not a philanthropic enterprise," insisted Allen W. Dulles, president of the Council on Foreign Relations and an energetic campaigner for the program. It was "a policy to contain the advance of Russia westward in Europe, an advance which would inevitably follow the economic breakdown of the West." This danger was raised by Truman himself after the communists seized total control in Czechoslovakia in February–March 1948. Linking this coup to the Soviet Union's earlier destruction of independence and democracy in other east European countries, the president denounced "this ruthless course of action, and the clear design to extend it to the remaining free nations of Europe." Speedy approval of the European Recovery Program (ERP) was the first of the measures he asked Congress to take in response, together with adoption of universal military training and the reintroduction (for five years) of Selective Service. In the crisis atmosphere, healthy majorities in both houses passed the Foreign Assistance Act in March.[42] In 1950, it took the announcement of Russia's atomic bomb test to persuade the House to approve one billion dollars of military assistance to countries in the North Atlantic pact.[43]

The Nature of America's Stake

What, then, was the nature of the American interest in the economic recovery and political stabilization of the west European democracies? Was it basically the fear that they would fall under the domination of the Soviet Union and that this would pose a dire threat to the United States itself? This is the interpretation advanced by Realist scholars. According to the political scientists Barry R. Posen and Stephen W. Van Evera, for example,

> the United States was motivated to contain Soviet expansion after World War II largely by the same concern that had earlier drawn it into war: the need to preserve the political division of industrial Eurasia. Other concerns also affected American decision making, but were much less important. American policymakers recognized that any state controlling the entire Eurasian landmass would command more industrial power than the United States. Such a state, they feared, could distill more military power from its national economy and thus could threaten the United States, even across the Atlantic.[44]

As historians have shown, there is much documentary evidence to support this interpretation.[45] Thus, one of the first papers drafted by the staff of the new National Security Council in 1948 maintained that "there are in Europe and Asia areas of great potential power which if added to the existing strength of the Soviet world would enable the latter to become so superior in manpower, resources and territory that the prospect for the survival of the United States as a free nation would be slight." A few months earlier, the Joint Strategic Survey Committee of the Joint Chiefs of Staff had portrayed the potential vulnerability of an isolated America in terms remarkably similar to Lippmann's four years earlier:

> The area of United States defense commitments includes, roughly, the lands and waters from Alaska to the Philippines and Australia in the Pacific and from Greenland to Brazil and Patagonia in the Atlantic. This area contains 40 percent of the land surface of the earth but only 25 percent of the population. The Old World (Europe, Asia and Africa) contains only 60 percent of the land surface of the earth but 75 percent of the population. The potential military strength of the Old World in terms of manpower and in terms of war-making capacity is enormously greater than that of our area of defense commitments, in which the United States is the only arsenal nation.[46]

Yet there are good reasons for doubting that a concern with national security in the most basic sense of protecting the American homeland from external attack provides an adequate explanation for the U.S. commitment to western Europe in the late 1940s—or even a major part of the explanation. In the first place, the posited danger was very remote. U.S. policymakers did not fear that the Soviet Union would mount an armed attack on western Europe in the near future. Kennan and other knowledgeable officials knew that, in the aftermath of the titanic struggle with Nazi Germany, the Russians were neither in the position nor in the mood to engage in another major conflict. Moreover, if the Soviet Union did become involved in a war with the United States, military planners recognized that it would be bound to lose. Even had the Red Army overrun western Europe in the postwar years, it would have annexed an area dependent on external sources of fuel and food that would not have added significantly to Soviet war capabilities. With no means of inflicting damage on the United States, Russia would be vulnerable to aerial attack, atomic and otherwise, that would gradually destroy its industry and war-making power. The Soviets would not start a war because they knew that an American victory would be simply a matter of time.[47]

Those who argued that America's security depended on a balance of power in Eurasia conceded that the loss of western Europe would not pose a threat to the United States in the short term. But they insisted that, because of the disproportion in the populations and resources of the two hemispheres, such a loss would inevitably develop into a threat once the countries of the Old World had recovered from the temporary effect of the war.[48] These comparative assessments of global resources were generally very loosely made. This applies, for example, to Kennan's often cited identification of the "five centers of industrial and military power in the world which are important to us from the standpoint of national security" because they possessed "the requisite conditions of climate, of industrial strength, of population and of tradition which would enable people there to develop and launch the type of amphibious power which would have to be launched if our national security were seriously affected."[49] In taking no account of the relative productive capacity of these "centers," Kennan was obscuring the scale of America's industrial preeminence—as well as the military advantages provided by its technological superiority.

Kennan's remark also illustrated how, although the potential danger was placed in the future, its portrayal harked back to the past. The implicit specter of a transatlantic invasion by "amphibious power" hardly seemed to belong to the era of Superfortresses and atomic bombs; indeed, it was more reminiscent of the preparedness propaganda of 1914–16 than of the debate preceding Pearl Harbor when the focus had mostly been on the possibility of air attack and the unreliable loyalty of Latin America. Generally, however, it was the geopolitical arguments of Spykman and others during World War II that constituted the basis for the claim that American security was dependent on the European balance of power. As on that earlier occasion, when the issue was subjected to professional military analysis, it became clear that the claim rested on a conception of the nation's security requirements that included the ability to project American power overseas as well as simply to defend the homeland. "Unless we can retain allies on the eastern side of the Atlantic strong enough, in the event of an ideological war, to hold the Soviets away from the eastern shores of the Atlantic," the planners observed in the April 1947 study, "the shortest and most direct avenue of attack against our enemies will almost certainly be denied to us."[50] At a sophisticated level, the strategic argument for the commitment to western Europe had a somewhat circular character; the United States needed friendly allies across the Atlantic if it was to have the capability to defend western Europe from attack (and defeat the aggressor power).

The element of replay in such arguments was in practice a strength. For the ultimate justification for the view that western Europe constituted a vital security interest was historical experience. Thus, the Joint Chiefs of Staff planners argued that:

> Two world wars in the past thirty years have demonstrated the interdependence of France, Great Britain and the United States in case of war with central or eastern European powers. . . . That the defense of the United States and Canada in North America and of Great Britain and France in western Europe is inseparable from the combined defense of them all is not a question of what men think now, but is something that has been demonstrated by what we have had to do, though tardily, and

therefore at greater risk and cost, in actual warfare in the past. In the light of this past experience, the burden of proof is upon anyone who opposes the thesis of the interdependence of these four countries.[51]

In public, too, great stress was laid on this apparent lesson of history. "Two great wars in this century have shown us beyond doubt that our prosperity, our security, and indeed our survival, are bound up with the fate of the nations of Western Europe," Truman declared to Congress as he requested funds for military assistance in June 1950.[52]

The persuasiveness of this appeal to recent history, and the related discrediting of "isolationism," helps to explain why the claim that western Europe constituted a vital security interest was rarely disputed in public debate. Thus, the North Atlantic treaty was supported by more than 80 percent of the public in opinion polls and gained Senate approval by 82 votes to 13 in July 1949. However, at that time, Acheson had explicitly assured the Senate Foreign Relations Committee that the treaty would not oblige the United States to keep ground troops in Europe, and polls showing that support for the treaty fell drastically when the phrase "promise to go to war" was included in the question confirm that it was generally seen as a form of psychological reassurance involving little real cost. When costs rose, the necessity of the commitment was less widely accepted. Thus, when Truman demanded universal military training and a supplemental defense appropriation following the Czech crisis in March 1948, the Republican Congress rejected UMT and trimmed the sums requested for the army and navy but upped by $822 million the allocation to the air force, always the service that ranked highest in public opinion polls. It would be wrong to say, as some scholars do (and Truman asserted), that this reflected a "Fortress America" outlook, but it did rest on the assumption that, while a friendly and democratic western Europe might be a real American interest, it was not one vital to the security of the United States itself.[53]

This viewpoint was articulated more clearly in the "great debate" of 1950–51 following the administration's decision to commit four U.S. divisions to continental Europe on a permanent basis and to establish a joint NATO command under General Eisenhower. An attack on this policy by Herbert Hoover in a nationwide radio broadcast in December 1950 elicited a generally favorable public and press reaction and helped to stimulate resistance to it by Republicans in Congress. Partisan and interbranch conflicts clearly played an important part in stimulating this controversy, but its substance revolved around the best strategy for maintaining American security. Hoover advocated the avoidance of land conflicts in Eurasia, on the grounds that such conflicts would be both cripplingly expensive and impossible to win, and reliance instead on America's own productive, naval, and air power to protect the country from the danger of attack. In making this case, he stressed that "we Americans alone with sea and air power can so control the Atlantic and Pacific Oceans that there can be no possible invasion of the Western Hemisphere by Communist armies. They can no more reach Washington in force than we can reach Moscow." Developing this point in a later broadcast, Hoover added, on the authority of his own expertise, that "with proper economic action this Hemisphere can be made self-contained in critical raw materials."[54]

"No responsible military man denies these two conclusions," Hoover declared, and administration spokesmen did not challenge the basic proposition that the United States could defend the Western Hemisphere against direct attack. But in response they reiterated the argument made by Wilson in 1919 that facing the prospect of having to do this unilaterally would be destructive of America's liberties at home. "We would have to take defense measures which might really bankrupt our economy, and change our way of life so that we wouldn't recognize it as American any longer," Truman asserted as he requested an extension of the Mutual Security Program in 1952. "It would require a stringent and comprehensive system of allocation and rationing in order to husband our smaller resources. It would require us to become a garrison state, and to impose upon ourselves a system of centralized regimentation unlike anything we have ever known." Arguing that "national security" requires the protection of "core values" as well as territory, some historians see this concern as the basic motivation for the commitments to western Europe.[55]

However, Truman's statement was clearly a riposte to the charge being mounted at the time by Republican critics like Taft that the budgetary costs of the administration's strategy would undermine both the nation's economic strength and the free enterprise system, thereby destroying the very "America we are trying to preserve." More broadly, as the historian Michael Hogan observes, "the image of the garrison state . . . became the dominant metaphor" for *both* sides in the debates in these years over the requirements of national security. The repeated calls for universal military training, the unification of the armed forces and their enhanced influence in policymaking, the institutions created by the National Security Act of 1947, the plans and agencies developed to mobilize the nation's production in wartime—these were all denounced by some as contrary to republican principles of government and as destructive of cherished liberties. To the libertarian publicist Frank Chodorov, they were leading the country "into that very totalitarianism which destroyed the civilization of Europe." In this situation, whether people saw the threat to the nation's traditional way of life as lying more in the scale of the commitments currently being undertaken or in the future possibility of an isolated, beleaguered America was surely determined by factors other than the comparative plausibility of the two scenarios.[56]

The extent to which the defense of the nation's territory and the preservation of its core values really depended on western Europe's not falling under the domination of a hostile power was, then, neither self-evident nor uncontested. Moreover, the danger of this situation arising was agreed not to be imminent and was seen by many as very remote. In these circumstances, fear for America's own security hardly seems to provide a sufficient explanation for the commitments made to promote the region's recovery and to ensure its defense.

Many of those skeptical of the security rationale, both at the time and in later scholarship, have argued that the real driver of U.S. policy was economic interest. In its simplest version, this approach sees the commitments to western Europe as the product of a desire to sustain American export markets in order to avoid a return to economic depression at home. Thus, some argue that the Marshall Plan was prompted by a desire to sustain the level of exports to Europe by redressing the dollar gap and averting the imposition of exchange controls.[57]

As usual with attempts to explain U.S. foreign policy in terms of a concern with overseas markets and investment opportunities, the most obvious objection to this explanation is the relatively small contribution that these made to the country's economic welfare. Exports to Europe constituted only 2.4 percent of GNP in 1947. Nor was the country at this time suffering from depression or unemployment; on the contrary, both economists and politicians were much more concerned about inflation fueled by the inability of production to meet domestic demand. Truman made this clear in the very address to Congress in which he requested interim aid in November 1947. In practice, the Marshall Plan did not increase the role of exports to Europe in the American economy; on the contrary, as a proportion of GNP, these fell after 1947 and in 1951 amounted to only 1.6 percent.[58]

In response to this objection, proponents of an economic interpretation point out that policymakers and other advocates of the Marshall Plan often spoke of America's need to export. Nevertheless, as a theme in the public campaign for the European Recovery Program, this was somewhat muted. Thus, the report of the President's Committee on Foreign Aid, which was chaired by Averell Harriman, described the idea "that we need to export our goods and services as free gifts to insure our own prosperity" as "nonsense." Harriman was rebutting communist propaganda portraying the Marshall Plan as a device to save American capitalism, but his committee's judgment was endorsed and reiterated by the Council of Economic Advisers. Meanwhile, conservative Republican opponents of the program predicted that aid on such a scale would not only increase the tax burden grievously but would also create "scarcity and high prices" at home; insofar as it produced prosperity, Taft argued, it would be a "false prosperity which cannot be permanently maintained," like that of the 1920s, which had collapsed when the Europeans defaulted on their loans and the export trade collapsed. The only domestic beneficiaries, western senators in particular declared, would be "the monopolists," "the very rich, the very top of the manufacturing, producing, and investment groups."[59]

This last argument accorded with the most plausible version of the economic interpretation, which sees the interest at stake as sectional rather than broadly national. As we have seen, it is striking how many of the officials shaping U.S. foreign policy during and after World War II had been drawn from Wall Street or were closely connected with it. Thus, Harriman, Forrestal, McCloy, Robert Lovell, and Paul Nitze had been investment bankers, while Thomas K. Finletter and John Foster Dulles, among others, were from large New York law firms. It was the Council on Foreign Relations and related organizations that took the lead in developing public support for the Marshall Plan rather than general business organizations such as the National Association of Manufacturers or the U.S. Chamber of Commerce. The nature of the congressional support for the administration's foreign policy commitments has been taken to provide further evidence for rooting it in sectional economic interest. Analysis of roll-call votes shows that, while party allegiance is by far the best predictor of how members of Congress voted, regional differences were also marked; in both parties, those from the Northeast supported the administration's measures to a significantly greater extent than those from Mountain and (in the case of Republicans) especially Midwestern states.[60]

Yet these regional differences should not be exaggerated. Although a Gallup poll in March 1948 found a higher percentage favoring the Marshall Plan in the Northeast than in the East Central states, the plan still enjoyed a two-to-one majority in the latter region. And, insofar as regional differences did exist, they are less easily explicable in terms of economic interest than is often suggested. The world economy mattered to many people in western states as well as in eastern ones. Indeed, it remained the case that in general a higher proportion of agricultural products were exported than of manufactured goods. In 1947, about 45 percent of American wheat was exported, compared to only 7 percent of automobiles and about 10 percent of rolled steel products. On the other hand, the international involvement of U.S. banks was remarkably small in comparison with their domestic activities. Loans to Europe constituted little over 1 percent of their total lending in 1950, and even for New York banks the figure was less than 3 percent. Such a marginal interest hardly seems sufficient to account for the undoubtedly strong support in the Eastern financial community for action to aid the economic recovery and political stabilization of Europe.[61]

This commitment should be understood in much broader terms. Even in the economic dimension, policymakers' concern was less with the direct profits of

Wall Street banks than with the maintenance of a liberal, multilateral system of international trade and investment. The establishment of state-controlled economies in the countries of western Europe would greatly reduce the scope of the open trading system the Bretton Woods agreements had been designed to establish, but this was hardly the only reason why the prospect of communist takeovers there was anathema to Americans.

Indeed, as we have seen, the creation of a flourishing international economy had become an objective of U.S. foreign policy in the war years largely because it was seen as the essential bedrock for a lasting peace. Similarly, in a memorandum on the European Recovery Program written by Charles P. Kindleberger and others for the Policy Planning Staff of the State Department in June 1947, the first of its aims was stated to be "that Germany should become a democratic, peaceful state." Earlier, in the influential paper in which he outlined what became the Marshall Plan, Kennan defined its purpose as "the restoration of the economic health and vigor of European society," deploring the impression given by the Truman Doctrine "that the United States approach to world problems is a defensive reaction to communist pressure and that the effort to restore sound economic conditions in other countries is only a by-product of this reaction and not something we would be interested in doing if there were no communist menace."[62]

Just as the goals of U.S. policy went well beyond the securing of overseas markets and investment opportunities, so the impetus for it came from a much broader segment of American society than the investment bankers of New York and those associated with them. Men like Kennan and Marshall, let alone Truman, had no connection with or particular sympathy for Wall Street. Similarly, the widespread support for their policies in the media and among the wider public is not easily attributable to economic interests. (Polls in the fall of 1947 showed substantial majorities of those who had an opinion in favor of the Marshall Plan.)[63] Clearly, many Americans who had no economic stake in the matter believed that a democratic and peaceful Europe was a national interest of sufficient importance to justify the commitment of significant resources to efforts to achieve and secure it.

As we have seen, this belief was commonly defended by an appeal to history, particularly the fact that the United States had been drawn into the two great European wars of the century. But this had by no means been a purely passive process. In both cases, it had resulted from actions—in the first case on the part of private interests as well as the administration—that reflected the extent to which influential Americans had felt involved in these foreign wars and sought to influence their outcome. As previous chapters attempted to show, these sentiments were not the product of hard-headed assessments of the nation's economic and strategic interest but arose in more complex ways from the extent to which Americans cared about what happened in the continent from which the great majority could trace their descent and with which they shared a religious, intellectual, and cultural tradition—indeed, what was commonly called a civilization.

The significance of this basic, if somewhat intangible, aspect of the nation's stake in the future of western Europe was rarely articulated in official documents, but it was by Kennan as he sought, while working on the Marshall Plan, to depict "the source of United States interest":

> Further deterioration might be disastrous to Europe. It might well bring such hardship, such bewilderment, such desperate struggle for control over inadequate resources as to lead to widespread repudiation of the principles on which modern European civilization has been founded.... The implications of such a loss would far surpass the common apprehensions over the possibility of "communist control." . . . The United States, in common with most of the rest of the world, would suffer a cultural and spiritual loss incalculable in its long-term effects.

To the students at the War College a few weeks earlier, Kennan had suggested that Americans' own commitment to liberal democracy would be imperiled:

> Remember that in abandoning Europe we would be abandoning not only the fountainheads of most of our own culture and tradition; we would also be abandoning almost all the other areas of the world where progressive representative government is a working proposition. We would be placing ourselves in the position of a lonely country, culturally and politically. To maintain confidence in our own traditions and institutions we would henceforth have to whistle loudly in the dark. I am not sure that whistling could be loud enough to do the trick.[64]

Kennan might be seen as an idiosyncratic figure in this respect, having spent much of his life in Europe and being in some ways more attracted to its traditional cultures than to that of his own country. Certainly, not all Americans felt as closely bonded with the Old World as did Kennan—or as did Acheson, at whose boyhood home Queen Victoria's birthday had been celebrated every year by his British-born father and Canadian mother. Yet even a broadly based official committee observed that "in the event of a totalitarian Europe . . . our spiritual loss would be incalculable," and Truman himself stressed to Congress that "our deepest concern with European recovery is that it is essential to the maintenance of the civilization in which the American way of life is rooted."[65]

In an era when college students were commonly required to take courses in "the history of western civilization," the belief that Europe and the United States shared distinctive values of fundamental importance was taken for granted by most Americans, and this cultural connection was invoked in discussion of foreign policy by people across the political spectrum. Thus John Foster Dulles warned Marshall in early 1947 that if the Soviet system should be extended across Europe, "western civilization and personal freedom, as we had known it, would be impossible." For Dulles, as for many others, what was at stake was the "Christian civilization" that Winston Churchill had declared to be in peril in his "iron curtain" speech of March 1946. The North Atlantic treaty, the State Department explained, had "its origins in the common heritage and civilization of the peoples living on both sides of the North Atlantic Ocean." Even as he opposed the stationing of U.S. troops in Europe the following year, Herbert Hoover insisted that "we are not blind to the need to preserve Western Civilization on the Continent of Europe or to our cultural and religious ties to it," arguing that this made it all the more important that "this Gibraltar of Western Civilization" not be overstretched and exhausted.[66]

The cultural connection with Europe went back, of course, to the origins of the American colonies, and it had over the years often found expression not only in affirmations of the difference and superiority of the ways of the New World but also in related justifications of isolationism. That this traditional way of asserting America's distinctive identity had lost much of its force by the late 1940s reflected two developments. The first was the shift in the balance of power between the Old World and the New World. As we have seen, well-informed Americans had been very conscious of the changing balance since the late nineteenth century. But the process climaxed after World War II when American dominance was apparent not only in the realms of financial, economic, and geopolitical power but also in scientific, intellectual, and cultural achievement; New York and Washington had clearly become the capitals of the western world. In relation to the nation's role in the world, this preeminent position produced an efflorescence of the image of maturity, already present in the rhetoric of Wilson and others at the turn of the century; according to this widely reiterated narrative, the United States, having passed through its adolescence of innocence and fecklessness, was now prepared to accept the (masculine) responsibilities of adulthood. In a culture in which the self-made man was an icon, these responsibilities were generally seen to demand not only a disciplined commitment but also an all-around capability, which included the readiness to protect those dependent on you from violent attack.

The second development related more specifically to the determination of foreign policy. This was that Americans were very largely united in their views about the European situation. This had emphatically not been the case in the past. The extent to which both sides in the war of 1914 had been passionately supported by different groups of Americans had made it difficult for Wilson to find a consensual basis for bringing the nation's power effectively to bear on that conflict. Thereafter, strong but divergent feelings about such matters as the justice of the German settlement and the benignity of Britain's world role had not only contributed to the failure to join the League of Nations but also remained an obstacle in the interwar period to the adoption of a firmer and more forceful policy. In the period preceding America's entry into World War II, these divisions had, of course, intensified. They became particularly bitter after Hitler's attack on the Soviet Union and Roosevelt's extension of Lend-Lease aid to that country which, Hoover had declared at the time, "makes the whole argument of our joining the war to bring the four freedoms to mankind a gargantuan jest."[67]

By contrast, the commitment to western Europe in the Truman years was strikingly uncontroversial. Certainly this owed something to the continuing concern to avoid a repeat of the partisan conflict that had disrupted the course of U.S. policy after World War I. Thus, leading Republicans were included in the delegations not only to the San Francisco conference establishing the United Nations but also to several of the foreign ministers' conferences about the postwar settlement in Europe. During the 1948 election campaign, John Foster Dulles, as the foreign policy adviser of the Republican candidate, Thomas E. Dewey, accompanied Marshall to the U.N. General Assembly. Following his much-heralded conversion from "isolationism," Vandenberg was the Republican politician most identified with a "bipartisan" or "nonpartisan" approach to foreign policy, and the administration worked with him in gaining congressional approval of their commitments to Europe, including aid to Greece and Turkey, the Marshall Plan, and the North Atlantic treaty.

These new commitments naturally met some opposition. Vandenberg's hold over Republicans in Congress, never complete, declined after the 1948 elections. A minority had consistently espoused the anti-British viewpoint propagated by Colonel R. R. McCormick's *Chicago Tribune*. However, the most politically weighty critics expressed a more nuanced dissent that focused on questions of cost and strategy rather than the nature and importance of the objective. Taft, for example, did not oppose the principle of Marshall aid; he wanted only to trim the appropriation. Hoover, who had taken the same position, called after the Czech coup for authorization of the full amount as "a major dam to Russian aggression." Similarly, while Taft was among the small minority of senators who voted against the North Atlantic treaty, he declared that he would favor a unilateral extension of the Monroe Doctrine "to let Russia know that if she attacked western Europe, the United States would be in the war." It was the anticommunist thrust of policy that brought such leading anti-interventionists of 1940–41 behind the administration's commitment to western Europe after World War II. It was difficult for them to oppose efforts to combat the spread of a doctrine that Hoover, for example, had denounced as "an evil thing . . . contrary to the spiritual, moral, and material aspirations of man."[68]

The popular support for the new consensus also reflected the fact that the different countries to which significant groups of Americans felt a special attachment were now all on the same side. Elite Anglo-Saxon Protestants who favored continuing the close relationship with the United Kingdom were now pulling in the same basic direction as both those who retained sympathy with Germany and the bitterly anti-Soviet east European ethnic groups, particularly Polish-Americans. The tireless anticommunist propaganda of the Catholic hierarchy melded ideological antipathy and ethnic loyalties while reinforcing both. Insofar as the support for the foreign policy commitments of the Truman administration represented the coming together of people with different interests and perspectives, analogous to the coalitions usually required to pass domestic legislation, the search for a single driving concern or motive is misguided.

Yet there were more general factors that form essential elements in an explanation of American actions. One, obviously, was the developing Cold War. Aggressive moves by Moscow, such as the Iran crisis, the Berlin blockade, and the Czech coup, produced a surge in support for aid to Europe. The confidence generally felt in policymaking circles that such crises would not lead to full-scale conflict was not shared by the general public. Polls in 1948 showed that a third of people believed that the United States would find itself in another war within a year, and two-thirds thought it would within ten years. Such apprehensions were the product not only of Soviet actions but also of the way that policymakers had stimulated a sense of threat and danger as they sought to develop political support for measures to achieve broader, long-term objectives. If the United States in these years was prepared to devote far more resources to the achievement of foreign policy objectives than it ever had before in peacetime, a good part of the reason was that Americans felt themselves to be in a quasi-war. Relatedly, they saw U.S. policy as essentially reactive in nature. Such "portentous new policies and departures" as the Truman Doctrine and the Marshall Plan, the historian Thomas A. Bailey wrote in 1950, were "not products of the American tradition or of basic American desires" but were "authored by the men in the Kremlin."[69]

American policy also reflected a confidence engendered by consciousness of the nation's power. This is not to say that there was no recognition that the exercise of this power would involve costs. On the contrary, this point was emphasized both in public debate and within government. As we have seen, conservative critics of the administration insisted that overspending on foreign aid and defense would impose crippling tax burdens that would damage the domestic economy and that fighting land wars in Eurasia would exhaust the nation's strength. Truman himself was concerned about the inflationary effect of government spending and borrowing and, on the vigorous advice of his economic advisers, set a firm ceiling of $15 billion on the defense budget in May 1948, reducing this to $13 billion in July 1949. Even in the State Department, Kennan advocated a "particularized" rather than "universalistic" approach on the grounds that "the limitations on [what] this nation, or any other single nation, can accomplish with that margin of its energies and material production which it can afford to devote to outside affairs are greater than we are often inclined to remember."[70]

Yet Kennan was at least as confident as other officials that the United States was much stronger than the Soviet Union and that it had the capacity to shape events abroad where its serious interests were involved. In designing the Marshall Plan, he reflected in December 1947, "I was conscious of the weakness of the Russian position, of the slenderness of the means with which they operated, of the ease with which they could be held and pushed back." Marshall saw the Berlin blockade as the product of "Russian desperation in face of success of ERP," and General Clay urged that the Kremlin's bluff be called, as "they are definitely afraid of our air power." "As long as we can outproduce the world, can control the sea and can strike inland with the atomic bomb," Secretary of the Navy James Forrestal wrote in 1947, "we can assume certain risks otherwise unacceptable." Consciousness of this primacy led in some quarters to an attitude of mind that can only be called imperial. "The United States is, by reason of its strength and political enlightenment, the natural leader of this hemisphere," the planners of the Joint Chiefs of Staff casually remarked, as they recommended the transfer of arms to "Latin American military men" who would be "very strong domestic political leaders." Outside the administration, belief in America's potential power was even greater. In March 1949, as communist armies were poised along the Yangtze for their final push southward, senators from both parties appealed publicly for "effective assistance to the Government of China."[71]

Doing More with More

During the course of Truman's second term, America's commitment to its world role grew in two dimensions—financial and geographic. Whereas in the fiscal year 1950 spending on defense and foreign assistance had constituted 32 percent of the federal budget and 5 percent of GNP, by the fiscal year 1952 it amounted to 68 percent of total government expenditure and 13.2 percent of GNP. This dramatic increase occurred while the United States was fighting a war in Korea, the cost of which also included the loss of 36,500 American lives. But both the great increase in national security expenditures and the readiness to deploy American power across the Pacific as well as the Atlantic had deeper causes than North Korea's invasion of South Korea in June 1950, and both outlasted the end of the Korean War in July 1953. By that date the United States had extended security guarantees to Japan, Taiwan, the Philippines, Australia, and New Zealand; in addition, it was meeting over 40 percent of the cost of the French war in Indochina against the insurgency led by Ho Chi Minh. A very substantial program of military assistance to allied nations had been established, and America's own armed forces had grown from one and a half million in 1948 to three and a half million.[72]

The most concrete evidence that these developments cannot simply be attributed to the Korean War is the famous memorandum, NSC-68, that had been written the previous spring in response to Truman's request for "a reexamination of our objectives in peace and war and of the effect of these objectives on our strategic plans." The request accompanied a directive to go ahead with the development of a hydrogen bomb and alluded to the prospect of this, together with the recently revealed Soviet atomic bomb capability, as part of the new strategic context that required appraisal. The lengthy document that was produced under the direction of the new head of the Policy Planning Staff, Paul H. Nitze, called for a "rapid and sustained build-up of the political, economic, and military strength of the free world," including "substantial" increases in U.S. spending for military purposes and military assistance and "some" increase in economic aid.[73]

Historians have disagreed over the extent to which NSC-68 represented a broadening of the scope of U.S. policy.[74] Certainly, the globalist implications of such statements as that "a defeat of free institutions anywhere is a defeat everywhere" seem at odds with the emphasis on the unique character of the commitment to western Europe in Kennan's early papers for the Policy Planning Staff. But that emphasis, which was an attempt to counter the sweeping terms of the Truman Doctrine, was in part a distinctively personal one in that it reflected Kennan's skepticism about the United Nations and the vision of world order that had been espoused by American internationalists since Woodrow Wilson's time, and also his strong sense that the United States and the countries of western Europe shared values that had little relevance or meaning to people of other cultures. He made this last point in opposing further commitment in China, and it was in the same context that he articulated the strategic rationale for a "particularized" approach referred to earlier. But this rationale itself extended America's vital interests beyond western Europe in that Japan was one of the "five centers of industrial and military power" identified as important, and Kennan was in the forefront of efforts to bind Japan to the West through the "reverse course" of occupation policy in 1948.[75]

Moreover, as the historian Melvyn P. Leffler has emphasized, these core commitments carried with them wider concerns insofar as the prosperity of west European countries and Japan was seen as dependent on access to overseas resources and markets. For this reason, among others, U.S. policymakers had sought to ensure that communist success in China was not replicated in Southeast Asia. In December 1948, Kennan himself had observed that "curiously enough, the most crucial issue of the moment in our struggle with the Kremlin is probably the problem of Indonesia." In that country, the United States responded to the perceived danger that communists would exploit anticolonialist sentiment by putting pressure on the Dutch to cede power to more moderate nationalists. But in French Indochina, where the insurgency led by the communist Ho Chi Minh enjoyed increasing success, Cold War concerns moderated the anticolonial thrust of American policy. After Communist China and the Soviet Union recognized Ho's as the legitimate government of Vietnam in January 1950, the United States recognized the French-sponsored regime of Bao Dai and began to provide economic and military aid to France and her allied governments in Indochina.[76]

However, this aid, like that earlier to China, hardly constituted a major item in the U.S. budget. If NSC-68 did not embody any clear enlargement of the general objectives of U.S. policy—indeed, it explicitly reiterated the definition of these in an NSC document of 1948—it did insist that a much greater national effort was needed if these objectives were to be achieved.[77] The West, it implied, was losing the Cold War, which was envisaged very much in military terms; without military superiority, containment was "no more than a policy of bluff." Accordingly, less stress was laid on the communist victory in China than on the build-up of Russian military strength. The Soviet Union was "devoting a far greater *proportion* of its resources to military purposes than are the free nations and, in significant components of military power, a greater *absolute* quantity of resources." Above all, its atomic and potentially thermonuclear capability made a major build-up of western military strength both vital and urgent.[78]

To some historians, the logic of this argument is self-explanatory. "With the breaking of the American nuclear monopoly in August 1949, everything changed practically overnight," Marc Trachtenberg writes. "The American nuclear monopoly was the one thing that had balanced Soviet superiority in ground forces in Europe; now, with the breaking of that monopoly, the Soviets were in a much better position to accept a showdown with the West." Consequently, they could be expected to adopt more aggressive stances in Europe and elsewhere, running the risk of war.[79] Yet matters were not really so simple. America's capacity to deliver a devastating atomic attack on the Soviet Union (which was much greater in 1950 than it had been a few years earlier) would lose plausibility as a deterrent only when the Soviet Union had developed the capability of itself making a similar attack on the United States, in retaliation or indeed preemptively. Although NSC-68 claimed that already by 1950 the Soviet Union had the capacity to attack "targets in Alaska, Canada, and the United States," in fact, as Trachtenberg admits, existing Soviet bombers (the TU-4) had the range to attack the American homeland only through one-way suicide missions. The prediction that the Soviet Union would by 1954 be able to deliver one hundred atomic bombs against U.S. targets was equally alarmist; the Russians did not possess truly intercontinental bombers until the late 1950s. By contrast, as Samuel Wells points out, in 1956 "the U.S. Strategic Air Command had operational at least 350 bombers with intercontinental range plus a force of 1,560 medium-range B-47s, most of which were based within range of the Soviet Union or were capable of refueling in flight."[80] In this situation, the United States could continue to rely on its atomic superiority to provide credible "extended deterrence" in Europe and elsewhere without fear of a retaliatory attack on its own homeland. American policymakers recognized this, as is shown by the serious consideration given to the use of atomic weapons both in the Korean War and the Taiwan Strait crisis of 1954 and by John Foster Dulles's advocacy of a strategy of "massive retaliation" in those years.[81]

If Soviet possession of an atomic bomb did not create a clear strategic need for large-scale rearmament, NSC-68's advocacy of such a program requires some further explanation. Revisionist historians like Curt Cardwell find this in the continuing need to bridge the dollar gap created by the imbalance of trade with Europe, to which the United States was exporting more than four times as much as it was importing. Another crisis in Britain's transatlantic balance of payments forced a 30 percent devaluation of sterling against the dollar in September 1949. With Marshall Plan aid due to end in 1952, Europe had to acquire dollars in other ways if transatlantic trade was not to be sharply reduced. The prime aim of NSC-68, it is argued, was to provide a justification for funneling dollars to Europe in the form of military assistance (something Congress was much more likely to view favorably than an extension of economic aid) and thus "to maintain the high level of U.S. exports necessary for free market capitalism to function at home."[82]

Again, this sort of argument does not stand up well to an examination of the statistics. In 1949, Nitze himself thought that American exports were at an "abnormally high" level. Even then, the trade surplus of the United States with Europe amounted to 1.25 percent of GNP—not a negligible sum but hardly a margin vital for the survival of free market capitalism. In 1950, as it happened, the value of American exports to Europe did decline by 25 percent— without perceptible effects on American prosperity or the political legiti- macy of its economic system. At this time, as part of its efforts to further west European integration, the United States was lending financial support to a system (the European Payments Union) that actually discriminated against dollar imports.[83]

Nevertheless, the argument that NSC-68 had causes other than the Soviet atomic bomb is strengthened by the fact that Nitze, who was to be its principal author, had begun work on a central feature—the comparative analysis of Russian and American military spending—in the summer of 1949, before the unexpect- edly early Soviet test was revealed by intelligence in September.[84] Nitze embarked on this study in the context of a battle within the administration over the defense budget.[85] The Joint Chiefs of Staff had long argued that the armed forces lacked the strength to meet all the nation's commitments, but their demands had been resisted by the Budget Bureau, which was supported by Truman himself. In 1948, Marshall, as secretary of state, had thrown his considerable weight against Secre- tary of Defense James Forrestal's strenuous attempts to increase military spend- ing. In the summer of 1949, however, the resistance to further cuts did not come from the Defense Department (where the new secretary, Louis A. Johnson, was firmly committed to Truman's budget ceiling) but from the State Department, where Acheson and other leading figures were convinced that the achievement of America's foreign policy objectives required the commitment of much larger resources.[86]

The State Department's change of position was connected to personnel changes. Nitze, whose influence was rising even before he was appointed head of the Policy Planning Staff in January 1950, saw the Cold War much more in mili- tary terms than Kennan did, and his perspective was largely shared by Acheson (who was later to observe that Kennan had "never, in my judgment, grasped the realities of power relationships"). This divergence no doubt owed something to personal temperament, but it can also be seen as reflecting differences in forma- tive experiences and, relatedly, in worldviews. Kennan and Marshall had been professionally concerned with U.S. foreign relations in the 1920s and 1930s, and at some level America's position in the prewar world remained for them a sort of norm. For Acheson and Nitze (and many other leading officials), involvement in international affairs had come only with World War II, and the default setting for their approach to policymaking thereafter seems to have been that the United States was involved in a global conflict requiring a high degree of national mobi- lization; thus, they conceived the Cold War in strategic terms that were essentially military.[87]

Linked to this were the differences over policy toward Europe that led to Kennan's loss of influence. Kennan's reiterated advocacy of German reunification and the withdrawal of both Soviet and Western forces from that country looked toward the restoration of an independent Europe, capable of balancing against Russian power without American assistance. However, Acheson and other leading policymakers did not believe that western Europe could be securely peaceful and democratic unless it were aligned with the United States. In October 1949, Acheson observed that for "the last 35 or 40 years . . . we have been holding a concept that . . . we would shortly return to 'normality', whereas . . . during that entire period the realities of the situation confronting us forced us to do nothing but 'abnormal' things." Taken together with his long-held views about the crucial role Britain had played in creating and maintaining the conditions of nineteenth-century prosperity, this may be seen as another indication that Acheson was an adherent of "hegemonic stability theory" *avant la lettre*. International order and a multilateral trading system depended upon management by a power possessing both financial strength and military muscle.[88]

From this perspective, the solidity of the American-led order seemed threatened in various ways in the latter part of 1949. If the dollar gap caused any serious concern, it was for foreign policy reasons rather than for domestic economic ones. The possibility that financial stringency might cause Britain to withdraw from its political and military commitments in the Middle East and Southeast Asia worried some, but the chief anxiety remained Europe. If a reduction in American exports to the continent led to a restoration of traditional trade patterns between western and eastern Europe, this could weaken political links with the United States and strengthen neutralist sentiment, particularly in Germany, where the Soviet Union was offering the bait of reunification. Countering this by integrating the newly established Federal Republic securely within a west European system ran up against French opposition to the restoration of German power in a structure that did not include Britain. But the British firmly resisted pressure to join the developing European economic institutions.[89]

At a meeting to discuss these problems in October 1949, Averell Harriman suggested that integration could best be promoted "not from the purely economic or the purely political standpoint but the standpoint of security." At the same time, he observed that "one of the most important psychological developments in the last year in western Europe had been the abatement of the fear of Soviet aggression." Such fear had, of course, done much to produce the readiness in the countries of western Europe to accept American leadership. That readiness also depended on confidence in America's ability and willingness to hold the line at the Rhine, if necessary—a confidence that the now forseeable end of its atomic monopoly was likely to weaken.[90]

To all these problems, the program outlined in NSC-68 offered some solution. An expansion of the Military Assistance Program that had been launched in July 1949 might help address the problem of the dollar gap after the end of Marshall Aid. Large-scale rearmament would not only augment the capabilities of the North Atlantic pact allies in the event of hostilities but also, more urgently, reassure Europeans that the United States would defend the continent in the event of war. German participation in this enterprise would heighten European tensions in the short run, but by advancing the process of integration would counter the danger of Germany's succumbing to neutralism or a revival of revanchist nationalism.[91]

NSC-68 began by framing its argument in the long-term context Acheson had emphasized. With "the defeat of Germany and Japan and the decline of the British and French Empires," power had gravitated to the United States and the Soviet Union. So the international system was now bipolar—but the two poles were not of equal strength. It was the United States that possessed "the greatest military potential of any single nation in the world," a point buttressed by tables showing how greatly its industrial production and resources of energy exceeded those of the Soviet Union. But whereas Soviet capabilities were being "mobilized close to the maximum possible extent," on the American side there was "a wide gap of unactualized power." This gap had to be narrowed if the United States was to possess the "superior overall power" necessary to achieve its policy objectives. These objectives were essentially two, and each was defined in ambitious terms. The first was "containment," a policy that sought not only to "block further expansion of Soviet power" but also to "induce a retraction of the Kremlin's control and influence" and "so foster the seeds of destruction within the Soviet system that the Kremlin is brought at least to the point of modifying its behavior to conform to generally accepted international standards." Second, there was the broader goal of developing "a healthy international community," described as "a policy which we would probably pursue even if there was no Soviet threat," as "in a shrinking world the absence of order among nations is becoming less and less tolerable."

The purpose of NSC-68 was to generate support for the greater national effort seen as necessary for the achievement of these goals. In the first place, the authors stressed that such an effort would not impose intolerable burdens on the American people. To counter the argument of Truman's budget advisers (and many in Congress) that the country could not afford to spend more on defense and foreign aid, they referred back to the World War II experience. This had shown that "the American economy, when it operates at a level approaching full efficiency, can provide enormous resources for purposes other than civilian consumption while simultaneously providing a high standard of living."[92]

The chief way in which NSC-68 attempted, in Acheson's later words, to "bludgeon the mind of 'top government'" was by heightening the sense of threat and danger.[93] As we have seen, it had been such a sense that had secured congressional approval for the British Loan, aid to Greece and Turkey, and the Marshall Plan. But in 1949, following the lifting of the Berlin blockade in the spring, the public anticipated a relaxation of tensions with Russia, and there was increasing pressure in Congress for a reduction of Marshall aid funding. "The American people have a false sense of security," Acheson complained in the spring of 1950. It was the desire to shatter this that gave parts of NSC-68 the rhetorical tone of a platform speech rather than an internal memorandum—indeed, despite its "top secret" status, its gist was conveyed by Acheson and others in public statements.[94]

The basic proposition was that "the cold war is in fact a real war in which the survival of the free world is at stake." Thus, over the objections not only of Kennan but of his fellow Russian expert Charles Bohlen, NSC-68 portrayed the Soviet Union as "animated by a new fanatic faith" and determined "to impose its absolute authority over the rest of the world." Because the United States was "the only major threat to the achievement of its fundamental design," it was seen by the Kremlin as "the principal enemy whose integrity and vitality must be subverted or destroyed by one means or another"; "the existence and persistence of the idea of freedom is a permanent and continuous threat to the foundation of the slave society; and it therefore regards as intolerable the long continued existence of freedom in the world."

Soviet capabilities were described as alarmingly as Soviet intentions—and as questionably. ("The task of a public officer seeking to explain and gain support for a major policy is not that of the writer of a doctoral thesis," Acheson later observed.) The physical safety of the United States itself was in danger, not only because of the Soviet Union's imminent capacity to deliver a devastating atomic attack on North America but also because, if Moscow gained control of most of Eurasia, it would "acquire a potential far superior to our own." In asserting that "this Republic and its citizens in the ascendancy of their strength stand in their deepest peril," NSC-68 pointed up the paradoxical, almost contradictory, nature of the case it was making. The United States was at once so vulnerable that it was "in greater jeopardy than ever before in our history" and so powerful that it could realistically aspire to change the behavior and nature of the Soviet Union and to establish world order.[95]

It is impossible to know how far NSC-68 would have succeeded in its purpose without the Korean War. Although Louis Johnson had been induced to add his signature to the report, Truman did not approve it immediately, instead asking for cost estimates (which had been deliberately omitted) and review by an ad hoc committee including representatives of the Budget Bureau and the Treasury Department. The president was clearly reluctant to incur deficits or sacrifice cherished Fair Deal programs, and in public he discounted suggestions of a large increase in the defense budget, observing that "we are not alarmed in any sense of the word." However, given Acheson's determination and influence, the breadth and strength of the bureaucratic coalition he and Nitze mustered, and their cultivation of allies in the media, it is likely that Truman would have requested some increase in military spending and foreign assistance in the budget for fiscal year 1952. Yet this would surely have fallen well short of the 40–50 billion dollars the authors of NSC-68 had estimated as the cost of the programs they thought necessary, a sum that Congress could hardly have been expected to approve in the absence of a war.[96]

This has led some to suggest that a desire to seize the chance to promote the rearmament program inspired the decision to send U.S. forces to counter North Korea's attack on South Korea in June 1950. They point out that Korea had long been judged as of slight strategic importance, that it was outside America's "defensive perimeter" as Acheson had defined this in a well-reported speech in January, and that the Joint Chiefs of Staff sought to avoid involvement in a ground war in Asia. It is true that Acheson, who promptly took the lead in shaping the U.S. response to the crisis, had anticipated that a communist attack somewhere would provide an opportunity to fulfill the NSC-68 program. But this is perhaps most relevant as evidence of the mindset that led to the immediate assumption that the North Korean invasion was a proxy move by the Kremlin. Acheson and his advisers saw it as a clear challenge that had to be met if nervous allies were not to doubt American resolve.[97] And on this issue Acheson had no difficulty in bringing the president along; indeed, Truman himself seems to have led the way over the use of force. There is no reason to doubt his sincerity in portraying this "naked, deliberate, unprovoked aggression" as "a clear challenge to the basic principles of the United Nations Charter" (which he certainly took more seriously than did some of his advisers), and in invoking the lesson of the 1930s "when aggression unopposed bred more aggression and eventually war."[98] Such arguments had resonance not only with the American public but also with foreign ones, and this helped the British and Commonwealth governments, in particular, to lend more than symbolic military support to what quickly became a United Nations mission.

Although the administration had been under fierce attack in Congress and parts of the media over its Asian policy since the "loss" of China, the decision to intervene in Korea probably owed little to domestic political considerations.

Becoming involved in a land war in Asia was not the favored strategy of Republican critics like Taft and Hoover, who were in any case much less interested in Korea than in support for Chiang Kai-shek's government in Taiwan. The administration went some way toward meeting this last concern by announcing that the Seventh Fleet would be interposed between Taiwan and the mainland. Although it was maintained publicly that this move did not constitute involvement in the Chinese civil war, it was followed up by the sending of a military mission and $125 million in aid to the Nationalist regime. The Korean War also stimulated accelerated support of the French war in Indochina and economic and military aid to the Philippines, where an insurgency was flourishing. These steps demonstrated a firmer determination to prevent further communist advances in Asia, a determination that was to lead naturally to larger and more formal commitments in the next few years.[99]

The actions of U.S. policymakers at this time are commonly attributed to anxiety, but they also reflected a striking confidence in the scale of American power. After all, the United States ended up with commitments to provide security across much of the globe—and to countries that had little reciprocal strength to offer in exchange. The real anxiety of policymakers concerned the translation of America's potential power into effective influence. This involved two issues—whether America's resolve to use its power would have credibility abroad and how much political will there would be at home to devote resources to the achievement of foreign policy goals. The issues were related in that the first was seen as depending to a significant extent on the second.

All these assumptions and concerns were manifested in the first six months of the Korean War. Intervention had been spurred by the desire to demonstrate American resolve, and it was soon used to muster domestic and allied support for rearmament. As Truman stressed to Congress, this was necessary "not only to deal with the aggression in Korea but also to increase our common defense, with other free nations, against further aggression." The sums the administration requested in July almost doubled the defense budget and more than tripled that for the military assistance program.[100] Decision-making with regard to the war itself manifested great confidence in American power—indeed, at times overconfidence. At the outset, officials not only anticipated that the North Korean forces would soon be defeated but were also sure that the Soviet Union, aware that it would lose a global war, would not counter U.S. intervention militarily. Although checking the North Korean assault proved considerably more difficult (and costly in terms of casualties) than had been expected, the tide was turned by General MacArthur's bold amphibious landing at Inchon in September. After this success, MacArthur was authorized to cross the 38th parallel, defeat the North Korean army, and reunite the country, despite the fears of some in Washington (including Nitze as well as Kennan) that this would provoke a reaction from China. MacArthur's prophecy that the war would be won by Christmas was belied in late November when more than two hundred thousand Chinese troops crossed the Yalu River and drove the U.N. forces back well south of the parallel. This development of the conflict into a major war created a more favorable climate for the further military build-up that was already being planned. Following the supplemental appropriations that Truman requested in December, the defense budget for fiscal year 1951 had risen from $13.3 billion to $44.3 billion and that for the military assistance program from $1.4 billion to $10.5 billion.[101]

Although the sweeping advance of the Chinese communists thus made a crucial contribution to the strengthening of western Europe's defenses, it also raised the question of how much of a commitment the United States was going to make in Asia. The beleaguered MacArthur called for the bombing of bases in Manchuria, blockading the Chinese coast, and augmenting his forces with nationalist troops from Taiwan. He implied that victory could be achieved without much greater deployment of U.S. troops, possibly through the use of atomic weapons. By making his case publicly in a manner that was to lead to his dismissal in April 1951, he aligned himself with the fierce Republican attacks on Truman and Acheson both for "losing" China and for sacrificing the lives of American boys through their ineptitude. The retreats and casualties had eroded public support for the war. The initial intervention had been widely acclaimed (even by former isolationists), enhancing Truman's standing; a poll in early October 1950 found a large majority in favor of invading North Korea and forcing its surrender. However, the president's poll ratings plummeted in November, and by January 1951 Gallup was reporting that two-thirds of Americans favored pulling "our troops out of Korea as fast as possible," while 44 percent of those with an opinion now thought it had been "a mistake" to intervene in the first place. Shortly after, an overwhelming majority (77%) declared their opposition to starting "an all-out war with Communist China." This provided a propitious climate for those urging a less ambitious and expensive strategy. "The whole Korean tragedy is developing proof that the way to punish aggressors is from the air and sea and not by land armies," Herbert Hoover declared.[102]

To this domestic pressure for restraint was added some from America's major ally. Following Truman's remark at a press conference that "active consideration" was being given to the use of atomic weapons, British Prime Minister Clement Attlee invited himself to Washington for urgent consultations. In broad historical perspective, this may be viewed as a turning point in transatlantic relations. Hitherto, as we have seen, the governments of the

European democracies had generally sought to encourage the United States to play a wider and more forceful role in world politics. In the second half of the twentieth century and beyond, Europeans more commonly saw America's behavior as overly belligerent and sought to restrain (or even deplored) its overseas interventions, especially in the Third World. Although Attlee failed in his attempt to secure an explicit commitment that atomic weapons would not be used without prior consultation, he did succeed in engaging the president and his top advisors in a discussion of wider policy issues. These discussions illuminated the reasons why the view from Washington differed in significant ways from that from London.

At this dark time, when both Truman and Acheson spoke of being "licked in this campaign," Attlee agreed that South Korea should not be abandoned and that the line should be held if at all possible. But he also pressed for concessions in order to achieve a negotiated ceasefire—particularly that the United States follow the United Kingdom by recognizing the People's Republic and allowing it to take China's seat in the United Nations. Emphasizing that, like Tito in Yugoslavia, the Chinese communists did not owe their power to the Red Army, and also the strength of nationalism in an old and proud civilization, Attlee said that the British hoped "to drive a wedge between China and Russia." Continued nonrecognition and sanctions, let alone the retaliatory actions of which the Americans were speaking in the event of their being forced out of Korea, would leave China "with Russia as her only friend." Acheson did not dissent from this assessment of the likely course of Sino-Soviet relations in the long run (remarking that "he had probably been more bloodied by announcing these views than anyone else"), but he insisted that the immediate question was "whether you start by accepting the results of aggression and say to the aggressors that they had licked us and can collect their price. Would we go on and say that we are friendly to the aggressors, that we want to trade with them and seat them in the UN?" Truman remarked that this would not go down well with "American opinion."[103]

The extent to which the divergence of views between American and British policymakers was rooted in different estimations of their own nation's power came out very clearly in the discussions. Urging consideration of "the balance of forces," the British participants observed that "it would not be easy to bring damage to China quickly" but that "considerable and rapid damage could be done to the UK in Hong Kong and Malaya." With regard to economic sanctions, Attlee thought that "they could hurt us more on this than we could hurt them." Acheson, by contrast, was confident that "if the Chinese Communists take an attitude of hostility to the United States they will suffer more than we do." The limits to American power of which he and Truman were most conscious were not external but internal. Whereas the British feared that confrontation with China would overextend the United States in an area of secondary strategic significance, Acheson argued that it was a necessary concomitant of measures to strengthen the defense of Europe because it "would provide a better chance to get our people behind the effort and to draw on the power from the United States which actually is the only source of power." With Truman observing that "we could not separate our discussion from the political problems we face," Acheson stressed that no administration "could possibly urge the American people to take vigorous action in its foreign policy on one ocean front while on the other ocean front they seemed to be rolled back and to accept a position of isolation."[104]

It would be wrong to attribute this American position to the influence of the China lobby. The fervent partisans of Chiang Kai-shek did indeed constitute a highly vocal presence both in Congress and in sections of the media, but the amount of support they enjoyed among the wider public was limited. Polls in 1948–49 had found that giving goods and military supplies to the Nationalists enjoyed only minority support, and that far more Americans had an unfavorable view of Chiang than a favorable view. To the British, Acheson emphasized that, in his characterization of American public opinion, "he was not referring to vociferous extremists but to the sound judgment of reasonable people."[105]

If, as Acheson indicated, it would be impossible to sustain broad political support for a regionally specific commitment to Europe, this was fundamentally because none of the justifications for an active American involvement in world politics provided a solid basis for such geographical discrimination or circumscription. This was obviously true of the aspiration to establish and uphold certain principles of international conduct, particularly the delegitimization of aggressive war. This objective, embodied in Wilson's League of Nations, the Kellogg-Briand Pact, and the UN Charter, provided the most commonly articulated case for intervention in Korea. But experience had proved that it was not sufficient in itself to generate the resources needed for the exercise of real power abroad.

Such resources had been forthcoming before 1945 only in times of war, and it took a quasi-war to produce them in the postwar period. The unique effectiveness of the Cold War in mobilizing national support for foreign policy enterprises arose from its combination of stark ideological conflict with existential security concerns. From at least the time of the Truman Doctrine, the traditional national mission to promote and defend freedom was evoked, with communism being equated with totalitarian tyranny. Given that the values at stake were seen as universal, this ideological contest was implicitly global in its scope—a fact that was quickly exploited by the friends of China in Congress. "Does the administration have less concern for human liberty in Asia that it does in Europe?" Senator William Knowland (R–Calif.) asked. Did it want "free men everywhere," or did it draw "a color line on freedom?"[106]

It might be thought that the needs of American security provided a better justification for discriminating between different parts of the world and prioritizing Europe. This had been the view of some officials, including military planners as well as the Policy Planning Staff, in the immediate postwar years. It was the thrust of Walter Lippmann's 1947 critique of the Truman Doctrine (and the X-Article), and it has been propounded in subsequent decades by "realist" critics of U.S. involvement in Third World conflicts.[107] Yet the fact that this viewpoint never established itself as an accepted basis for policymaking reflected intrinsic difficulties with the argument. To gain real political traction as a motive for strenuous foreign policy actions, "security" had to be defined narrowly, as protecting the American homeland from direct attack. Kennan had recognized this, and it was in these terms that he sought in his lectures and private briefings in 1948–49 to develop a rationale for a regionally discriminatory approach. But Kennan had rested his argument on a scenario—a possible attack on North America by an amphibious force—that had little credibility in an era of modern airpower and atomic weapons. Even the Joint Chiefs of Staff study of April 1947 had relied on the earlier experience of the two world wars in making the case that the countries of western Europe were the most important ones with respect to America's own security. In 1950, with Hoover, Taft, and others stressing the ability of the United States to protect its homeland from attack through its own air and naval power, arguments that rested on the comparative narrowness of the Atlantic and the military-industrial potential of western Europe hardly possessed the credibility necessary to sustain a Eurocentric approach. Thus, the *Chicago Tribune* thought it was sufficient to point out that Russia lacked the surface navy and merchant marine to invade the United States in order to denounce as unjustified Truman's declaration of a state of national emergency in December 1950.[108]

Given the generally recognized unlikelihood of an external attack in the short term, the only way that the country's existential security could be seen as threatened was by positing a future situation in which Soviet Russia, intent on world domination, gained control over so much of the rest of the world that it could overpower the United States. This is what Truman did as he sought to gain approval of the long-term commitment of American forces to Europe and the vastly increased budgets for defense and foreign assistance in 1950–52. But in doing so, he did not discriminate between different overseas continents; on the contrary, he portrayed them all as vital to "our own national security":

> If Western Europe were to fall to Soviet Russia, it would double the Soviet supply of coal and triple the Soviet supply of steel. If the free countries of Asia and Africa should fall to Soviet Russia, we would lose the sources of many of our most vital raw materials, including uranium, which is the basis of our atomic power. And Soviet command of the manpower of the free nations of Europe and Asia would confront us with military forces which we could never hope to equal.[109]

This sort of argument made undeveloped countries in Asia and Africa as vital for American security as the advanced industrial nations of western Europe.

In truth, it was hard to justify the scale of the nation's involvement in world politics through the need to ensure the basic safety of North America, as some policymakers privately recognized. "If we had objectives only for the purpose of repelling invasion and not to create a better world, the will to fight would be lessened," Nitze remarked during the drafting of NSC-68.[110] Nitze was surely right that the expansion of the nation's commitments, and the concomitant readiness to become involved in overseas conflicts, did not arise simply from the requirements of self-defense. Yet his observation is also misleading insofar as it suggests that this readiness was produced by a general aspiration to establish a world order that accorded with American ideals and values (including free enterprise). Such an aspiration certainly existed but, as we have seen, on its own it had not been strong enough to generate the scale of resources needed to influence the course of events on other continents in a significant way. This happened only when the desire "to create a better world" was focused on a particular overseas situation (commonly a conflict) where a sufficient number of Americans felt sufficiently strongly about the outcome to provide the necessary political will to bring the nation's great potential power to bear.

The historical record shows that the United States was initially led to commit resources to the achievement of foreign policy enterprises on a scale unprecedented in peacetime by concern with conditions in Europe after 1945. The importance attached by policymakers to the establishment of a prosperous, democratic, and peaceful western Europe derived from several sources. Basic was the desire to avoid being dragged into another European war, but at a deeper level it was a product (as those earlier interventions had been) of the deep and complex connections between the United States and Europe. These derived from much more than material economic and possible security interests. Conscious of their country's enormous potential power and the weakness of the formerly great powers of western Europe, influential Americans felt a responsibility for the fate of the civilization of which they were inescapably a part. As we have seen, as the Cold War came to be envisaged as a global conflict, this initial commitment grew and spread to other continents, but when they came under pressure these more extensive involvements proved to lack the depth of support of the original one.

Conclusion

The expansion of the scale and scope of America's involvement in world politics during the last years of the Truman administration was to continue in the decades that followed. Although the proportion of GNP devoted to national security declined somewhat after its 1951–54 peak, it did not come back down to the 1949 level until the late 1970s—and then only briefly. The armed forces continuously numbered somewhere between two and a half and three and a half million until the draft was ended in 1973.[1] In addition, other instrumentalities for exerting influence abroad were developed further. The operational capabilities of the Central Intelligence Agency grew from their beginnings in 1947 with covert propaganda and funding to include more direct and sometimes violent means of intervention in the politics of target countries; the agency's budget increased tenfold in real terms between 1963 and 2005.[2] Aid to foreign governments, particularly military assistance and arms supplies, became more widely employed not only as a form of diplomatic leverage but also to help sympathetic regimes battle internal opposition. Geographically, America's political involvement overseas spread, notably in the Middle East, where the United States supplanted Britain as the dominant outside power in the 1950s, a process taken forward with the establishment of Central Command in 1983. Exercising influence also through bilateral diplomatic relations and its leading role in numerous international bodies, the United States was clearly the dominant player in world politics.

The momentum of this global involvement was sustained by interests it had itself brought into existence. Participation in international organizations generated ongoing, and in some cases growing, commitments. The country's allies and clients became accustomed to demanding continued American support in meeting the problems and threats that confronted them. From inside the country, upward pressure on the national security budget was exerted by what President Dwight Eisenhower called "the military-industrial complex"— composed of the large defense establishment itself, corporations manufacturing arms and military equipment, and the allies of both in Congress from states benefiting from defense contracts and military bases. The nation's expanded role in world affairs not only increased the attention paid to foreign policy by politicians but also produced over time a whole class of people professionally concerned with the subject, working in universities, think tanks, and the media as well as at times in government, and playing a prominent part in public debate. Coming to think of themselves, in the words of one, as "the foreign-policy elite" whose role now resembled that of "the management" of a firm, they generally tended to promote active engagement with the problems of the world. A quite different source of domestic pressure for high defense spending, and on some occasions overseas interventions too, came from the increased importance attached by most Americans to their country's preeminent status. "Our identity as a nation," David Calleo observed in 2009, "is intimately bound up with seeing ourselves as the world's most powerful country, at the heart of a global system."[3]

These various interests and attitudes, which either had not existed or had been less influential before America's assumption of a global role, contributed significantly to its maintenance and expansion. But the factors that had brought the role into being also continued to shape—and constrain—the way it was played.

As earlier, political support for strenuous action entailing significant costs depended very largely on the existence of conflict and a sense of threat. For over four decades, this was provided by the Cold War. When that ended, there was a reduction not only in the national security budget but also in the attention paid to foreign affairs generally by the public, the media, Congress and even the executive.[4] It took the terrorist attacks of September 2001 and the subsequent wars in Afghanistan and Iraq to reverse these trends again.

This correlation reinforced two preexisting tendencies. One was a propensity—more in popular attitudes and public debate than among professionals—to favor military responses to perceived threats. This bias was reflected in the high and increasing proportion of the national security budget allotted to the Pentagon. Whereas appropriations for foreign aid had been equal to 21.5 percent of the defense budget in fiscal years 1946–48 and as much as 31.5 percent in 1949–52, thereafter this figure fell back to 11.6 percent in 1953–61, 9.8 percent in 1970, and 8.2 percent in 1982. Moreover, much foreign aid took the form of military assistance—by 1956 this had risen to about 70 percent of the total, though the proportion fell back during the 1960s before rising again in the 1980s.[5]

The second preexisting tendency that was reinforced by the difficulty of securing resources or wide political attention for foreign policy in the absence of a conflict was the widespread assumption that America's global role should be seen as simply a defensive reaction to threats from the outside world. How valid is that assumption?

Certainly, it is highly unlikely that the American role in the second half of the twentieth century would have been as large had there not been the two world wars in the first half. Imagining away such world-historical events is too large a counterfactual to be profitably pursued, but from a more narrowly American perspective the broad political support for the extensive and expensive commitments undertaken after 1945 was, as we have seen, largely the product of the country's involvement in these two world wars. It was above all the apparent vindication of the view that in the modern world it was impossible for the United States to escape involvement in such conflicts that led to the discrediting of "isolationism" and the creation of a national consensus that the United States should take the lead in establishing an international order that would prevent their occurrence.

That the assumption of a global role grew out of America's experience in the two world wars might seem to confirm the essentially defensive character of U.S. policy. For in both wars the United States became a belligerent in response to a direct attack—on its own shipping in 1917 and on its territory in 1941. However, it is necessary to remember that the countries making those attacks saw the United States as already participating in the war against them—in the first case by supplying Germany's enemies and in the second by using economic pressure to force Japan to abandon its ambitions. In World War I, the alignment can be attributed in part to external circumstances—Britain's command of the sea. But this is by no means the whole story. In allowing loans that facilitated the huge Allied purchases of supplies as well as in its differential response to British and German violations of international maritime law, the United States had made policy decisions that helped Germany's enemies. In 1941, the economic and military support being given to the countries fighting the Axis Powers was obvious and overt. In other words, participation in the two wars was not something forced on the country out of the blue. Before it entered them as a belligerent, it had involved itself in these overseas conflicts. In the case of the Cold War, the role of American initiative was even more evident.

As we have seen in earlier chapters, there were particular causes of the involvement in each of these specific cases, but there were also some that reflected aspects of American policymaking that have been apparent at other times. One of these is the influence of emotional ties with other countries—ties that are naturally intensified when these countries are under threat. In World War I, both the financing of Allied purchases and the climate of opinion that shaped the response to U-boat warfare owed much to the Anglophilia of many East Coast WASPs. Such circles also took the lead in promoting aid to the allies and intervention in World War II and later in mobilizing support for the Marshall Plan and NATO. A comparable example is the relationship with Israel in recent decades. In the case of both Britain and Israel, people with personal, ethnic, or cultural connections with the country in question sought actively to shape opinion and policy but only succeeded to a significant extent when Americans generally came to see it as an ideologically compatible ally whose survival and empowerment would strengthen the cause of democracy in the world. There were naturally particular elements in each case—in the Israeli one, the significance in some Christian theologies of the fate of the Jews. But both examples show that concern with another country's security may precede, rather than derive from, its definition as a vital American interest—something that those who take a more rigorously materialist view of the national interest tend to deplore.

A second recurrent feature is the uncompromising character of American diplomacy. Manifest in both the response to submarine warfare in 1915–16 and the conduct of negotiations with Japan in 1941, this formed the background to the attacks that brought the United States into the two world wars. It also characterized dealings with the Soviet Union, particularly between 1946 and 1962. More generally, it has been difficult to obtain domestic support for a "realist" approach to foreign policy when this was seen to involve compromising American principles to accommodate the interests of other powerful countries—a problem faced both by Roosevelt over the post–World War II settlement and by Henry Kissinger in the years of détente.

Basic also to American policy in the two world wars and after 1945 was a concern with the nature of the wider environment in which the country had to live. The primary concern was with Europe, the continent with which Americans had uniquely strong personal, cultural, and religious as well as economic connections. From World War I on, policymakers viewed a peaceful and stable Europe in which liberal democracies could survive and prosper as an important American interest.

The concern with Europe had a unique depth and emotional strength but also accorded with a wider desire for a law-governed world order in which international trade could flourish and all states could enjoy security. From the 1890s on, prominent Americans, including presidents, argued that the nation should do more to promote and sustain such an order, but no strenuous efforts were made in this direction before the clear breakdown of world order in 1914 produced much greater concern with the issue. Within two years, the establishment of a peaceful, liberal world order after the war through the creation of a league of nations had become the strategic objective of Wilson's foreign policy. Despite Wilson's failure, the goal of a law-governed world remained the proclaimed objective of American policymakers in the 1920s, and it was the threat to this posed by the aggressions of the 1930s that led FDR to begin his attempt to persuade Americans that they needed to do more to affect the course of events overseas. During World War II, Wilson's project of building a liberal world order through the creation of international institutions underpinned by American power was brought to fruition. Maintaining such an order has remained the most basic and enduring goal of U.S. foreign policy ever since, through the Cold War and after. As he sent American forces to reverse Iraq's aggression against Kuwait in 1991, President George H. W. Bush stressed the need for "a world where the rule of law, not the law of the jungle, governs the conduct of nations."[6]

Each of these features of American policy, varied as they are, may be seen as reflections of the country's uniquely powerful and secure position in the international system. It is this that has led Americans to feel that they can act on the basis of their sentiments and values rather than strategic calculation—an assumption strikingly manifest in the essential failure of Arab attempts to use the "oil weapon" to weaken American support for Israel. Similarly, if American diplomacy has been particularly intransigent, this is surely not because the United States has had more at stake than the countries with which it was (or was not) negotiating. Rather, it has reflected both an expectation that other states would have to yield if the United States stood firm and a confidence that failure to reach agreement would not seriously damage its own interests. The aspiration to create and maintain a system of world order rested not only on a confidence in the capacities of America's power to achieve such an ambitious goal but also on an implicit assumption that this power was substantially greater than that needed to secure what Paul Nitze described as its "narrow competitive interests." In Wolfers's terminology, world order was a "milieu goal" rather than a "possession goal"; from a systemic perspective, it constitutes the provision of a "collective good."[7]

Translating the broad goal of a law-governed world into effective policy has always faced two basic difficulties. The first is securing agreement among those who favor the general goal about the means through which it should be achieved. Thus, Republicans like Theodore Roosevelt, Elihu Root, and Henry Cabot Lodge strongly favored American action to uphold a law-governed world order but opposed Wilson's League of Nations; instead, they favored a more limited and traditional alignment with Britain and France. This difference grew out of, and was embittered by, the conflict during World War I between those who wholeheartedly endorsed the Allied cause and those who took a more neutral view of the war and its causes. The joint war effort of 1917–18 strengthened the first viewpoint temporarily, but disillusionment with the Versailles settlement then served to distance U.S. opinion and policy from the other victor powers. A comparable tension emerged during World War II over the extent to which the nation's traditional anti-imperialist principles should be compromised in order to maintain the great power alliance as the basis of international peace and world order in the postwar period. The Cold War altered the context of this conflict between "idealism" and "realism" but it nonetheless persisted.

The second, and greater, difficulty has been that of gaining political support for actions in pursuit of this general goal that entail significant costs. This difficulty constrained Theodore Roosevelt's foreign policy actions, defeated Wilson, and obstructed FDR's attempts from 1937 on to bring American power to bear against what he called the "international lawlessness" threatening "the very foundations of civilization."[8] At times, as between 1931 and 1941 with regard to Japanese expansion, it has created a notable gap between the nation's declared policy and its effective actions. Most Americans were naturally reluctant to devote resources to foreign policy enterprises, let alone risk the lives of American servicemen, unless the nation's own safety or prosperity was directly at stake. So those who believed that the United States should pursue the wider goal of world order regularly argued that these core interests were dependent on such an order. In doing so, they provided the evidence drawn upon by those historical accounts that explain the expansion of American policy in terms of those interests.

Such explanations are unpersuasive. As we saw in the introduction, the dependence of America's core interests on the achievement of foreign policy objectives has always been very questionable. It is not necessary to doubt the sincerity with which people believed that America's safety from attack depended on Britain's command of the Atlantic, a balance of power in Eurasia—or, indeed, a law-governed world order—in order to insist that such beliefs are not self-explanatory. As we have seen, most of those who developed and propagated them were predisposed to favor the policies and actions that were said to follow from them. The reasons for such predispositions are therefore a necessary part of any explanation of the policies such beliefs justified. On the other hand, those not already predisposed to favor the policies that were seen as following from such beliefs commonly challenged the reasoning on which the beliefs were based—often quite effectively. This reduced the effectiveness of such arguments in building support for strenuous action abroad.

This analysis helps to explain certain key features of the historical record. Thus the very real possibility between the summer of 1940 and the fall of 1941 that Nazi Germany might achieve uncontested control of the whole of Europe did not lead the United States to enter the war against it as a full-scale belligerent. It did so only in response to a direct attack rather than to achieve a broader foreign policy goal—as had been the case also in 1917. Indeed, something in addition to such general goals as world order or a Eurasian balance of power has always been required to produce the will to exercise American power in a substantial way. The nature of such extra ingredients has varied from case to case. In World War I, it was the mixture of moral and patriotic outrage aroused by Germany's manner of conducting the war (as this was portrayed) and apparently aggressive intentions, culminating in the sinking of American ships and the Zimmermann Note. In World War II, it was abhorrence of the Nazi regime and alarm at the apparently limitless expansionism of Germany and Japan. In the Cold War, it was the intense hatred and fear of communism felt by almost all Americans. And in each of these supremely important cases, these emotions were focused by the special concern felt by most Americans of that period with events in Europe.

Seeing the expansion of American policy goals as the product of various concomitants of a sense of power rather than as arising from the requirements of America's own safety and prosperity also helps explain the recurrent pattern of advance and retreat. Manifested first over imperialism and the involvement in world politics in 1917–18, this pattern persisted even during the period of American globalism, most notably over Vietnam (1961–75) and in the Middle East since 9/11 but also in minor cases such as the interventions in Lebanon (1982–84) and Somalia (1992–94). That the United States suffered no apparent damage to its core interests as a result of its retreats in such cases was taken by many to show that the advances had been unnecessary and unwise.

If the link between world order on the one hand and American prosperity and security (in the basic sense in which security is popularly understood) on the other has always been hard to sustain when subjected to skeptical questioning, further explanation is required for the scale of the efforts that the United States has made to establish and maintain such an order. As already noted, by far the greatest of these efforts have been in the context of major war or quasi-war. But the successive conflicts in which the United States has been involved do not by any means explain the totality of the global role it has played. The commitment to world order has had an independent dynamic, giving rise to significant actions, notably the international institution-building during World War II, the devotion of resources to the pacification and stabilization of Europe and Japan in the postwar period, and the Balkan interventions of the 1990s. As we have seen, this commitment reflected the belief that the scale of America's power brought with it a responsibility to promote "public goods" beyond its own narrow interests. Among influential members of the American elite, this belief can be traced back to the early twentieth century. It was often associated with the view that the peace and prosperity of the nineteenth century owed much to the role played by Britain and that, as British power declined, it was both the duty and the destiny of the United States to take over the role.

This was, however, only one strand in the mentalities that inspired the projection of American power and influence across the globe. The link Wilson had forged between the establishment of international order and the spread of America's own liberal values persisted and developed, as did the activist interpretation of the nation's historic mission that he had articulated so eloquently. The teleology implicit in the assumption that the United States provided a model to the whole world of a better future found expression in the "modernization theory" that was developed in the 1950s and 1960s to counter the perceived appeal of communism to the postcolonial world. A skeptical historian of this process, Odd Arne Westad, confesses that in his researches, he had been "astonished at the sense of duty and sacrifice" with which those involved sought to improve the lives of people "in faraway places" through spreading American values and practices.[9]

Such idealism was one important impulse, but another was the desire to hold sway in the world. From Wilson on, American "leadership" has been seen as a central and essential feature of world order.[10] As we have seen, Spykman's rigorous analysis concluded that the danger facing the United States in 1941 was that it would become "merely a buffer state between the mighty empires of Germany and Japan"; in military circles the fear was that the United States would become "a second class power." Likewise in 1940–41 and in the early Cold War, planning documents made it clear that it was for the projection of power to Europe rather than the defense of North America that a friendly Britain was a strategic necessity. The rejection of the possibility of a neutral, reunited Germany in 1949–52 seems to have been influenced by the desire to maintain an America-aligned western Europe. All this is grist to the mill of those who see the United States as having been engaged since the 1940s in a consistent drive for "geopolitical dominance."[11] Explaining U.S. policy in terms of such a "grand strategy" neglects the extent to which the shape and limits of American actions in the world derive from pressures generated by domestic politics. Nevertheless, the satisfactions and gratifications of wielding power do seem at times to have given an expansionist thrust to U.S. policy, independent of any instrumental purpose or agenda. "Empire" is an inappropriate description of something as variable in its potency and as imprecisely defined geographically as America's influence in world politics, but the role the United States has played has given rise to an "imperial" mentality.

If these various impulses and ambitions may all be seen as products, to a greater or less extent, of a subjective consciousness of America's potential power, the way that the sheer scale of this power has in practice reduced the costs of wielding influence has also been crucial. The greatest efforts to reform, support, and police the world order were made when America's relative wealth and power was at its apogee. The Marshall Plan and other postwar aid to Europe amounted to about 20 billion in current dollars, but such was the scale of the nation's trade surpluses in those years that its reserves nonetheless increased by nearly $6 billion between 1946 and 1949. In 1950, the U.S. possessed half the world's monetary gold, reserve currencies, and IMF reserves. But the proportion declined to 33 percent in 1960, 22 percent in 1965, and 16 percent in 1970. As the margin of America's economic superiority declined, so did the extent to which resources were devoted to wider foreign policy goals. From the 1960s on, the budgets for foreign aid, including even military assistance, decreased substantially in constant dollars, let alone as a proportion of GNP. In 1971, the country's visible trade balance, which had been in surplus almost every year since 1893, moved into deficit, and the deficits grew greatly thereafter. In the same year, by taking the dollar off gold, President Nixon removed the indispensable foundation of the Bretton Woods system for limiting exchange rate fluctuations. Secretary of the Treasury John Connolly warned an international group of bankers that Washington "would no longer engage in international actions in which the true long-run interests of the U.S. are not just as clearly recognized as those of the nations with which we deal." The days were over when, in trade relations with its European allies, the United States had been prepared to sacrifice its own economic interests for the sake of political objectives.[12]

This correlation could be taken to indicate that the goal of an American-led world order (or "geopolitical dominance") has been, in economists' parlance, a "luxury good"—rather than a necessity in the way that safety from external attack and national prosperity are. Luxury goods are, of course, desirable—when one can afford them. From this perspective, the future of America's world role is likely to depend less on how much America's potential power continues to exceed that of any rival than on how far the demands of playing that role can compete with its domestic priorities.

Notes

PREFACE

1. For some of Lyndon Johnson's statements to this effect, see Andrew Preston, "Monsters Everywhere: A Genealogy of National Security," *Diplomatic History* 38.3 (2014): 477–79.

2. Henry R. Luce, "The American Century," *Life* (February 17, 1941), 61–62. For the full passage, see page 173 in this volume.

INTRODUCTION: THE PROBLEM

1. *Statistical Abstract of the United States, 2002: The National Data Book*, table 495.

2. The crucial character of this factor in determining the outcome is well argued in Correlli Barnett, *The Sword Bearers: Supreme Command in the First World War* (Bloomington, 1963), 356.

3. Paul Kennedy, *The Rise and Fall of the Great Powers: Economic Change and Military Conflict from 1500 to 2000* (London, 1988), 353–56.

4. For the scholarly debate on this issue, see Stephen G. Brooks, G. John Ikenberry, and William C. Wohlforth, "Don't Come Home, America: The Case against Retrenchment," *International Security* 37.3 (Winter 2012/13): 7–51, and the works referenced there. For a recent contribution to the wider public debate, see Robert Kagan, "Superpowers Don't Get to Retire: What Our Tired Country Still Owes the World," *New Republic*, June 9, 2014, 14–21.

5. For justifications of this definition of power, see Kenneth N. Waltz, *Theory of International Politics* (Reading, MA, 1979), 191–92; William Curti Wohlforth, *The Elusive Balance: Power and Perceptions during the Cold War* (Ithaca, 1993), 3–5. As Wohlforth points out, the alternative "relational" definition of power as control or influence means it can only be inferred from outcomes and that "a relationship of power can never be known until after power is exercised." Such a definition makes it difficult to identify occasions on which a state might possess power without exercising it, and also limits the concept's capacity to *explain* behavior that involves such exercise.

6. Paul Bairoch, "International Industrialization Levels from 1750 to 1980," *Journal of European Economic History* 11 (Fall 1982): 296, 304; G. John Ikenberry, ed., *America Unrivalled: The Future of the Balance of Power* (Ithaca, 2002), 105.

7. Michael Mandelbaum, *The Fate of Nations: The Search for National Security in the Nineteenth and Twentieth Centuries* (Cambridge, UK, 1988), 129, 133.

8. Robert Gilpin, *War and Change in World Politics* (Cambridge, UK, 1981), 106–7.

9. Morgenthau seems to have seen this as one of the "objective laws that have their roots in human nature" upon which he sought to erect his "theory of international politics." Hans J. Morgenthau, *Politics Among Nations*, 3rd ed. (New York, 1965), 33–35, 3–4.

10. For example, Martin Wight, *Power Politics,* ed. Hedley Bull and Carsten Holbraad (Harmondsworth, 1979), 144.

11. Waltz, *Theory of International Politics*, 195–209, quotations 207, 195. That great powers have "managerial responsibilities" with regard to "the peace and security of the

international system as a whole" is also argued by Hedley Bull. See *The Anarchical Society: A Study of Order in World Politics* (London, 1977), 202.

12. Robert Gilpin, *The Political Economy of International Relations* (Princeton, 1987), 86. The quoted formulation covers both Gilpin's version of the theory that emphasizes the liberalism of the resulting system and Charles P. Kindleberger's version that emphasizes its stability. Hegemonic stability theory derives from Kindleberger's *The World in Depression, 1929–1939*, revised and enlarged edition (Berkeley and Los Angeles, 1986), ch. 14, and "Dominance and Leadership in the International Economy: Exploitation, Public Goods and Free Rides," *International Studies Quarterly* 25 (1981): 242–54. For a critical theoretical analysis, see Duncan Snidal, "The Limits of Hegemonic Stability," *International Organization* 39 (Autumn 1985): 579–613.

13. The only exception to this generalization may be what has become known as "soft power"—that is, the appeal of a nation's culture or ideology to the citizens or governments of other countries. However, this resource, to the extent that it exists independently of "hard" power, is difficult to wield as a means of effective leverage for specific purposes in particular situations. We owe the concept of "soft power" to Joseph S. Nye Jr. See in particular *Bound to Lead: The Changing Nature of American Power* (New York, 1990), 32, 193–95; *The Paradox of American Power: Why the World's Only Superpower Can't Go It Alone* (New York, 2002), 8–11.

14. See Klaus Knorr, *The Power of Nations: The Political Economy of International Relations* (New York, 1975), 94.

15. Gilpin, *War and Change in World Politics*, 51.

16. Such an assumption forms part of the basis of the theory that democracies are less prone to war than are autocratic governments. For an introduction to this literature, see Bruce Russett, *Grasping the Democratic Peace* (Princeton, 1993); Michael E. Brown, Sean M. Lynn-Jones, and Steven E. Miller, eds., *Debating the Democratic Peace* (Cambridge, MA, 1996).

17. Gideon Rose, "Neoclassical Realism and Theories of Foreign Policy," *World Politics* 51 (October 1998): 144–72, quotations 146–47, 152.

18. Gilpin, *War and Change in World Politics*, 95.

19. This point is made in David Reynolds, "Power and Superpower: The Impact of Two World Wars on America's International Role," in *America Unbound: World War II and the Making of a Superpower*, ed. Warren F. Kimball (New York, 1992), 22.

20. U.S. Department of Commerce, Bureau of the Census, *Historical Statistics of the United States: Colonial Times to 1970* (Washington, D.C., 1975), 229.

21. Harold G. Vatter, *The U.S. Economy in World War II* (New York, 1985), 20.

22. David A. Baldwin, *Economic Statecraft* (Princeton, 1985), 296.

23. Susan Strange, *States and Markets* (London, 1988), 220.

24. Gilpin, *War and Change in World Politics*, 95.

25. See the table in Michael Edelstein, "War and the American Economy in the Twentieth Century," in *The Cambridge Economic History of the United States*, vol. 3, *The Twentieth Century*, ed. Stanley L. Engerman and Robert E. Gallman (Cambridge, UK, 2000), 342. In addition to the wars listed there (World Wars I and II, Korea, and Vietnam), the United States was involved in several minor wars, of which the most significant in terms of casualties were the Spanish-American War of 1898 and that against the subsequent insurgency in the Philippines.

26. Edelstein, "War and the American Economy in the Twentieth Century," 331–33.

27. According to Niall Ferguson's calculations in *The Pity of War* (London, 1998), 110–11. Ferguson's estimates for the other major states are 3.9 percent for France, 3.5 percent for Germany, and 3.1 percent for Britain. For a year-by-year tabulation, see David Stevenson, *Armaments and the Coming of War: Europe, 1904–1914* (Oxford, UK, 1996), 6. Slightly different figures, but of the same order of magnitude, are given in Nazli Choucri

and Robert C. North, *Nations in Conflict: National Growth and International Violence* (San Francisco, 1975), table 7.1, 116.

28. Niall Ferguson, *Colossus: The Rise and Fall of the American Empire* (New York, 2004), 16; Geir Lundestad, *The Rise and Decline of the American "Empire": Power and Its Limits in Comparative Perspective* (Oxford, UK, 2012), 50; Robert J. Lieber, *Power and Willpower in the American Future* (New York, 2012), 42–45.

29. For example, Nicholas John Spykman, *America's Strategy in World Politics* (New York, 1942), 17; Robert Endicott Osgood, *Ideals and Self-Interest in America's Foreign Relations: The Great Transformation of the Twentieth Century* (Chicago, 1953), 5; Waltz, *Theory of International Politics*, 91–92.

30. C. Vann Woodward, "The Age of Reinterpretation," *American Historical Review* 66 (October 1960): 2–3.

31. Spykman, *America's Strategy in World Politics*, 66.

32. Frederick H. Hartmann, *The New Age of American Foreign Policy* (New York, 1970), 16.

33. For representative statements of this view, see John Lewis Gaddis, *The Long Peace: Inquiries into the History of the Cold War* (New York, 1987), 25; Barry R. Posen and Stephen W. Van Evera, "Reagan Administration Defense Policy: Departure from Containment," in *Eagle Resurgent? The Reagan Era in American Foreign Policy*, ed. Kenneth A. Oye, Robert J. Lieber and Donald Rothschild (Boston, 1987), 77–78; Arthur A. Stein, "Domestic Constraints, Extended Deterrence, and the Incoherence of Grand Strategy: The United States, 1938–1950," in *The Domestic Bases of Grand Strategy*, ed. Richard Rosecrance and Arthur A. Stein (Ithaca, 1993), 97.

34. Arthur M. Schlesinger Jr., *The Cycles of American History* (London, 1987), 53. For earlier, fuller arguments for this continuity, see William T. R. Fox, "American Foreign Policy and the Western European Rimland," *Proceedings of the American Academy of Political Science* 22 (January 1948): 74; Gordon A. Craig, "The United States and the European Balance," *Foreign Affairs* 55 (October 1976): 189–90.

35. Woodward himself linked the two claims: "Throughout most of its history the United States has enjoyed a remarkable degree of military security, physical security from hostile attack and invasion. This security was not only remarkably effective, but it was relatively free. . . . The age of security and the age of free security ended almost simultaneously." "The Age of Reinterpretation," 2–3.

36. Fareed Zakaria, "The Myth of America's 'Free Security,'" *World Policy Journal* 14 (Summer 1997): 35–43; Fareed Zakaria, *From Wealth to Power: The Unusual Origins of America's World Role* (Princeton, 1998), 177–78.

37. John Keegan, *The Price of Admiralty: The Evolution of Naval Warfare* (Harmondsworth, 1988), 41–42.

38. Spykman, *America's Strategy in World Politics*, 393.

39. Spykman, *America's Strategy in World Politics*, 397–98, 442.

40. Woodward, "The Age of Reinterpretation," 4.

41. Mark A. Stoler, *Allies and Adversaries: The Joint Chiefs of Staff, the Grand Alliance, and U.S. Strategy in World War II* (Chapel Hill and London, 2000), 259.

42. Mandelbaum, *Fate of Nations*, 138–40.

43. John J. Mearsheimer, "Back to the Future: Instability in Europe after the Cold War," *International Security* 15 (Summer 1990): 12; John J. Mearsheimer, *The Tragedy of Great Power Politics* (New York, 2001), 21, 35.

44. For classic expositions of the first possibility, see John H. Herz, "Idealist Internationalism and the Security Dilemma," *World Politics* 2 (1950): 157; Arnold Wolfers, "'National Security' as an Ambiguous Symbol," *Political Science Quarterly* 67 (December 1952): 494–98. On the second, see Kennedy, *Rise and Fall of the Great Powers*, esp. 515; Jack Snyder, *Myths of Empire: Domestic Politics and International Ambition* (Ithaca, 1991), 1, 6–9.

45. Mearsheimer, *Tragedy of Great Power Politics*, 234–36, 44, 77, 114–28. Mearsheimer recognizes (264–65) that the case of imperial Japan brings into question "the stopping power of water" but attributes the difference to the absence in east Asia of the sort of great powers that would have faced Britain and the United States in continental Europe. For fuller critiques of Mearsheimer's argument as a whole, see Barry R. Posen, "The Best Defense," *National Interest* (Spring 2002): 119–26; Richard N. Rosecrance, "War and Peace," *World Politics* 55.1 (October 2002): 137–66.

46. Mearsheimer, *Tragedy of Great Power Politics*, 127. See Christopher Layne, *The Peace of Illusions: American Grand Strategy from 1940 to the Present* (Ithaca, 2006), 10.

47. Mearsheimer, *Tragedy of Great Power Politics*, 141–43, 237, 265–66.

48. Mackinder's 1904 lecture, "The Geographical Pivot of History," is reprinted in *Democratic Ideals and Reality* (New York, 1962), 241–64, esp. 262. For fuller treatment of these sources, see chapters 4 and 5 in this volume; for the genealogy, see John A. Thompson, "The Geopolitical Vision: The Myth of an Outmatched USA," in *Uncertain Empire: American History and the Idea of the Cold War*, ed. Joel Isaac and Duncan Bell (New York, 2012), 91–114, esp. 100–107.

49. See JCS 1769/1, "United States Assistance to Other Countries from the Standpoint of National Security," April 29, 1947, in *Foreign Relations of the United States* (hereafter *FRUS*), *1947*, (Washington, D.C., 1973), 739. For other articulations of this argument by officials in the Truman administration, see Melvyn P. Leffler, *A Preponderance of Power: National Security, the Truman Administration, and the Cold War* (Stanford, 1992), 11–13, 163–64, 322, 370, 401, 406.

50. Thompson, "Geopolitical Vision," 103–5, 108.

51. For such arguments, see Stephen M. Walt, *The Origins of Alliances* (Ithaca, 1987), ch. 5; Stephen M. Walt, "Alliance Formation and the Balance of World Power," *International Security* 9 (Spring 1985): 3–43; Waltz, *Theory of International Politics*, 125–28.

52. Gilpin, *War and Change in World Politics*, 86–88.

53. Mearsheimer, *Tragedy of Great Power Politics*, 41.

54. Melvyn P. Leffler, "National Security," in *Explaining the History of American Foreign Relations*, ed. Michael J. Hogan and Thomas G. Paterson (Cambridge, UK, 1991), 202–13; Leffler, *Preponderance of Power*, xi.

55. Robert H. Johnson, "Exaggerating America's Stake in Third World Conflicts," *International Security* 10 (Winter 1985–86): 40–44; Robert Jervis, "Domino Beliefs and Strategic Behavior," in *Dominoes and Bandwagons*, ed. Robert Jervis and Jack Snyder (New York, 1991), 31.

56. Robert W. Tucker, *The Purposes of American Power: An Essay on National Security* (New York, 1981), 119–20; Robert Jervis, *The Illogic of American Nuclear Strategy* (Ithaca and London, 1984), 67–70.

57. "Cooperation under the Security Dilemma," *World Politics* 30 (January 1978), 198–99; see also Kenneth N. Waltz, "Nuclear Myths and Political Realities," *American Political Science Review* 84 (September 1990), 732–34.

58. Tucker, *Purposes of American Power*, 116–18; see also Johnson, "Exaggerating America's Stake," 36–37; Waltz, "Nuclear Myths and Political Realities," 739.

59. It is sometimes countered that the balance of world productive resources has relevance even in this context. See Stephen M. Walt, "The Case for Finite Containment: Analyzing U.S. Grand Strategy," *International Security* 14 (1989), 29. Given the comparative cheapness of nuclear weapons, this is not a convincing argument.

60. Charles Krauthammer, "The Poverty of Realism," *New Republic*, February 17, 1986, 16.

61. Tucker, *A New Isolationism: Threat or Promise?* (New York, 1972), 46–47; Tucker, *Purposes of American Power*, 121.

62. Tucker, *Purposes of American Power*, 121.

63. Wolfers, "The Goals of Foreign Policy" in *Discord and Collaboration* (Baltimore, 1962), 73–77.

64. On the wider importance of defining "security as a policy objective distinguishable from others," see David A. Baldwin, "The Concept of Security," *Review of International Studies* 23 (January 1997): 5–26.

65. George W. Bush, Second Inaugural Address, January 20, 2005. *Public Papers of the Presidents of the United States: George W. Bush 2005* (Washington, D.C., 2007), 66.

66. Quoted in Robert W. Tucker, *Nation or Empire?: The Debate over American Foreign Policy* (Baltimore, 1968), 37–38.

67. *Public Papers and Addresses of Franklin D. Roosevelt* (hereafter *PPA*), 8:202–3.

68. Notably in *The Idea of National Interest: An Analytical Study in American Foreign Policy*, with the collaboration of G. H. E. Smith (Chicago, 1966), esp. 112–20, 166–67, 228–30, 390–99, 434–39. The book was originally published in 1934.

69. The classic statement of Williams's thesis is *The Tragedy of American Diplomacy* (Cleveland, 1959; rev. eds. 1962, 1972). For an assessment of its reception, see Bradford Perkins, "*The Tragedy of American Diplomacy*: Twenty-Five Years After," in *Redefining the Past: Essays in Diplomatic History in Honor of William Appleman Williams*, ed. Lloyd C. Gardner (Corvallis, 1986), 21–34. For recent works by political scientists that adopt Williams's "open door empire" thesis, see Andrew J. Bacevich, *American Empire: The Realities and Consequences of U.S. Diplomacy* (Cambridge, MA, 2002), 30–31, 71, 85–91; Layne, *Peace of Illusions*, 9, 29–36, 118–20, 216.

70. Robert E. Lipsey, "U.S. Foreign Trade and the Balance of Payments, 1800–1913" in *The Cambridge Economic History of the United States*, vol. 2, *The Long Nineteenth Century*, ed. Stanley Engerman and Robert E. Gallman (Cambridge, UK, 2000), 685–91; *Historical Statistics*, 887, 903.

71. Peter H. Lindhert, "U.S. Foreign Trade and Trade Policy in the Twentieth Century," *The Cambridge Economic History of the United States*, vol. 3, *The Twentieth Century*, ed. Engerman and Gallman, 454.

72. *Historical Statistics*, 887.

73. Robert Pollard, *Economic Security and the Origins of the Cold War, 1945–50* (New York, 1985), chs. 1–2; Alfred E. Eckes Jr., "Open Door Expansionism Reconsidered: The World War II Experience," *Journal of American History* 59 (March 1973): 909–24.

74. The agreement was the European Payments Union. On this issue, see Francis J. Gavin, *Gold, Dollars, and Power: The Politics of International Monetary Relations, 1958–1971* (Chapel Hill, 2004), esp. 3–4, 93–94, 200.

75. Alfred E. Eckes, "Trading American Interests," *Foreign Affairs* 71 (1992): 135–37.

76. *Historical Statistics*, 903.

77. For some examples of the asymmetries involved, see Kenneth N. Waltz, "The Myth of National Interdependence," in *The International Corporation*, ed. Charles P. Kindleberger (Cambridge, MA, 1970), 213. Robert O. Keohane points out that, strictly speaking, the relative strengths of bargaining positions depends on the opportunity costs involved, which will not necessarily be a function simply of the statistical value of the trade. He nevertheless accepts that "other things being equal, one might expect that the country with the larger market would have more leverage." See Keohane, *After Hegemony: Cooperation and Discord in the World Political Economy* (Princeton, 1984), 198.

78. On the German case, see Gavin, *Gold, Dollars, and Power*, esp. 65–66.

79. Jeff Frieden, "Sectoral Conflict and Foreign Economic Policy, 1914–1940," *International Organization* 42 (Winter 1988): 63–64.

80. Frieden, "Sectoral Conflict and Foreign Economic Policy," 81–82.

81. In addition, the development of government-sponsored expropriation insurance from the late 1940s provided a means of protecting the interests of those who invested overseas that had no direct impact on foreign policy. See Charles Lipson, *Standing Guard: Protecting Foreign Capital in the Nineteenth and Twentieth Centuries* (Berkeley, Los Angeles, and London, 1985), 232–48.

82. Stephen L. Gwynn, ed., *Letters and Friendships of Sir Cecil Spring-Rice* (London, 1929), 2:196.

83. I do not mean here to discount the possible influence of cultural or political differences also.

84. Waltz, *Theory of International Politics*, 158.

85. Raymond Vernon, *Sovereignty at Bay* (New York, 1971), 186.

86. This started with the "dollar diplomacy" of the Taft administration. According to the historian Odd Arne Westad, "during the Cold War the government always wanted private companies to increase their investments abroad—and especially in the Third World—in order to create influence and 'development,' but with limited success. One of the main reasons why Washington had to turn to direct and indirect aid to Third World countries in the 1950s and 1960s was the lack of a willingness to invest on the side of U.S. business." Westad, *The Global Cold War: Third World Interventions and the Making of Our Times* (Cambridge, UK, 2007), 30.

87. See chapter 3 in this volume and Gilpin, *U.S. Power and the Multinational Corporation: The Political Economy of Foreign Direct Investment* (London, 1976), chs. 7–8.

88. See chapter 3 in this volume and Stephen D. Krasner, *Defending the National Interest: Raw Materials Investments and U.S. Foreign Policy* (Princeton, 1978), 97–119.

89. Alfred E. Eckes Jr., *The United States and the Global Struggle for Minerals* (Austin and London, 1979), 49.

90. Krasner, *Defending the National Interest*, 9.

91. Michael Shafer has claimed that "each generation of U.S. foreign policy makers since Theodore Roosevelt has discovered—and then forgotten—a strategic minerals crisis of its own." Shafer, "Mineral Myths," *Foreign Policy* 47 (Summer 1982), 155. See also Johnson, "Exaggerating America's Stakes in Third World Conflicts," 34, 37–38; Walt, "Case for Finite Containment," 20–21; and, for a history of the concern, Eckes, *United States and the Global Struggle for Minerals*.

92. Spykman, *America's Strategy in World Politics*, 468, also 297–98, 314. For a fuller consideration of Spykman's argument, see chapters 4 and 5 in this volume.

93. Kennedy, *Rise and Fall of the Great Powers*, 356.

94. See particularly Peter Trubowitz, *Defining the National Interest: Conflict and Change in American Foreign Policy* (Chicago, 1998); Frieden, "Sectoral Conflict and Foreign Economic Policy"; Thomas Ferguson, "From Normalcy to New Deal: Industrial Structure, Party Competition, and American Public Policy in the Great Depression," *International Organization* 38 (Winter 1984): 41–94.

95. Address in Independence Hall, February 22, 1861; Annual Message to Congress, December 1, 1862. Roy P. Basler, ed., *Abraham Lincoln: His Speeches and Writings* (New York, 1962), 577, 688.

96. For this argument, see Robert W. Tucker, "Exemplar or Crusader?: Reflections on America's Role," *National Interest* 5 (Fall 1986): 64–75. For a similar view, see Robert Kagan, *Dangerous Nation: America and the World, 1600–1898* (New York, 2006), esp. 52.

97. Ole R. Holsti, "Promotion of Democracy as Popular Demand?" in Michael Cox, G. John Ikenberry, and Takashi Inoguchi, eds., *American Democracy Promotion: Impulses, Strategies, and Impacts* (New York, 2000), 151–80; John Tures, "The Democracy-Promotion Gap in American Public Opinion," *Journal of American Studies* 41 (December 2007): 557–79.

98. *Historical Statistics*, 224, 1114 (U.S. Department of State, Office of the Historian), http://history.state.gov/about/faq/department-personnel.

1. A NEW SENSE OF POWER

1. U.S. Department of Commerce, Bureau of the Census, *Historical Statistics of the United States: Colonial Times to 1970* (Washington, D.C., 1975), 8, 224, 511–12, 520–21, 592–94, 690–91, 693–94; Robert E. Gallman, "Economic Growth and Structural Change in the Long Nineteenth Century" and Moses Abramovitz and Paul A. David, "American Macroeconomic Growth in the Era of Knowledge-Based Progress: The Long-Run Perspective," in *The Cambridge Economic History of the United States*, ed. Stanley L. Engerman and Robert E. Gallman (Cambridge, UK, 2000), 2:6–7, 23; 3:66–68; Walter LaFeber, *The American Search for Opportunity, 1865–1913* (Cambridge, UK, 2013), 25.

2. Gallman, "Economic Growth and Structural Change," 2–6; Paul Bairoch, "International Industrialization Levels from 1750 to 1980," *Journal of European Economic History* 11 (Fall 1982): 296, 304; Paul Kennedy, *The Rise and Fall of the Great Powers: Economic Change and Military Conflict from 1500 to 2000* (London, 1988), 200; "Special Report: The World Economy," *The Economist*, September 24–30, 2011. The Churchill quotation is from Peter G. Boyle, ed., *The Churchill-Eisenhower Correspondence, 1953–1955* (Chapel Hill and London, 1990), 179.

3. George C. Herring, *From Colony to Superpower: U.S. Foreign Relations since 1776* (New York, 2008), 291–95, 306–7; Robert E. Hannigan, *The New World Power: American Foreign Policy, 1898–1917* (Philadelphia, 2002), 56–60; Ernest R. May, *Imperial Democracy: The Emergence of America as a Great Power* (New York, 1973), 10; Olney to Thomas F. Bayard, July 20, 1895, quoted in Norman A. Graebner, ed., *Ideas and Diplomacy: Readings in the Intellectual Tradition of American Foreign Policy* (New York, 1964), 254.

4. Allan R. Millett and Peter Maslowski, *For the Common Defense: A Military History of the United States of America*, revised and expanded edition (New York, 1994), 249, 267–70, 274–77; Harold Sprout and Margaret Sprout, *The Rise of American Naval Power, 1776–1918* (Princeton, 1967), 183–222; Edward Rhodes, "Sea Change: Interest-Based vs. Cultural-Cognitive Accounts of Strategic Choice in the 1890s," *Security Studies* 5 (Summer 1996): 123.

5. Philip A. Crowl, "Alfred Thayer Mahan: The Naval Historian," in *Makers of Modern Strategy: From Machiavelli to the Nuclear Age*, ed. Peter Paret (Princeton, 1986): 444–77; A. T. Mahan, *The Interest of America in Sea Power: Present and Future* (1897; repr. Freeport, 1970).

6. Henry Cabot Lodge, "Our Blundering Foreign Policy," *The Forum* 19 (March 1895): 17.

7. William C. Widenor, *Henry Cabot Lodge and the Search for an American Foreign Policy* (Berkeley and Los Angeles, 1980), 66–110; Peter Karson, "The Nature of 'Influence': Roosevelt, Mahan, and the Concept of Sea Power," *American Quarterly* (October 1971): 586–90; Henry Cabot Lodge, "Our Blundering Foreign Policy": 8–17; Paul T. McCartney, *Power and Progress: American National Identity, the War of 1898, and the Rise of American Imperialism* (Baton Rouge, 2006), 255; Theodore Roosevelt address at the Naval War College, June 2, 1897.

8. McCartney, *Power and Progress*, 87–113; May, *Imperial Democracy*, 69–159, 196–219; Warren Zimmermann, *First Great Triumph: How Five Americans Made Their Country a World Power* (New York, 2002), 154–55, 240; Widenor, *Lodge*, 108–9; Walter LaFeber, *The New Empire: An Interpretation of American Expansion, 1860–1898* (Ithaca, 1963), 405–6.

9. McCartney, *Power and Progress*, 109–10, 134–42; McKinley, Annual Message, December 6, 1897; Special Message to Congress, April 11, 1898, *FRUS, 1898* (Washington, D.C., 1901), 750–60.

10. McCartney, *Power and Progress*, 199–257; May, *Imperial Democracy*, 243–62; Richard Hofstadter, "Cuba, the Philippines, and Manifest Destiny," in *The Paranoid Style in American Politics and other Essays* (London, 1966), 162–71; David Healy, *U.S. Expansionism: The Imperialist Urge in the 1890s* (Madison, 1970), 61–67.

11. Memorandum, "What Ought We to Do?" (c. August 1, 1898). Arthur S. Link et al., eds., *The Papers of Woodrow Wilson* (hereafter *PWW*) (Princeton, 1966–94), 10:575; *The Times*, May 12, 1898, quoted in May, *Imperial Democracy*, 221; John H. Latané, *America as a World Power, 1897–1907* (New York and London, 1907); Archibald Cary Coolidge, *The United States as a World Power* (New York, 1908).

12. For a full account of this process, see David Healy, *Drive to Hegemony: The United States in the Caribbean, 1898–1917* (Madison, 1988).

13. Herring, *From Colony to Superpower*, 369–74.

14. Herring, *From Colony to Superpower*, 324–35; Millett and Maslowski, *For the Common Defense*, 306–13.

15. Herring, *From Colony to Superpower*, 360–63; Lewis L. Gould, *The Presidency of Theodore Roosevelt* (Lawrence, 1991), 179–84, 186–95.

16. Herring, *From Colony to Superpower*, 346–50, 371–72; Millett and Maslowski, *For the Common Defense*, 319–28; Rhodes, "Sea Change," 123–24; *Historical Statistics*, 1114; Walter LaFeber, "The 'Lion in the Path': The U.S. Emergence as a World Power," *Political Science Quarterly* 101.5 (1986): 716.

17. Gould, *Presidency of Theodore Roosevelt*, 192–94; Roosevelt, Annual Message, December 3, 1906; Taft, Annual Message, December 3, 1912, *FRUS, 1906* I (Washington, D.C., 1909), LI; *1912* (Washington, D.C., 1919), xix–xx.

18. Millett and Maslowski, *For the Common Defense*, 323; Richard D. Challener, *Admirals, Generals, and American Foreign Policy, 1898–1914* (Princeton, 1973), 41–43, 233–43, 262–64; Hannigan, *New World Power*, 109–15; Herring, *From Colony to Superpower*, 353–55; Fareed Zakaria, *From Wealth to Power: The Unusual Origins of America's World Role* (Princeton, 1998), 163; Roosevelt to W. H. Taft, August 21, 1907, Elting E. Morison et al., ed., *The Letters of Theodore Roosevelt* (Cambridge, MA, 1951–54), 5:761–62.

19. Hannigan, *New World Power*, 112–33; Roosevelt to Taft, December 22, 1910, Morison, ed., *Letters of Theodore Roosevelt*, 7:189–92.

20. Hannigan, *New World Power*, 52–89, 298; Challener, *Admirals, Generals, and American Foreign Policy*, 57; TR to Archibald Bulloch Roosevelt, December 2, 1914, Morison et al., ed., *Letters of Theodore Roosevelt*, 8:851–52.

21. TR to Archibald Bulloch Roosevelt, December 2, 1914, to C. W. Eliot [unsent], April 4, 1904, to J. B. Bishop, February 23, 1904, Morison et al., ed., *Letters of Theodore Roosevelt*, 8:852; 4:769–70, 734; Emily S. Rosenberg and Norman L. Rosenberg, "From Colonialism to Professionalism: The Public Private Dynamic in United States Financial Advising, 1898–1929," *Journal of American History* 74 (June 1987): 61; H. Herwig and D. F. Trask, "Naval Operations Plans between Germany and the USA, 1898–1913: A Study of Strategic Planning in the Age of Imperialism," in *The War Plans of the Great Powers, 1880–1914*, ed. Paul M. Kennedy (London, 1979), 40–60; Nancy Mitchell, *The Danger of Dreams: German and American Imperialism in Latin America* (Chapel Hill, 1999), 46–52; Bradford Perkins, *The Great Rapprochement: England, and the United States, 1895–1914* (London, 1969), 157–58; Jay Sexton, *The Monroe Doctrine: Empire and Nation in Nineteenth-Century America* (New York, 2011), 237–38.

22. Millett and Maslowski, *For the Common Defense*, 320; Rachel West, *The Department of State on the Eve of the First World War* (Athens, GA, 1978), 4.

23. Zakaria, *From Wealth to Power*, 8–9, 32, 35–41, 59–62, 67–70, 90–180, 187–92; Robert L. Beisner, *From the Old Diplomacy to the New, 1865–1900* (New York, 1975), 48–50.

24. *Historical Statistics*, 1104; Richard Franklin Bensel, *Yankee Leviathan: The Origins of Central State Authority in America, 1859–1877* (Cambridge, UK, 1990), 138–42, 162–63, 168–73, 243–48.

25. Beisner, *From the Old Diplomacy to the New*, 6–7, 30–33, 57–64; David M. Pletcher, "1861–1898: Economic Growth and Diplomatic Adjustment," in *Economics and World Power: An Assessment of American Diplomacy since 1780*, ed. William H. Becker and Samuel F. Wells (New York, 1984), 128–29; Robert H. Wiebe, *The Search for Order, 1877–1920* (New York, 1967), 225–28; Millett and Maslowski, *For the Common Defense*, 248–49.

26. George Washington, Farewell Address, September 17, 1796; James Monroe, Annual Message, December 2, 1823; Grover Cleveland, Inaugural Address, March 4, 1885, James D. Richardson, ed., *Messages and Papers of the Presidents* (Washington, D.C.) I (1896), 221–23; II (1896), 217–19; VII (1898), 301; Beisner, *From the Old Diplomacy to the New*, 10.

27. E. Berkeley Tompkins, *Anti-Imperialism in the United States: The Great Debate, 1890–1920* (Philadelphia, 1970), 123–95, 273–82; Robert L. Beisner, *Twelve against Empire: The Anti-Imperialists, 1898–1900* (New York, 1968), quotation 113.

28. Perkins, *Great Rapprochement, passim*, quotations 57–58, 107, 98; Widenor, *Lodge*, 126. See also Howard K. Beale, *Theodore Roosevelt and the Rise of America to World Power* (New York, 1962), esp. ch. 3, quotation 145; William N. Tilchin, *Theodore Roosevelt and the British Empire: A Study in Presidential Statecraft* (Houndmills, 1997).

29. *Historical Statistics*, 105.

30. Stuart Anderson, *Race and Rapprochement: Anglo-Saxonism and Anglo-American Relations, 1895–1904* (East Brunswick, 1981), 55–57, 78–82; John Higham, *Strangers in the Land: Patterns of American Nativism, 1860–1925* (New York, 1963), 101–5; Widenor, *Lodge*, 44–49.

31. Widenor, *Lodge*, 79–81, 37–39; Beale, *Theodore Roosevelt*, 148–56; Perkins, *Great Rapprochement*, 29, 87; Anderson, *Race and Rapprochement*, 83, 110.

32. David S. Patterson, *Toward a Warless World: The Travail of the American Peace Movement, 1887–1914* (Bloomington, 1976); Calvin DeArmand Davis, *The United States and the Second Hague Peace Conference: American Diplomacy and International Organization, 1899–1914* (Durham, 1975), esp. 32–33, 285–86.

33. Roosevelt to Taft, August 21, 1907, Morison et al., ed., *Letters of Theodore Roosevelt*, 5:761; Beale, *Theodore Roosevelt*, 388.

34. Claude G. Bowers, *Beveridge and the Progressive Era* (Cambridge, MA, 1932), 64.

35. LaFeber, *New Empire*, esp. ch. 4; William Appleman Williams, *The Tragedy of American Diplomacy*, 2nd revised and enlarged ed. (New York, 1972), esp. ch. 1; Williams, *The Roots of the Modern American Empire: A Study of the Growth and Shaping of Social Consciousness in a Marketplace Society* (London, 1970).

36. Pletcher, "1861–1898," 130–31, 139–41; LaFeber, *New Empire*, 192–94; Paul S. Holbo, "Economics, Emotion, and Expansion: An Emerging Foreign Policy," in *The Gilded Age*, revised and enlarged edition, ed. H. Wayne Morgan (Syracuse, 1970), 211–12.

37. Marc-William Palen, "The Imperialism of Economic Nationalism," *Diplomatic History* 39 (January 2015), 157–85.

38. Alfred E. Eckes Jr., *Opening America's Market: U.S. Foreign Trade Policy since 1776* (Chapel Hill, 1995), 46–47; William H. Becker, "1899–1920: America Adjusts to World Power," in *Economics and World Power*, ed. Becker and Wells, 185–86; Holbo, "Economics, Emotion, and Expansion," 204–7; Pletcher, "1861–1898," 135–37, 145. Compare LaFeber, *New Empire*, 48–49, 112–21, 159–72, 189–90, 202, 376.

39. Beisner, *Twelve against Empire*, 103–5; *Historical Statistics*, 903–4, 890; LaFeber, *New Empire*, 301–2, 354; Pletcher, "1861–1898," 146–48; Becker, "1899–1920," 176–78, 182–83.

40. TR to N. M. Butler, September 24, 1907. Morison et al., ed., *Letters of Theodore Roosevelt*, 5:805–6.

41. *Historical Statistics*, 885, 887, 903–4; LaFeber, *American Search for Opportunity*, 25; Becker, "1899–1920," 177; LaFeber, *New Empire*, 192–93; Holbo, "Economics, Emotion, and Expansion," 202.

42. Robert Seager II, "Ten Years before Mahan: The Unofficial Case for a New Navy, 1880–1890," *Mississippi Valley Historical Review* 40 (December 1953): 502–4; Sprout, *Rise of American Naval Power*, 184, 206–8; Rhodes, "Sea Change," 81; *Congressional Record*, 51st Congress, 2nd session, 1891, 22, pt. 2, 1804.

43. *Congressional Record*, 53rd Congress, 3rd session, 1895, 27, part 4, 3082–3084; part 2, 1210–1213; Henry Cabot Lodge, *Speeches and Addresses, 1884–1909* (Boston, 1909), 182–83.

44. *Congressional Record*, 54th Congress, 1st session, 1895, 28, part 1, 419–20.

45. Richard Olney to Thomas F. Bayard, July 20, 1895, *FRUS, 1895*, I (Washington, D.C., 1896), 553–62.

46. Lord Salisbury to Sir Julian Pauncefote, November 26, 1895, *FRUS, 1895*, I, 563–67; Cleveland Message to Congress, December 17, 1895, Richardson, *Messages and Papers of the Presidents*, 9:656–58; Widenor, *Lodge*, 137.

47. *FRUS, 1895*, I, 553–62; *Congressional Record*, 54th Congress, 1st session, 1895, 28, part 1, 420; Mitchell, *Danger of Dreams*, 64–107.

48. Roosevelt to Lodge, March 27, 1901, *Selections from the Correspondence of Theodore Roosevelt and Henry Cabot Lodge* (New York, 1925), 484–85; Mitchell, *Danger of Dreams*, 53–62, 218. Mitchell takes the reasoning of the Navy's Black War Plan more seriously than other scholars—or than seems warranted.

49. Fred Greene, "The Military View of National Policy, 1904–1940," *American Historical Review* 66.2 (January 1961): 364.

50. Platt quoted in May, *Imperial Democracy*, 19–20 (Platt was speaking in favor of the annexation of Hawaii); Lodge to Elihu B. Hayes, May 18, 1898, quoted in Christopher McKnight Nichols, *Promise and Peril: America at the Dawn of a Global Age* (Cambridge, 2011), 51; Wilson, "The Significance of American History," September 9, 1901. *PWW* 12:184.

51. Taft, Annual Message, December 3, 1912, *FRUS, 1912* (Washington, D.C., 1919), vii–xxvii; McKinley speech at the Pan-American Exposition, Buffalo, New York, September 5, 1901.

52. Frank Ninkovich, "Theodore Roosevelt: Civilization as Ideology," *Diplomatic History* 10 (Summer 1986): 221–45, esp. 225–26, 228–29; Annual Message, December 2, 1902, *FRUS, 1902* (Washington, D.C., 1903), xxi–xxii.

53. Ninkovich, "Theodore Roosevelt," 225–26; *The Outlook*, April 1, 1911; "National Duties," address at Minnesota State Fair, September 2, 1901, in Theodore Roosevelt, *The Strenuous Life: Essays and Addresses* (London and New York, 1911), 324–25.

54. Ernest R. May, *American Imperialism: A Speculative Essay* (New York, 1968), *passim*; Frank Ninkovich, *Global Dawn: The Cultural Foundation of American Internationalism, 1865–1890* (Cambridge, MA, 2009), 2–3, *passim*; A. T. Mahan, *The Interest of America in Sea Power: Present and Future* (Boston, 1898), 258–59; Roosevelt address at the Methodist Episcopal Church, Washington, D.C., January 18, 1909, quoted in William N. Tilchin, "Setting the Foundation: Theodore Roosevelt and the Construction of an Anglo-American Special Relationship," in *Artists of Power: Theodore Roosevelt, Woodrow Wilson and Their Enduring Impact on U.S. Foreign Policy*, ed. Tilchin and Charles E. Neu (Westport, 2006), 58–59; Brooks Adams, *America's Economic Supremacy* (New York, 1900), v, 2–8, 50–51.

55. Adams, *America's Economic Supremacy*, 11; "Washington" [Lewis D. Einstein], "The United States and Anglo-German Rivalry," *National Review* 60 (January 1913): 736–50; "A Diplomatist" [Lewis D. Einstein], *American Foreign Policy* (Boston, 1909), 47–66.

56. Wilson, campaign address in Jersey City, New Jersey, May 25, 1912, *PWW* 24:443; Olney quoted in Healy, *U.S. Expansionism*, 39.

57. Roosevelt to Elihu Root, May 20, 1904. Morison et al., ed., *Letters of Theodore Roosevelt*, 4:801; Roosevelt, Annual Message, December 3, 1906, *FRUS, 1906*, I, xlvii; Wilson, address on Latin American policy, Mobile, Alabama, October 27, 1913; Fourth of July address, July 4, 1914, *PWW* 28:450; 30:251.

58. Herbert Croly, *The Promise of American Life* (New York, 1909), 289–314.

2. ADVANCE AND RETREAT, 1914–1920

1. Robert H. Ferrell, *Woodrow Wilson and World War I, 1917–1921* (New York, 1985), 18, 48, 53, 84–90; Niall Ferguson, *The Pity of War* (London, 1998), 316; Michael Edelstein, "War and the American Economy in the Twentieth Century," in *The Cambridge Economic History of the United States*, vol. 3, *The Twentieth Century*, ed. Stanley Engerman and Robert E. Gallman (Cambridge, UK, 2000), 337; U.S. Department of Commerce, Bureau of the Census, *Historical Statistics of the United States: Colonial Times to 1970* (Washington, D.C., 1975), 867, 1104, 1114.

2. The following paragraphs are indebted to the masterly overview and analysis of Americans' initial reactions to the war in Arthur S. Link, *Wilson: The Struggle for Neutrality, 1914–1915* (Princeton, 1960), 6–31.

3. John A. Thompson, *Reformers and War: American Progressive Publicists and the First World War* (Cambridge, 1987), 83–89; Thomas J. Knock, *To End All Wars: Woodrow Wilson and the Quest for a New World Order* (Princeton, 1992), 50–55; C. Roland Marchand, *The American Peace Movement and Social Reform, 1898–1918* (Princeton, 1972), chs. 6–7.

4. *Wabash Plain-Dealer*, cited in Eric F. Goldman, *Rendezvous with Destiny: A History of Modern American Reform* (rev. ed., New York, 1956), 180.

5. Kathleen Burk, *Britain, America, and the Sinews of War* (London, 1985), 6–7, 15–27.

6. Priscilla Roberts, "The Anglo-American Theme: American Visions of an Atlantic Alliance, 1914–1933," *Diplomatic History* 21 (Summer 1997): 341–42; for more detail, see Roberts, "The American 'Eastern Establishment' and World War I: The Emergence of a Foreign Policy Tradition," unpublished Ph.D. thesis, University of Cambridge, 1981. J. P. Morgan Jr. himself spent six months of the year in England, where he had a country house. Burk, *Britain, America and the Sinews of War*, 20–21. On the Anglo-French loan of 1915, see Link, *Struggle for Neutrality*, 616–28.

7. Henry F. May, *The End of American Innocence: A Study of the First Years of Our Own Time* (London, 1960), 363.

8. As May suggests, the intensity of pro-Allied feeling seems to have reflected concern about the internal character of the United States as much as with its international environment. In a particularly striking example of this, the passionately pro-Allied ambassador to Britain (and former magazine editor) Walter Hines Page wrote to his son on the eve of U.S. intervention: "My mind keeps constantly on the effect of the war and especially of our action on our own country. Of course that is the most important end of the thing for us." Among the benefits that Page foresaw was that participation in the war "will make us less promiscuously hospitable to every kind of immigrant; . . . reestablish in our minds and conscience and policy our true historic genesis, background, kindred, and destiny—i.e. kill the Irish and German influence; . . . bring men of a higher type into our political life." W. H. Page to Arthur W. Page, March 25, 1917, in Burton J. Hendrick, *The Life and Letters of Walter H. Page* (London, 1924), 2:218–19.

9. Quoted in Ross A. Kennedy, *The Will to Believe: Woodrow Wilson, World War I, and America's Strategy for Peace and Security* (Kent, 2009), 37. Root's faith in international law and his belief that a nation as powerful as the United States had a responsibility to uphold it were of long standing and were widely shared in the more conservative wing of the prewar peace movement. See Sondra R. Herman, *Eleven against War: Studies in American Internationalist Thought, 1898–1921* (Stanford, 1969), 40–44, 52–54; Marchand, *American Peace Movement and Social Reform*, 39–73.

10. *The New York Times*, September 24, 1914, cited in William C. Widenor, *Henry Cabot Lodge and the Search for an American Foreign Policy* (Berkeley, 1980), 188.

11. *Congressional Record,* 63rd Congress, 3rd sess., 1915, 52, pt. 2:1610.

12. For details, see John A. Thompson, "The Exaggeration of American Vulnerability: The Anatomy of a Tradition," *Diplomatic History* 16 (Winter 1992): 25–27, and the sources cited there.

13. Warren F. Kuehl, *Seeking World Order: The United States and International Organization to 1920* (Nashville, 1969), 172–92, 214–16; Marchand, *American Peace Movement and Social Reform*, 153–57; Knock, *To End All Wars*, 56.

14. In January 1918, the British Ambassador reported the president saying that at the beginning of the war "his chief preoccupation was not external but internal. There was imminent danger of civil discord, the country was divided into groups which did not understand one another, which were of different origin and which at any moment might fly at each other's throats. . . . That was his main preoccupation during the first year of the war." Sir Cecil Spring Rice to A. J. Balfour, January 4, 1918. Arthur S. Link et al., eds., *The Papers of Woodrow Wilson* (hereafter *PWW*) (Princeton, 1966–94), *PWW* 45:455.

15. "An Appeal to the American People," August 18, 1914, *PWW* 30:393–94.

16. Wilson to W. H. Page, October 28, 1914, *PWW* 31:243.

17. Burk, *Britain, America, and the Sinews of War,* 6, 14–27; John W. Coogan, *The End of Neutrality: The United States, Britain, and Maritime Rights, 1899–1915* (Ithaca and London, 1981), 160–67, 195–97, 223.

18. Link, *Struggle for Neutrality*, 62–64, 162–70.

19. Coogan, *End of Neutrality*, esp. 181, 236; Robert W. Tucker, *Woodrow Wilson and the Great War: Reconsidering America's Neutrality 1914–1917* (Charlottesville, 2007), 86–87.

From a somewhat different perspective, Edward H. Buehrig also sees a direct connection between the failure of the United States to moderate the Allied blockade through "drastic pressure" and the German resort to submarine warfare against merchant shipping, and thus U.S. entry into the war. Edward H. Buehrig, *Woodrow Wilson and the Balance of Power* (Bloomington, 1955), 83.

20. Buehrig, *Woodrow Wilson and the Balance of Power*, viii–ix, 103; Link, *Struggle for Neutrality*, 129; Kennedy, *Will to Believe*, 69–71.

21. House diary, August 30, 1914; House diary, November 4, 1914, *PWW* 30:462, 31:265.

22. Annual Message to Congress, December 8, 1914, *PWW* 31:421–24; Link, *Struggle for Neutrality*, 138–40.

23. Annual Message to Congress, December 8, 1914, *PWW* 31:422.

24. Link, *Struggle for Neutrality*, 214–19; House diary, February 10, 1915, in Charles Seymour, *The Intimate Papers of Colonel House* (London, 1926), 1:375.

25. For this characterization, see Reinhard R. Doerries, *Imperial Challenge: Ambassador Count Bernstorff and German-American Relations, 1908–1917* (Chapel Hill, 1989), 131–32, 308.

26. Secretary of State to Ambassador Gerard, February 10, 1915, *FRUS, 1915, Supplement: The World War* (Washington, D.C., 1928), 98–100; Link, *Struggle for Neutrality*, 320–23.

27. The value of U.S. exports to the United Kingdom and France rose from $754 million in 1914 to $2,748 million in 1916. *Historical Statistics*, 903.

28. American-registered tonnage constituted 12 percent of the world's shipping in 1914, but 87 percent of it operated on the Great Lakes and rivers or in coastal trade. See Link, *Struggle for Neutrality*, 81–82.

29. Link, *Struggle for Neutrality*, 312, 335; Patrick Devlin, *Too Proud to Fight: Woodrow Wilson's Neutrality* (London, 1974), 201–3.

30. For this suggestion, see Kennedy, *The Will to Believe*, 85.

31. Memorandum, April 7, 1915, quoted in Link, *Struggle for Neutrality*, 362.

32. See the thorough analysis in Tucker, *Wilson and the Great War*, 99–100.

33. *FRUS: The Lansing Papers, 1914–1920* (Washington, D.C., 1939), 1:365–80.

34. *Struggle for Neutrality*, 367.

35. For instance, *The Nation*, May 13, 1915, p. 527; *Metropolitan Magazine*, June 1915, p. 3. For the general reaction, see Link, *Struggle for Neutrality*, 372–75.

36. A few weeks later, Roosevelt wrote to an English correspondent, "If we had done what we ought to have done after the sinking of the *Lusitania*, I and my four boys would now be in an army getting ready to serve with you." TR to Arthur A. Lee, June 17, 1915. E. E. Morison et al., eds., *The Letters of Theodore Roosevelt* (Cambridge, MA, 1954), 8:937.

37. Quoted in Robert Endicott Osgood, *Ideals and Self-Interest in America's Foreign Relations: The Great Transformation of the Twentieth Century* (Chicago, 1953), 140.

38. Address in Philadelphia to Newly Naturalized Citizens, May 10, 1915, *PWW* 33:149.

39. W. J. Bryan to James W. Gerard, May 13, 1915, *FRUS, 1915, Supplement*, 393–96.

40. House to Wilson, May 9, 1915; Wilson to Bryan, May 10, 1915, *PWW* 33:134, 139.

41. Remarks to the Associated Press of New York, April 20, 1915, *PWW* 33:41.

42. On this, see John A. Thompson, *Woodrow Wilson* (London, 2002), 35–38.

43. Link, *Struggle for Neutrality*, 396–97.

44. Wilson to Bryan, June 7, 1915, *PWW* 33:349.

45. Bryan to Wilson, June 5, 1915, *PWW* 33:342.

46. Wilson to Melancthon Williams Jacobus, July 20, 1915, *PWW* 33:535.

47. Link, *Struggle for Neutrality*, 590–93; Wilson, Address to the Manhattan Club, November 4, 1915, *PWW* 35:167–73; Arthur S. Link, *Wilson: Confusions and Crises, 1915–1916* (Princeton, 1964), 15–48.

48. Addresses in Cleveland, Ohio, January 29, 1916, Chicago, Illinois, January 31, 1916, Topeka, Kansas, February 2, 1916, *PWW* 36:47, 64–66, 72–73, 92–95.

49. "For my own part, I cannot consent to any abridgement of the rights of American citizens in any respect. The honor and self-respect of the nation is involved. We covet peace and shall preserve it at any cost but the loss of honor. To forbid our people to exercise their rights for fear we might be called upon to vindicate them would be a deep humiliation indeed. . . . What we are contending for in this matter is of the very essence of the things that have made America a sovereign nation. She cannot yield them without conceding her own impotency as a nation and making virtual surrender of her independent position among the nations of the world." Wilson to Senator W. J. Stone, February 24, 1916, *PWW* 36:213–14.

50. Link, *Confusions and Crises*, 319.

51. Osgood, *Ideals and Self-Interest*, 216–22; John A. S. Grenville and George B. Young, *Politics, Strategy, and American Diplomacy: Studies in American Foreign Policy, 1873–1917* (New Haven, 1966), 325–26, 333–35.

52. Address in St. Louis on Preparedness, February 3, 1916, *PWW* 36:116.

53. That it was possible for submarines to operate against merchant ships in an acceptable manner was conceded by Wilson in the third *Lusitania* Note of July 21, 1915. *FRUS, 1915, Supplement*, 480–82.

54. Wilson to House, July 14, 1915, enclosing Warren Worth Bailey to Wilson, July 12, 1915, *PWW* 33:506, 494–95; Link, *Struggle for Neutrality*, 439–41.

55. Wilson to Edith Bolling Galt, August 19, 1915; Wilson to House, August 21, 1915, *PWW* 34:261, 271.

The German ambassador reported to Berlin in late July that "Mr. Wilson was carried away by his emotions about the sinking of the Lusitania. Stimulated by this emotion, he has taken such an inflexible position that he cannot retreat without making himself impossible in the eyes of public opinion here. . . . However, it must be stressed that Mr. Wilson does not want to wage war against us or to become a partisan of England. About this matter one should not be fooled by the eastern press in the United States." Ambassador von Bernstorff to the Foreign Office, July 28, 1915, quoted in Link, *Struggle for Neutrality*, 451–53.

56. Link, *Confusions and Crises*, 132–36, 616–25.

57. Link, *Confusions and Crises*, 102–4; Sir E. Grey to E. M. House, September 22, 1915, *PWW* 35:71n–72n. To a greater extent than Wilson and House realized, Grey's desire for a postwar league of nations represented his personal feelings rather than an agreed British policy. See Keith Robbins, *Sir Edward Grey: A Biography of Lord Grey of Fallodon* (London, 1971), 319–20.

58. Link, *Confusions and Crises*, 105–7; House to Wilson, November 10, 1915, Wilson to House, November 11, November 12, 1915; House diary, November 28, 1915, *PWW* 35:186–87, 192, 261.

59. Wilson to House, December 24, 1915, *PWW* 35:387–88.

60. Link, *Confusions and Crises*, 101–41; House to Wilson, February 15, 1916; House to Grey, March 7, 1916, *PWW* 36:180, 266. For a contrary interpretation, see Kennedy, *The Will to Believe*, esp. 95–96.

61. Link, *Confusions and Crises*, 278–79.

62. Address to the League to Enforce Peace, May 27, 1916, *PWW* 37:113–16. On House and freedom of the seas, see Link, *Struggle for Neutrality*, 223–27.

63. Wilson to House, July 2, 1916; Wilson to House, July 23, 1916, *PWW* 37:345, 466–67; Viscount Grey of Fallodon to House, August 28, 1916, *PWW* 38:89–92; Link, *Wilson: Campaigns for Progressivism and Peace, 1916–1917* (Princeton, 1965), 10–23, 32–38, 65–71.

Publicly, Wilson had never departed from impartiality. Even in his speech to the League to Enforce Peace he had offended Allied opinion by reiterating with regard to the war that "with its causes and its objects we are not concerned. The obscure fountains from which its stupendous flood has burst forth, we are not interested to search for or explore." *PWW* 37:113.

64. Link, *Wilson: Campaigns*, 43–48, 106–11.

65. Campaign addresses, October 5, 7, 14, 26, 1916, *PWW* 38:345–48, 364–65, 436–37, 538–41.

66. Link, *Campaigns*, 160–62, 170–75, 192.

67. House diary, November 14, November 15, 1916, *PWW* 38:646–47, 656–60; Link, *Campaigns*, 187–90, 199–200.

68. Memorandum by Walter Hines Page [September 23, 1916], *PWW* 38:241. Of course, Wilson in this interview was seeking to ensure that Page understood how little he and most Americans shared the Ambassador's passionate pro-Allied partisanship. But there is other evidence that, as a careful scholar has observed, "By the end of 1916, the president had come close to, perhaps even achieved, the neutrality in thought he had urged upon his fellow citizens at the outset of the war." Tucker, *Wilson and the Great War*, 188.

69. "Have you ever heard what started the present war? If you have, I wish you would publish it, because nobody else has. So far as I can gather, nothing in particular started it, but everything in general. There had been growing up in Europe a mutual suspicion, an interchange of conjectures about what this government and that government was going to do, an interlacing of alliances and understandings, a complex web of intrigue and spying,

that presently was sure to entangle the whole of the family of mankind on that side of the water in its meshes." Luncheon Address to Women in Cincinnati, October 26, 1916, *PWW* 38:531.

70. In October 1916, British Chancellor of the Exchequer Reginald McKenna had warned the Cabinet that "by next June or earlier, the President of the American Republic will be in a position, if he wishes, to dictate his own terms to us." This followed intra-governmental studies in London on the extent of the British dependence on American financing. Link, *Campaigns*, 178–84.

71. Link, *Campaigns*, 200–206; Spring Rice to the Foreign Office, December 3, 1916, *PWW* 40:136–37.

72. Link, *Campaigns*, 165–219; Secretary of State to Ambassadors and Ministers in belligerent countries, December 18, 1916, *FRUS, 1916, Supplement*, 97–99. Wilson's Note did stress that it had been long considered and was in no way associated with the German overture.

73. Link, *Campaigns*, 220–61, quotation 236–37.

74. Address to the Senate, January 22, 1917, *PWW* 40:533–39.

75. The establishment of a Polish kingdom was part of Germany's peace terms, as these had been communicated privately to Wilson. Constrained by the Russian alliance, the Allies in their reply to Wilson's Note had referred only to the Czar's intention to create a "free" and united Poland, but there was a good deal of sympathy for the Polish cause in London. Link, *Campaigns*, 238–39, 255–57; Sterling J. Kernek, "Distractions of War during Peace: The Lloyd George Government's Reactions to Woodrow Wilson, December 1916–November 1918," *Transactions of the American Philosophical Society* New Series 65, Part 2 (1975) 29n.; V. H. Rothwell, *British War Aims and Peace Diplomacy, 1914–1918* (Oxford, 1971), 55–57, 65.

76. Memorandum by Herbert Bruce Brougham, December 14, 1914, *PWW* 31:458–60. Wilson developed this line of thought most fully in a document he wrote (but did not publish) in late November 1916. "An Unpublished Prolegomenon to a Peace Note," c. November 25, 1916, *PWW* 40:67–70.

77. Address to the Senate, January 22, 1917, *PWW* 40:533–39.

Wilson had delayed giving the speech until it had been transmitted in code to U.S. embassies in Europe so that they could ensure its full publication locally, and he explained to a correspondent that "the real people I was speaking to was neither the Senate nor foreign governments, but the *people* of the countries now at war." Wilson to J. P. Gavit, January 29, 1917, *PWW* 41:55; Link, *Campaigns*, 253–55.

78. Address to the Senate, January 22, 1917; Wilson to C. H. Dodge, January 25, 1917, *PWW* 40:533–39, 41:11; Link, *Campaigns*, 269–71; *Congressional Record*, 64th Congress, 2nd session, 2364–2370.

79. As we shall see, the strategic version of this thesis was developed in the debate over entry into World War II, but it became widely accepted and remains so. See, for example, Arthur M. Schlesinger Jr., "Foreign Policy and the American Character," in *Cycles of American History* (London, 1987), 53; Arthur A. Stein, "Domestic Constraints, Extended Deterrence and the Incoherence of Grand Strategy: The United States, 1938–1950," in *The Domestic Bases of Grand Strategy*, ed. Richard Rosecrance and Arthur A. Stein (Ithaca, 1993), 97; Michael C. Desch, *When the Third World Matters: Latin America and United States Grand Strategy* (Baltimore, 1993), 39.

80. Page memorandum, [September 23, 1916], *PWW* 38:241.

81. Link, *Wilson: Campaigns*, 110–11, 135–36.

82. Osgood, *Ideals and Self-Interest*, 217–22.

83. Osgood, *Ideals and Self-Interest*, 253–54; Link, *Campaigns*, 302–3, 396, 410–11; *New Republic*, February 17, 1917, 57.

On the initial reading of the Russian Revolution as pro-war, see George F. Kennan, *Russia and the West under Lenin and Stalin* (New York and Toronto, 1961), 18–24. On March 16, Lansing forwarded to Wilson an assessment along these lines by Samuel N. Harper, the best-known American authority on Russia.

84. House to Wilson, February 10, 1917; Lansing Memorandum on the Severance of Relations with Germany, February 4, 1917; W. H. Page to Wilson, March 9, 1917, *PWW* 41:190, 122, 373.

85. Page to Secretary of State, March 5, 1917, *PWW* 41:336–37. In this and a later telegram, Page (who, of course, reflected what he had been told by British authorities) stressed that the danger presented by German submarines made it impossible to send further large shipments of gold to America rather than that the reserves were almost exhausted (as they in fact were). U.S. Department of State, *Foreign Relations of the United States: 1917.* Supplement 2, I (Washington, D.C., 1931), 516–18.

86. For example, Richard M. Abrams, *The Burdens of Progress, 1900–1929* (Glenview, 1978), 101, 107–8.

87. Edward B. Parsons, *Wilsonian Diplomacy: Allied-American Rivalries in War and Peace* (St. Louis, 1978), 10.

88. Luncheon Address in Cincinnati, [October 26, 1916], *PWW* 40:528.

89. *Historical Statistics*, 903, 225. Exports to the United Kingdom and France constituted more than half of America's total exports in 1916.

90. Link, *Struggle for Neutrality*, 616–25; *Campaigns*, 380–82.

91. *Congressional Record*, 65th Congress, 1st session, Senate, 213–14.

92. John Milton Cooper Jr., "The Command of Gold Reversed: American Loans to Britain, 1915–1917," *Pacific Historical Review* 45 (May 1976): 223.

93. Ernest R. May, *The World War and American Isolation, 1914–1917* (Cambridge, 1959), 432. See also Link, *Campaigns*, ix, 414; Devlin, *Too Proud to Fight*, 678–82.

94. See Link, *Campaigns*, 414.

95. Devlin, *Too Proud to Fight*, 680.

96. Jane Addams, *Peace and Bread in Time of War* (New York, 1922), 63–64.

97. House diary, February 1, 1917, *PWW* 41:87; Link, *Campaigns*, 296.

98. Ibid., 293–97.

99. Link, *Campaigns*, 297–99.

100. F. K. Lane to G. W. Lane, February 25, 1917, *PWW* 41:282; Address in Topeka, February 2, 1916; Wilson to Senator W. J. Stone, February 24, 1916, *PWW* 36:92, 213–14. For Lodge, see *Congressional Record*, 65th Congress, 1st session, 207–8.

101. Addresses to Congress, February 3, April 2, 1917, *PWW* 41:111, 521: Herbert Hoover, *The Ordeal of Woodrow Wilson* (New York, 1958), 7.

102. See, for example, Norman K. Risjord, "1812: Conservatives, War Hawks, and the Nation's Honor," *William and Mary Quarterly*, 3rd series, 18 (April 1961): 196–210; Walter Russell Mead, *Special Providence: American Foreign Policy and How It Changed the World* (New York, 2001), 231–32, 250–51.

103. Ross Gregory, *The Origins of American Intervention in the First World War* (New York, 1971), 135–36. See also May, *The World War and American Isolation*, 427; Link, *Campaigns*, 411–12. In an article arguing that the values of a code of honor underlay the decisions for war of European countries in 1914, Avner Offer observes that "a sequence of insults also provoked the United States into the war, by means of unrestricted submarine warfare." Offer, "Going to War in 1914: A Matter of Honor?" *Politics and Society* 23.2 (June 1995): 213–41, quotation 234–35.

104. Address to Congress, February 3, 1917, *PWW* 41:111; Link, *Campaigns*, 314–18, 385–87.

105. Address to Congress, February 26, 1917, *PWW* 41:283–87; Link, *Campaigns*, 310–13, 340–42, 346–50, 376–77.

106. Link, *Campaigns*, 240–46, 342–46, 353–59; Justus D. Doenecke, *Nothing Less Than War: A New History of America's Entry into World War I* (Lexington, 2011), 267–68.

107. *PWW* 41:436–45; Link, *Campaigns*, 396–408, 415–17; Doenecke, *Nothing Less Than War*, 280–81, 284.

108. For example: "Wilson was the weight that would bring down either scale. He was not only the President: he was the casting vote of the nation." Devlin, *Too Proud to Fight*, 660. See also John Milton Cooper Jr., *Pivotal Decades: The United States, 1900–1920* (New York, 1990), 266, and *Woodrow Wilson: A Biography* (New York, 2009), 381.

109. Link, *Campaigns*, 398–400; Charles Seymour, ed., *The Intimate Papers of Colonel House* (London, 1926), 2:467.

110. Lansing Memorandum of the Cabinet Meeting, March 20, 1917, *PWW* 41:438.

111. The amendment was lost by 293 votes to 125. For a thorough analysis of the division, see John Milton Cooper Jr., *The Vanity of Power: American Isolationism and the First World War* (Westport, 1969), 179–81, 233–35.

112. J. P. Tumulty to Wilson, March 24, 1917, *PWW* 41:462.

113. For the condemnation by some progressive publicists of national honor as a reason for fighting, see Thompson, *Reformers and War*, 131, 151.

114. Address to Congress, April 2, 1917, *PWW* 41:519–27.

115. The votes were 82 to 6 in the Senate and 373 to 50 in the House of Representatives.

116. *Congressional Record*, 65th Congress, 1st session, 253; Robert David Johnson, *The Peace Progressives and American Foreign Relations* (Cambridge, MA, 1995), 68.

117. Wilson remarks at the dedication of the Red Cross Building, May 12, 1917; J. T. Heflin to Wilson, May 17, 1917; Wilson to J. T. Heflin, May 22, 1917, *PWW* 42:282, 323–24, 370–71.

118. Osgood, *Ideals and Self-Interest in America's Foreign Relations*, 257–61.

119. Robert H. Ferrell, *Woodrow Wilson and World War I, 1917–1921* (New York, 1985), 18, 48, 84–87; Michael Edelstein, "War and the American Economy in the Twentieth Century," *The Cambridge Economic History of the United States*, vol. 3, 331, 337, 342; *Historical Statistics*, 1104.

120. Lansing Memorandum, March 20, 1917, *PWW* 41:436–44; Walter Millis, *Road to War: America 1914–1917* (Boston, 1935), 435; *Congressional Record*, 65th Congress, 1st session, 207–8; Ferrell, *Wilson and World War I*, 14. See also David M. Esposito, *The Legacy of Woodrow Wilson: American War Aims in World War I* (Westport, 1996), 92–93; Frederick Palmer, *Newton D. Baker: America at War* (New York, 1931), 1, 108–9.

121. Esposito, *Legacy of Wilson*, 100, 123–24. See also Frank Ninkovich, *The Wilsonian Century: U.S. Foreign Policy since 1900* (Chicago, 1999), 62.

122. Victor S. Mamatey, *The United States and East Central Europe, 1914–1918: A Study in Wilsonian Diplomacy and Propaganda* (Princeton, 1957), 90; Murray L. Eiland III, *Woodrow Wilson: Architect of World War II* (New York, 1991), 66; David Steigerwald, "The Reclamation of Woodrow Wilson," *Diplomatic History* 23 (Winter 1999): 81–82. For contemporary comments, see Thompson, *Reformers and War*, 157–58.

123. Wilson to House, July 21, 1917, *PWW* 43:237–38, emphasis in original. For Wilson's explanation of his position on an agreement not to make a separate peace, see "A Memorandum by John Howard Whitehouse," April 14, 1917, *PWW* 42:65–67.

124. Address to Congress, April 2, 1917, *PWW* 41:522.

125. John Whiteclay Chambers Jr., *To Raise an Army: The Draft Comes to Modern America* (New York and London, 1987), 125, 130–42.

126. Wilson to E. W. Pou, April 13, 1917, *PWW* 42:52.

127. Chambers, *To Raise an Army*, 144–50; Ferrell, *Wilson and World War I*, 52.

128. Wilson to N. D. Baker, December 4, 1917; David Lloyd George to Lord Reading, April 14, 1918; also March 28, March 29, April 2, April 9, 1918, *PWW* 45:208, 47, 338–41, 181–83, 203–5, 229–30, 307; Ferrell, *Wilson and World War I*, 69–77, 53.

129. Arno J. Mayer, *Political Origins of the New Diplomacy, 1917–1918* (New Haven, 1959), 194–95; Pope Benedict XV to the Rulers of the Belligerent Peoples, August 1, 1917, enclosed in W. H. Page to Lansing, August 15, 1917, *PWW* 43:482–85.

130. Wilson to His Holiness the Pope, August 27, 1917, to H. B. Brougham, September 29, 1917, to David Lawrence, October 5, 1917; *New York Times*, October 9, 1917, *PWW* 44:57–59, 279, 309, 325–27. See also "To the Provisional Government of Russia," May 22, 1917, Flag Day address, June 14, 1917, *PWW* 42:366, 501–3.

These many statements are hard to reconcile with the claim of some historians that Wilson continued until the spring of 1918 to want a negotiated peace. On this claim, see Arthur S. Link, *Woodrow Wilson: Revolution, War, and Peace* (Arlington Heights, 1979), 77–80; Cooper, *Woodrow Wilson*, 395.

131. Address to Congress, January 8, 1918, *PWW* 45:534–39. The terms of the secret treaties were known to the authors of the Memorandum on which Wilson based the territorial Points. See Memorandum by S. E. Mezes, D. H. Miller, and Walter Lippmann, *PWW* 45:459–85; Ronald Steel, *Walter Lippmann and the American Century* (Boston, 1980), 130–36, 609–10.

132. For Roosevelt's support of the nationalities, see Mamatey, *The United States and East Central Europe*, 133–35, 156–57, 162–63. On the position of the European allies, see Betty Miller Unterberger, *The United States, Revolutionary Russia, and the Rise of Czechoslovakia* (Chapel Hill, 1989), 35, 62–63, 168, 233, 269–70, 284–86, 314–15. On Wilson's earlier opposition to the dismemberment of the Habsburg empire, see J. J. Jusserand to the French Foreign Ministry, March 7, 1917; "A Memorandum by John Howard Whitehouse," April 14, 1917, *PWW* 41:356–57, 42, 65–66.

133. Address to Congress, February 11, 1918, *PWW* 46:323. On the impact of this and other of Wilson's statements on anti-colonial leaders in Egypt, India, and East Asia, see Erez Manela, *The Wilsonian Moment: Self-Determination and the International Origins of Anticolonial Nationalism* (New York, 2007).

134. "I would be very much obliged if you would issue instructions that 'Our Associates in the War' is to be substituted. I have been very careful about this myself because we have no allies and I think I am right in believing that the people of the country are very jealous of any intimation that there are formal alliances." Wilson to Herbert Hoover, December 10, 1917, *PWW* 45:256–57.

135. Wilson to House, September 2, 1917, *PWW* 44:120–21. Members of the Inquiry produced the memorandum that Wilson used in formulating the Fourteen Points.

136. Diary of Josephus Daniels, October 17, 1918, *PWW* 51:372.

137. Wilson to House, July 21, 1917, *PWW* 43:238.

138. Diary of W. C. Bullitt, December 10, 1918, *PWW* 53:352.

139. This remark was made to newspaper reporters traveling with him. Diary of Dr. Grayson, December 8, 1918, *PWW* 53:337.

140. T. W. Lamont Memorandum of Conversation with the President, October 4, 1918, *PWW* 51:222–26.

141. Address to the Senate, January 22, 1917, *PWW* 40:538–39.

142. Thompson, *Reformers and War*, 91–103, 181, 202–12; Address in the Metropolitan Opera House, September 27, 1918, *PWW* 51:127–33; Arthur Walworth, *America's Moment: 1918: American Diplomacy at the End of World War I* (New York, 1977), 72. On the possible influence of Baker's reports to House and the State Department, see Inga

Floto, *Colonel House in Paris: A Study of American Policy at the Paris Peace Conference 1919* (Princeton, 1980), 32–33.

143. *The Collected Writings of John Maynard Keynes,* vol. 2, *The Economic Consequences of the Peace* (London, 1971), 24; H. G. Wells, *The Shape of Things to Come: The Ultimate Revolution* (London, 1933), 96.

144. *Collected Writings* 2, 24.

145. Carter Glass to Wilson [December 19, 1918], *PWW* 53:441–42. Having recently come from the House of Representatives, Glass wrote with special authority about the attitudes of Congress.

146. Arno J. Mayer, *Politics and Diplomacy of Peacemaking: Containment and Counter-revolution at Versailles, 1918–1919* (New York, 1969), 266–73. For further discussion of this point, see Klaus Schwabe, *Wilson, Revolutionary Germany, and Peacemaking, 1918–1919* (Chapel Hill, 1985), 166–67; William R. Keylor, "Versailles and International Diplomacy" in *The Treaty of Versailles: A Reassessment after 75 Years,* ed. Manfred F. Boemeke, Gerald D. Feldman, and Elisabeth Glaser (Cambridge, 1998), 477–78.

147. "If you had made your fight in the open, instead of behind closed doors, you would have carried with you the public opinion of the world, which was yours," the young William C. Bullitt told the president as he resigned in protest from the American delegation. Bullitt to Wilson, May 17, 1919, *PWW* 59:232–33.

148. Wilson statement on the Adriatic question, April 23, 1919; Ambassador T. N. Page to American Mission in Paris, April 24, 1919, *PWW* 58:5–8, 91–93.

149. Knock, *To End All Wars,* 176–77.

150. Bullitt later asserted that had Wilson had the virility to employ this threat in Paris, "he might possibly have obtained the 'just and lasting peace' he had promised to the world." Sigmund Freud and William C. Bullitt, *Thomas Woodrow Wilson: A Psychological Study* (London, 1967), 180–81.

151. Wilson to House, October 30, 1918, *PWW* 51:513; Walworth, *America's Moment,* 61.

152. On the attitudes of the American military, see Schwabe, *Wilson, Revolutionary Germany, and Peacemaking,* 224–27.

153. "The ordering of the *George Washington* to return to France looked upon here as an act of impatience and petulance on the President's part and not accepted here in good grace either by friends or foes. It is considered as evidence that the President intends to leave the conference if his views are not accepted.... Up to this time the world has been living on stories coming out of Paris that there was to be an agreement on the League of Nations.... A withdrawal at this time would be a desertion." J. P. Tumulty to C. T. Grayson, April 9, 1919, *PWW* 57:177.

154. Wilson had assured members of the Inquiry at his shipboard meeting with them that as "the only disinterested people at the peace conference," the Americans would be courted for their support by the leaders of other countries; the European allies were divided by rivalries and mutual hostility but "all were anxious to cooperate with us." Diary of W. C. Bullitt, December 10, 1918, Memorandum by Isaiah Bowman, December 10, 1918, *PWW* 51:351, 353.

155. At his first meeting with Wilson, Lloyd George formed the impression that the League of Nations "was the only thing that he cared much about." Minutes of the Imperial War Cabinet, December 30, 1918, *PWW* 53:558–69.

156. Sterling J. Kernek, "Woodrow Wilson and National Self-determination: A Study of the Manipulation of Principles in the Pursuit of Political Interests," *Proceedings of the American Philosophical Society* 126 (1982): 255–62.

157. Lansing Memorandum, April 28, 1919; Diary of Ray Stannard Baker, April 30, 1919, *PWW* 58:185, 270–71.

158. Address at Des Moines, September 6, 1919, *PWW* 63:79. Wilson placed much more emphasis on the implications of America's great power than on the "structural

interdependence" created by modern communications, which is seen as the crucial factor by the historian Frank Ninkovich. See Ninkovich, *Modernity and Power: A History of the Domino Theory in the Twentieth Century* (Chicago, 1994), esp. xiii–xiv, 38–39, 51.

159. Minutes of the 8th meeting of the League of Nations Commission, February 11, 1919, Cecil diary, [February 11, 1919], *PWW* 55:72–80; David Hunter Miller, *The Drafting of the Covenant* (New York, 1928), 1, 175–81.

160. Wilson to House, March 22, 1918, *PWW* 47:105.

161. Thompson, *Reformers and War*, 239–42.

162. Lamont diary, July 5, 1919, quoted in Schwabe, *Woodrow Wilson, Revolutionary Germany, and Peacemaking*, 531.

163. Tumulty to Wilson, [May 8, 1919], [May 22, 1919]; R. S. Baker diary, May 23, May 31, [1919], *PWW* 58:561, 59:419, 447, 645–47. Tumulty's view of the favorable response to the Versailles treaty in the American press was confirmed by the authoritative surveys in the *Literary Digest*. See *Literary Digest* 61, May 17, 1919, 11–15, May 24, 1919, 9–13, May 31, 1919, 15–16.

164. William Appleman Williams, *The Tragedy of American Diplomacy*, rev. ed. (New York, 1962), 106, 139–40.

165. Alexander De Conde, *A History of American Foreign Policy* (New York, 1963), 487.

166. John Milton Cooper Jr., *Breaking the Heart of the World: Woodrow Wilson and the Fight for the League of Nations* (Cambridge, 2001), 57–58, 84–85, 126–29, 425; Ralph Stone, *The Irreconcilables: The Fight against the League of Nations* (New York, 1970).

167. The fullest account and analysis of the debates and votes in the Senate is in Cooper, *Breaking the Heart of the World*, esp. 264–69, 340–70.

168. Thomas A. Bailey, *Woodrow Wilson and the Great Betrayal* (Chicago, 1963), 271, 277.

169. Bailey, *Woodrow Wilson and the Great Betrayal*, 388–89.

170. William C. Widenor, *Henry Cabot Lodge and the Search for an American Foreign Policy* (Berkeley, 1980), 339. Much official opinion in London believed that the Lodge reservations destroyed the value of the League from the British point of view and that, if they were adopted, Britain itself should give notice of withdrawal from the organization. The French government, too, was disillusioned by the Senate's attitude. Lloyd E. Ambrosius, *Woodrow Wilson and the American Diplomatic Tradition: The Treaty Fight in Perspective* (Cambridge, UK, 1987), 236–39, 214–15. For Wilson's reference to "a debating society," see Press Conference, July 10, 1919; Conversation with Members of the Senate Foreign Relations Committee, August 19, 1919, *PWW* 61:421, 62:343.

171. Address in Cheyenne, September 24, 1919, *PWW* 62:480. Wilson used the term *nullification* in his letters to the Democratic leader in the Senate on the occasion of both votes. Wilson to Senator Gilbert Hitchcock, November 18, 1919, March 8, 1920. *PWW* 64: 58; 65: 67–71. Arthur S. Link emphasizes the effects of Wilson's stroke on his personality and behavior but he nonetheless admits that "even a healthy Wilson might have concluded that this reservation amounted, as he put it, to nullification of the Treaty." Link, *Wilson: Revolution, War, and Peace*, 123.

172. In early August, Lodge assured a correspondent of his confidence that the Republican senators would unite behind reservations that would "take the United States out of the treaty entirely on all the parts where we wish to refuse obligations." Ambrosius, *Wilson and the American Diplomatic Tradition*, 160.

173. For a thorough account and analysis of these tortuous negotiations, see Cooper, *Breaking the Heart of the World*, 147–48, 154–55, 303–15; Herbert F. Margulies, *The Mild Reservationists and the League of Nations Controversy in the Senate* (Columbia, 1989).

174. Root to Lodge, June 19, 1919, quoted in Widenor, *Lodge and the Search for an American Foreign Policy*, 331.

175. Knox first articulated his "doctrine" in December 1918 and incorporated it in a Senate resolution in June 1919. Cooper, *Breaking the Heart of the World*, 40–41, 101, 155.

176. George C. Herring, *From Colony to Superpower: U.S. Foreign Relations since 1776* (New York, 2008), 428; Link, *Wilson: Revolution, War, and Peace*, 108.

177. Henry White to Wilson, April 16, 1919, *PWW* 57:416–17.

178. Lodge to Bryce, April 20, 1920, quoted in Ambrosius, *Wilson and the American Diplomatic Tradition*, 252.

179. Cooper, *Breaking the Heart of the World*, 384–96. Harding speech at Des Moines, Iowa, October 7, 1920, quotation 392.

180. For classic expositions of the historical interpretation, see Walter Lippmann, *U.S. Foreign Policy: Shield of the Republic* (Boston, 1943), 30–33, 47–70; Hans J. Morgenthau, *In Defense of the National Interest: A Critical Examination of American Foreign Policy* (New York, 1951), ch. 1.

For the concept of "free security," see C. Vann Woodward, "The Age of Reinterpretation," *American Historical Review* 66 (October 1960): 2–3.

181. Addresses in San Diego, September 19, 1919, San Francisco, September 17, 1919, Salt Lake City, September 23, 1919, St. Louis, September 5, 1919, Bismarck, September 10, 1919, *PWW* 63:377, 314–18, 452–53, 38–39, 155–56.

182. Addresses in Indianapolis, September 4, 1919, Salt Lake City, September 23, 1919, Bismarck, September 10, 1919, *PWW* 63:27, 455, 161.

183. Address in San Diego, September 19, 1919. In this connection, Wilson rather misleadingly claimed that the treaty "provides for the destruction of autocratic power as an instrument of international control" and asserted that, if Germany restored the Hohenzollerns, she would be "forever excluded from the League of Nations." Addresses in Minneapolis, September 9, 1919, Oakland, September 18, 1919, *PWW* 62:372, 135, 358.

In fact, the only criterion for eligibility to membership in the Covenant (Article 7) was that it "shall be limited to fully self-governing countries including Dominions and Colonies."

184. Addresses in San Francisco, September 17, 1919, Helena, September 11, 1919, Oakland, September 18, 1919, St. Paul, September 9, 1919, *PWW* 62:333, 184, 358, 148.

185. Addresses in Sioux Falls, September 8, Bismarck, September 10, 1919, and St. Louis, September 5, 1919, *PWW* 63:115–16, 159, 43–48.

186. Addresses in Omaha, September 8, 1919, Tacoma, September 13, 1919, Denver, September 25, 1919, Helena, September 11, 1919, *PWW* 63:102, 243–44, 495, 183.

187. Addresses in Omaha, September 8, Spokane, September 12, 1919, Oakland, September 18, 1919, Shrine Auditorium, Los Angeles, September 20, 1919, Denver, September 25, 1919, *PWW* 63:101, 225, 359, 411, 495.

188. Address in St. Louis, September 5, 1919, *PWW* 63:35. This argument, which Wilson did not repeat, is the closest he came to articulating what became known as "the domino theory," which Frank Ninkovich regards as central to Wilson's thinking about national security. Ninkovich, *Modernity and Power*, esp. 51–53.

189. Wilson dropped the argument that the League would give the United States the right to "mind other people's business" after being told that it had provoked "rather severe criticism on the Hill." Rudolph Forster to J. P. Tumulty, September 5, 1919, *PWW* 63:51–52.

190. Cooper, *Breaking the Heart of the World*, 341–43, 379–80.

191. Address in Spokane, September 12, 1919, *PWW* 63:229–30.

192. Addresses in Sioux Falls, September 8, 1919, Spokane, September 12, 1919, Shrine Auditorium in Los Angeles, September 20, 1919, *PWW* 63:115, 229–30, 415–16.

193. Address to Republican Convention, June 8, 1920, quoted in Ambrosius, *Wilson and the American Diplomatic Tradition*, 264.

194. Address in Free Trade Hall, Manchester, December 30, 1918, *PWW* 53:550.

195. Addresses in Billings and Helena, September 11, 1919, the Shrine Auditorium in Los Angeles, September 20, 1919, *PWW* 63:172, 181–82, 418.

196. See, for example, Osgood, *Ideals and Self-Interest*, 295–98, 309–11; Selig Adler, *The Isolationist Impulse: Its Twentieth Century Reaction* (New York, 1961), 90–96.

197. See, in particular, Manela, *The Wilsonian Moment, passim.*

3. A RESTRAINED SUPERPOWER, 1920–1938

1. Barry Eichengreen, "U.S. Foreign Financial Relations in the Twentieth Century," in *The Cambridge Economic History of the United States*, vol. III, *The Twentieth Century*, ed. Stanley L. Engerman and Robert E. Gallman (Cambridge, UK, 2000), 476; Melvyn P. Leffler, "1921–1932: Expansionist Impulses and Domestic Constraints" in *Economics and World Power: An Assessment of American Diplomacy since 1780*, ed. William H. Becker and Samuel F. Wells, Jr. (New York, 1984), 227; *Statistical History of the United States*, 867; Patrick O. Cohrs, *The Unfinished Peace after World War I: America, Britain and the Stabilisation of Europe, 1919–1932* (Cambridge, UK, 2006), 16. U.S. gold imports, 1920–29, amounted to $1,355 million. John Braeman, "The New Left and American Foreign Policy during the Age of Normalcy: A Re-Examination," *Business History Review* 57 (Spring 1983): 86.

2. Duncan Burn, *The Steel Industry, 1939–1959: A Study in Competition and Planning* (Cambridge, UK, 1961), table 105; Paul Bairoch, "International Industrialization Levels from 1750 to 1980," *Journal of European Economic History* 11 (1982), 296, 304. See also the tables on comparative pig-iron production and energy consumption by the major powers in 1920 and 1930 from "Correlates of War Printout Data," in Ernest R. May, "The United States' Underuse of Military Power," in *History and Neorealism*, ed. Ernest R. May, Richard Rosecrance, and Zara Steiner (Cambridge, 2010), 229–32.

3. Kenneth N. Waltz, *Theory of International Politics* (Reading, MA, 1979), 215.

4. Cohrs, *Unfinished Peace*, 16; Zara Steiner, *The Lights that Failed: European International History, 1919–1933* (Oxford, UK, 2005), 620.

5. William Appleman Williams, *The Tragedy of American Diplomacy* (revised and enlarged edition, New York, 1962); Walter LaFeber, *The New Empire: An Interpretation of American Expansion, 1860–1898* (Ithaca, 1963); Lloyd C. Gardner, *Economic Aspects of New Deal Diplomacy* (Madison, 1964); Thomas J. McCormick, *China Market: America's Quest for Informal Empire, 1893–1901* (Chicago, 1967); Carl P. Parrini, *Heir to Empire: United States Economic Diplomacy, 1916–1923* (Pittsburgh, 1969); William Appleman Williams, ed., *From Colony to Empire: Essays in the History of American Foreign Relations* (New York, 1972); Patrick J. Hearden, *Roosevelt Confronts Hitler: America's Entry into World War II* (DeKalb, 1987).

6. Williams, *Tragedy of American Diplomacy*, 106; Williams, "The Legend of Isolationism in the 1920s," *Science and Society* 18 (1954): 1–20.

7. "Problems of Our Economic Evolution," address to Stanford University seniors, June 22, 1925, cited in Frank Ninkovich, *The Wilsonian Century: U.S. Foreign Policy since 1900* (Chicago, 1999), 78–79.

8. Herbert Feis, *The Diplomacy of the Dollar, 1919–1932* (New York, 1966), 7–14; Emily Rosenberg, *Financial Missionaries to the World: The Politics and Culture of Dollar Diplomacy, 1900–1930* (Durham, 2003), 106–7.

9. Robert Freeman Smith, "Republican Policy and the Pax Americana, 1921–1932," in *From Colony to Empire*, ed. Williams, 287.

10. For details, see Lester V. Chandler, *Benjamin Strong: Central Banker* (Washington, D.C., 1958), 251–331.

11. Cohrs, *Unfinished Peace*, 2, 269. Cohrs provides a very full account of the whole process.

12. L. Ethan Ellis, *Republican Foreign Policy, 1921–1933* (New Brunswick, 1968), 65–68, 182–85, 323–63; U.S. Note to China and Japan, January 7, 1932, *FRUS, 1932*, 1 (Washington, D.C., 1948), 1.

13. Warren I. Cohen, *Empire without Tears: America's Foreign Relations, 1921–1933* (New York, 1987), xii.

14. Cohen, *Empire without Tears*, 2; *Statistical History of the United States*, 1141; John Braeman, "Power and Diplomacy: The 1920s Reappraised," *Review of Politics* 44 (1982): 347–50; Michael Edelstein, "War and the American Economy in the Twentieth Century," in *The Cambridge Economic History of the United States*, III, *The Twentieth Century*, ed. Engerman and Gallman (Cambridge, UK, 2000), 331–32.

15. Michael J. Hogan, *Informal Entente: The Private Structure of Cooperation in Anglo-American Economic Diplomacy, 1918–1928* (Columbia, 1977), 29–33; Joseph S. Tulchin, *The Aftermath of War: World War I and U.S. Policy toward Latin America* (New York, 1971), 160–64; Cohrs, *Unfinished Peace*, 84, 298; Feis, *Diplomacy of the Dollar*, 6.

16. Melvyn P. Leffler, *The Elusive Quest: America's Pursuit of European Stability and French Security, 1919–1933* (Chapel Hill, 1979), 122, 127–29.

17. This point stands even though the actual effects of these tariffs in curtailing imports may well have been less than commonly thought. Leffler, "1921–1932," 249–50.

18. Harding to Fred Starek, November 2, 1922, quoted in Leffler, *Elusive Quest*, 68.

19. Ellis, *Republican Foreign Policy*, 333–42.

20. Gerald E. Wheeler, *Prelude to Pearl Harbor: The United States Navy and the Far East, 1921–1931* (Columbia, 1963); John Braeman, "Power and Diplomacy: The 1920s Reappraised," *Review of Politics* 44 (1982): 353–57; Leffler, "1921–1932," 237.

21. Smith, "Republican Policy and the Pax Americana," 255.

22. Stephen D. Krasner, *Defending the National Interest: Raw Materials Investments and U.S. Foreign Policy* (Princeton, 1978), 98–106; Hogan, *Informal Entente*, 191–94.

23. Krasner, *Defending the National Interest*, 106–19; Tulchin, *Aftermath of War*, 118–34; Hogan, *Informal Entente*, 159–66, 171–85; John A. DeNovo, *American Interests and Policies in the Middle East, 1900–1939* (Minneapolis, 1963), 167–209.

24. Krasner, *Defending the National Interest*, 156–78; Tulchin, *Aftermath of War*, 72–78, 96–97; Ellis, *Republican Foreign Policy*, 229–52.

25. Braeman, "New Left and American Foreign Policy," 96; Leffler, "1921–1932," 250.

26. Hogan, *Informal Entente*, 92–93; Cohen, *Empire without Tears*, 98–99.

27. *Statistical History of the United States*, 869, 884; Braeman, "New Left and American Foreign Policy," 82–84; Leffler, "1921–1932," 229, 246–48.

28. Braeman, "New Left and American Foreign Policy," 82–87; *Statistical History of the United States*, 903; Waltz, *Theory of International Politics*, 213. National Income is the net National Product (GNP minus the value of commodities consumed in the process of production). The market value of U.S. investments abroad rose from $12.2 billion in 1914 to $35.1 billion in 1929—but had declined to $14.2 billion by 1933. Eichengreen, "U.S. Foreign Financial Relations in the Twentieth Century," 476–79.

29. For this claim, see William Russell Mead, *Special Providence: American Foreign Policy and How It Changed the World* (New York, 2001), xv–xvii.

30. Leffler, "1921–1932," 251.

31. Cohen, *Empire without Tears*, 23.

32. Leffler, *Elusive Quest*, 55–56.

33. Cohrs, *Unfinished Peace*, 190.

34. Imperial War Cabinet Minutes, December 30, 1918, *PWW* 53:558–69; Hogan, *Informal Entente*, 89–91, 198.

35. Leffler, *Elusive Quest*, 89–90.

36. Geir Lundestad, "Empire by Invitation? The United States and Western Europe, 1945–1952," *Journal of Peace Research* 23 (September 1986): 263–77.

37. Robert D. Schulzinger, *The Wise Men of Foreign Affairs: The History of the Council on Foreign Relations* (New York, 1984), 1–30; Robert D. Schulzinger, *The Making of the*

Diplomatic Mind: The Training, Outlook, and Style of United States Foreign Service Officers, 1908–1931 (Middletown, 1975), 3–11, 107–8; Priscilla Roberts, "The Transatlantic American Foreign Policy Elite: Its Evolution in Generational Perspective," *Journal of Transatlantic Studies* 7.2 (June 2009): 163–83.

38. Jeff Frieden, "Sectoral Conflict and Foreign Economic Policy, 1914–1940," *International Organization* 42.1 (Winter 1988): 67–78; Joan Hoff Wilson, *American Business and Foreign Policy, 1920–1933* (Lexington, 1971), 28–29.

39. Schulzinger, *Making of the Diplomatic Mind*, 10.

40. Jeffrey J. Matthews, *Alanson B. Houghton: Ambassador of the New Era* (Lanham, 2004), quotations 32, 42, 47.

41. Warren F. Kuehl and Lynne K. Dunn, *Keeping the Covenant: American Internationalists and the League of Nations, 1920–1939* (Kent, 1997), 50–53, 190–91; Selig Adler, *The Isolationist Impulse: Its Twentieth Century Reaction* (New York, 1961), 190; Andrew Preston, *Sword of the Spirit, Shield of Faith: Religion in American War and Diplomacy* (New York, 2012), 297–98.

42. Charles DeBenedetti, *Origins of the Modern Peace Movement, 1915–1929* (Millwood, 1978), 158–59, 113, 239, 251.

43. Kuehl and Dunn, *Keeping the Covenant*, 31; Cohrs, *Unfinished Peace*, 111–12, 538; Leffler, *Elusive Quest*, 100; Williams, *Tragedy of American Diplomacy*, 150.

44. The classic critique here remains Charles P. Kindleberger, *The World in Depression, 1929–1939* (revised and enlarged edition, Berkeley and Los Angeles, 1986), ch. 14.

45. Charles E. Hughes, *The Pathway of Peace: Representative Addresses Delivered during His Term as Secretary of State (1921–1925)* (New York and London, 1925), 55, 105; Cohrs, *Unfinished Peace*, 88; Leffler, *Elusive Quest*, 64–66.

46. Robert David Johnson, *The Peace Progressives and American Foreign Relations* (Cambridge, MA, 1995), esp. 119, 158–66; Rosenberg, *Financial Missionaries to the World*, 122–50.

47. DeBenedetti, *Origins of the Modern Peace Movement*, esp. 61–63, 66–68, 135–36, 203–4.

48. For a detailed exploration of this theme, see John E. Moser, *Twisting the Lion's Tail: American Anglophobia between the World Wars* (New York, 1999).

49. Leffler, *Elusive Quest*, 84, 80.

50. Wilson, *American Business and Foreign Policy*, 115–17; Tulchin, *Aftermath of War*, 109–17.

51. Leffler, *Elusive Quest*, 133–38; Cohrs, *Unfinished Peace*, 310–11.

52. Speech at the Pilgrims' Dinner in London, July 21, 1924, in Hughes, *Pathway of Peace*, 105–6.

53. Leffler, *Elusive Quest*, 115–16; Cohrs, *Unfinished Peace*, 303.

54. Leffler, *Elusive Quest*, 41; Hughes, *Pathway of Peace*, 53; Coolidge address to the Chicago Commercial Club, December 4, 1924, quoted in Hogan, *Informal Entente*, 39.

55. Hughes, *Pathway of Peace*, 53; Annual Message to Congress, December 8, 1925, *FRUS, 1925*, I (Washington, D.C., 1940), xvi–xvii.

56. Leffler, *Elusive Quest*, 79–81, 195–96; Leffler, "1921–1932," 260–62. U.S. exports declined as a percentage of GNP from 5 percent in 1929 to 3.2 percent in 1931. *Statistical History of the United States*, 887.

57. The quotation is from Akira Iriye, *The Cambridge History of American Foreign Relations*, Volume III, *The Globalizing of America, 1913–1945* (Cambridge, 1993), 139.

58. Albert K. Weinberg, "The Historical Meaning of the American Doctrine of Isolation," *American Political Science Review* 34 (June 1940): 539.

59. See, for example, John H. Latané, *From Isolationism to Leadership: A Review of American Foreign Policy* (Garden City, 1918). When a revised edition appeared in 1922,

Latané observed that "some of my readers may question the propriety of the title.... But I do not regard the verdict of 1920 as an expression of the final judgment of the American people. The world still waits on America, and sooner or later we must recognize and assume the responsibilities of our position as a great world power."

60. George Washington, Farewell Address, September 17, 1796, James D. Richardson, ed., *Messages and Papers of the Presidents* (Washington D.C., 1896–99): 221–23.

61. Charles A. Beard, *Giddy Minds and Foreign Quarrels: An Estimate of American Foreign Policy* (New York, 1939), 74.

62. Charles A. Beard, "Collective Security—A Debate: A Reply to Mr. Browder," *New Republic*, February 2, 1938, 359; *A Foreign Policy for America* (New York, 1940), 152.

63. John Quincy Adams, *An Address Delivered at the Request of the Citizens of Washington ... on the Fourth of July, 1821* (Washington, D.C., 1821).

64. See, in particular, Robert W. Tucker, *A New Isolationism: Threat or Promise?* (Washington, D.C., 1971); Earl C. Ravenal, *Never Again: Learning from America's Foreign Policy Failures* (Philadelphia, 1978); Eric A. Nordlinger, *Isolationism Reconfigured: American Foreign Policy for a New Century* (Princeton, 1995); Patrick J. Buchanan, *A Republic, Not an Empire: Reclaiming America's Destiny* (Washington, D.C., 1999).

65. Manfred Jonas, *Isolationism in America 1935–1941* (Ithaca, 1966), 3–16, quotation 5.

66. Maurice Matloff, "The American Approach to War, 1919–1945," in *The Theory and Practice of War: Essays presented to Captain B. H. Liddell Hart*, ed. Michael Howard (London, 1965), 215–18. The "color plans" were those drawn up to deal with the eventuality of war with particular countries, each of which was identified by a given color.

67. A process illuminated in Robert A. Divine's authoritative study, *The Illusion of Neutrality* (Chicago, 1962), to which the following account is greatly indebted. The Chamberlain quotation is on 196.

68. Divine, *Illusion of Neutrality*, 2–13.

69. Divine, *Illusion of Neutrality*, 13–20, 32–35; Henry L. Stimson and McGeorge Bundy, *On Active Service in Peace and War* (New York, 1948), 233.

70. Divine, *Illusion of Neutrality*, 32–56; Lippmann, "The Defeat of the World Court," *New York Tribune*, February 2, 1935.

71. "Arms and the Men," *Fortune*, March 1934; H. C. Engelbrecht and F. C. Hanighen, *Merchants of Death* (New York, 1934); George Seldes, *Iron, Blood, and Profits* (New York, 1934).

72. Divine, *Illusion of Neutrality*, 62–67, 74–76, 111.

73. Divine, *Illusion of Neutrality*, 82–133.

74. Divine, *Illusion of Neutrality*, 180–81.

75. Warren I. Cohen, *The American Revisionists: The Lessons of Intervention in World War I* (Chicago, 1967), 189, 170–72; Hadley Cantril, *Public Opinion, 1935–1946* (Princeton, 1951), 201.

76. Cohen, *American Revisionists*, 172–74, 181–84; Divine, *Illusion of Neutrality*, 93–94.

77. Charles A. Beard with the collaboration of G. H. E. Smith, *The Open Door at Home: A Trial Philosophy of National Interest* (New York, 1935), esp. 211–15, 230, 286–94, vii. On Beard's view of the necessary connection between the search for export markets and imperialism and war, see also Charles A. Beard with the collaboration of G. H. E. Smith, *The Idea of National Interest: An Analytical Study in American Foreign Policy* (New York, 1934); Divine, *Illusion of Neutrality*, 146–48; Moser, *Twisting the Lion's Tail*, 92–93, 99, 103–4.

78. Beard, *Idea of National Interest*, 410–31; Beard, *Open Door at Home*, 234–37; Thomas C. Kennedy, *Charles A. Beard and American Foreign Policy* (Gainesville, 1975), 70–74.

79. Walter Lippmann, "Self-Sufficiency: Some Random Reflections," *Foreign Affairs* 12.2 (January 1934): 212–13. See also Herbert Feis, "The Open Door at Home," *Foreign Affairs* 13.4 (July 1935): 600–611.

80. *Statistical History of the United States*, 887.

81. Divine, *Illusion of Neutrality*, 149–52.

82. Allen W. Dulles and Hamilton Fish Armstrong, *Can America Stay Neutral?* (New York, 1939), 108, 153–54; Divine, *Illusion of Neutrality*, 184; Address at Chautauqua, New York, August 14, 1936. *Public Papers and Addresses of Franklin D. Roosevelt* (hereafter *PPA*), ed. Samuel I. Rosenman, vol. 5, *1936* (New York, 1938–50), 291.

83. Divine, *Illusion of Neutrality*, 134–67, 173–99.

84. Divine, *Illusion of Neutrality*, 166, 174–75, 185–86. The other four of the six negative votes were cast by New Englanders, expressing their section's traditional opposition to measures that restricted exports.

85. Cohen, *American Revisionists*, 161, 164; Divine, *Illusion of Neutrality*, 86–88, 119–20, *passim*.
Roosevelt's letter to House is hard to square with Robert A. Divine's assertion that he "pursued an isolationist policy out of genuine conviction" in the mid-1930s. Divine, *Roosevelt and World War II* (Baltimore, 1969), 5–10.

86. Address at Chautauqua, New York, August 14, 1936, *PPA*, 5, *1936* (New York, 1938), 288, 292.

87. David M. Kennedy, *Freedom from Fear: The American People in Depression and War, 1929–1945* (New York, 1999), 402–3; Jonas, *Isolationism in America*, 158–66.

88. Schulzinger, *Wise Men of Foreign Affairs*, 40–46, 53–57; Divine, *Illusion of Neutrality*, 63–64, 92–95, 117–19, 182–83.

89. Divine, *Illusion of Neutrality*, 223–27, 96.

90. Lippmann, "Rough-Hew Them How We Will," *Foreign Affairs* 15 (July 1937), 590–91.

91. Divine, *Illusion of Neutrality*, 200–210, 219, 227; Kennedy, *Freedom From Fear*, 401–2.

92. Divine, *Illusion of Neutrality*, 117. Even in his Chautauqua speech, the closest he ever came to endorsing an isolationist position, Roosevelt had stated that "we must remember that so long as war exists on earth there will be some danger that even this Nation which most ardently desires peace may be drawn into war." *PPA*, 5, *1938, 288*.

93. Address at Chicago, October 5, 1937, *PPA*, 6, *1937* (New York, 1941), 406–11.

94. Divine, *Illusion of Neutrality*, 213.

95. Robert Dallek, *Franklin D. Roosevelt and American Foreign Policy, 1932–1945* (New York, 1979), 19; Speech at the Woodrow Wilson Foundation Dinner, Washington, D.C., Edgar B. Nixon, ed., *Franklin D. Roosevelt and Foreign Affairs*, I (Cambridge, MA, 1969), 558–64.

96. Dallek, *Roosevelt and American Foreign Policy*, 84–85, 91–93; Annual Message to the Congress, January 3, 1936; Annual Message to the Congress, January 6, 1937, *PPA*, 5, *1936*, 8–12, 640–42.

97. Dallek, *Franklin D. Roosevelt and American Foreign Policy*, 76–77.

98. Dallek, *Franklin D. Roosevelt and American Foreign Policy*, 116–17, 129–30, 138–39, 155–57; Divine, *Illusion of Neutrality*, 132–33; Richard A. Harrison, "A Presidential *démarche*: Franklin D. Roosevelt's Personal Diplomacy and Great Britain, 1936–37," *Diplomatic History* 5.3 (Summer 1981): 245–72; David Reynolds, *The Creation of the Anglo-American Alliance 1937–1941: A Study in Competitive Cooperation* (London, 1981), 31–33, 10–23.

99. Chamberlain to his sister, Hilda, December 17, 1937, quoted in Reynolds, *Creation of the Anglo-American Alliance*, 297.

100. Reynolds, *Creation of the Anglo-American Alliance*, 297, 30–33, 60. See also Kennedy, *Freedom from Fear*, 402; Dallek, *Franklin D. Roosevelt and American Foreign Policy*, 153–55.

101. Cohrs, *Unfinished Peace*, 10–11, 296–324; Rosenberg, *Financial Missionaries to the World*, 247–53, 258–59.

4. LESSENING RESTRAINT, 1938–1941

1. William L. Langer and S. Everett Gleason, *The World Crisis and American Policy: The Undeclared War, 1940–1941* (New York, 1953).

2. Robert E. Osgood, *Ideals and Self-Interest in America's Foreign Relations: The Great Transformation of the Twentieth Century* (Chicago, 1953), 403; Melvyn P. Leffler, *A Preponderance of Power: National Security, the Truman Administration, and the Cold War* (Stanford, 1992), 22–23; John M. Schuessler, "The Deception Dividend: FDR's Undeclared War," *International Security* 34 (Summer 2010): 163.

3. Fireside Chat on National Security, December 29, 1940; Fireside Chat following the *Greer* incident, September 11, 1941, *PPA*, vol. 9, *1940* (New York, 1941), 633–44; vol. 10, *1941* (New York, 1950), 384–92.

4. H. R. Stark, "Memorandum for the Secretary," November 12, 1940, in Steven R. Ross, ed., *American War Plans, 1919–1941* (New York and London, 1992), 3:228–29; *PPA*, vol. 9, *1940*, 640.

5. Churchill to Anthony Eden, May 2, 1941, quoted in David Reynolds, *The Creation of the Anglo-American Alliance 1937–41: A Study in Competitive Co-operation* (London, 1981), 199. On the fundamental importance to Churchill of an expectation of future American participation in the war, see David Reynolds, "Churchill and the British 'Decision' to Fight On in 1940: Right Policy, Wrong Reasons," in *Diplomacy and Intelligence during the Second World War: Essays in Honour of F. H. Hinsley,* ed. Richard Langhorne (Cambridge, UK, 1985), 147–67, esp. 160–65.

6. "Joint Board Estimate of United States Over-All Production Requirements," September 11, 1941, in Ross, ed., *American War Plans*, 5:163.

7. For this argument, see Bruce M. Russett, *No Clear and Present Danger: A Skeptical View of the U.S. Entry into World War II* (New York, 1972), esp. 24–34.

8. Only a further 7 percent was bought from the United States for cash; 84 percent came from Britain. Reynolds, *Creation of the Anglo-American Alliance*, 167.

9. Robert E. Sherwood, *Roosevelt and Hopkins: An Intimate History* (New York, 1948), 264–74; Reynolds, *Creation of the Anglo-American Alliance*, 182–83.

10. Sherwood, *Roosevelt and Hopkins*, 227.

11. Steven Casey, *Cautious Crusade: Franklin D. Roosevelt, American Public Opinion, and the War against Nazi Germany* (Oxford, 2001), 18–19.

12. *Public Opinion Quarterly* 5 (June 1941): 326–27; (Fall 1941): 482; (Winter 1941): 680; Hadley Cantril, *Public Opinion, 1935–1946* (Princeton, 1951), 971–77.

13. On the difference of views between the heirs of Theodore Roosevelt and of Wilson in "the foreign policy elite," see Priscilla Roberts, "The Transatlantic American Foreign Policy Elite: Its Evolution in Generational Perspective," *Journal of Transatlantic Studies* 7 (June 2009): esp. 167–71.

14. David M. Kennedy, *Freedom From Fear: The American People in Depression and War, 1929–1945* (New York, 1999), 410–16; Barbara Rearden Farnham, *Roosevelt and the Munich Crisis: A Study of Political Decision-Making* (Princeton, NJ, 1997), 152–56.

15. This change is particularly striking in view of the fact that "American public opinion in regard to the foreign policy of the United States remained virtually unaffected by international developments from the fall of 1935 until after the Munich crisis in September 1938." Philip E. Jacob, "Influence of World Events on U.S. 'Neutrality' Opinion,"

Public Opinion Quarterly 4 (March 1940): 48, 51–54; *Public Opinion Quarterly* 3 (October 1939): 600.

16. Farnham, *Roosevelt and the Munich Crisis*, 91, 146–56, 175–80, 190–92; "Annual Message to the Congress," January 4, 1939, *PPA*, vol. 8, *1939*, 3; Reynolds, *Creation of the Anglo-American Alliance*, 47; Robert Dallek, *Franklin D. Roosevelt and American Foreign Policy, 1932–1945* (New York, 1979), 183.

17. Dallek, *Franklin D. Roosevelt and American Foreign Policy*, 173; press conference, November 15, 1938, *PPA*, 7, *1938*, 598–600; Reynolds, *Creation of the Anglo-American Alliance*, 41.

18. Reynolds, *Creation of the Anglo-American Alliance*, 43–44.

19. Farnham, *Roosevelt and the Munich Crisis*, 103, 152–58, 163–66; William L. Langer and S. Everett Gleason, *The Challenge to Isolation: The World Crisis of 1937–1940 and American Foreign Policy* (New York, 1952), 51; Reynolds, *Creation of the Anglo-American Alliance*, 43–44.

20. In her thorough study of Roosevelt's decision-making at this time, Barbara Rearden Farnham writes that "he stressed rearmament partly as a way to mask his intention to help Britain and France, and his attempts to inform the public of his reaction to the Munich crisis were framed as general warnings about the potential threat from the dictators that included little or nothing about aiding the allies as a means of combating it." Farnham, *Roosevelt and the Munich Crisis*, 192–93.

21. Langer and Gleason, *Challenge to Isolation*, 37; Mark Skinner Watson, *United States Army in World War II. The War Department. Chief of Staff: Plans and Preparations* (hereafter *Chief of Staff*) (Washington, D.C., 1950), 136–43; John Morton Blum, *From the Morgenthau Diaries: Years of Urgency, 1938–1941* (Boston, 1965), 46–49; Farnham, *Roosevelt and the Munich Crisis*, 175–86.

22. Farnham, *Roosevelt and the Munich Crisis*, 190–92. "Let's either give them the good stuff or tell them to go home, but don't give some stuff which the minute it goes up in the air it will be shot down," Secretary of the Treasury Henry Morgenthau had urged the president. Blum, *Years of Urgency*, 68.

23. Annual Message to Congress, January 4, 1939, *PPA*, 8, *1939*, 1–2.

24. Transcript, "Conference with the Senate Military Affairs Committee, Executive Offices of the White House, January 31, 1939," cited in Wayne S. Cole, *Roosevelt and the Isolationists, 1932–45* (Lincoln, 1983), 304–8; Farnham, *Roosevelt and the Munich Crisis*, 192–96; Langer and Gleason, *Challenge to Isolation*, 49–50.

25. Cole, *Roosevelt and the Isolationists*, 306; Cantril, *Public Opinion*, 202; press conference with members of the American Society of Newspaper Editors, April 18, 1940, *Complete Press Conferences of Franklin D. Roosevelt* (hereafter *CPC*) (New York, 1972), 15:278.

26. Langer and Gleason, *Challenge to Isolation*, 139–40, 143.

27. Langer and Gleason, *Challenge to Isolation*, 137–39.

28. Meeting with the American Society of Newspaper Editors, April 20, 1939, *CPC*, 13:309, 313.

29. Robert A. Divine, *The Illusion of Neutrality* (Chicago, 1962), 248; Livingston Hartley, *Is America Afraid? A New Foreign Policy for the United States* (New York, 1937), 140–41, 113–40, 175–79; Walter Lippmann, "Britain at Bay" and "The Doors of America," *New York Herald Tribune*, October 15, 1938, January 12, 1939.

30. *Public Opinion Quarterly* 4 (March 1940): 102; Edward Mead Earle, "American Military Policy and National Security," *Political Science Quarterly* 53 (March 1938): 1–13; Walter Lippmann, "American Foreign Policy in the Making: The Critical Choice," *New York Herald Tribune*, January 31, 1939; Roosevelt to A. Hitler (and B. Mussolini), April 14, 1939, *PPA*, 8, *1939*, 202–3.

31. Langer and Gleason, *Challenge to Isolation*, 130, 136–47; Divine, *Illusion of Neutrality*, 273–78; *Public Opinion Quarterly* 3 (October 1939): 597, 600; 4 (March 1940): 103–5; Cantril, *Public Opinion*, 1157; Jacobs, "U.S. 'Neutrality' Opinion," 54–55.

32. In the polls, there was consistently a slightly higher percentage supporting a bigger air force than a bigger navy or army. See *Public Opinion Quarterly* 3 (October 1939): 597; 4 (March 1940): 103–4.

33. Baldwin, "Our New Long Shadow," *Foreign Affairs* 17 (April 1939): 476. Baldwin more explicitly dismissed alarmist scenarios of "bombs crashing about our heads, the Panama Canal destroyed and the Nazi swastika rampant on our prostrate nation" in his review of Livingston Hartley's *Our Maginot Line: The Defense of the Americas*, New York *Times Book Review*, April 9, 1939, p. 19. See also Divine, *Illusion of Neutrality*, 249.

34. Watson, *Chief of Staff*, 150–51.

35. Message to Congress, September 21, 1939, *PPA*, 8, *1939*, 512–22.

36. "We Must Keep Out," *Saturday Evening Post*, October 27, 1939; *Congressional Record*, 76th Congress, 2nd session, 250 (October 10, 1939), 631 (October 20, 1939); "Defense of the Western Hemisphere," Study Group Report, February 14, 1940. Papers of the Council on Foreign Relations, box 39, Seeley G. Mudd Library, Princeton, New Jersey.

37. Vandenberg quoted in Cole, *Roosevelt and the Isolationists*, 328; Divine, *Illusion of Neutrality*, 333.

38. Fireside Chat on the War in Europe, September 3, 1939, *PPA*, 8, *1939*, 463; *Public Opinion Quarterly* 4 (March 1940): 99, 102, 106–9; Cantril, *Public Opinion*, 1075–1076, 1057–1059; Divine, *Illusion of Neutrality*, 303–5; Walter Johnson, *The Battle against Isolation* (Chicago, 1944), 47–48.

39. Divine, *Illusion of Neutrality*, 325–31.

40. Divine, *Illusion of Neutrality*, 332; Reynolds, *Creation of the Anglo-American Alliance*, 73–75.

41. Press conference with members of the Business Advisory Council, May 23, 1940, *CPC*, 15:359; *Public Opinion Quarterly* 4 (March 1940): 101; Osgood, *Ideals and Self-Interest*, 407; Joseph P. Lash, *Roosevelt and Churchill, 1939–1941: The Partnership That Saved the West* (London, 1977), 87.

Stark's estimate was both conventional and reasonable. On the unlikely nature of the German defeat of France and the unpredictable contingencies that produced it, see Ernest R. May, *Strange Victory: Hitler's Conquest of France* (New York, 2000).

42. *Public Opinion Quarterly* 4 (September 1940): 550; (December 1940): 711–12; Cantril, *Public Opinion*, 1186.

43. *Public Opinion Quarterly* 4 (June 1940): 357. Almost 60 percent had said in September 1939 that they believed a victorious Germany would start a war against the United States; thereafter the proportion declined to less than 50 percent in April 1940. It rose again in May 1940 to about 55 percent and remained at that level through the summer. Hadley Cantril, "America Faces the War: A Study in Public Opinion," *Public Opinion Quarterly* 4 (September 1940): 398.

44. Meeting with the American Society of Newspaper Editors, April 18, 1940, *CPC*, 15:277–81; Message to Congress, May 16, 1940, Fireside Chat, May 26, 1940, *PPA*, 9, *1940*, 198–205, 238.

45. Fireside Chat, May 26, 1940, Address at University of Virginia, Charlottesville, Virginia, June 10, 1940, *PPA*, 9, *1940*, 232–37, 259–64.

46. A series of polls on conscription indicated that even in December 1938 as many as 37 percent had favored the proposition that "every able-bodied young man 20 years old should be made to serve in the army or the navy for one year"; the proportion rose to 50 percent in early June 1940 and to 67 percent in late July. *Public Opinion Quarterly* 4 (September 1940): 394, 550–51.

47. Robert A. Divine, *The Reluctant Belligerent: American Entry into World War II* (New York, 1965), 86; Ira Katznelson, *Fear Itself: The New Deal and the Origins of Our Time* (New York, 2013), 308–13.

48. The officer was Major (later General) Walter Bedell Smith. Watson, *Chief of Staff*, 109–11, 138–39, 306–13, quotation 312. See also Reynolds, *Creation of the Anglo-American Alliance*, 109–13; Langer and Gleason, *Challenge to Isolation*, 483, 513, 521–22, 568–69; Maurice Matloff and Edwin M. Snell, *Strategic Planning for Coalition Warfare* (Washington, D.C., 1953), 12–21; David G. Haglund, "George C. Marshall and the Question of Military Aid to England, May–June 1940," *Journal of Contemporary History* 15 (December 1980): 745–60.

49. Cantril, "America Faces the War," 391–92; Cantril, *Public Opinion*, 1159–1160; Reynolds, *Creation of the Anglo-American Alliance*, 146, 153.

50. *New York Times*, August 19, 1940. Bullitt received twenty-two thousand letters and telegrams in response to his speech and also monetary contributions that helped him to print and distribute over two million copies. Langer and Gleason, *Challenge to Isolation*, 756.

51. Mark A. Stoler, *Allies and Adversaries: The Joint Chiefs of Staff, the Grand Alliance, and U.S. Strategy in World War II* (Chapel Hill, 2000), 21, 24–25; Watson, *Chief of Staff*, 105–6, 370–71.

52. Robert A. Divine, *Foreign Policy and U.S. Presidential Elections: 1940–1948* (New York, 1974), 34–35, 62–89.

53. Langer and Gleason, *Challenge to Isolation*, 40–42; David G. Haglund, *Latin America and the Transformation of U.S. Strategic Thought, 1936–1940* (Albuquerque, 1984), 101–8; Watson, *Chief of Staff*, 94.

54. Reynolds, *Creation of the Anglo-American Alliance*, 64–67; Lash, *Roosevelt and Churchill*, 63–66.

55. Langer and Gleason, *Challenge to Isolation*, 744–76, quotation 770.

56. Langer and Gleason, *Undeclared War*, 422–32, 575–78; Richard W. Steele, *The First Offensive: Roosevelt, Marshall, and the Making of American Strategy* (Bloomington, 1973), 10–18.

57. Stark, Memorandum for the Secretary, November 12, 1940, in Ross, *American War Plans*, 3:225–50; Stoler, *Allies and Adversaries*, 24–40, quotations 30, 28; Mark A. Stoler, "From Continentalism to Globalism: General Stanley D. Embick, the Joint Strategic Survey Committee, and the Military View of American National Policy during the Second World War," *Diplomatic History* 6 (Summer 1982): 305. On Stark, see Forrest C. Pogue, *George C. Marshall: Ordeal and Hope, 1939–1942* (London, 1968), 125.

58. It seems doubtful that Lothian used these exact words. See David Reynolds, "Lord Lothian and Anglo-American Relations, 1939–1940," *Transactions of the American Philosophical Society* 73.2 (1983): 48n.

59. Fireside Chat on National Security, December 29, 1940, *PPA*, 9, *1940*, 633–44; *Hearings before the Committee on Foreign Affairs, House of Representatives, 77th Congress. 1st session, on HR 1776* (hereafter *House Hearings on Lend-Lease*) (Washington, D.C., 1941), 6, 86, 97–102, 158–59, 172.

60. *House Hearings on Lend-Lease*, 231–32, 262, 371–74.

61. Langer and Gleason, *Challenge to Isolation*, 275, 283–84; *Public Opinion Quarterly* 5 (June 1941): 322–24; Cantril, *Public Opinion*, 409–10.

62. Henry R. Luce. "The American Century," *Life* (February 17, 1941), 61–62. A broadly similar argument was made by the editors of *Fortune*. See "The Zero Hour," *Fortune* 23.4 (April 1941): 59.

63. Hanson W. Baldwin, *United We Stand! Defense of the Western Hemisphere* (New York, 1941), 74–82, *passim*. While recognizing that the Western Hemisphere was much

smaller than the Eastern in both area and population, Baldwin pointed out that the two were much more evenly matched in terms of steel production and (even more) steelmaking capacity: 128–29, 325. Baldwin explicitly endorsed Lindbergh's dismissal of the danger of air attack. "U.S. Air Power," *Fortune* 23.3 (March 1941): 76. On Baldwin and the anti-interventionists, see Justus D. Doenecke, *Storm on the Horizon: The Challenge to American Intervention, 1939–1941* (Lanham, 2000), 246.

64. On this, see Edward M. Earle, "American Security—Its Changing Conditions," *Annals of the American Academy of Political and Social Science* (November 1941): 191; Nicholas John Spykman, *America's Strategy in World Politics: The United States and the Balance of Power* (New York, 1942), 443. Although this work was not published until 1942, it is clear that Spykman wrote it as a contribution to the "great debate" before the entry of the United States into the war.

65. The figure dropped from 68 percent to 56 percent. Cantril, *Public Opinion*, 775, 976.

66. For instance, Roosevelt's radio broadcast, May 26, 1940, *PPA*, vol. 9, *1940*, 238–39; Edward Mead Earle, *Against This Torrent* (Princeton, 1941), 22–23.

67. *House Hearings on Lend-Lease*, 6. Lord Lothian quoted in Nicholas John Cull, *Selling War: The British Propaganda Campaign against American "Neutrality" in World War II* (New York, 1995), 115. According to one thorough study of the foreign policy debate in Chicago, the possibility of a direct military attack upon the United States if Britain fell "already was beginning to fade from CDAAA [Committee to Defend America by Aiding the Allies] arguments" by October 1940. James C. Schneider, *Should America Go to War? The Debate over Foreign Policy in Chicago, 1939–1941* (Chapel Hill, 1989), 78.

68. Beatrice Bishop Berle and Travis Beal Jacobs, eds., *Navigating the Rapids: From the Papers of Adolf A. Berle* (New York, 1973), 332, 335, 352, 370.

69. Cantril, *Public Opinion*, 973–74, 1127–28; *Public Opinion Quarterly* 5 (Fall 1941): 485; (Winter 1941): 680.

70. *Public Opinion Quarterly* 5 (June 1941): 322–24; Cantril, *Public Opinion*, 409–10.

71. Cantril, *Public Opinion*, 969–74; *Public Opinion Quarterly* 4 (December 1940): 714; 5 (June 1941): 318, 325. See also Alfred O. Hero Jr., *The Southerner and World Affairs* (Baton Rouge, 1965), 91–103; Peter Trubowitz, *Defining the National Interest: Conflict and Change in American Foreign Policy* (Chicago, 1998), 130–33; Katznelson, *Fear Itself*, 280–87, 301–6, 309–16.

72. *House Hearings on Lend-Lease*, 378–80, 165–67; *Hearings before the Committee on Foreign Relations, U.S. Senate, 77th Congress, 1st session, on S. 275* (Washington, D.C., 1941) (hereafter *Senate Hearings on Lend-Lease*), 180–96.

73. Arthur H. Vandenberg Jr., ed., *The Private Papers of Senator Vandenberg* (London, 1953), 9–11.

74. Justus D. Doenecke, *Not to the Swift: The Old Isolationists in the Cold War Era* (Cranbury, 1979), 30; *House Hearings on Lend-Lease*, 652. For other statements by anti–Lend Lease witnesses expressing support for the principle of aiding Britain, see 441–42, 482, 488. Even Senator Robert A. Taft (R–Oh.), who said that a German victory would be preferable to U.S. entry into the war, favored cash loans to Britain and Canada. James T. Patterson, *Mr. Republican: A Biography of Robert A. Taft* (Boston, 1972), 242–44.

75. By contrast, most polls in this period found less than 20 percent anticipating an Axis victory. Cantril, *Public Opinion*, 1186–1187; *Public Opinion Quarterly* 4 (December 1940): 711–12; 5 (March 1941): 156; (Fall 1941): 479; (Winter 1941): 676. Churchill's phrase comes from a broadcast speech in February 1941. See Langer and Gleason, *Undeclared War*, 280.

76. Reynolds, *Creation of the Anglo-American Alliance*, 111–13; David G. Haglund, "George C. Marshall and the Question of Military Aid to England, May–June 1940," *Journal of Contemporary History* 15 (December 1980): 745–60. Likewise, Ambassador

Lothian's public warning in June 1940 that the defeat of Britain would mean the loss of its fleet seems to have backfired. See Reynolds, "Lord Lothian," 21–22.

In April 1941, Adolf Berle feared that another successful German blitzkrieg would strengthen isolationist sentiment in the United States. See Waldo Heinrichs, *Threshold of War: Franklin D. Roosevelt and American Entry into World War II* (New York, 1988), 51, 231.

77. *Public Opinion Quarterly* 5 (June 1941): 319.

78. A poll in early September 1940 found slightly more (45%) disbelieving Bullitt's prediction that a victorious Germany would invade the United States than believing it (42%). *Public Opinion Quarterly* 4 (December 1940): 712.

79. Cantril, *Public Opinion*, 976.

80. Patrick J. Hearden, *Roosevelt Confronts Hitler: America's Entry into World War II* (DeKalb, 1987), ix–x.

81. Radio address, May 27, 1941, *PPA*, 10, *1941*, 183–84.

82. Douglas Miller, *You Can't Do Business with Hitler: What a Nazi Victory Would Mean to Every American* (Boston, 1941), 49–50, 91–92, 152–55, 170–71, 191, 204–11.

83. Hearden, *Roosevelt Confronts Hitler*, 159–62, 185–86; Justus D. Doenecke, "Power, Markets, and Ideology: The Isolationist Response to Roosevelt Policy, 1940–1941," in *Watershed of Empire: Essays on New Deal Foreign Policy*, ed. Leonard P. Liggio and James J. Martin (Colorado Springs, 1976), 132–34.

84. Miller, *You Can't Do Business with Hitler*, 139–41, 151–67.

85. Doenecke, "Power, Markets, and Ideology," 137; James T. Patterson, "Robert A. Taft and American Foreign Policy, 1939–1945," in *Watershed of Empire*, ed. Liggio and Martin, 196.

86. Adam Tooze, *The Wages of Destruction: The Making and Breaking of the Nazi Economy* (London, 2007), 88; U.S. Department of Commerce, Bureau of the Census, *Historical Statistics of the United States: Colonial Times to 1970* (Washington, D.C., 1975), 903; Robert M. Hathaway, "1933–1945: Economic Diplomacy in a Time of Crisis," in *Economics and World Power: An Assessment of American Diplomacy since 1789*, ed. William H. Becker and Samuel F. Wells Jr. (New York, 1984), 300–305; Mira Wilkins, *The Maturing of Multinational Enterprise: American Business Abroad from 1914 to 1970* (Cambridge, 1974), 185–89; Arnold A. Offner, "Appeasement Revisited: The United States, Great Britain, and Germany, 1933–1940," *Journal of American History* 64.2 (September 1977): 374–78; John M. Blum, *From the Morgenthau Diaries: Years of Crisis, 1928–1938* (Boston, 1959), 149–55; *Years of Urgency*, 78–82.

87. *House Hearings on Lend-Lease*, 465–77; Justus D. Doenecke, ed., *In Danger Undaunted: The Anti-Interventionist Movement of 1940–1941 as Revealed in the Papers of the America First Committee* (Stanford, 1990), 159–63. On Emeny, see Alfred E. Eckes Jr., *The United States and the Global Struggle for Minerals* (Austin, 1979), 74–75.

88. These percentages are averages based on the annual figures of exports as a proportion of GNP, adjusted by deducting the exports to three other North American countries (Canada, Mexico, and Cuba). *Historical Statistics*, 887, 903.

89. *Fortune* 22.3 (September 1940): 50.

90. Wilkins, *The Maturing of Multinational Enterprise: American Business Abroad from 1914 to 1970* (Cambridge, MA, 1974), 253–55; Eckes, *United States and the Global Struggle*, 76–77, 99–100.

91. Spykman, *America's Strategy in World Politics*, 292–317, 451, 456, quotations 299–300, 456.

92. See, for example, Baldwin, *United We Stand!*, 54–55, 86–87, 311–14.

93. *Fortune* (December 1940): 154.

94. Remarks to the Business Advisory Group, May 23, 1940, quoted in Langer and Gleason, *Challenge to Isolation*, 477.

95. Spykman, *America's Strategy in World Politics*, 305. For the dramatic increases in the U.S. output of minerals during World War I, see Eckes, *United States and the Global Struggle*, 16–17, 45.

96. Robert J. Art, "The United States, the Balance of Power, and World War II: Was Spykman Right?" *Security Studies* 14 (July–September 2005): 381–87.

97. Table in Baldwin, *United We Stand!*, 311.

98. Trubowitz, *Defining the National Interest*, 96–168. For a related analysis, see Jeff Frieden, "Sectoral Conflict and Foreign Economic Policy, 1914–1940," *International Organization* 42 (Winter 1988): 60–90.

99. For example, by Frieden, "Sectoral Conflict and Foreign Economic Policy," 63–67, 70–75; Trubowitz, *Defining the National Interest*, 107–9.

100. The distinctiveness and consequential importance of the South's strong support for the move from isolationism is emphasized in Katznelson, *Fear Itself*, 281–91, 303–16. See also Hero, *Southerner and World Affairs*, 95; Joseph A. Fry, *Dixie Looks Abroad: The South and U.S. Foreign Relations, 1789–1973* (Baton Rouge, 2002), 201–9; Alexander DeConde, "The South and Isolationism," *Journal of Southern History* 24 (August 1958): 343–45; Trubowitz, *Defining the National Interest*, 135.

101. Frieden, "Sectoral Conflict and Foreign Economic Policy"; Thomas Ferguson, "From Normalcy to the New Deal: Industrial Structure, Party Competition, and American Public Policy in the Great Depression," *International Organization* 38 (Winter 1984): 41–94.

102. Doenecke, *In Danger Undaunted*, 17.

103. Cantril, *Public Opinion*, 966, 974.

104. Miller, *You Can't Do Business with Hitler*, preface.

105. Cantril, *Public Opinion, 1935–1946*, 974. The address had also contained, in the words of Waldo Heinrichs, the president's "only fully developed exposition in 1941 of the strategic threat as he saw it." Heinrichs, *Threshold of War*, 84.

106. *Fortune* 21.1 (January 1940): 88, 90.

107. *Fortune* 22.1 (July 1940): insert.

108. "The Fortune Forum of Executive Opinion," *Fortune* 22.3 (September 1940): 114. Interestingly, there was a correlation between responses to this question and the executives' political preferences, with Roosevelt supporters being significantly more pessimistic than those (the large majority) who backed Willkie.

109. Doenecke, *Not to the Swift*, 114–15.

110. Spykman, *America's Strategy in World Politics*, 3–4.

111. Richard W. Steele, *Propaganda in an Open Society: The Roosevelt Administration and the Media, 1933–1941* (Westport, 1985), 82; radio address, May 27, 1941, *PPA*, vol. 10, *1941*, 193; Lindbergh, San Francisco address, July 2, 1941, quoted in Doenecke, "Power, Markets, and Ideology," 152.

112. *Life* (June 3, 1940), 25.

113. Adolf A. Berle diary, September 5, 1940, quoted in Hearden, *Roosevelt Confronts Hitler*, 244.

114. Luce, "American Century," 64.

115. Arthur Sweetser, Memorandum on Approaches to Postwar International Organization, September 17, 1941, War and Peace Studies of the Council on Foreign Relations, quoted in Hearden, *Roosevelt Confronts Hitler*, 242; Robert D. Schulzinger, *The Wise Men of Foreign Affairs: The History of the Council on Foreign Relations* (New York, 1984), 60–79.

116. Miller, *You Can't Do Business with Hitler*, 224, 218.

117. Luce, "American Century," 63.

118. *House Hearings on Lend-Lease*, 648.

119. Stimson Diary, December 19, 1940, quoted in Steele, *Propaganda in an Open Society*, 113.

120. *Senate Hearings on Lend-Lease*, 170. See also Reinhold Niebuhr, *Christianity and Power Politics* (New York, 1940), esp. 39–41. On the defection from the isolationist position of anti-Fascist liberals, see Manfred Jonas, *Isolationism in America 1935–1941* (Ithaca, 1966), 217–21.

121. *Senate Hearings on Lend-Lease*, 169.

122. Schneider, *Should America Go to War?*, 42–43.

123. *Senate Hearings on Lend-Lease*, 182–83.

124. Mark Lincoln Chadwin, *The Warhawks: American Interventionists before Pearl Harbor* (New York, 1970), ch. 3.

125. Douglas to Conant, October 9, 1940, quoted in Hearden, *Roosevelt Confronts Hitler*, 243.

126. Chadwin, *Warhawks*, 62. Officially, the Century Group's aim was to attack isolationism and develop support for a policy of aid to the Allies, but they clearly hoped that the United States would become involved in the war as a full belligerent. In March 1941, Hobson became chairman of the Fight for Freedom Committee which explicitly called for American intervention. Chadwin, *Warhawks*, 43–45, 163–66.

127. Chadwin, *Warhawks*, 19–20.

128. Address at Yale University, November 28, 1939, in Dean Acheson, *Morning and Night* (Boston, 1965), 267–75; Hearden, *Roosevelt Confronts Hitler*, 244–45.

129. Doenecke, *In Danger Undaunted*, 88–89, 116–17, 215–17, *passim*; Justus D. Doenecke, *The Battle against Intervention, 1939–1941* (Malabar, 1997), 110–22, 137–38; Doenecke, *Storm on the Horizon*, 203–11.

130. Doenecke, "Power, Markets, and Ideology," 146–48.

131. Senate speech, June 25, 1941, quoted in Patterson, "Taft and American Foreign Policy," 200.

132. Doenecke, "Power, Markets, and Ideology," 142–45.

133. Berle diary, October 11, 17, 1940, quoted in Hearden, *Roosevelt Confronts Hitler*, 244; Luce, "American Century," 63; Diary of Colonel Paul Robinett, September 12, 1941, quoted in Stoler, *Allies and Adversaries*, 50.

134. Fireside Chat on National Security, December 29, 1940, *PPA*, 9, *1940*, 638–39. For analyses of the purposes of the Welles Mission, see Dallek, *Franklin D. Roosevelt and American Foreign Policy*, 216–18; Reynolds, *Creation of the Anglo-American Alliance*, 69–72.

135. Annual Message to Congress, January 6, 1941; Atlantic Charter, August 14, 1941, *PPA*, 9, *1940*, 672; 10, *1941*, 314–15.

136. Acting Chief of Staff, War Plans Division to Chief of Staff, July 16, 1941, quoted in Watson, *Chief of Staff*, 341; Stark, "Memorandum for the Secretary," Ross, *American War Plans*, 3:241, 229.

137. Fireside Chat on National Security, December 29, 1940; Message to Congress on the operations of Lend-Lease, June 10, 1941, *PPA*, vol. 9, *1940*, 643; vol. 10, *1941*, 214; FDR to Stimson, August 30, 1941, quoted in Richard Overy, *Why the Allies Won* (London, 1995), 206; Roosevelt to Secretary of War, July 9, 1941, in Ross, *American War Plans*, 5:160–61.

138. "Joint Board Estimate of United States Over-All Production Requirements," September 11, 1940, in Ross, *American War Plans*, 5:160–201.

139. Compare Dallek, *Franklin D. Roosevelt and American Foreign Policy*, 285–89, and Casey, *Cautious Crusade*, 41–45, with Reynolds, *Creation of the Anglo-American Alliance*, 219–20, and *From Munich to Pearl Harbor: Roosevelt's America and the Origins of the Second World War* (Chicago, 2001), 157–58, and Heinrichs, *Threshold of War*, 78, 151.

140. Stoler, *Allies and Adversaries*, 57; Richard M. Leighton and Robert W. Coakley, *Global Logistics and Strategy, 1940–1943* (Washington, D.C., 1955), 140. Just at this time, indeed, Walter Lippmann publicly advocated reducing the size of the army and

concentrating on providing material, naval, and air support to Britain and Russia. Lippmann, "The Case for a Smaller Army," *New York Herald Tribune*, September 20, 1941.

141. "Joint Board Estimate," Ross, *American War Plans*, 5:193–203.

142. See Reynolds, *From Munich to Pearl Harbor*, 10–11, 53–54, 90–91, 106–7, 131–32, 142.

143. For a brief, authoritative account of these developments, see Reynolds, *From Munich to Pearl Harbor*, 158–66.

144. Charles C. Tansill, *Back Door to War: The Roosevelt Foreign Policy, 1933–1941* (Chicago, 1952); Marc Trachtenberg, *The Craft of International History: A Guide to Method* (Princeton, 2006), ch. 4; Schuessler, "Deception Dividend," 145–62.

145. For this, see Heinrichs, *Threshold of War*, chs. 6–7; Akira Iriye, *The Origins of the Second World War in Asia and the Pacific* (London and New York, 1987), ch. 5.

146. For a full analysis of why this was so, see Iriye, *Origins of the Second World War*, 165–84.

147. Quoted in Langer and Gleason, *Undeclared War*, 652.

148. Memorandum, October 2, 1940, quoted in Henry L. Stimson and McGeorge Bundy, *On Active Service in Peace and War* (New York, 1948), 385. A year later, Stimson made the same point to a cabinet meeting with vivid, if dubious, historical detail: "In the autumn of 1919 President Wilson got his dander up and put an embargo on all cotton going to Japan and a boycott on her silk, with the result that she crawled down within two months and brought all of her troops out from Siberia like whipped puppies." Quoted in Norman A. Graebner, "Hoover, Roosevelt, and the Japanese" in *Pearl Harbor as History: Japanese-American Relations 1931–1941,* ed. Dorothy Borg and Shumpei Okamato (New York and London, 1973), 51.

149. Michael S. Sherry, *The Rise of American Air Power: The Creation of Armageddon* (New Haven, 1987), 104–15.

150. Heinrichs, *Threshold of War*, 193–97, 211–17.

151. Spykman, *America's Strategy in World Politics*, 27.

152. Hugh Rockoff, "The United States: From Ploughshares to Swords" in *The Economics of World War II: Six Great Powers in International Comparison,* ed. Mark Harrison (Cambridge, UK, 1998), 83; Watson, *Chief of Staff*, 16.

153. Luce, "American Century," 62.

5. FULL-SCALE INVOLVEMENT, 1941–1945

1. The votes was 82 to 0 in the Senate, 288 to 1 in the House of Representatives; the sole dissentient was Representative Jeanette Rankin (R–Mont.), a pacifist opposed to all wars.

2. Wayne S. Cole, *America First: The Battle against Intervention, 1940–1941* (New York, 1971), 194–95; Robert A. Dallek, *Franklin D. Roosevelt and American Foreign Policy, 1932–1945* (New York, 1979), 311.

3. Robert Sherwood, citing a contemporary memorandum by Harry Hopkins, argues that it would in fact have been politically very difficult for Roosevelt to have led the United States into the war in response to a Japanese attack on British or Dutch possessions in Southeast Asia. Robert E. Sherwood, *Roosevelt and Hopkins: An Intimate History* (New York, 1948), 427–30; Dean Acheson, *Present at the Creation: My Years in the State Department* (New York, 1969), 37.

4. Dallek, *Roosevelt and American Foreign Policy*, 312; Fireside Chat, December 9, 1941, *PPA*, vol. 10, *1941*, 529.

5. The survey was an unpublished one undertaken for the Office of Facts and Figures. Richard W. Steele, *The First Offensive: Roosevelt, Marshall, and the Making of American Strategy* (Bloomington, 1973), 52, 202. In a Gallup poll, the question "which country is

the greater threat to America's future?" elicited a more lopsided response, with 64 percent saying Germany and only 15 percent Japan. George H. Gallup, *The Gallup Poll: Public Opinion, 1935–1971* (New York, 1972), 312.

6. Mark Skinner Watson, *United States Army in World War II. The War Department. Chief of Staff: Plans and Preparations* (hereafter *Chief of Staff*) (Washington, D.C., 1950), 16; I. C. B. Deer and M. R. D. Foot, eds., *The Oxford Companion to the Second World War* (Oxford, 1995), 1192, 1198.

7. Richard Overy, *Why the Allies Won* (London, 1995), 331; Deer and Foot, eds., *Oxford Companion*, 1181–1182, 1199; *Jane's Fighting Ships of World War II* (New York, 1989), 267, 270.

8. Overy, *Why the Allies Won*, 210, 223–25, 241–42, 331; Albert Seaton, *The Russo-German War, 1941–1945* (London, 1971), 589.

9. Paul Kennedy, *The Rise and Fall of the Great Powers: Economic Change and Military Conflict from 1500 to 2000* (London, 1988), 355; Overy, *Why the Allies Won*, 44, 192, 214, 254, 336.

10. Overy, *Why the Allies Won*, 228–34; Deer and Foot, eds., *Oxford Companion*, 1180.

11. U.S. Department of Commerce, Bureau of the Census, *Historical Statistics of the United States: Colonial Times to 1970* (Washington, D.C., 1975), 126, 224; Hugh Rockoff, "The United States: From Ploughshares to Swords" in *The Economics of World War II: Six Great Powers in International Comparison,* ed. Mark Harrison (Cambridge, UK, 1998), 81, 98–104; Overy, *Why the Allies Won*, 192; Deer and Foot, eds., *Oxford Companion*, 1181–1182.

12. Instead of the traditional dockside construction from the hull upwards, Kaiser's shipyards were designed with a long assembly line stretching back from the coast to which pre-fabricated parts of the ship and components were fed by conveyors and overhead pulleys. Overy, *Why the Allies Won*, 193–97. See also Rockoff, "United States," 104–6; Deer and Foot, eds., *Oxford Companion*, 1181–1182.

13. Michael Edelstein, "War and the American Economy in the Twentieth Century," in *The Cambridge Economic History of the United States,* III *The Twentieth Century,* ed. Stanley L. Engerman and Robert E. Gallman (Cambridge, UK, 2000), 331–32; Rockoff, "United States," 88–89.

14. Mark A. Stoler, *Allies and Adversaries: The Joint Chiefs of Staff, the Grand Alliance, and U.S. Strategy in World War II* (Chapel Hill, 2000), 64–66; George C. Herring, *From Colony to Superpower: U.S. Foreign Relations Since 1776* (New York, 2008), 542–44; James T. Sparrow, *Warfare State: World War II Americans and the Age of Big Government* (New York, 2011), 261.

15. Phillips P. O'Brien, "East versus West in the Defeat of Nazi Germany," *Journal of Strategic Studies* 23 (June 2000): 89–113.

16. State of the Union Address, January 6, 1942, *PPA*, vol. 11, *1942*, 36–37.

17. Fireside chat, December 29, 1940, *PPA*, vol. 9, *1940*, 640, 643; Kent Roberts Greenfield, *American Strategy in World War II: A Reconsideration* (Baltimore, 1963), 74; David M. Kennedy, *Freedom from Fear: The American People in Depression and War, 1929–1945* (New York, 1999), 618–19, 630–37.

18. Steven Casey, *Cautious Crusade: Franklin D. Roosevelt, American Public Opinion, and the War against Nazi Germany* (Oxford, 2001), 98–100; Deer and Foot, eds., *Oxford Companion*, 1181, 1183; Overy, *Why the Allies Won*, 293–94; *Historical Statistics*, 1140; "World War II Casualties," *Wikipedia: The Free Encyclopedia*, accessed August 30, 2014.

19. Fireside chats, February 23, 1942, December 9, 1941, *PPA*, vol. 11, *1942*, 113; vol. 10, *1941*, 527.

20. For this expectation, see Marquis W. Child, *This Is Your War* (Boston, 1942), esp. p. 4.

21. Kennedy, *Freedom from Fear*, 624–26; Edelstein, "War and the American Economy," 351.

22. Kennedy, *Freedom from Fear*, 644–47; Rockoff, "United States," 90–94. Rockoff provides a more detailed analysis of the situation with respect to various elements in the standard of living.

23. "Farming in the 1940s," *Wessels Living History Farm*, York, Nebraska, *www. livinghistoryfarm.org*; Casey, *Cautious Crusade*, 48, 75. Roosevelt continued to refer to "this war of survival," for example in State of the Union Address, January 7, 1943, *PPA*, vol. 12, *1943*, 31.

24. State of the Union Address, January 11, 1944, *PPA*, vol. 13, *1944–1945*, 36; Hadley Cantril, *Public Opinion 1935–1946* (Princeton, 1951), 1175; Dallek, *Roosevelt and American Foreign Policy*, 440.

25. Cantril, *Public Opinion*, 1174; Steele, *First Offensive*; Gallup, *Gallup Poll*, 370; Casey, *Cautious Crusade*, 76–77.

26. Casey, *Cautious Crusade*, 49–50; Gallup, *Gallup Poll*, 388; Steele, *First Offensive*, 52; John Dower, *War without Mercy: Race and Power in the Pacific War* (New York, 1986).

27. Dallek, *Roosevelt and American Foreign Policy*, 319, 324–27; Steele, *First Offensive*, 93–98, 106–7, 121–22, 134–41; John Lewis Gaddis, *The United States and the Origins of the Cold War, 1941–1947* (New York, 1972), 135–39, 157–65.

28. An analysis by the historian Melvin Small of the way the Soviet Union was portrayed in American magazines and journals revealed how sensitive this was to international developments. During the period of the Nazi-Soviet pact, there were almost ten times as many unfavorable as favorable articles, but between June 1941 and December 1944, almost twice as many favorable as unfavorable ones. Melvin Small, "How We Learned to Love the Russians: American Media and the Soviet Union during World War II," *The Historian* 36 (1974): 460, 478. See also Gaddis, *United States and the Origins of the Cold War*, 33–49; Andrew Preston, *Sword of the Spirit, Shield of Faith: Religion in American War and Diplomacy* (New York, 2012), 354–62; Roosevelt, "Extemporaneous Remarks to Advertising War Council Conference," March 8, 1944, *PPA*, vol. 13, *1944–1945*, 99.

29. When liberals criticized the "deal" done with the Vichy Admiral Jean Darlan to end the opposition of French forces to the North African landings, Roosevelt responded not by engaging with the question of who should rule in liberated Europe but by proclaiming the doctrine of "unconditional surrender." Casey, *Cautious Crusade*, 112–22.

30. Fireside Chats, December 24, 1943, December 9, 1941, State of the Union Addresses, January 6, 1942, January 7, 1943, *PPA*, vol. 10, *1941*, 522, 526; vol. 11, *1942*, 35; vol. 12, *1943*, 554, 33; Emily S. Rosenberg, *A Date Which Will Live: Pearl Harbor in American Memory* (Durham, 2003), 11–15, 32–33.

31. Richard W. Steele, "American Popular Opinion and the War against Germany: The Issue of Negotiated Peace, 1942," *Journal of American History* 65 (December 1978): 704–6.

32. Otto Friedrich, "Day of Infamy," *Time*, December 2, 1991, 15.

33. Herring, *From Colony to Superpower*, 538. See also, for example, Gaddis Smith, *Morality, Reason, and Power: American Diplomacy in the Carter Years* (New York, 1986), 14; Thomas A. Bailey, *A Diplomatic History of the American People*, 9th ed. (Englewood Cliffs, 1974), 740.

34. Arthur H. Vandenberg Jr., ed., *The Private Papers of Senator Vandenberg* (London, 1953), 1.

35. Vandenberg, ed., *Private Papers of Senator Vandenberg*, 19; Justus D. Doenecke, *Storm on the Horizon: The Challenge to American Intervention, 1939–1941* (Lanham, 2000), 321–22.

36. State of the Union Address, January 6, 1941, The Atlantic Charter, August 14, 1941, *PPA*, vol. 9, *1940*, 663–72; vol. 10, *1941*, 314–15; Department of State *Bulletin* 2 (January 6, 1940), 11–12.

37. Harley A. Notter, *Postwar Foreign Policy Preparation, 1939–1945* (Washington, D.C., 1949), 20; Robert D. Schulzinger, *The Wise Men of Foreign Affairs: The History of the Council on Foreign Relations* (New York, 1984), 60–70; Papers of the Council on Foreign Relations, Seeley G. Mudd Library, Princeton, New Jersey; Harley A. Notter to Leo Pasvolsky, September 24, 1941, quoted in Patrick J. Hearden, *Architects of Globalism: Building a New*

World Order during World War II (Fayetteville, 2002), 37. See also J. Simon Rofe, "Pre-war Post-war Planning: The Phoney War, the Roosevelt Administration, and the Case of the Advisory Committee on Problems of Foreign Relations," *Diplomacy and Statecraft* 23 (2012): 254–79.

38. David Ekbladh, "Present at the Creation: Edward Mead Earle and the Depression-Era Origins of Security Studies," *International Security* 36 (Winter 2011/12), 107–41; Inderjeet Parmar, "The Carnegie Corporation and the Mobilisation of Opinion in the United States' Rise to Globalism, 1939–1945," *Minerva: A Review of Science, Learning and Policy* 37 (December 1999): 355–78.

39. Percy W. Bidwell, *Our Foreign Policy in Peace and War* (New York, 1942), quoted in Robert A. Divine, *Second Chance: The Triumph of Internationalism in America during World War II* (New York, 1967), 69. See also Justus D. Doenecke, *Not to the Swift: The Old Isolationists in the Cold War Era* (Cranbury, 1979), 9, 37.

40. See chapter 4 in this volume.

41. Contrary to Douglas T. Stuart's claim that Pearl Harbor as "one of those rare cases in which historical events prove one side unequivocally right and the other indisputably wrong." Stuart, *Creating the National Security State: A History of the Law that Transformed America* (Princeton, 2008), 40.

42. For a similar argument by a political scientist that we "need to do more than invoke shock as the cause" of the change "in the dominant American episteme on how best to provide for security," see Jeffrey W. Legro, "Whence American Internationalism," *International Organization* 54 (Spring 2000): 253–89, quotations 263, 256.

43. Fireside Chat, December 9, 1941, *PPA*, vol. 10, *1941*, 522–30.

44. Speech given at Yale, November 28, 1939, in Dean Acheson, *Morning and Noon: A Memoir* (Boston, 1965), 270; Fireside Chat, February 23, 1942, *PPA*, vol. 11, *1942*, 106–8.

45. Melvyn P. Leffler, "The American Conception of National Security and the Beginnings of the Cold War, 1945–48," *American Historical Review* 89 (April 1984): 349–50; Michael S. Sherry, *Preparing for the Next War: American Plans for Postwar Defense, 1941–45* (New Haven, 1977), 44–47.

46. Lippmann, *U.S. Foreign Policy: Shield of the Republic* (Boston, 1943), 94–95, 131–33.

47. Lippmann, *U.S. Foreign Policy*, 109–12.

48. Ronald Steel, *Walter Lippmann and the American Century* (London, 1981), 406.

49. Nicholas John Spykman, *America's Strategy in World Politics: The United States and the Balance of Power* (New York, 1942), 195, 18, 8, *passim*.

50. Nicholas John Spykman, *The Geography of the Peace*, ed. Helen R. Nicholl (New York, 1944), 7; Edward Mead Earle, "Introduction" to Halford J. Mackinder, *Democratic Ideals and Reality: A Study in the Politics of Reconstruction* (New York, 1942), xxi–xxvi. See also Robert Strausz-Hopé, *Geopolitics: The Struggle for Space and Power* (New York, 1942); Hans W. Weigert, *Generals and Geographers: The Twilight of Geopolitics* (New York, 1942). On Roosevelt, see chapter 4 in this volume.

51. Frederick Sherwood Dunn, "An Introductory Statement" in Spykman, *Geography of the Peace*, x; Frederick S. Dunn et al., "A Security Policy for Postwar America," March 1945, quoted in Stoler, *Allies and Adversaries*, 227–29.

52. Lippmann, "America and the World," *Life* (June 3, 1940), 103–6; "The Outlook for America," lecture at Bar Harbor, Maine [c. August 1940], Robert O. Anthony Collection, Walter Lippmann papers, Yale University Library; Lippmann, "The Atlantic and America: The Why and When of Intervention," *Life* (April 7, 1941), 84–88, 90–92; Forrest Davis, *The Atlantic System: The Story of Anglo-American Control of the Seas* (New York, 1941); Edward M. Earle, *Against This Torrent* (Princeton, 1941), 33–44; Earle, "American Security: Its Changing Conditions," a lecture delivered, August 13, 1941, *Annals of*

the American Academy of Political and Social Science (November 1941): 186–93. See also Lippmann, "Seapower: The Weapon of Freedom," *Life* (October 28, 1940), 45, 110–12; Lippmann, "America's Great Mistake," *Life* (July 21, 1941), 74–80; Earle, "National Security and Foreign Policy," Earle, "The Threat to National Security," *Yale Review* 29 (March 1940): 444–59; 30 (March 1941): 469–73.

53. Earle, "National Security and Foreign Policy," 451–52. See also Earle, "The Future of Foreign Policy," *New Republic* 51 (November 8, 1939), Part II, 86–94; Earle, *Against This Torrent*, 48–50.

54. Lippmann, "The Generation That Was Duped," *New York Herald Tribune*, June 15, 1940; "The Atlantic and America: The Why and When of Intervention," 85–88. The origins and validity of Lippmann's thesis is subjected to skeptical appraisal in Robert E. Osgood, *Ideals and Self-Interest in America's Foreign Relations: The Great Transformation of the Twentieth Century* (Chicago, 1953), esp. 115–25, 328–29, 397–400.

55. Alfred Vagts, "The United States and the Balance of Power," *Journal of Politics* 3 (November 1941), 433; Davis, *Atlantic System*, 236–45.

56. See, for example, Dean Acheson, *Present at the Creation: My Years in the State Department* (New York, 1969), 4.

57. Jerome Bruner, *Mandate from the People* (New York, 1944), 15–16. The change of opinion had been gradual but steady. As late as November 1939, two months after the outbreak of a war in Europe for which the great majority blamed Germany, 68 percent still thought it a mistake for the United States to have entered World War I. But by December 1940, only 39 percent took this view, now slightly outnumbered by the 42 percent who thought that the United States had done the right thing in 1917. Gallup, *Gallup Poll*, 54, 189, 253.

58. For this common view, see John Lewis Gaddis, *The Long Peace: Inquiries into the History of the Cold War* (New York, 1987), 25.

59. Address to the League to Enforce Peace, May 27, 1916; Addresses in Omaha, September 8; Denver, September 25; St. Louis, September 5, 1919, *PWW*, 37:113–14; 63:102, 495, 42.

60. Divine, *Second Chance*, 28.

61. Divine, *Second Chance*, 36, 43, 45, 100–101, 168–71, *passim*; Thomas J. Knock, "'History with Lightning': The Forgotten Film *Wilson*," *American Quarterly* 28 (1976): 523–43.

62. Schulzinger, *Wise Men of Foreign Affairs*, 56–57; Parmar, "Carnegie Corporation and the Mobilisation of Opinion," 355–78; Divine, *Second Chance*, 37, 57–58, 134.

63. Preston, *Sword of the Spirit*, 398–402; Divine, *Second Chance*, 160–66.

64. Parmar, "Carnegie Corporation and the Mobilisation of Opinion," 355–78; Ekbladh, "Present at the Creation," 119–26; Divine, *Second Chance*, 150, 190–91, 244–47; Hearden, *Architects of Globalism*, 187.

65. Parmar, "Carnegie Corporation and the Mobilisation of Opinion," 378.

66. Divine, *Second Chance*, 63–64, 70–74; Child, *This Is Your War*, 11; Steele, "American Popular Opinion," 705–6; Sparrow, *Warfare State*, 54.

67. Divine, *Second Chance*, 130–33; Vandenberg, ed., *Private Papers of Senator Vandenberg*, 34–36; *Public Opinion Quarterly* 8 (Fall 1944): 454; Gallup, *Gallup Poll*, 283, 451–52, 497, 446; *Public Opinion Quarterly* 7 (Spring 1943): 173; 7 (Winter 1943): 759.

68. Vandenberg, ed., *Private Papers of Senator Vandenberg*, 19.

69. Gallup, *Gallup Poll*, 446.

70. Minutes of the Advisory Committee on Postwar Foreign Policy, May 2, 1942, quoted in Hearden, *Architects of Globalism*, 147.

71. Richard N. Gardner, *Sterling-Dollar Diplomacy: Anglo-American Collaboration in the Reconstruction of Multilateral Trade* (Oxford, 1956), 8, 16–17.

72. Notter, *Postwar Foreign Policy Preparation*; Hearden, *Architects of Globalism*, xi–xv, 36–38.

73. Gardner, *Sterling-Dollar Diplomacy*, 4–22; Robert A. Pollard, *Economic Security and the Origins of the Cold War, 1945–1950* (New York, 1985), 4–14; Hearden, *Architects of Globalism*, 19–23, 41–43, 150, 257–58.

74. Gardner, *Sterling-Dollar Diplomacy*, 42–47, 54–62, 107–9.

75. Gardner, *Sterling-Dollar Diplomacy*, 71–144; Hearden, *Architects of Globalism*, 31–33, 42–51, 59–64; Georg Schild, *Bretton Woods and Dumbarton Oaks: American Economic Planning and Postwar Political Planning in the Summer of 1944* (Houndsmills, 1995), 84–138, 184.

76. "The American Challenge," *The Economist*, July 18, 1942, quoted in Schild, *Bretton Woods and Dumbarton Oaks*, 107.

77. Hearden, *Architects of Globalism*, 28–29, 39–41, 63–64, 68–69, *passim*, quotations 40–41, 63; Schild, *Bretton Woods and Dumbarton Oaks*, 184.

78. William Appleman Williams, *The Tragedy of American Diplomacy*, second revised and enlarged edition (New York, 1972), 169–73, 231–36, *passim*.

79. Schild, *Bretton Woods and Dumbarton Oaks*, 99–100, 182–83; Hearden, *Architects of Globalism*, 61–63.

80. Gardner, *Sterling-Dollar Diplomacy*, 76, 134–36.

81. A crucial group of Republican legislators that switched sides from protection to liberalization represented Northern districts in which exports had grown substantially in importance and the threat of imports had faded. Doug Irwin and Randall Kroszner, "Interests, Institutions, and Ideology in Securing Policy Change: The Republican Conversion to Trade Liberalization after Smoot-Hawley," *Journal of Law and Economics* 42 (October 1999): 643–73.

82. Gardner, *Sterling-Dollar Diplomacy*, 158–59, 176–77.

83. Alfred E. Eckes Jr., *Opening America's Market: U.S. Foreign Trade Policy since 1776* (Chapel Hill, 1995), 156; Gardner, *Sterling-Dollar Diplomacy*, 140–43; Elizabeth Borgwardt, *A New Deal for the World: America's Vision for Human Rights* (Cambridge, MA, 2005), 127–33.

84. Leo Pasvolsky, "The Problem of Economic Peace," in *A Basis for the Peace to Come*, ed. Francis J. McConnell et al. (New York, 1942), 84, quoted in Schild, *Bretton Woods and Dumbarton Oaks*, 14–15.

85. Franklin D. Roosevelt to Adolf A. Berle, June 26, 1941, quoted in Hearden, *Architects of Globalism*, 149.

86. Divine, *Second Chance*, 43–44; The Atlantic Charter, August 14, 1941, *PPA*, vol. 10, *1941*, 314–15; Speech at the Mayflower Hotel, Washington, December 28, 1933, in Edgar B. Nixon, ed., *Franklin D. Roosevelt and Foreign Affairs* (Cambridge, MA, 1969), 1:561–62; Address to the Canadian Parliament, August 25, 1943; State of the Union Address, January 7, 1943, *PPA*, vol. 12, 368, 32–33.

87. White House conferences, May 29, 1942, June 1, 1942, *FRUS, 1942* (Washington, D.C., 1961), 568–69, 581.

88. Herbert Hoover and Hugh Gibson, *The Problems of Lasting Peace* (New York, 1942), 252–67, 277–79; Lippmann, *U.S. War Aims* (Boston, 1944), 170–82; Lippmann, *U.S. Foreign Policy*, 71–76, 164–66; Divine, *Second Chance*, 60–61, 124–27.

89. Schild, *Bretton Woods and Dumbarton Oaks*, 25–26; Divine, *Second Chance*, 114; memorandum of conversation at the British Embassy, Washington, May 22, 1943, quoted in Hearden, *Architects of Globalism*, 157–58. Interestingly, Spykman had made the same argument before the war. See Spykman, "Geography and Foreign Policy, II," *American Political Science Review* 32 (April 1938): 228.

90. John Lamberton Harper, *American Visions of Europe: Franklin D. Roosevelt, George F. Kennan, and Dean G. Acheson* (Cambridge, UK, 1994), 94–97; Divine, *Second Chance*,

114; Hearden, *Architects of Globalism*, 156–58; Robert C. Hilderbrand, *Dumbarton Oaks: The Origins of the United Nations and the Search for Postwar Security* (Chapel Hill, 1990), 24–25; Schild, *Bretton Woods and Dumbarton Oaks*, 26; Cordell Hull, *The Memoirs of Cordell Hull* (London, 1948), 2:1639–1645.

91. Hilderbrand, *Dumbarton Oaks*, 25–26; Hearden, *Architects of Globalism*, 159–64; Divine, *Second Chance*, 136–37, 141–55; Hull, *Memoirs of Cordell Hull*, 2:1314–15.

92. Divine, *Second Chance*, 216–20.

93. Divine, *Second Chance*, 198; Dallek, *Roosevelt and American Foreign Policy*, 463–66, 479, 503–6; Gaddis, *United States and the Origins of the Cold War*, 149–57.

94. Sherwood, *Roosevelt and Hopkins*, 710; Hearden, *Architects of Globalism*, 295, 286, 292, 302–3, 317–18. See also Eduard Mark, "American Policy toward Eastern Europe and the Origins of the Cold War, 1941–1946: An Alternative Interpretation," *Journal of American History* (September 1981): 313–36.

95. For example, Secretary of State Edward Stettinius warned Eden in February 1945 that failure to reach agreement with the Soviet Union on a broadly based Polish government "would greatly disturb public opinion in America especially among the Catholics and might prejudice the whole question of American participation in the postwar world organization." Hearden, *Architects of Globalism*, 305.

96. State of the Union Address, January 6, 1945, *PPA*, vol. 13, *1944–1945*, 498.

97. Daniel Yergin, *Shattered Peace: The Origins of the Cold War and the National Security State* (Harmondsworth, 1980), 42–68, quotation 68; address to Congress on the Yalta Conference, March 1, 1945, *PPA*, vol. 13, *1944–1945*, 579–82. See also Gaddis, *United States and the Origins of the Cold War*, 133–73.

That Roosevelt, like Churchill, effectively conceded eastern Europe to Stalin in 1944–45 is argued by Warren F. Kimball, *The Juggler: Franklin Roosevelt as Wartime Statesman* (Princeton, 1991), ch. 8. For Roosevelt's focus on the need to prevent Germany and Japan from regaining the potential for aggression, see Fireside Chat, December 24, 1943, *PPA*, vol. 12, *1943*, 556–60. Ernest R. May argues that Roosevelt's thinking about the postwar was in every way shaped by his understanding of what had gone wrong after World War I. Ernest R. May, *"Lessons" of the Past: The Use and Misuse of History in American Foreign Policy* (New York, 1973), ch. 1.

98. Acheson, *Present at the Creation*, 48–62; Hearden, *Architects of Globalism*, 151, 162–63, 46–48, 84, 295–96, 85–88, 183–84, 304, 308–9; George C. Herring Jr., *Aid to Russia, 1941–1946: Strategy, Diplomacy, the Origins of the Cold War* (New York, 1973), 144–78; Harry S. Truman, *Memoirs of Harry S. Truman*, vol. 1, *Year of Decisions* (New York, 1955), 70–71.

99. Richard H. Pells, *The Liberal Mind in a Conservative Age: American Intellectuals in the 1940s and 1950s* (New York, 1985), 12–13.

100. Sherwood, *Roosevelt and Hopkins*, 832–34.

101. Dallek, *Roosevelt and American Foreign Policy*, 433, 443; Hearden, *Architects of Globalism*, 167, 206.

102. See, for example, James T. Shotwell, *The Great Decision* (New York, 1944).

6. ASSUMING "THE RESPONSIBILITIES OF POWER," 1945–1952

1. G. John Ikenberry, *After Victory: Institutions, Strategic Restraint, and the Rebuilding of Order after Major Wars* (Princeton, 2001), 201; Ikenberry, *Liberal Leviathan: The Origins, Crisis, and Transformation of the American World Order* (Princeton, 2011), 167.

2. Paul Kennedy, *The Rise and Fall of the Great Powers: Economic Change and Military Conflict from 1500 to 2000* (London, 1988), 357–59; Mark Harrison, ed., *The Economics of World War II: Six Great Powers in International Comparison* (Cambridge, UK, 1998), 10; Melvyn P. Leffler, "The Emergence of an American Grand Strategy, 1945–1952," in *The*

Cambridge History of the Cold War, volume I *Origins*, ed. Leffler and Odd Arne Westad (Cambridge, UK, 2010), 67. In 1945, the assistant secretary of the navy estimated that the United States had built 443 bases and other facilities during the war. Ikenberry, *Liberal Leviathan*, 163n.

3. Paul Bairoch, "International Industrialization Levels from 1750 to 1980," *Journal of European Economic History* 11.2 (Spring 1982): 304. On the "anomalous" character of U.S. economic preponderance in the postwar years, see Joseph S. Nye Jr., *Bound to Lead: The Changing Nature of American Power* (New York, 1990), 5–6.

4. Michael S. Sherry, *Preparing for the Next War: American Plans for Postwar Defense, 1941–45* (New Haven, 1977), 191–94; John Lewis Gaddis, *The United States and the Origins of the Cold War, 1941–1947* (New York, 1972), 261–62; Benjamin O. Fordham, *Building the Cold War Consensus: The Political Economy of U.S. National Security Policy, 1949–51* (Ann Arbor, 1998), 176.

5. Robert A. Pollard, *Economic Security and the Origins of the Cold War, 1945–1950* (New York, 1985), 256–61; John Lewis Gaddis, *Strategies of Containment: A Critical Appraisal of American National Security Policy during the Cold War*, revised and expanded edition (New York, 2005), 393.

6. Address in San Francisco, June 26, 1945. *Public Papers of the Presidents of the United States: Harry S. Truman* (hereafter *PP:HST*), *1945* (Washington, D.C., 1961–66), 141; Marshall address, February 22, 1947, quoted in Joseph Marion Jones, *The Fifteen Weeks [February 21–June 5, 1947]* (New York, 1955), 107–9; Acheson press conference, June 29, 1951, quoted in John Lamberton Harper, *American Visions of Europe: Franklin D. Roosevelt, George F. Kennan, and Dean G. Acheson* (New York, 1994), 280. Truman's 1939 comment is quoted in Michael H. Hunt, *Ideology and U.S. Foreign Policy* (New Haven, 1987), 156. On Taft, see his comments on the Anglo-American Financial Agreement, March 13, 1946, in *Hearings before the Committee on Banking and Currency*, United States Senate, 79th Congress (Washington, D.C., 1946), 333–34.

7. Interestingly, two of Acheson's successors as secretary of state, John Foster Dulles (1953–59) and Dean Rusk (1961–69) were also the sons of Protestant ministers, as of course was Woodrow Wilson.

8. Jones, *Fifteen Weeks*, 116–17. For another example of this reading of history, see Dexter Perkins, "The Department of State and American Public Opinion," in *The Diplomats, 1919–1939*, ed. Gordon A. Craig and Felix Gilbert (Princeton, 1953), 282–308.

9. Sherry, *Preparing for the Next War*, 36–37, 4, 101–19; Michael J. Hogan, *A Cross of Iron: Harry S. Truman and the Origins of the National Security State, 1945–1954* (Cambridge, 1998), 23–68, 74–77; Melvyn P. Leffler, *A Preponderance of Power: National Security, the Truman Administration, and the Cold War* (Stanford, 1992), 56–60. A full account of the evolution of the National Security Act can be found in Douglas T. Stuart, *Creating the National Security State: A History of the Law that Transformed America* (Princeton, 2008).

10. General Henry Harley Arnold, "Third Report of the Commanding General of the Army Air Forces," November 12, 1945, in *The War Reports of General of the Army George C. Marshall, . . . General of the Army H. H. Arnold . . . Fleet Admiral Ernest R. King* (Philadelphia and New York, 1947); "The 36–Hour War: Arnold Report Hints at the Catastrophe of the Next Great Conflict," *Life* (November 19, 1945), 27–35; Truman, Address to Congress on Universal Military Training, *PP:HST, 1945*, 405–6.

11. Truman, Address to Congress on Universal Military Training, *PP:HST, 1945*, 412; Hogan, *Cross of Iron*, chs. 4–6; Stuart, *Creating the National Security State*; Hanson W. Baldwin, *The Price of Power* (New York, 1947), 63–69; Aaron L. Friedberg, *In the Shadow of the Garrison State: America's Anti-Statism and Its Cold War Grand Strategy* (Princeton, 2000), 155–62.

12. Hogan, *Cross of Iron*, 25. For a more formal statement of this point, see the JCS memorandum of September 19, 1945 in *FRUS, 1946*, vol. 1 (Washington, D.C., 1972), 1161.

13. Melvyn P. Leffler, "The American Conception of National Security and the Beginnings of the Cold War, 1945–48," *American Historical Review* 89 (April 1984): 356–58; Mark A. Stoler, *Allies and Adversaries: The Joint Chiefs of Staff, the Grand Alliance, and U.S. Strategy in World War II* (Chapel Hill, 2000), 226–29; Sherry, *Preparing for the Next War*, 213–16.

14. Leffler, *Preponderance of Power*, 39. As late as 1948, more than a third of those polled by Gallup agreed that "since the war this country has gone too far in concerning itself with problems in other parts of the world." Jeffrey A. Frieden, "From the American Century to Globalization," in *The Short American Century: A Postmortem*, ed. Andrew J. Bacevich (Cambridge, MA, 2012), 149.

15. Friedberg, *In the Shadow of the Garrison State*, 155–72; Marc Trachtenberg, *A Constructed Peace: The Making of the European Settlement, 1945–1963* (Princeton, 1999), 87.

16. Richard N. Gardner, *Sterling-Dollar Diplomacy: Anglo-American Collaboration in the Reconstruction of Multinational Trade* (Oxford, 1956), 176–77.

17. Hogan, *Cross of Iron*, 71–73, 122–58; U.S. Department of Commerce, Bureau of the Census, *Historical Statistics of the United States: Colonial Times to 1970* (Washington, D.C., 1975), 1141; Friedberg, *In the Shadow of the Garrison State*, 97, 155–72; Robert A. Pollard, "The National Security State Reconsidered: Truman and Economic Containment, 1945–1950," in *The Truman Presidency*, ed. Michael J. Lacey (Cambridge, UK, 1989), 224–26.

18. The term *garrison state* was coined by the political scientist Harold Lasswell in the years preceding World War II. Friedberg, *In the Shadow of the Garrison State*, 51–52, 56–58; Hogan, *Cross of Iron*, 8–9, 28–30, 63, 120–22, 150–52.

19. M. J. Heale, *American Anticommunism: Combating the Enemy Within, 1830–1970* (Baltimore, 1990), 110–35; Gaddis, *United States and the Origins of the Cold War*, 32–33, 56–61; James T. Patterson, *Grand Expectations: The United States, 1945–1974* (New York, 1996), 179–82.

20. *New York Herald Tribune* in Christopher Thorne, *Allies of a Kind: The United States, Britain, and the War against Japan, 1941–1945* (Oxford, 1978), 503; MacLeish in George C. Herring, *From Colony to Superpower: U.S. Foreign Relations Since 1776* (New York, 2008), 598; Baruch to Truman, June 8, 1945, in Gaddis, *United States and the Origins of the Cold War*, 224.

21. Trachtenberg, *Constructed Peace*, 13–15; Hadley Cantril and Mildred Strunk, eds., *Public Opinion, 1935–1946* (Princeton, 1951), 371; Gaddis, *United States and the Origins of the Cold War*, 273–74, 289–91, 296–99; Leffler, *Preponderance of Power*, 31, 49, 100.

22. Gaddis, *United States and the Origins of the Cold War*, 282–312, 336–37; Leffler, *Preponderance of Power*, 81–88, 100–104, 106–10, 123–25; Trachtenberg, *Constructed Peace*, 34–41; Kennan to Byrnes, February 22, 1946, *FRUS, 1946*, vol. 6 (Washington, D.C., 1970), 696–709; Herring, *From Colony to Superpower*, 606–7, 609–10.

23. Leffler, *Preponderance of Power*, 86–87, 102, 110–11, 123–25, 127–30, 168–70.

24. Walter Lippmann put the term *cold war* into common usage in the fall of 1947. See Anders Stephanson, "Cold War Degree Zero," in *Uncertain Empire*, ed. Joel Isaac and Duncan Bell (New York, 2010), 26–27.

25. Statement of Assistant Secretary of State Dean Acheson, June 12–13, 1945. *Hearings before the Committee on Banking and Currency*, U.S. Senate, 79th Congress (Washington, D.C., 1945), 19–22, 48–49; Dean Acheson, *Present at the Creation: My Years in the State Department* (New York, 1969), 28, 122; Pollard, *Economic Security*, 25–31, 66–70; H. Bradford Westerfield, *Foreign Policy and Party Politics: Pearl Harbor to Korea* (New Haven, 1955), 206.

26. McCloy Memorandum for the President, April 26, 1945; Potter/Hyndley report, June 7, 1945; Truman to Dwight D. Eisenhower, July 26, 1945, quoted in Melvyn P. Leffler, *The Struggle for Germany and the Origins of the Cold War* (Washington, D.C., 1996), 16–21; Leffler, *Preponderance of Power*, 63–65.

27. Leffler, *Struggle for Germany*, 28–40; Leffler, *Preponderance of Power*, 151–54; Trachtenberg, *Constructed Peace*, 41–62; Pollard, *Economic Security*, 94–106.

28. Marshall radio address, April 28, 1947, *Department of State Bulletin*, May 11, 1947, 924; Michael J. Hogan, *The Marshall Plan: America, Britain, and the Reconstruction of Western Europe, 1947–1952* (New York, 1987), 29–35; Leffler, *Preponderance of Power*, 151–60.

29. Marshall speech at Harvard, June 5, 1947, Jones, *Fifteen Weeks*, 281–84; Hogan, *Marshall Plan*, 40–46, 51–53.

30. Pollard, *Economic Security*, 146–52; Thomas J. Christensen, *Useful Adversaries: Grand Strategy, Domestic Mobilization, and Sino-American Conflict, 1947–1958* (Princeton, 1996), 48–49.

31. Truman, "Special Message to Congress on the Threat to the Freedom of Europe," *PP:HST, 1948*, 185; Leffler, *Preponderance of Power*, 206–13, 215–18, 233–35, 280–82; Trachtenberg, *Constructed Peace*, 72–78, 84–86; Timothy P. Ireland, *Creating the Entangling Alliance: The Origins of the North Atlantic Treaty Organization* (Westport, 1981), chs. 1–3; Lawrence S. Kaplan, *The United States and NATO: The Formative Years* (Lexington, 1984), chs. 4–6. *New York Times* quoted in Justus D. Doenecke, *Not to the Swift: The Old Isolationists in the Cold War Era* (Cranbury, 1979), 153.

32. Clay quoted in Trachtenberg, *Constructed Peace*, 52; James McAllister, *No Exit: America and the German Problem, 1943–1954* (Ithaca, 2002), 110–11; Daniel Yergin, *Shattered Peace: The Origins of the Cold War and the National Security State* (Harmondsworth, 1978), 191, 212–13, 226; Truman to Heads of War Agencies, May 22, 1945, *PP:HST, 1945*, 61.

33. Charles S. Maier, "The Two Postwar Eras and the Conditions for Stability in Twentieth-Century Europe," *American Historical Review* 86 (April 1981): 327–52; Michael J. Hogan, "Revival and Reform: America's Twentieth-Century Search for a New Economic Order Abroad," *Diplomatic History* 8 (Fall 1984): 287–310; Hogan, *Marshall Plan*, 1–10.

34. A point made by Melvyn P. Leffler in *Preponderance of Power*, x–xi. The "empire by invitation" thesis was first advanced in Geir Lundestad, "Empire by Invitation? The United States and Western Europe, 1945–1952," *Journal of Peace Research* 23 (September 1986): 263–77.

35. Michael Wala, "Selling the Marshall Plan at Home: The Committee for the Marshall Plan to Aid European Recovery," *Diplomatic History* 10.3 (Summer 1986): 259.

36. Bruce Robellet Kuniholm, *The Origins of the Cold War in the Near East: Great Power Conflict and Diplomacy in Iran, Turkey, and Greece* (Princeton, 1980), 98, 188, *passim*; Leffler, *Preponderance of Power*, 142–44; Jones, *Fifteen Weeks*, 76.

37. Pollard, *Economic Security*, 120–21.

38. Acheson, *Present at the Creation*, 219; Jones, *Fifteen Weeks*, 138–43; Dean Acheson, *Morning and Noon* (London, 1965), 267–75; Leffler, *Preponderance of Power*, xi.

39. Jones, *Fifteen Weeks*, 141–43; Truman address to joint session of Congress, March 12, 1947, *PP:HST, 1947*, 176–80; Pollard, *Economic Security*, 119–25.

40. Gardner, *Sterling-Dollar Diplomacy*, 236–53; *Public Opinion Quarterly* 10.1 (Spring 1946): 117; Westerfield, *Foreign Policy and Party Politics*, 215.

41. Jones, *Fifteen Weeks*, 139, 283; Pollard, *Economic Security*, 145–52; *Public Opinion Quarterly* 11.4 (Winter 1947–48): 675–76; 12.1 (Spring 1948): 172–73. As Christensen points out, the unique power of the anticommunist justification for the Marshall Plan was particularly evident among the least-informed members of the public. Christensen, *Useful Adversaries*, 57–58.

42. Allen W. Dulles, *The Marshall Plan*, edited and with an introduction by Michael Wala (Providence, 1993), 116, 122; Truman, Special message to the Congress on the Threat to the Freedom of Europe, March 17, 1948, *PP:HST, 1948*, 182–86.

Dulles completed the manuscript of his little book in January 1948, but its publication was cancelled after the unexpectedly early passage of the legislation in March 1948.

43. Doenecke, *Not to the Swift*, 155–57.

44. Posen and Van Evera go on to state that "the logic behind containment would have required American opposition to Soviet expansion even if the Soviet Union had abandoned communism for democracy." Posen and Van Evera, "Reagan Administration Defense Policy: Departure from Containment," in *Eagle Resurgent? The Reagan Era in American Foreign Policy*, ed. Kenneth A. Oye, Robert J. Lieber, and Donald Rothschild (Boston, 1987), 77–78.

45. See, for example, Gaddis, *Strategies of Containment*, 57–60; and especially Leffler's magisterial study of policymaking in the Truman years, *Preponderance of Power*.

46. NSC-7, "The Position of the United States with Respect to Soviet-Directed World Communism," March 30, 1948, *FRUS, 1948*, vol. 1, part 2 (Washington, D.C., 1976), 546; JCS 1769/1, "United States Assistance to Other Countries from the Standpoint of National Security," *FRUS, 1947*, vol. 1 (Washington, D.C., 1973), 734–50, quotation 739. For the similar passage in Lippmann's *U.S. Foreign Policy: Shield of the Republic*, see pages 208–9 in this volume.

47. Leffler, *Preponderance of Power*, 96, 149, 182, 209–11, 218–20, 261–62, 276–77, 282, 305–8; Trachtenberg, *Constructed Peace*, 89, and the sources cited there.

48. Baldwin, *Price of Power*, 296, 164; Leffler, "American Conception of National Security," 356–58; Leffler, *Preponderance of Power*, 60–61.

49. National War College lecture, "Contemporary Problems of Foreign Policy," September 17, 1948; Gaddis, *Strategies of Containment*, 30.

50. "United States Assistance to Other Countries from the Standpoint of National Security," *FRUS, 1947*, vol. 1, 739. The argument was similar to that in Stark's November 1940 memorandum.

51. "United States Assistance to Other Countries from the Standpoint of National Security," *FRUS, 1947*, vol. 1, 739–40.

52. Special Message to Congress on Military Aid, June 1, 1950, *PP:HST, 1950*, 446.

53. Ted Galen Carpenter, "United States' NATO Policy at the Crossroads: The 'Great Debate' of 1950–1951," *International History Review* 8 (August 1986): 389–415; Acheson, *Present at the Creation*, 285; Christensen, *Useful Adversaries*, 83; Hogan, *Cross of Iron*, 100–107, 112–13, 324–29.

Christensen characterizes congressional advocates of an air-based deterrent strategy as a "'Fortress America' coalition" in *Useful Adversaries*, 47–48.

54. Herbert Hoover, nationwide broadcasts from New York City, December 20, 1950, February 9, 1951, in Hoover, *Addresses Upon the American Road, 1950–1955* (Stanford, 1955), 3–22.

55. Hoover broadcast, February 9, 1951. *Addresses 1950–1955*, 15; Truman, Radio and Television address, March 6, 1952, Special Message to the Congress on the Mutual Security Program, March 6, 1952. *PP:HST, 1952–53*, 195, 189.

For the stress on the crucial importance of this concern to American policymakers, see particularly Leffler, *Preponderance of Power*, 11, 13–14; and Leffler, "American Conception of National Security," 202–13.

56. Hogan, *Cross of Iron*, 99–100, 18, *passim*; Doenecke, *Not to the Swift*, 116.

Aaron L. Friedberg has shown how this traditional anti-statism served to limit the build-up of America's military power in these years. More questionable, however, is Friedberg's argument that were it not for this "the United States might have moved during the late 1940s and early 1950s toward more thoroughgoing preparations for fighting, surviving, and winning a war against the Soviet Union, whether fought with or without atomic and thermonuclear weapons." *In the Shadow of the Garrison State*, 81–82, *passim*.

57. Fred Block, "Economic Instability and Military Strength: The Paradoxes of the 1950 Rearmament Decision," *Politics and Society* 10.1 (1980): 42–43; Curt Cardwell, *NSC 68 and the Political Economy of the Early Cold War* (New York, 2011), 58–69, 85–86.

58. Percentages calculated from *Historical Statistics*, 887, 903; Truman Address to Congress opening the Special Session, November 17, 1947, *PP:HST, 1947*, 494–98.

59. Leffler, *Preponderance of Power*, 160–61; Hogan, *Marshall Plan*, 95–97, 190–91.

60. Fordham, *Building the Cold War Consensus*, 95–96; Hogan, *Marshall Plan*, 97–99. For the analysis of congressional roll-call votes, see Westerfield, *Foreign Policy and Party Politics*, 32–36, 415–18. Fordham provides a more thorough analysis of roll-call votes in the Senate but includes also those on commercial policy and military spending. *Building the Cold War Consensus*, 78–85. For the opinion poll, see Christensen, *Useful Adversaries*, 264.

61. Leffler, *Preponderance of Power*, 160–61; Fordham, *Building the Cold War Consensus*, 96.

62. Memorandum, June 12, 1947, in *Marshall Plan Days* (Boston, 1987), 18; PPS/1, "Policy with Respect to American Aid to Western Europe," May 23, 1947, in *The State Department Policy Planning Staff Papers 1947*, ed. Anna K. Nelson (New York, 1983), 5, 11. John Lewis Gaddis describes PPS/1 as "certainly the most influential" paper produced by the Policy Planning Staff. John Lewis Gaddis, *George F. Kennan: An American Life* (New York, 2011), 267.

63. *Public Opinion Quarterly* 11.4 (Winter 1947–48): 675–76; 12.1 (Spring 1948): 365–66.

64. PPS/4, "Certain Aspects of the European Recovery Program from the United States Standpoint," July 23, 1947, Nelson, ed., *The State Department Policy Planning Staff Papers 1947*, 30–32; George F. Kennan, *Memoirs, 1925–1950* (Boston, 1967), 318–19.

65. Robert J. McMahon, *Dean Acheson and the Creation of an American World Order* (Washington, D.C., 2009), 7; memorandum by Advisory Steering Committee on European Recovery Program, September 29, 1947, *FRUS, 1947*, vol. 3 (Washington, D.C., 1972), 476–77; Truman, Special Message to Congress on the Marshall Plan, December 19, 1947, *PP:HST, 1947*, 516.

66. Dulles memorandum, March 7, 1947, cited in Leffler, *The Struggle for Germany*, 37; Churchill, Speech at Fulton, Missouri, March 3, 1946, *The Collected Works of Sir Winston Churchill* (London, 1975), vol. 28, 74–84, quotation at 82; State Department White Paper on the North Atlantic Treaty; Hoover, nationwide broadcast, December 20, 1950, *Addresses Upon the American Road, 1950–1955*, pp. 8, 5.

67. Hoover address, June 29, 1941, quoted in *Addresses Upon the American Road, 1950–1955*, 12.

68. Westerfield, *Foreign Policy and Party Politics*, 269–324, quotation 287; Robert David Johnson, *Congress and the Cold War* (Cambridge, UK, 2006), 1–34; Taft, July 26, 1949; Hoover, nationwide broadcast, January 27, 1952, in *Addresses Upon the American Road, 1950–1955*, 42; Doenecke, *Not to the Swift*, 131, 224.

69. *Public Opinion Quarterly* 13.3 (Fall 1949): 554; 13.4 (Winter 1949–50): 728; Thomas A. Bailey, *America Faces Russia: Russian-American Relations from Early Times to Our Day* (Ithaca, 1950), 345–46.

70. Friedberg, *In the Shadow of the Garrison State*, 101–6; Gaddis, *Strategies of Containment*, 27–31.

71. Kennan, "Notes on the Marshall Plan," December 15, 1947, Marshall to Cabinet, July 23, 1948 in Leffler, "The Emergence of an American Grand Strategy," 77–78, 80–81; Forrestal to Chan Gurney, December 8, 1947, in Gaddis, *Strategies of Containment*, 62; "United States Assistance to Other Countries from the Standpoint of National Security," *FRUS, 1947*, vol. 1, 743–44; Westerfield, *Foreign Policy and Party Politics*, 347–48.

Stalin apparently warned Mao, through Anastas Mikoyan, that crossing the Yangtze might lead the United States to enter the war against him. Christensen, *Useful Adversaries*, 142.

72. John Lewis Gaddis, *Strategies of Containment: A Critical Appraisal of American National Security Policy during the Cold War,* revised and expanded edition (New York, 2005), 393; Pollard, *Economic Security and the Origins of the Cold War,* 256–61; *Historical Statistics,* 1141; Acheson, *Present at the Creation,* 676–77; Lawrence S. Kaplan, *A Community of Interests: NATO and the Military Assistance Program, 1948–1951* (Washington, D.C., 1980); Fredrik Logevall, *Embers of War: The Fall of an Empire and the Making of America's Vietnam* (New York, 2012), 311.

73. Truman to Acheson, January 31, 1950; NSC-68, "United States Objectives and Programs for National Security," April 14, 1950, *FRUS, 1950,* vol. 1 (Washington, D.C., 1950), 141–42, 234–92. See also Ernest R. May, ed., *American Cold War Strategy: Interpreting NSC 68* (Boston and New York, 1993).

74. For example, Gaddis, *Strategies of Containment,* 90–106, cf. Leffler, *Preponderance of Power,* 355–60.

75. For example, PPS/1, May 23, 1947; PPS/4, July 23, 1947; PPS/23, February 24, 1948. Nelson, ed., *Policy Planning Staff Papers 1947,* 11, 65–66, *1947–1949* (New York and London, 1983), 121–26. See also Wilson Miscamble, *George F. Kennan and the Making of American Foreign Policy, 1947–1950* (Princeton, 1992), 252–68.

76. Leffler, *Preponderance of Power,* 258–61, 300–304, 338–41; Logevall, *Embers of War,* 217–29.

77. The earlier document was NSC-20/4 of November 23, 1948. This itself was a shortened version of NSC-20/1 of August 18, 1948, which had been drafted by Kennan's Policy Planning Staff.

78. NSC-68, *FRUS, 1950,* vol. 1, 237–92.

79. Trachtenberg, *Constructed Peace,* 95–101. See also Leffler, *Preponderance of Power,* 356–57.

80. Samuel F. Wells Jr., "Sounding the Tocsin: NSC 68 and the Soviet Threat," *International Security* 4 (Fall 1979): 153–54.

81. See John Lewis Gaddis, "The Origins of Self-Deterrence: The United States and the Non-Use of Nuclear Weapons, 1945–1958," in *The Long Peace: Inquiries into the History of the Cold War* (New York, 1987), 104–46.

82. Curt Cardwell, *NSC 68 and the Political Economy of the Early Cold War* (New York, 2011), 65, *passim.* See also Fordham, *Building the Cold War Consensus,* 43–53.

83. Cardwell, *NSC 68,* 175; *Historical Statistics,* 224, 887, 903, 905; Pollard, *Economic Security and the Origins of the Cold War,* 160, 165–67. Moreover, as Cardwell admits, the rearmament program initially aggravated the dollar gap by leading to a sharp rise in the world prices of raw materials. Cardwell, *NSC 68,* 230.

84. Paul Y. Hammond, "NSC-68: Prologue to Rearmament," in Warner R. Schilling, Paul Y. Hammond, Glenn H. Snyder, *Strategy, Politics, and Defense Budgets* (New York, 1962), 289. See also Acheson, *Present at the Creation,* 345; Fordham, *Building the Cold War Consensus,* 33–35.

85. This point is fully argued in Fordham, *Building the Cold War Consensus,* 26–40.

86. Leffler, *Preponderance of Power,* 223–25, 262–64, 308–11; Warner R. Schilling, "The Politics of National Defense: Fiscal 1950," in Schilling, Hammond, Snyder, *Strategy, Politics, and Defense Budgets,* 139–51, 185–95.

87. Hammond, "NSC-68," 280, 287–89. Acheson's statement in the *New York Times,* January 12, 1958, is quoted in Gaddis, *Kennan,* 528.

88. Acheson to the Policy Planning Staff, October 11, 1949, quoted in Cardwell, *NSC 68,* 170. For Acheson's view of the role Britain had played, see page 185 in this volume. This was the conventional wisdom in the circles within which Acheson moved. See David P. Calleo and Benjamin M. Rowland, *America and the World Political Economy: Atlantic*

Dreams and National Realities (Bloomington, 1973), esp. 17–19, 46–48. For hegemonic stability theory, see the introduction to this volume.

For an insightful account of Kennan's and Acheson's different approaches to Europe, see John Lamberton Harper, *American Visions of Europe: Franklin D. Roosevelt, George F. Kennan, and Dean G. Acheson* (New York, 1994), parts 2 and 3.

89. Leffler, *Preponderance of Power*, 312–23, 345–46; Luke Fletcher, "The Collapse of the Western World: Acheson, Nitze, and the NSC 68/Rearmament Decision," *Diplomatic History*, forthcoming.

90. Meeting of the U.S. Ambassadors at Paris, October 21–22, 1949, *FRUS, 1949*, vol. 4 (Washington, D.C., 1975), 478, 494; Harper, *American Visions of Europe*, 291–97.

91. Leffler, *Preponderance of Power*, 314–16; Fordham, *Building the Cold War Consensus*, 42–48; Fletcher, "The Collapse of the Western World."

92. NSC-68, *FRUS, 1950*, vol. 1 (Washington, D.C., 1977), 1, 237–92.

93. Acheson, *Present at the Creation*, 374–75.

94. Westerfield, *Foreign Policy and Party Politics*, 332–33; Christensen, *Useful Adversaries*, 101–2, 122–24; Harper, *American Visions of Europe*, 291; Acheson, *Present at the Creation*, 375–80. See also McGeorge Bundy, ed., *The Pattern of Responsibility* (Cambridge, 1951), esp. ch. 2.

95. NSC-68, *FRUS, 1950*, vol. 1, 237–92; May, *American Cold War Strategy*, 12–13; Acheson, *Present at the Creation*, 375; Gaddis, *Strategies of Containment*, 108.

96. News conference, May 4, 1950, *PP:HST, 1950*, 285–86; Hammond, "NSC-68," 327–44; Acheson, *Present at the Creation*, 377.

Historians have differed over whether Truman would have accepted the recommendations of NSC-68 in the absence of Korea. May (*American Cold War Strategy*, 13–15) and Fordham (*Building the Cold War Consensus*, 54–65) suggest that he would, Leffler (*Preponderance of Power*, 358) and Pollard (*Economic Security*, 239–40) that he had not been persuaded that a large increase in military spending was necessary. I agree with Cardwell's balanced assessment, *NSC 68*, 206.

97. Fordham, *Building the Cold War Consensus*, 65–71, 114–18; Christensen, *Useful Adversaries*, 124; Leffler, *Preponderance of Power*, 366–67.

98. Special message to Congress, July 19, 1950, *PP:HST, 1950*, 529. See also *Memoirs of Harry S. Truman*, II, *Years of Trial and Hope* (New York, 1956), 332–33; Ernest R. May, *"Lessons" of the Past: The Use and Misuse of History in American Foreign Policy* (New York, 1973), ch. 3.

99. Leffler, *Preponderance of Power*, 368–69, 374–76, 380–83, 394–95; Gaddis, "Drawing Lines: The Defensive Perimeter Strategy in East Asia, 1947–1951," in *The Long Peace*, 72–103; Christensen, *Useful Adversaries*, 133–37; Fordham, *Building the Cold War Consensus*, 123–24; Herring, *From Colony to Superpower*, 646–47.

100. *PP:HST, 1950*, 532; Fordham, *Building the Cold War Consensus*, 104; Hammond, "NSC-68," 353, 356–57.

101. Leffler, *Preponderance of Power*, 367–80, 395–403; Herring, *From Colony to Superpower*, 641–47; Gaddis, "Drawing Lines," 94–100; Fordham, *Building the Cold War Consensus*, 118–21.

According to Secretary of the Army Frank Pace's later recollection, Marshall (now secretary of defense) had greeted MacArthur's prediction that the war would soon be over as bad news because "the American people" would not yet have "learned their lesson." Fordham, *Building the Cold War Consensus*, 175–76.

102. *Public Opinion Quarterly* 15.1 (Spring 1951): 170; 15.3 (Summer 1951): 386–87; Doenecke, *Not to the Swift*, 190–91; Hoover broadcast, February 9, 1951, *Addresses 1950–1955*, 20.

103. Meetings of President Truman and Prime Minister Attlee, December 4–8, 1950, *FRUS, 1950*, vol. 3 (Washington, D.C., 1977), 1706–1782; Acheson, *Present at the Creation*, 478–85; Leffler, *Preponderance of Power*, 399–401; Christensen, *Useful Adversaries*, 181–91.

104. *FRUS, 1950*, vol. 3, 1716, 1727–1728, 1731–1735; Acheson, *Present at the Creation*, Christensen, *Useful Adversaries*, 181–91.

105. *Public Opinion Quarterly* 13.1 (Spring 1949): 158–59, 13.3 (Fall 1949): 543–44; 13.4 (Winter 1949–50), 721–22; George H. Gallup, *The Gallup Poll, 1935–1971* (New York, 1972), 2:818, 852–53; Christensen, *Useful Adversaries*, 267; *FRUS, 1950*, vol. 3, 1720.

106. Christensen, *Useful Adversaries*, 110n, also 49–76.

107. Walter Lippmann, *The Cold War: A Study in U.S. Foreign Policy* (New York, 1947); Stephen M. Walt, "The Case for Finite Containment: Analyzing U.S. Grand Strategy," *International Security* 14 (1989): 19–21; Robert H. Johnson, "Exaggerating America's Stake in Third World Conflicts," *International Security* 10 (1984/85): 32–68; Stephen Van Evera, "American Strategic Interests: Why Europe Matters, Why the Third World Doesn't," testimony prepared for hearings before the Panel on Defense Burdensharing, Committee on Armed Services, U.S. House of Representatives, March 2, 1988.

108. Gaddis, *Strategies of Containment*, 30–31; JCS 1769/1, "United States Assistance to Other Countries from the Standpoint of National Security," April 29, 1947, *FRUS, 1947*, vol. 1, 734–50; Doenecke, *Not to the Swift*. 196.

109. State of the Union Message, January 8, 1951, *PP:HST, 1951* (Washington, D.C., 1965), 8. See also Radio and Television Address to the American People on the Mutual Security Program, March 6, 1951, *PP:HST, 1952–53*, 192.

110. Nitze to James B. Conant, cited in Gaddis, *Strategies of Containment*, 108.

CONCLUSION

1. John Lewis Gaddis, *Strategies of Containment: A Critical Appraisal of American National Security Policy during the Cold War*, revised and expanded edition (New York, 2005), 393–94; *Historical Statistics of the United States*, 1141.

2. Perry Anderson, "American Foreign Policy and Its Thinkers," *New Left Review* 83 (September–October 2013): 107.

3. Michael Mandelbaum, "The Inadequacy of American Power," *Foreign Affairs* (September–October 2002): 67; David Calleo, *Follies of Power: America's Unipolar Fantasy* (Cambridge, UK, 2009), 4, both quoted in Anderson, "American Foreign Policy and Its Thinkers," 114n, 109n.

4. David Halberstam, *War in a Time of Peace: Bush, Clinton, and the Generals* (New York, 2001), esp. 70–75, 109, 490, 494.

5. David A. Baldwin, *Economic Statecraft* (Princeton, 1985), 296; George M. Guess, *The Politics of United States Foreign Aid* (London, 1987), 34, 37–38, 51.

6. Address to the Nation Announcing Allied Military Action in the Persian Gulf, January 16, 1991. *PP: George Bush, 1991* (Washington, D.C., 1992), 44.

7. Arnold Wolfers, "The Goals of Foreign Policy," in *Discord and Collaboration* (Baltimore, 1962), 73–77, quotation 74n. On "collective goods," see Kenneth N. Waltz, *Theory of International Politics* (Reading, MA, 1979), 198. For a recent analysis emphasizing the distinction between the "defense of the territory, prosperity, and sovereign independence of the American people" and "the promotion of a liberal world order," see Robert Kagan, "Superpowers Don't Get to Retire: What Our Tired Country Still Owes the World," *New Republic* (June 9, 2014), 14–31, esp. 20.

8. "Quarantine" speech at Chicago, Illinois, October 5, 1937, *Public Papers and Addresses of Franklin D. Roosevelt*, edited by Samuel I. Rosenman, vol. 6, *1937* (New York, 1937), 407.

9. Odd Arne Westad, *The Global Cold War: Third World Interventions and the Making of Our Times* (Cambridge, UK, 2005), 5, 32–37, 111.

10. Robert W. Tucker and David C. Hendrickson, *The Imperial Temptation: The New World Order and America's Purpose* (New York, 1992), 41–43.

11. Christopher Layne, *The Peace of Illusions: American Grand Strategy from 1940 to the Present* (Ithaca, 2006), 1–5, *passim*.

12. Francis J. Gavin, *Gold, Dollars, and Power: The Politics of International Monetary Relations, 1958–1971* (Chapel Hill, 2004), 193, also 3, 33–34, 68, 93, 95, 188; Barry Eichengreen, "U.S. Foreign Financial Relations in the Twentieth Century," in *The Cambridge Economic History of the United States*, III, *The Twentieth Century*, ed. Stanley L. Engerman and Robert E. Gallman (Cambridge, UK, 2000), 489–90, 493–94; Alan Wolfe, *America's Impasse: The Rise and Fall of the Politics of Growth* (New York, 1981), 153.

Index

Acheson, Dean, 14, 185, 207, 218–19, 232, 239, 245–46, 250, 255, 263–71
Adams, Brooks, 52–53
Adams, Charles Francis, 40
Adams, John Quincy, 133
Addams, Jane, 58, 82
Afghanistan, 276
African-Americans, 144
Aguinaldo, Emilio, 30, 32
Algerçiras conference (1906), 33–34
America First Committee, 168, 173, 177–78, 180, 185, 204; dissolved, 193
American Bankers' Association, 219
American Expeditionary Force (1917–19), 88–89
American Legion, 236
American mission, 20–21, 92, 103, 173, 271–72; expansive version of, 53–54; isolationist interpretation, 21, 133; Wilson's invocation of, 69–70, 74, 86, 282
American nationalism: imperial mentality, 259, 282; nature of, 20–21; sense of national honor, 70, 83–85, 297n49; stake in U.S. primacy, 186, 276, 282; strength of, 186
American power: byproduct of economic growth, 122–23; confidence in, 24, 57, 68–69, 92–93, 105, 107–8, 143, 156, 182–91, 225–28, 236, 258–59, 268–71; growth of, 4, 25–26, 122–23, 197, 230; scale of resources, 26, 110–11, 195–97, 230, 283. *See also* power
Anglo-Japanese alliance, 118, 123
Anglophilia, 42–43, 52–53, 185, 258, 278
anticommunism, 202; effect in weakening isolationism, 258; nature and depth of, 236
arbitration treaties, 43, 51, 97
armaments reduction, 77, 112–13, 146, 148, 220
Armenia, 104
Armstrong, Hamilton Fish, 141–42
Arnold, Henry H., 207–8, 233
Art, Robert J., 179
Atkinson, Edward, 46
Atlantic Charter, 186, 205, 217, 220–21
atomic bomb. *See* nuclear weapons
Attlee, Clement, 269–70
Austro-Hungarian Empire, 90–91

Axis powers, 141, 152–58, 160–61, 166, 186–87, 191, 194, 199

Bailey, Thomas A., 99, 258
Baker, Ray Stannard, 58, 93, 97
Baldwin, Hanson W., 163, 173, 210, 234, 314n63
Bao Dai, 261
Baruch, Bernard, 141, 236
Battle of Britain, 153, 170
Bayard, Thomas F., 40
Beard, Charles A., 16, 132–33, 139–40, 149
Bedell Smith, Walter, 122, 314n48
Berle, Adolf A., 174, 183, 186, 217, 220, 224
Berlin blockade and airlift, 241, 258–59, 266
Beveridge, Albert J., 44
Blaine, James G, 36, 45
Bohlen, Charles E., 238, 266
Bone, Homer T., 138
Borah, William E., 78, 86, 102, 117, 128, 134, 141–42, 149, 163, 165
Borchard, Edwin, 140
Bowman, Isaiah, 222
Brazil, 36, 169–70
Bretton Woods: conference (1944), 218–19; system, 17, 220, 229, 239, 254, 283
Briand, Aristide, 117
Bristol, Admiral Mark L., 131
Brookings Institution, 178, 210
Brussels Pact, 242
Bryan, William Jennings, 40, 43, 69; as secretary of state, 43, 62, 66–68, 142
Bryce, James, 60, 101
Budget Bureau, 263, 267
Bullitt, William C., 169
Bush, George H. W., 279
Bush, George W., 15
Byrnes, James F., 238

Calleo, David, 276
Canada, 16, 22, 41, 48, 157, 160, 170, 249, 262; as source of raw materials, 19
Cantril, Hadley, 155, 215
Cardwell, Curt, 262